ACCA

PAPER F8

AUDIT AND ASSURANCE

P
R
A
C
T
I
C
E

&

R
E
V
I
S
I
O
N

K
I
T

> BPP Learning Media is an **ACCA Approved Content Provider** for the ACCA qualification. This means we work closely with ACCA to ensure our products fully prepare you for your ACCA exams.
>
> In this Practice & Revision Kit, which has been reviewed by the **ACCA examination team**, we:
>
> - Discuss the **best strategies** for revising and taking your ACCA exams
> - Ensure you are well **prepared** for your exam
> - Provide you with **lots of great guidance** on tackling questions
> - Provide you with **three** mock exams
>
> Our **Passcard** product also supports this paper.

FOR EXAMS IN SEPTEMBER 2017, DECEMBER 2017, MARCH 2018 AND JUNE 2018

BPP
LEARNING MEDIA

First edition 2007
Tenth edition February 2017

ISBN 9781 5097 0859 8
(previous ISBN 9781 4727 4440 1)

e-ISBN 9781 5097 0997 7
(previous e-ISBN 9781 4727 4655 9)

Cataloguing-in-Publication Data
A catalogue record for this book
is available from the British Library

Published by

BPP Learning Media Ltd
BPP House, Aldine Place
London W12 8AA

www.bpp.com/learningmedia

Printed and bound by
CPI Group (UK) Ltd
Croydon
CR0 4YY

Your learning materials, published by BPP Learning Media Ltd, are printed on paper obtained from traceable sustainable sources.

We are grateful to the Association of Chartered Certified Accountants for permission to reproduce past examination questions. The suggested solutions in the Practice & Revision Kit have been prepared by BPP Learning Media Ltd, except where otherwise stated.

BPP Learning Media is grateful to the IASB for permission to reproduce extracts from the International Financial Reporting Standards including all International Accounting Standards, SIC and IFRIC Interpretations (the Standards). The Standards together with their accompanying documents are issued by:

The International Accounting Standards Board (IASB) 30 Cannon Street, London, EC4M 6XH, United Kingdom. Email: info@ifrs.org Web: www.ifrs.org

Disclaimer: The IASB, the International Financial Reporting Standards (IFRS) Foundation, the authors and the publishers do not accept responsibility for any loss caused by acting or refraining from acting in reliance on the material in this publication, whether such loss is caused by negligence or otherwise to the maximum extent permitted by law.

About this Practice & Revision Kit

ACCA have commenced the transition of F5–F9 to computer-based examination (CBE), beginning with a pilot in limited markets in September 2016. Students will initially have the choice of CBE or paper exams and as a result, changes will be made to BPP's learning materials to ensure that we fully support students through this transition.

This Practice & Revision Kit is valid for exams from the September 2017 sitting through to the June 2018 sitting and in this Practice & Revision Kit you will find questions in both multiple choice question (MCQ) and objective testing question (OTQ) format. OTQs include a wider variety of questions types including MCQ as well as number entry, multiple response and drag and drop. More information on these question types will be available on the ACCA website.

OTQs will only appear in computer-based exams but these questions will still provide valuable practice for all students whichever version of the exam is taken. These are clearly marked on the contents page as either CBE style OTQ bank or CBE style OTQ case.

More information on the exam formats can be found on page xv.

All timings given throughout this Practice & Revision Kit are based on the paper-based exam which is 3 hours and 15 minutes long. Time management is a key skill for success in this exam and so we recommend you use these indicative timings when attempting questions to time on paper.

ACCA are recommending that all students consult the ACCA website on a regular basis for updates on the launch of the new CBEs.

Contents

Question index

The headings in this checklist/index indicate the main topics of questions, but questions are expected to cover several different topics.

Questions set under the old syllabus *Audit and Internal Review* (AIR) paper are included because their style and content are similar to those which appear in the F8 exam. The questions have been amended to reflect the current exam format.

Part E: Review and reporting

Mock exam 1 (Specimen exam)

Mock exam 2 CBE style (September 2016 exam)

Mock exam 3 (December 2016 exam)

Topic index

Listed below are the key Paper F8 syllabus topics and the numbers of the questions in this Kit covering those topics. If you need to concentrate your practice and revision on certain topics or if you want to attempt all available questions that refer to a particular subject, you will find this index useful.

Syllabus topic	Question numbers
Accounting estimates	137-141, 169-173, 174-178
Analytical procedures	41-45, 75, 79, 108, 113, 157, 179-183
Assurance engagement	1-5, 76, 114, 151
Audit acceptance	56-60
Audit evidence	46-50, 108, 110, 117-121, 122-126, 132-136, 147, 148, 149, 152, 153, 154, 155, 156, 157
Audit planning and documentation	36-40, 46-50, 51-55, 77, 80
Audit regulation	11-15
Audit reporting	149, 155, 159-163, 164-168, 169-173, 179-183, 184-188, 189-193, 194-198
Audit risk	36-40, 41-45, 46-50, 51-55, 71, 73, 74, 75, 76, 78, 80, 127-131, 147, 153, 154
Audit sampling	72, 127-131, 137-141
CAATs	91-95, 127-131, 142-146, 148, 150
Cash and bank	81-85, 117-121, 132-136, 157, 158
Corporate governance	6-10, 16-20, 26-30, 31-35, 80
Directors' emoluments	156
Engagement letters	56-60, 61-65
Ethics	1-5, 11-15, 21-25, 26-30, 151, 61-65
Experts	117-121, 154
External audit	1-5, 66-70
Fraud, laws and regulations	1-5, 41-45, 76, 106, 109
Going concern	75, 76, 179-183, 184-188
Interim audit	66-70, 110
Internal audit	6-10, 31-35, 86-90, 91-95, 106, 107, 112, 127-131
Internal controls	41-45, 81-85, 86-90, 91-95, 101-105, 106, 107, 109, 110, 112, 113, 114, 115
Inventory	36-40, 71, 73, 74, 75, 77, 96-100, 114, 155
Materiality and misstatements	36-40, 79, 169-173, 179-183, 184-188
Non-current assets	51-55, 71, 75, 96-100, 112, 117-121, 155, 156, 157
Not-for-profit organisations	41-45, 157
Outsourcing	78
Payables and accruals	132-136, 152, 156, 158
Provisions and contingencies	46-50, 71, 77, 106, 122-126, 152
Purchases systems	86-90, 96-100, 107, 111, 112, 115
Quality control	56-60, 72
Receivables and revenue	41-45, 51-55, 109, 137-141, 152, 159-163, 164-168
Sales systems	81-85, 101-105, 109, 116, 142-146,
Subsequent events	151, 152, 164-168, 194-198
Wages systems	91-95, 106, 108, 110, 113
Written representations	132-136, 169-173, 174-178

Helping you with your revision

Tackling revision and the exam

Using feedback obtained from ACCA examination team review:

- We look at the dos and don'ts of revising for, and taking, ACCA exams

- We focus on Paper F8; we discuss revising the syllabus, what to do (and what not to do) in the exam, how to approach different types of question and ways of obtaining easy marks

Selecting questions

We provide signposts to help you plan your revision.

- A full **question index**

- A **topic index** listing all the questions that cover key topics, so that you can locate the questions that provide practice on these topics, and see the different ways in which they might be examined

Making the most of question practice

At BPP Learning Media we realise that you need more than just questions and model answers to get the most from your question practice.

- Our **Top tips** included for certain questions provide essential advice on tackling questions, presenting answers and the key points that answers need to include.

- We show you how you can pick up **easy marks** on some questions, as we know that picking up all readily available marks often can make the difference between passing and failing.

- We include **marking guides** to show you what the examination team rewards.

- We include **comments from the examination team** to show you where students struggled or performed well in the actual exam.

- We refer to the **BPP Study Text for exams in September 2017, December 2017, March 2018 and June 2018** for detailed coverage of the topics covered in questions

Attempting mock exams

There are three mock exams that provide practice at coping with the pressures of the exam day. We strongly recommend that you attempt them under exam conditions. **Mock exam 1** is the Specimen exam paper. **Mock exam 2** is the September 2016 computer-based exam. **Mock exam 3** is the December 2016 exam paper.

Revising F8

The F8 paper assumes knowledge of Paper F3 *Financial Accounting*. It is important, therefore, that candidates can apply the knowledge they have gained in this paper to the audit and assurance context of Paper F8.

All questions are compulsory so you must revise the **whole** syllabus. Since the exam includes 3 10 mark OT case questions (each comprising five OT questions of 2 marks each) in Section A, you should expect questions to cover a large part of the syllabus. Selective revision **will limit** the number of questions you can answer and hence reduce your chances of passing. It is better to go into the exam knowing a reasonable amount about most of the syllabus rather than concentrating on a few topics to the exclusion of the rest.

In Section B, all questions will require a written response but there may be questions requiring the calculation and interpretation of some basic ratios in the context of audit planning or review.

In short, remember that **all** the questions in this paper are compulsory. Therefore, we **strongly advise** that you do not selectively revise certain topics – any topic from the syllabus could be examined. Selective revision will limit the number of questions you can answer and hence reduce your chances of passing this paper.

Question practice

Practising as many exam-style questions as possible will be the key to passing this exam. You must do questions under **timed conditions** and ensure you write full answers to the discussion parts as well as doing the calculations.

Avoid looking at the answer until you have finished a question. Your biggest problem with F8 questions may be knowing how to start, and this needs practice.

Also ensure that you attempt all three mock exams under exam conditions.

Passing the F8 exam

Displaying the right qualities and avoiding weaknesses

In order to pass this paper it is important that you get some of the basics right. These include the following:

Read the question

Again this sounds obvious but is absolutely critical. When you are reading the question think about the following:

- Which technical area is being tested?

  This should let you identify the relevant areas of technical knowledge to draw on.

- What am I being asked to do?

  (We will take a more detailed look at the wording of requirements later.)

- Are there any key dates?

  This is important in questions on inventory. If the inventory count takes place at a time other than the year-end you need to be aware of this.

- What is the status of your client?

  For example is it large or small, is it a new or existing client? This might affect issues such as risk.

- What is the nature of the business?

  This is particularly relevant in planning questions as it will have an impact on risk areas.

- How many marks are allocated to each part of the question so approximately how many points do I need to make?

  When you think about the number of points you need to achieve you need to consider this in relation to the requirement. If you are asked for explanation it is likely that you will score more marks per point than if you are simply asked for a list of points.

You also need to think about the order in which you read information in the question. Particularly in Section B it is important that you read the requirement first so that as you read through the rest of the information you are aware of the key matters/issues which you are looking out for. For example if you are asked for risks in a scenario you can try to identify as many risk factors as possible as you read the detailed information.

You should also try to read the question as 'actively' as possible. Underline key words, annotate the question and link related points together. These points can often serve as the basis for an outline plan.

Understand the requirements

It is important that you can understand and differentiate between the requirements and terms that the examination team typically uses. Here are some examples:

Requirement	Meaning
Explain	Make a point clear, justify a point of view
Describe	Give an account of something, including the key features
Define	Give the meaning of
Recommend	Advise the appropriate actions to pursue in terms the recipient will understand
Discuss	Critically examine an issue
List	Normally punchier points than 'explain' or 'discuss'
Illustrate	Explain by using examples
Audit procedures/audit tests	Actions
Enquiries	Questions
Evidence	Source (eg document) and what it proves

Think and plan

No matter how well prepared you are you are going to have to do some thinking in the exam. Obviously you will be under time pressure, but if used effectively thinking and planning time should not be seen as a waste of time.

Generating ideas can often be a problem at this stage. Remember that your knowledge of key ISAs can serve as a good starting point.

In audit evidence questions you may think about the financial statement assertions (completeness, accuracy, existence etc). You could also think about the different types of procedures (inspection, observation, inquiry, confirmation, recalculation/reperformance and analytical procedures).

In risk questions it might be helpful to think about the different elements of risk (inherent risk, control risk, detection risk).

Repeating this knowledge will not be sufficient in most cases to pass the question but these ideas can form a very sound basis for developing a good answer.

Keep going back to the requirement and make sure that you really are answering the question. One of the most common errors in auditing papers is identifying the correct point but using it in the wrong way. Make sure that your answer is focused on the requirements. It may be tempting to write everything you know about a particular point but this will not help you to pass the exam. This 'scattergun' approach will attract few, if any, marks.

Producing your answer

Although much of the hard work has been done by the time you get to this stage you need to think carefully about how you put down each point on paper. The way you make the point can make a difference to the number of marks scored. You need to make sure your answers do not suffer from a lack of clarity and precision. This is particularly the case regarding questions on audit evidence. For example lists of tests stating 'check this' and 'check that' without explaining what is being checked and why is likely to score few marks. If you find it difficult to gauge the right level of detail try to imagine that you are explaining the procedure to a junior member of staff. Would they be able to perform the procedure based on your description?

Think about your style. A well structured answer with clearly identifiable points is generally preferable to long paragraphs of text. However, do not fall into the trap of producing note-form answers. This is rarely sufficiently detailed to score marks.

Gaining the easy marks

Easy marks in this paper tend to fall into two categories.

Objective test questions (OTQs)

Some OTQs are easier than others, particularly MCQs. Answer those that you feel fairly confident about as quickly as you can. Come back later to those you find more difficult. This could be a way of making use of the time in the examination most efficiently and effectively.

Make sure that you understand the wording of OTQs before selecting your answer.

Discussions in Section B questions

A Section B question may separate discussion requirements from calculations, so that you do not need to do the calculations first in order to answer the discussion part. This means that you should be able to gain marks from making sensible, practical comments without having to complete the calculations.

Discussions that are focused on the specific organisation in the question will gain more marks than regurgitation of knowledge. Read the question carefully and more than once, to ensure you are actually answering the specific requirements.

Pick out key words such as 'describe', 'evaluate' and 'discuss'. These all mean something specific.

- 'Describe' means to communicate the key features of
- 'Evaluate' means to assess the value of
- 'Discuss' means to examine in detail by argument

Clearly label the points you make in discussions so that the marker can identify them all rather than getting lost in the detail.

Provide answers in the form requested. Use a report format if asked for and give recommendations if required.

Tackling Objective Test Case Questions

In the paper-based exam you will only see MCQs in the objective test case questions. In the CBE you will see other styles of question in addition to MCQs including number entry, multiple response and drag and drop.

First, read the whole case scenario. Make a note of any specific instructions or assumptions, such as key dates.

Then skim through the requirements of the five questions. The questions are independent of each other and can be answered in any order.

Some of the questions will be easier than others. For example, you may be asked to identify risks to independence from a given scenario.

Other questions will be more difficult and/or complex. There are two types of question that may take you longer to answer.

The first more time-consuming question is one where you are asked to consider two related issues. The best approach to adopt here is a step-by-step approach, dealing with each issue in turn. For example you could be asked to consider whether a potential adjustment is material and the impact of this on the audit report based on circumstances set out in the scenario. The first step would be to assess the materiality of the adjustment using your technical knowledge, but also applying any information given to you in the scenario. Having made a decision it should be possible to discount at least one of the distracters. Then think about the impact on the auditor's report. Does the audit opinion need to be modified or not? If it is, is the issue pervasive or not? If possible, try to come to your own conclusion before looking at the options available, then check whether your answer is one of the options listed. (Obviously if you are struggling looking at the remaining available options may help to jog your memory.) Having selected your answer always check the remaining distracters to ensure that you haven't made a common mistake.

The second more time-consuming question is one where you are asked to consider a number of statements and identify which one (or more) of them is correct. Make sure that you read each statement at least twice before making your selection. Be careful to follow the requirements of the question exactly, for example if you are asked to identify **two** correct statements. Make sure that you have spotted any negative questions eg 'Which **TWO** of the following are **NOT**....'

Exam information

Computer-based exams

ACCA have commenced the launch of computer-based exams (CBEs) for F5–F9. They have been piloting computer-based exams in limited markets since September 2016 with the aim of rolling out into all markets internationally over a five-year period. Paper-based examinations will be run in parallel while the CBEs are phased in and BPP materials have been designed to support you, whichever exam option you choose.

Exam duration

The Skills module examinations F5–F9 contain a mix of objective and longer type questions with a duration of three hours for 100 marks. For paper-based exams there are an extra 15 minutes to reflect the manual effort required.

Extensive analysis has been undertaken to ensure that paper- and computer-based exams are educationally equivalent and that students are assessed with the same rigour in both formats. As part of the quality assurance process, ACCA has undertaken a number of tests with external stakeholders including learning providers and students across the globe, including exam trials (where exam-ready students sit both formats and statistical analysis is performed on both sets of results) and focus groups (where students and learning providers supplied feedback on their experience of taking computer exams compared to paper exams). It is this work that has given ACCA, and should give students, assurance that CBE and paper exams are fair and equivalent with regards to time and standard.

As ACCA increases its offering of F5–F9 session CBEs, it will be introducing seeded content to further guarantee all exams are equivalent and fair. When the seeded content is introduced, students will be given more time to complete the exams – increasing to 3 hours and 20 minutes to take into account the inclusion of additional seeded content.

For more information on these changes and when they will be implemented, please visit the ACCA website: www.accaglobal.com/gb/en/student/exam-entry-and-administration/computer-based-exams/session-cbes.html

Format of the exam

The exam format is the same irrespective of the mode of delivery and will comprise two exam sections:

Section	Style of question type	Description	Proportion of exam, %
A	Objective test (OT) case	3 questions × 10 marks Each question will contain 5 subparts each worth 2 marks	30
B	Constructed Response (Long questions)	1 question × 30 marks 2 questions × 20 marks	70
Total			100

Section A questions will be selected from the entire syllabus. The paper versions of these objective test questions contain multiple choice only and the computer-based versions will contain a variety. The responses to each question or subpart in the case of OT cases are marked automatically as either correct or incorrect by computer.

Section B questions will mainly focus on the following syllabus areas but a minority of marks can be drawn from any other area of the syllabus

- Planning and risk assessment (syllabus area B)
- Internal control (syllabus area C)
- Audit evidence (syllabus area D)

The responses to these questions are human marked.

Additional information

The study guide provides more detailed guidance on the syllabus and can be found by visiting the exam resource finder on the ACCA website: www.accaglobal.com/uk/en/student/exam-support-resources.html

Useful websites

The websites below provide additional sources of information of relevance to your studies for *Audit and Assurance*.

- www.accaglobal.com

  ACCA's website. The students' section of the website is invaluable for detailed information about the qualification, past issues of *Student Accountant* (including technical articles) and a free downloadable Student Planner App.

- www.bpp.com

  Our website provides information about BPP products and services, with a link to the ACCA website.

- www.ifac.org

  This website provides information on international accounting and auditing issues.

- www.ft.com

  This website provides information about current international business. You can search for information and articles on specific industry groups as well as individual companies.

Questions

AUDIT FRAMEWORK AND REGULATION

Questions 1–35 cover Audit framework and regulation, the subject of Part A of the BPP Study Text for F8.

BJM Co
20 mins

The following scenario relates to questions 1–5.

You are an audit senior of YHT & Co and have worked on the external audit of BJM Co (BJM), an unlisted company, since your firm was appointed external auditor two years ago.

BJM owns a chain of nine restaurants and is a successful company. BJM has always been subject to national hygiene regulations, especially in relation to the food preparation process. Non-compliance can result in a large fine or closure of the restaurant concerned.

The Board of BJM have recently notified you that the national hygiene regulations have been updated and are now much more stringent and onerous than before.

With this in mind, the Board have asked your firm to conduct a review of BJM's compliance with hygiene regulations, in order to allow the Board to assess whether the appropriate processes have been implemented at each of the nine restaurants. The review is not expected to include the provision of accounting advice or the preparation of figures in the financial statements.

The work is likely to be very lucrative. Your firm has sufficient experience to undertake the above review engagement.

1   Despite running a successful company, BJM's Board have often needed to be reminded of some fundamental principles and you often have to explain key concepts.

Which of the following statements best defines the external audit?

√ A   The external audit is an exercise carried out by auditors in order to give an opinion on whether the financial statements of a company are fairly presented.

B   The external audit is an exercise carried out in order to give an opinion on the effectiveness of a company's internal control system.

C   The purpose of the external audit is to identify areas of deficiency within a company and to make recommendations to mitigate those deficiencies.

D   The external audit provides negative assurance on the truth and fairness of a company's financial statements.

2   The Board has also struggled to differentiate between their responsibilities and those of the external auditor in circumstances such as the prevention and detection of fraud and error, and compliance with regulations.

Which of the following statements best describes YHT & Co's responsibility regarding BJM's compliance with hygiene regulations, in line with ISA 250 *Consideration of laws and regulations in an audit of financial statements*?

A   YHT & Co should actively prevent and detect non-compliance with the regulations.

√ B   YHT & Co should perform specific audit procedures to identify possible non-compliance.

C   YHT & Co should obtain sufficient appropriate audit evidence about BJM's compliance with the regulations as they have a direct effect on the financial statements.

D   YHT & Co does not have any responsibility as the hygiene regulations do not have a direct effect on the financial statements.

3   The partner responsible for the review of hygiene compliance has informed you that the engagement is an assurance engagement.

Which of the following would **NOT** have been relevant to the partner in forming this opinion?

    A   The existence of a three-party relationship
    B   The existence of suitable criteria
   ✓C   The determination of materiality
    D   The subject matter

---

4   The partner responsible for the review engagement has asked you to tell him what level of assurance you believe YHT & Co should provide, and also what type of opinion the firm should give.

What is the level of assurance and type of opinion that can be provided on this review engagement?

	Level of assurance	Report wording
A	Reasonable	Positive
B	Reasonable	Negative
C	Limited	Positive
✓ D	Limited	Negative

---

5   The audit partner has told you that the independence threats arising from YHT & Co performing the review engagement should be monitored carefully.

Which of the following is likely to cause the audit partner most concern?

    A   According to the ACCA Code of Ethics and Conduct, YHT & Co is prohibited from providing other assurance services to an audit client.

    B   The review engagement is likely to give rise to a self-review threat, as the outcomes of the review could form the basis of the financial statements which the audit team will audit.

   ✓C   The lucrative nature of the review engagement may make the external audit team less inclined to require management to make adjustments or to issue a modified audit opinion, for fear of losing the review engagement.

    D   If the new review engagement causes YHT & Co's fee income from BJM to exceed 15% of the firm's total fees, the ACCA Code of Ethics and Conduct states that the new engagement must be turned down.

(Total = 10 marks)

Conoy (CBE)   20 mins

The following scenario relates to questions 6–10.

Conoy designs and manufactures luxury motor vehicles. It is not a listed company and its shares are held equally by 12 individuals, most of whom belong to the same family. Many of these shareholders are also executive directors.

Conoy has an internal audit department, although the chief internal auditor frequently comments that Conoy's Board does not understand his reports, and does not provide sufficient support for his department and for the company's internal control systems. RWG & Co, Conoy's external auditors, have also expressed concern in this area.

The Board is considering a proposal from the chief internal auditor to establish an audit committee. The committee would consist of one executive director, the chief internal auditor, and three new appointees. One appointee would have a non-executive seat on the board of directors.

The board is also considering a significant expansion of the company. However, the company's bank is concerned by the standard of financial reporting as Conoy's finance director recently left the company. The board is delaying providing the bank with financial information until a new finance director has been appointed.

6   One of the shareholders, who is not an executive director, has heard about Conoy's plans to establish an audit committee. He has drawn up a list of statements which he feels the Board should review before making any decisions:

Which **TWO** of the statements made by the shareholder are **TRUE** in relation to the establishment of the audit committee?

- ☐ Those remaining shareholders who are not already executive directors should be appointed as non-executive directors and should be part of the audit committee
- ☑ The chief internal auditor should not be part of the audit committee
- ☑ Establishing an audit committee will mean that there is a specialist group of individuals which is responsible for monitoring high quality internal controls
- ☐ Establishing an audit committee will mean that the external audit fee will be reduced

7   Once established, the audit committee will have many objectives.

Which of the following does **NOT** form part of the audit committee's objectives?

- ☐ Safeguarding the privacy of whistleblowers
- ☑ Appointing the external auditor
- ☐ Monitoring the independence of the external auditor
- ☐ Implementing a policy on the supply of non-audit services by the external auditor

8   Conoy's internal audit department is currently not well understood or supported by the Board.

Which **TWO** of the following statements describe the main advantages of establishing an audit committee?

- ☑ The position of the internal audit department will be strengthened within the organisation
- ☐ Corporate governance will be enhanced as the board of directors will report to the audit committee
- ☑ The effectiveness of the internal audit department will be improved as the audit committee will monitor and review its performance on a regular basis
- ☐ The workload of the internal audit department will be better managed as the audit committee will be able to minimise the extent to which the external auditors rely on the work of the internal auditors

9   Which of the following statements best describes why having an audit committee could help Conoy raise additional finance by addressing the concerns of the bank?

- ☐ The independent non-executive members of the audit committee can provide guarantees to the bank concerning Conoy's financial viability.
- ☐ The audit committee will have at least one member who has relevant financial experience. This person will be able to stand in for as Conoy's finance director before a new finance director is appointed.
- ☑ The audit committee will have at least one member who has relevant financial experience, so that they can monitor the integrity of the financial statements
- ☐ The audit committee will review all the available evidence to substantiate information in financial reporting, thus improving the credibility of the financial statements

10   RWG & Co, Conoy's external auditor, believes that Conoy establishing an audit committee would bring the external auditor additional benefits.

Which of the following is **NOT** an advantage to RWG & Co of Conoy establishing an audit committee?

☐   RWG & Co would be able to report its audit findings and recommendations to an independent sub-committee

☐   RWG & Co would have a sub-committee with which it could raise issues of concern

☑   The audit committee will support RWG & Co's viewpoint in the event of any disputes with the management of Conoy

☐   The audit committee would have more time to examine RWG & Co's reports and recommendations and so providecomfort that recommendations and other matters are being considered and reviewed

(Total = 10 marks)

Stark

20 mins

The following scenario relates to questions 11–15.

You are an audit manager of Ali & Co and have just been assigned the audit of Stark Co (Stark). Stark, a listed company, provides investment advice to individuals, and is regulated by the relevant financial conduct authority.

Mr Day, a partner in Ali & Co, has been the audit engagement partner for Stark for the previous nine years and has excellent knowledge of the client. Mr Day has informed you that he would like his daughter Zoe to be part of the audit team this year; Zoe is currently studying for her first set of fundamentals papers for her ACCA qualification.

In an initial meeting with the finance director of Stark, you learn that the audit team will not be entertained on Stark's yacht this year, instead, he has arranged a balloon flight costing less than one-tenth of the expense of using the yacht and hopes this will be acceptable.

Ali & Co has always carried out tax advisory work for Stark. The tax advisory services do not have an impact on the figures reported in the financial statements. The finance director has stated that he feels strongly that the firm that offers taxation services this year should charge a fee which is based on a percentage of tax saved. He also trusts that your firm will accept a fixed fee for representing Stark in a dispute regarding the amount of sales tax payable to the taxation authorities.

11   From a review of the information above, your audit assistant has highlighted some of the potential risks to independence in respect of the audit of Stark.

(1)   Mr Day would like his daughter Zoe to be part of the audit team
(2)   Audit team to be offered a balloon flight
(3)   Tax fee to be based on a percentage of tax saved
(4)   Firm to represent Stark in a dispute with the tax authorities

Which of the following options best identifies the valid threats to independence and allocates the threat to the most appropriate category?

	Advocacy	Intimidation	Self-interest
A	(3) and (4)	(3) only	(1) and (2)
✓ B	(4) only	(3) only	(2) and (3)
C	(3) only	(3) and (4)	(2)
D	(3) and (4)	(1) and (4)	(1) and (2)

12   In relation to the audit team being offered a balloon ride:

Which of the following actions should be taken to ensure the firm complies with ACCA's Code of Ethics and Conduct?

A   The gift may be accepted as Stark has taken appropriate measures to reduce the value of the gift compared to previous years.

B   The value of the gift should be assessed to determine whether it is of material value to the financial statements.

✓C   The gift should only be accepted if its value is trivial and inconsequential to the recipients.

D   Only the audit partner and audit manager should accept the gift.

13   In relation to the audit engagement partner holding the role for nine years:

Which of the following safeguards should be implemented in order to comply with ACCA's Code of Ethics and Conduct?

A   An independent review partner should be appointed to the audit.

B   The audit engagement partner should be removed from the audit team but may serve as a quality control reviewer.

C   Ali & Co should not audit Stark for a two year period.

✓D   The audit engagement partner should be removed from the audit team.

14   Mr Day's daughter, Zoe, is currently learning about International Standards on Auditing (ISAs) in her studies. She has asked you for clarification of the following.

Which is the correct order of the following stages involved in the development of an ISA?

(1)   Distribution of exposure draft for public comment
(2)   Consideration of comments received from the public
(3)   Approval by IAASB members
(4)   Establishment of task force to develop draft standard
(5)   Discussion of proposed standard at a public meeting

A   1, 5, 4, 3, 2
B   2, 4, 1, 3, 5
✓C   4, 5, 1, 2, 3
D   5, 4, 2, 1, 3

15   Zoe is also concerned that Ali & Co might breach confidentiality were the audit firm to represent Stark in its dispute with the tax authorities.

Which of the following statements best reflects the auditor's duty of confidentiality?

A   Auditors must never, under any circumstances, disclose any matters of which they become aware during the course of the audit to third parties, without the permission of the client.

B   Auditors may disclose any matters in relation to criminal activities to the police or taxation authorities, if requested to do so by the police or a tax inspector.

✓C   Auditors may disclose matters to third parties without their client's consent if it is in the public interest, and they must do so if there is a statutory duty to do so.

D   Auditors may only disclose matters to third parties without their client's consent if the public interest or national security is involved.

(Total = 10 marks)

Tangerine Tech Co (Mar/Jun 16) (amended)   20 mins

The following scenario relates to questions 16–20.

You are an audit manager of Satsuma & Co and have been assigned to the audit of Tangerine Tech Co (Tangerine), a company which is planning to list on a stock exchange within six months. The listing rules of the stock exchange require compliance with corporate governance principles, and the directors are unsure whether they are following best practice in relation to this. They have asked the audit engagement partner for their view on this matter.

Tangerine's board is comprised of six executive directors, a non-executive chairman and three other non-executive directors (NEDs). The chairman and one of the NEDS are former directors of Tangerine and on reaching retirement age were asked to take on non-executive roles. The company has established an audit committee, and all NEDs are members including the chairman who chairs the committee. All four members of the audit committee were previously involved in sales or production related roles.

All of the directors have been members of the board for at least four years. As the chairman does not have an executive role, he has sole responsibility for liaising with the shareholders and answering their questions. The company has not established an internal audit function to monitor internal controls.

16   Which of the following features are corporate governance weaknesses which Tangerine Co would need to address prior to their listing?

    (1)   The chairman has sole responsibility for liaising with shareholders
    (2)   The company has not established an internal audit function
    (3)   The chairman and one of the NEDs are former executive directors of Tangerine Co

    A   1 and 2 only
✓ B   1 and 3 only
    C   2 and 3 only
    D   1, 2 and 3

---

17   The audit engagement partner's review has identified the following additional corporate governance weaknesses:

    (1)   All the directors have been members of the board for at least four years
    (2)   The board is comprised of six executive and four non-executive directors

Which of the following would the engagement partner recommend to address these weaknesses to ensure compliance with corporate governance principles?

	Weakness 1	Weakness 2
✓ A	The directors should be subject to re-election at regular intervals not exceeding three years	At least 50% of the board must be comprised of non-executive directors
B	The directors must be re-appointed annually by the chairman	At least 75% of the board must be comprised of executive directors
C	The directors should be subject to re-election at regular intervals not exceeding three years	At least 75% of the board must be comprised of executive directors
D	The directors must be re-appointed annually by the chairman	At least 50% of the board must be comprised of non-executive directors

---

18   The engagement partner has assessed the make-up of the audit committee.

Which of the following would be valid conclusions from this assessment?

    (1)   It is acceptable for the chairman to chair the audit committee
    (2)   A new member of the audit committee with relevant financial experience must be recruited

    A   1 only
✓ B   2 only
    C   1 and 2
    D   Neither 1 nor 2

19   The directors are aware that in accordance with corporate governance provisions they have responsibilities for internal control but are unclear as to the extent of these responsibilities.

Which of the following correctly describes their responsibilities?

	To review internal controls annually	To report on internal controls to shareholders
A	No	No
B	Yes	No
C	No	Yes
✓ D	Yes	Yes

20   The board of Tangerine is considering establishing an internal audit function.

Which of the following factors would be relevant in making this decision?

(1)   It would help the audit committee to discharge its responsibilities for monitoring internal control

(2)   The board would no longer need to take responsibility for the prevention and detection of fraud and error

(3)   The costs of establishing an internal audit function should be considered against the benefits gained

A	1 and 2 only
✓ B	1 and 3 only
C	2 and 3 only
D	1, 2 and 3

(Total = 10 marks)

LV Fones (6/10) (amended) (CBE)   20 mins

The following scenario relates to questions 21–25.

You are the audit manager of Jones & Co and you are planning the audit of LV Fones Co, a listed company, which has been an audit client for four years and specialises in manufacturing luxury mobile phones.

During the planning stage of the audit you have obtained the following information. The employees of LV Fones Co are entitled to purchase smartphones at a discount of 10%. The audit team has in previous years been offered the same level of staff discount.

During the year the financial controller of LV Fones was ill and hence unable to work. The company had no spare staff able to fulfil the role and hence a qualified audit senior of Jones & Co was seconded to the client for three months to cover the work of the financial controller. The audit partner has recommended that the audit senior work on the audit as he has good knowledge of the client. The fee income derived from LV Fones was boosted by this engagement and along with the audit and tax fee, now accounts for 16% of the firm's total fees, (15.7% last year).

From a review of the correspondence files you note 20% of last year's audit fee is still outstanding.

Based on the information above you have summarised some of the potential risks to independence in the audit of LV Fones as follows.

(1)   The audit team has been offered a discount on luxury phones
(2)   The audit senior was seconded to LV to cover for the financial controller
(3)   Total fees from LV is over 15% of the total fees of the firm for the second consecutive year
(4)   Fees are overdue in respect of last year's audit

21 Which of the following options best identifies the valid potential threats to independence in the audit of LV Fones and allocates the threat to the most appropriate category?

Self-interest	**Self-review**
1 and 2 only	3 and 4 only
3 and 4 only	1 and 2 only
✓ 1, 3 and 4	2 only
3 only	1, 2 and 4

22 You have also discovered that the engagement partner and the finance director have known each other socially for many years, and in fact went on holiday together last summer with their families to the finance director's villa.

Which **TWO** threats to independence are raised by this relationship and what safeguards should be applied?

Threats	**Safeguards**
Familiarity and self-interest	Jones & Co to resign as auditors
Self-review and intimidation	Rotation of audit partner
Self-review and intimidation	Jones & Co to resign as auditors
✓ Familiarity and self-interest	Rotation of audit partner

23 In relation to the audit team being offered a 10% discount on mobile phones:

Which of the following statements is true in accordance with ACCA's Code of Ethics and Conduct?

☐ The audit team can accept the discount as it is on the same terms as that offered to staff

☐ Junior members of the audit team are allowed to accept the discount, but the audit manager and audit partner should not

✓ Unless the value of the discount is trivial and inconsequential to the audit team members, the offer should be declined

☐ The audit team is only allowed to accept a discount of up to 5%

24 Which of the following steps must Jones & Co take, as the fees from LV have exceeded 15% for the last two years?

(1) Resign from the audit
(2) Disclose the matter to those charged with governance
(3) Arrange for a pre- or post-issuance review

☐ 1 only
☐ 2 only
☐ 3 only
✓ 2 and 3

25   The finance director of LV has made some enquiries about the other services that Jones & Co may be able to assist with.

In the table below indicate whether Jones & Co would or would not be able to provide the other services.

	Service can be provided	Service cannot be provided
Design and implementation of IT systems over financial reporting		☑
Assistance with preparation of tax return	☑	
Accounting services		☑
Recruiting service for the position of credit controller	☑	

(Total = 10 marks)

Orange (CBE)   20 mins

The following scenario relates to questions 26–30.

You are the audit manager of Currant & Co and you are planning the audit of Orange Financials Co (Orange), who specialise in the provision of loans and financial advice to individuals and companies. Currant & Co has audited Orange for many years.

The directors are planning to list Orange on a stock exchange within the next few months and have asked if the engagement partner can attend the meetings with potential investors. In addition, as the finance director of Orange is likely to be quite busy with the listing, he has asked if Currant & Co can produce the financial statements for the current year.

During the year, the assistant finance director of Orange left and joined Currant & Co as a partner. It has been suggested that due to his familiarity with Orange, he should be appointed to provide an independent partner review for the audit.

Once Orange obtains its stock exchange listing it will require several assignments to be undertaken, for example, obtaining advice about corporate governance best practice. Currant & Co is very keen to be appointed to these engagements, however, Orange has implied that in order to gain this work Currant & Co needs to complete the external audit quickly and with minimal questions/issues.

The finance director has informed you that once the stock exchange listing has been completed, he would like the engagement team to attend a weekend away at a luxury hotel with his team, as a thank you for all their hard work. In addition, he has offered a senior member of the engagement team a short-term loan at a significantly reduced interest rate.

Orange is aware that subsequent to the stock exchange listing it will need to establish an audit committee, and has asked for some advice in relation to this.

26   As part of your planning work you have identified a number of potential risks to independence:

(1)   The engagement partner has been asked to attend meetings with potential investors

(2)   Currant & Co has been offered the opportunity to provide other services to Orange Financials

(3)   Currant & Co have been asked to produce the financial statements of Orange Financials

(4)   There is a suggestion that a partner who previously worked for Orange Financials should be the review partner

Which of these issues could give rise to an advocacy threat?

☑ 1 only
☐ 2 and 3
☐ 4 only
☐ 2 and 4

27 Orange Financials has been offered work by Orange Financials. This is dependent on the audit being completed with minimal issues.

Which **TWO** of the following threats does this situation create?

- [✓] Intimidation
- [✓] Self-interest
- [ ] Familiarity
- [ ] Advocacy

---

28 The finance director has made two offers to members of the audit team:

(1) Weekend away
(2) Loan at reduced rates

Which of the following correctly summarises which of the offers, if any can be accepted?

	(1)	**(2)**
[ ]	Accepted	Accepted
[ ]	Accepted	Not accepted
[✓]	Not accepted	Accepted
[✓]	Not accepted	Not accepted

---

29 In accordance with ACCA's Code of Ethics and Conduct you have concluded that if you win the additional work you will need to disclose the proportion of fees obtained from Orange Financials to those charged with governance and conduct a post-issuance review.

Which of the following explains the basis for your conclusion?

- [ ] Total fees from Orange Financials will make up more than 10% of Currant Co's total fees for the first time since your appointment
- [ ] Total non-audit fees from all Currant Co's clients make up more than 5% of the total fees of the firm
- [✓] Total fees from Orange Financials make up more than 15% of Currant Co's total fees for the second consecutive year
- [ ] The disclosure and review are required in all circumstances where services other than audit are offered, irrespective of the level of fees

---

30 The board has noted down a number of statements relating to the audit committee and have asked you to confirm whether their understanding is correct.

Indicate whether the following statements are true or false.

	True	False
The audit committee should be made up of independent non-executive directors	✓	
The audit committee normally appoints the external auditors at the AGM		✓
The audit committee monitors and reviews the internal audit function	✓	
The audit committee sets out the scope of the external auditor's work		✓

(Total = 10 marks)

SGCC (CBE)

20 mins

The following scenario relates to questions 31–35.

You are an audit manager in HTQ & Co. One of your clients, SGCC, has recently become a listed company and has asked for your advice regarding the changes they should make to achieve appropriate compliance with corporate governance codes.

The Board

Mr Sheppard is the Chief Executive Officer and Chairman of the Board of SGCC. He appoints and maintains a board of five executive and two non-executive directors. While the board sets performance targets for the senior managers in the company, no formal targets are set for each director and no review of board policies is carried out. Board salaries are therefore set and paid by Mr Sheppard based on his assessment of all the board members, including himself, and not their actual performance.

Internal controls

Internal controls in SGCC are monitored by the senior accountant, although the company assumes that, as external auditors, your firm will carry out a detailed review of internal controls. SGCC does not have an internal audit department or an audit committee.

Annual financial statements are produced, providing detailed information on past performance.

31   From a review of the information above, your audit assistant has highlighted some weaknesses in SGCC's corporate governance especially concerning the composition of the Board.

Which of the following actions are appropriate to improve SGCC's corporate governance compliance?

- [ ] SGCC should appoint an external consultant to review board policies
- [✓] SGCC should appoint a new Chief Executive Officer or board Chairman
- [ ] SGCC should create a Remuneration Committee to oversee the appointment of new directors
- [ ] SGCC should implement a formal and rigorous evaluation of its directors' performance once every two years

32   Which **ONE** of the following statements is correct with regards to the composition of the board at SGCC?

- [✓] SGCC should appoint three new non-executive directors to the board
- [ ] SGCC should re-appoint two of its executive directors as non-executive directors
- [ ] SGCC should appoint three new executive directors to the board
- [ ] SGCC should re-appoint three of its executive directors as non-executive directors

33   Your audit assistant does not feel that SGCC's approach to internal controls is sufficiently robust to comply with corporate governance principles and has drawn up a list of recommendations.

Which **TWO** of the following recommendations are valid?

- [ ] SGCC should establish an audit committee with at least four directors as is required for all listed companies
- [ ] SGCC must establish an internal audit department as is required for all listed companies
- [✓] Once SGCC has an audit committee and an internal audit department, the head of the internal audit department should report to the audit committee
- [✓] SGCC should not rely on the external audit to inform them of deficiencies in internal controls

34   You are aware that SGCC is considering establishing an internal audit department.

With which of the following activities should the internal audit function **NOT** be involved?

- [ ] Monitoring of management's performance
- [ ] Reviewing adequacy of management information for decision-making purposes
- [✓] Taking responsibility for the implementation of a new sales ledger system
- [ ] Assessing compliance with regulation relevant to SGCC

---

35   If SGCC's Board decides to establish an internal audit department they will also need to decide whether they will employ members of staff or outsource the department to an external firm. You have drawn up a list of the advantages of outsourcing as compared to the advantages of employing staff directly including the following points:

(1)   Greater availability of specialist industry skills as required
(2)   Flexibility regarding staff numbers in response to changing circumstances
(3)   Elimination of direct training costs
(4)   Development of skills increasing the value of the human resource asset

For each advantage indicate whether it relates to the employment of internal auditors by SGCC or the outsourcing of the department.

Consideration	Employed	Outsourced
(1)	[ ]	[✓]
(2)	[ ]	[✓]
(3)	[ ]	[✓]
(4)	[✓]	[ ]

(Total = 10 marks)

PLANNING AND RISK ASSESSMENT

Questions 36–80 cover Audit planning and risk assessment, the subject of Part B of the BPP Study Text for F8.

Bridgford (CBE)   20 mins

The following scenario relates to questions 36–40.

You are an audit senior of Ovette & Co and your firm has recently been appointed as the auditor to Bridgford Products (Bridgford), a large company which sells televisions, DVD players and Blu-ray Disc players to electrical retailers.

You are planning the audit for the year ended 31 January 20X9 and your audit manager has asked you to produce both the audit strategy document and the detailed audit plan, including an assessment of materiality.

In order to assist you in your planning work you have visited Bridgford, where you obtained the following information.

Sales have increased during the year ended 31 January 20X9 following a move to attract new customers by offering extended credit. The new credit arrangements allow customers three months' credit, rather than the one month credit period allowed previously. As a result of this change, you have calculated that trade receivables days have increased from 49 days to 127 days.

Bridgford installed a new computerised inventory control system, which began operating on 1 June 20X8. Since the inventory control system records both inventory movements and current inventory quantities, Bridgford is proposing to use the inventory quantities on the computer to value the inventory at the year-end rather than carrying out an inventory count.

The production director informed you that in the last month or so there have been reliability problems with the company's products which have resulted in some customers refusing to pay for the products.

As part of the planning process you also undertake a risk assessment. Based on the information you have obtained to date you have identified several audit risks which you feel your team will need to address. The first risk relates to the extended credit terms offered by Bridgford to its customers, and the recent product reliability problems resulting in customers' refusal to pay.

A second audit risk relates to the computerised inventory control system which was implemented on 1 June 20X8. You are concerned about whether data was accurately transferred into the new system, and whether it is sufficiently reliable to determine the quantity of inventory for the year-end financial statements.

36   The audit manager has requested that you cover the following areas in the audit planning documentation:

(1)   The availability of the client's data and staff (including internal audit)
(2)   The allocation of responsibility for specific audit procedures to audit team members
(3)   The audit procedures to be undertaken for each area of the financial statements
(4)   The potential for using computer assisted audit techniques (CAATs) to gather evidence

Which of the following options correctly identifies which information would be included in the audit strategy and the detailed audit plan?

	Audit strategy	Detailed audit plan
☐	(1) and (2)	(3) and (4)
☑	(1) and (4)	(2) and (3)
☐	(2) and (4)	(1) and (3)
☐	(1) only	(2), (3) and (4)

37   You have set the level of materiality for the financial statements as a whole, and now need to determine performance materiality.

Which of the following statements about performance materiality is **NOT** true?

☐ Performance materiality is used to reduce the risk that the aggregate of uncorrected and undetected misstatements exceeds materiality for the financial statements as a whole to an acceptable level

☑ Performance materiality refers to the amounts set by the auditor at higher than the materiality level for particular classes of transactions, account balances or disclosures where the materiality level might otherwise mean that such items are not tested.

☐ Once the materiality for the financial statements as whole has been set, a lower level of performance materiality is determined by the auditor using his or her professional judgement.

☐ The performance materiality level is affected by the auditor's understanding of the entity and the nature and extent of misstatements identified in prior audits.

38   ISA 520 *Analytical procedures* states that where analytical procedures identify fluctuations or relationships that are inconsistent with other relevant information or that differ significantly from the expected results, the auditor shall investigate the reason for this.

Which of the following audit responses to the increase in trade receivables days of Bridgford is the **LEAST** relevant?

☐ Make enquiries of management to understand the likely reason why trade receivables days exceed the extended credit period

reduction in receivables

☐ Perform detailed substantive testing on the aged receivables listing, to determine whether any amounts should be written off

☑ Perform a trend analysis on current year and prior year monthly revenue, to identify whether revenue is overstated as a result of fraud or error

☐ Perform further working capital ratio analysis, to determine the effect of the extended credit on Bridgford's cash position

39   Which of the following statements summarises your key concern regarding the risk relating to the extended credit terms and refusal of certain customers to pay?

☐ That the directors may have presented Bridgford as a going concern when this is not the case
☐ Existence of receivables
☐ Completeness of receivables
☑ Valuation of receivables

40   Which of the following procedures is **NOT** a relevant response to the risk that inventory quantities are misstated by the new computerised inventory system?

☐ Determine the process by which information was input in to the new system and the level of testing performed by Bridgford to ascertain the accuracy of the transfer

☐ Determine how often inventory counts are performed and the level of corrections required to the inventory system

☑ Review sales prices of inventory sold after the year end to identify inventory where cost exceeds net realisable value

☐ Test the operation of the inventory system using computer assisted audit techniques

(Total = 10 marks)

EuKaRe (12/08) (amended) (CBE)

20 mins

The following scenario relates to questions 41–45.

You are an audit senior of TEY & Co and are responsible for planning the audit of EuKaRe for the year ended 30 September 20X8.

EuKaRe is a charity which was established over five years ago. The charity's aim is to provide support to children from disadvantaged backgrounds who wish to take part in sports such as tennis, badminton and football.

EuKaRe has a detailed constitution which explains how the charity's income can be spent. The constitution also notes that expenditure relating to the administration of the charity cannot exceed 10% of the charity's income in any year. EuKaRe currently employs three permanent members of staff. At present, 100 volunteers work for EuKaRe: some commit up to three days a week and others help out on an ad hoc basis. The organisation, including its finance department, is primarily run by volunteers.

The charity's income is derived wholly from voluntary donations. Sources of donations include the public in the form of cash collected in buckets by volunteers in shopping areas, and from generous individuals.

41   Based on your understanding of the nature of EuKaRe you have identified that income is primarily in the form of cash.

Which element of audit risk is increased by this fact?

☐	Detection risk
☑	Inherent risk
☐	Control risk
☐	Business risk

42   Your audit partner has highlighted to you that it is imperative that TEY & Co acts in line with ISA 315 *Identifying and assessing the risks of material misstatement through understanding the entity and its environment*. This means it must identify and assess the risks of material misstatement at both the financial statements level and at the assertion level, for classes of transactions, events and their related disclosures, and account balances and their related disclosures.

Which of the following statements is **NOT** an explanation of why ISA 315 *Identifying and assessing the risks of material misstatement through understanding the entity and its environment* requires a risk assessment to be carried out at the planning stage?

☐	The risk assessment will help the audit team gain an understanding of the entity for audit purposes
☑	The risk assessment will enable the audit senior to produce an accurate budget for the audit assignment
☐	The risk assessment will form the basis of the audit strategy and the detailed audit plan
☐	Once the risks have been assessed, TEY & Co can select audit team members with sufficient skill and experience to maximise the chance of those risks being addressed

43 You have identified several audit risks which you feel your team will need to address. One such audit risk relates to the risk that income may be understated in the financial statements. You are concerned that not all income may be recorded.

Which of the following statements is **NOT** a valid response to this audit risk?

- ☑ Obtain a breakdown of the income recorded from the cash that was collected in buckets, and vouch a sample of entries back to the volunteer in order to determine which volunteer collected the relevant donations

- ☐ Perform analytical procedures on the level of donations in shopping areas per volunteer

- ☐ Review the internal controls relating to cash collected in buckets to determine whether buckets are sealed, sequentially numbered and signed in and out by EuKaRe's volunteers

- ☐ Observe the counting and recording of proceeds from collections, to determine whether appropriate segregation of duties is in place

---

44 Another identified audit risk is the susceptibility of EuKaRe's business to fraud due to the high levels of cash involved.

Which of the following statements correctly describes the auditor's responsibilities in accordance with ISA 240 *The auditor's responsibilities relating to fraud in an audit of financial statements*?

- ☐ The auditor is responsible for the prevention and detection of fraud and error

- ☐ The auditor is not responsible for the prevention of fraud and error but is responsible for detection

- ☑ The auditor is responsible for obtaining reasonable assurance that the financial statements are free from material misstatement whether caused by fraud or error

- ☐ The auditor is responsible for detecting all errors and should attempt to detect fraud where information comes to light as a result of standard audit procedures

---

45 The audit manager has noted in the detailed audit plan that EuKaRe's control environment may be weak.

Which **TWO** of the following statements are valid reasons as to why EuKaRe may have a weak control environment?

- ☐ EuKaRe has a detailed constitution which explains how the charity's income can be spent

- ☑ EuKaRe's finance department relies on volunteers who may not have accounts experience

- ☐ A high proportion of the income of EuKaRe is cash

- ☑ Understaffing in the finance department at certain times is due to the ad hoc nature of volunteer working hours

(Total = 10 marks)

South

20 mins

The following scenario relates to questions 46–50.

You are an audit senior of KLT & Co, and your firm has recently been appointed as the auditor to South, a private company that runs seven supermarkets in the UK. You are currently planning your firm's first audit of South and are shortly due to make a preliminary visit to South's head office.

46   Your audit partner has highlighted to you that because South is a new audit client, it is particularly important that every member of the audit team has a good understanding of South's business.

Which of the following procedures must you use to obtain an understanding of the South and its environment in accordance with ISA 315 *Identifying and assessing the risks of material misstatement through understanding the entity and its environment*?

(1)   Analytical procedures
(2)   Inquiry
(3)   Confirmation
(4)   Reperformance

A   1, 2 and 3
B   1 and 2
C   2, 3 and 4
D   1 and 4

---

47   Having established a good understanding of South and its environment, the audit partner will need you to produce the planning documentation for the audit.

Which of the following statements describe the objectives / benefits of planning an audit according to ISA 300 *Planning an audit of financial statements* ?

(1)   To ensure appropriate attention is devoted to important areas of the audit
(2)   To assist in the coordination of work done by experts
(3)   To facilitate the assignment of work to audit team members
(4)   To ensure the audit is completed within budget restraints

A   1, 2, 3 and 4
B   1, 3 and 4
C   1, 2 and 3
D   2 and 3

Following your preliminary visit to South's head office you are now aware of the following information.

The company installed a new till system in all supermarkets four months before the year end. The new till system is linked to the accounting system at head office and automatically posts transactions to the accounting system. Previously journals were made manually based on totals on till rolls.

48   Having reviewed this information you have identified several audit risks which you feel your team will need to address. The first risk relates to the cost of the new till system which South has capitalised as a non-current asset. You are concerned that South may have included within the capitalised costs some items which are revenue in nature, leading to the overstatement of non-current assets.

Which of the following statements is a valid response to this audit risk?

A   Obtain a copy of the training manual relating to the new till system and discuss with directors the extent of training staff have received on the new system

B   Agree the capitalised costs from the trial balance back to invoices to confirm their value

C   Inspect invoices capitalised within the cost of the new till system to determine whether they are directly attributable to the cost of the new till system

D   Recalculate the depreciation charged on the new till system

49   A second audit risk relates to how well the new till system is operating. You are concerned that the system may not be reliable, and that consequently not all sales have been recorded, resulting in an understatement of revenue. You are also concerned that staff may not yet be familiar with the system, leading to an increased risk of errors relating to data entry.

Which of the following statements represent valid responses to this audit risk?

(1)   Perform analytical procedures by comparing daily / weekly sales by store with both the prior year and with expectations, in order to determine whether any unusual patterns have occurred following the installation of the new system

(2)   Vouch the sales revenue per the system to the till receipts to confirm the accuracy of the sales

(3)   Obtain a copy of the training manual relating to the new till system and discuss with directors the extent of training staff have received on the new system

(4)   Test the internal controls relating to the till system and the transfer of data into the accounting system

A   2 and 4
B   3 and 4
C   1, 2 and 4
D   1, 3 and 4

After a number of people living close to one of South's stores became seriously ill, the source of the illness was traced back to meat the customers had purchased from South. Legal proceedings were commenced against South by a number of customers during the financial year, demanding $1m in compensation.

50   You plan to review the legal correspondence relating to the claims made by customers to whom South sold contaminated meat.

Which of the following are valid objectives of this audit procedure?

(1)   To determine whether South's reputation will have been damaged within the local area

(2)   To confirm whether there are deficiencies in South's internal controls relating to food hygiene

(3)   To assess whether a provision for customer compensation is required in South's financial statements

(4)   To determine whether disclosure of the nature and financial effect of the legal claim is required in South's financial statements

A   2 and 3 only
B   3 and 4 only
C   2, 3 and 4 only
D   1, 2 , 3 and 4

(Total = 10 marks)

Mason   20 mins

The following scenario relates to questions 51–55.

You are an audit senior of IBN & Co and you are planning the audit of Mason Air Services (Mason) for the year ended 31 December 20X3.

Mason is a company that provides specialist helicopter support to the police force, the ambulance service, the fire service and the coastguard. Each of Mason's four contracts is equal in value. Mason owns and maintains the helicopter fleet which is held at cost. Each aircraft carries specialist equipment and is operated by a highly skilled specialist pilot.

51   Mason has secured a five year contract with each of its four customers (the police force, ambulance service, fire service and the coastguard). The contracts in place are all of equal value. Under the terms of the contract Mason charges customers an annual fee to cover the maintenance, storage and testing of the aircraft and equipment. The annual fee is payable in advance each year with the first annual payment being paid on the date the contract commences.

Based on the above information, which of the following statements summarises a key audit risk?

A   Mason's assets could be undervalued if the market value of the helicopter fleet exceeds its cost

B   Mason could breach the terms of its contracts with its customers and be liable to pay penalties, so provisions may be understated

√ C   Revenue may be overstated if it is recognised according to the contract date rather than over the relevant accounting period

D   An expert valuer is required to value the helicopters in the financial statements

---

52   Mason has not purchased any new helicopters during the year to 31 December 20X3; however there has been a lot of re-fitting, replacement and adding of specialist equipment to some of the existing aircraft. This has been necessary to keep up with the latest developments in search and rescue, and to maintain the aircraft to the high standard required under the contracts in place. This information has led you to be concerned that property, plant and equipment may be overstated in the financial statements.

Which of the following statements represents a valid response to this audit risk?

A   Perform a proof in total calculation of the depreciation charge for the year and investigate any significant differences

B   Review minutes of training meetings to determine whether the pilots have been trained how to use the specialist equipment

√ C   Obtain a breakdown of the capitalised costs and agree a sample of items to invoices to determine the nature of the expenditure

D   Discuss with directors how the acquisition of specialist equipment has been financed

---

53   From reading the prior year audit file you have just realised that Mason funded the original purchase of each aircraft with a secured loan carrying substantial interest charges. The loan is in the process of being renegotiated and the bank have indicated that finance costs will increase further.

Furthermore, the directors have told you that Mason's contract with the police force expires in March 20X4, at a time when the police are trying to substantially reduce the amount they pay in the wake of government cuts. It is thought that the contract will be put out to tender, and it is possible that another aircraft provider may also bid for the contract.

From the above information, which is the **MOST** important audit risk that should be documented in the detailed audit plan?

A   Disclosure relating to the secured loan may be omitted from the financial statements
√ B   Mason's going concern status may be at risk if the contract is not renewed
C   That interest charges may be understated
D   That the bank will rely on the audited financial statements when deciding whether to renew the loan

54 Which of the following are valid responses to the fact that Mason's contract with the police force is due for renewal?

    (1)   Review Mason's contracts with its other three customers to determine whether they contain a break clause, in order to determine the likelihood of losing any further contracts to other aircraft providers

    (2)   Contact the police force directly and request confirmation as to whether the contract is to be renewed

    (3)   Review the short-term and long-term funding facilities which are available to Mason

    (4)   Review correspondence with the police force to determine the likelihood of the contract being renewed

    A   1, 2 and 3
    B   1, 2 and 4
✓ C   1, 3 and 4
    D   2, 3 and 4

55 Mason also holds around $2 million of aircraft spares which are included within inventory. Mason sells the aircraft spares to amateur flying associations. Aircraft spares which are not sold after three years are scrapped.

Approximately a quarter of this value is made up of specialist equipment taken out of aircraft when it was replaced by newer or more advanced equipment. Such specialist equipment is transferred from non-current assets to inventory without adjustment, and continue to be recognised at amortised cost.

Which of the following summarises the key audit concern arising from the matter described?

    A   Accuracy, valuation and allocation of non-current assets
    B   Completeness of non-current assets
    C   Existence of inventory
✓ D   Accuracy, valuation and allocation of inventory

(Total = 10 marks)

Severn

20 mins

The following scenario relates to questions 56–60.

You are an audit manager of Rivers & Co. Your firm has been invited to tender for the audit of Severn Co, a listed company. Your firm does not have any other listed clients, and Severn will represent the biggest client of your firm (by client annual revenue) if your tender is successful.

A member of the audit committee of Severn Co informed your audit partner that the current auditors were not being invited to stand for re-election as the audit committee felt that the relationship between the firm and the company had begun to lose objectivity due to over-familiarity. You have reviewed past financial statements of Severn and have noted that the company applies IFRS, and that the audit committee reports on its responsibilities with regard to internal control annually. The director confirmed that the board would be happy to confirm their responsibilities in writing with Rivers & Co as they are aware of the relevant audit requirements.

56 The audit partner has asked you to prepare some information ready for the tender.

Which of the following would **NOT** be included in the tender for the audit of Severn Co?

    A   The proposed fee for the initial audit of Severn Co

    B   A description of Rivers & Co, including the curriculum vitae of key staff likely to be assigned to the client

✓ C   Overall level of materiality to be used in the audit

    D   A summary of potential other services Rivers & Co could provide to Severn Co

57   You have identified a number of issues which should be considered prior to tendering for a new client, whether:

(1)   The firm is independent of the potential client
(2)   The firm has the appropriate resources to conduct the audit of the potential client
(3)   The preconditions of audit will be met
(4)   The outgoing auditors will give Rivers & Co access to working papers

Given what you already know of Severn Co, which of these are most important to consider further prior to tendering for the audit?

A   1 and 2
B   2 and 3
C   3 and 4
D   1 and 4

Your firm has tendered for the engagement and has been successful. You have been asked to follow through the acceptance procedures for the firm.

58   You are re-appraising whether it is appropriate for the firm to accept the engagement.

Which of the following issues arising would cause Rivers & Co to decline the engagement?

A   The engagement letter has not been received by Rivers & Co.

B   Rivers & Co losing a major client meaning Severn's audit fee would represent 20% of annual firm income.

C   A reply from the outgoing auditors stating that they declined to seek reappointment to the audit of Severn Co due to a disagreement over accounting policies.

D   A request from Severn Co that the audit be carried out in March, when Rivers & Co already works at maximum capacity.

59   You are drafting an engagement letter in respect of Severn Co. You have identified four issues that could be included in the engagement letter:

(1)   Scope of the audit
(2)   Responsibilities of management of Severn Co
(3)   Timetable for the provision of accounting information by Severn Co
(4)   Fees and billing arrangements

Which of the above issues **MUST** be included in the engagement letter for it to comply with ISA 210 *Terms of audit engagements*?

A   1 and 4
B   2 and 3
C   3 and 4
D   1 and 2

60   Rivers & Co has now accepted the audit of Severn Co.

Which of the following actions in relation to Severn Co is **NOT** necessary at this stage?

A   Obtain references concerning the directors
B   Submit the letter of engagement
C   Carry out procedures to obtain an understanding of the entity
D   Appoint a quality control reviewer

(Total = 10 marks)

Goofy Co

20 mins

The following scenario relates to questions 61–65.

You are an audit manager in NAB & Co, a large audit firm which specialises in the audit of retailers. The firm currently audits Goofy Co (Goofy), a food retailer, but Goofy's main competitor, Mickey Co (Mickey), has approached the audit firm to act as auditors. Both Goofy and Mickey are listed companies. Goofy is concerned that if NAB & Co audits both companies then confidential information could pass across to Mickey.

The audit engagement partner for Goofy has been in place for approximately six years and her daughter, Emma, has just accepted a job offer from Goofy as a warehouse manager. Emma's employment contract states that if a bonus is to be paid it will be awarded as shares in Goofy rather than in cash. Goofy is offering NAB & Co a 5% bonus on top of the audit fee if this year's audit can be completed three weeks earlier than last year. This is to reduce the demands on the finance director's time as he is busy working on other projects.

61 The ACCA Code of Ethics and Conduct requires that an external auditor implement appropriate safeguards to ensure that a conflict of interest is properly managed.

Which of the following actions should NAB & Co take regarding the potential confidentiality issue?

(1) Inform the audit committees of both Goofy and Mickey of the potential conflict of interest and obtain their consent to act for both parties

(2) Use separate audit teams for each audit with a common independent review partner to determine whether confidentiality has been maintained

(3) Draw up confidentiality agreements to be signed by the Board of Directors of Goofy and Mickey

(4) Prevent unauthorised physical access to the information relating to the both company audits

A   1, 3 and 4
√B   1 and 4 only
C   1, 2 and 4
D   1, 2 and 3

---

62 From a review of the information above, your audit assistant has highlighted some of the potential risks to independence in respect of the audit of Goofy.

(1) Audit engagement partner has been in the position for six years
(2) Audit engagement partner's daughter works for Goofy
(3) Audit engagement partner's daughter's bonus would be in the form of shares
(4) 5% bonus offered if audit is completed three weeks earlier than last year

Which of the following options correctly identifies the valid threats to independence and allocates the threat to the appropriate category?

	Familiarity	Self-interest
A	1 and 3	2 and 4
B	2 and 4	1 and 3
√C	1 and 2	3 and 4
D	2 and 3	1 and 4

---

63   NAB & Co have decided that they would like to accept nomination as Mickey's auditors and Mickey's existing auditors have agreed to resign rather than be removed from office. The audit manager in charge of the tender has set out a list of procedures that the firm must undertake before Mickey can be approved as an audit client.

(1)   Ensure that the existing auditor's resignation has been properly conducted
(2)   Communicate with Mickey's existing auditors
(3)   Submit an engagement letter to Mickey's management
(4)   Perform client screening procedures, including an assessment of Mickey's risk profile

Which of the following summarises the correct order in which the above procedures should be undertaken?

A   1, 3, 2, 4
B   4, 3, 2, 1
C   1, 4, 2, 3
D   2, 4, 1, 3

64   Before NAB & Co can accept appointment as Mickey's auditors they must determine whether the preconditions for an audit are met and obtain management's agreement that it acknowledges and understands its responsibilities.

Which of the following is **NOT** included in the agreement obtained by the auditor?

A   Management's responsibility for preparing the financial statements

B   Management's responsibility for internal control to enable the preparation of financial statements which are free from material misstatement

C   Management's responsibility to provide the auditor with all information relevant to the preparation of the financial statements

D   Management's responsibility to prevent and detect fraud

65   Once NAB & Co has accepted appointment as Mickey's auditor they must draw up an engagement letter.

Which of the following must be included in the audit engagement letter?

A   Arrangements concerning the use of experts such as inventory counters
B   Obligations to make audit working papers available to other parties
C   Expected form and content of any reports
D   Basis on which fees are computed

(Total = 10 marks)

Carlise (CBE)   20 mins

The following scenario relates to questions 66–70.

You are an audit senior of UYE & Co and your firm is the external auditor of Carlise, a large private company that runs major sports venues in the UK. Carlise has a year-end of 31 December and you are currently planning the interim audit of Carlise for the six months ended 30 June 20X4.

This year you will have another audit senior, James, working with you who has recently joined UYE & Co. James did not work on any interim audits with his previous audit firm and your audit manager has asked you to train him to use the different approach used in interim audits.

James has drawn up the following list of audit procedures:

(1)   Update documentation relating to Carlise's accounting systems which has been prepared in prior year audits

(2)   Obtain third party confirmations relating to receivables, payables and cash at bank

(3)   Review the directors' assessment of whether Carlise is a going concern. Consider whether the assumptions made by the directors are reasonable and whether it is appropriate to prepare the accounts on the going concern basis

(4) Perform preliminary analytical procedures in order to identify any major changes in the business or unexpected trends

In July 20X4 Carlise established an internal audit department. The Board is still planning the exact responsibilities the internal audit department will have, but it is likely that, among other things, they will be involved in monitoring the internal controls relating to Carlise's online ticket sales system.

66 Indicate whether the procedures identified by James above will be conducted during the interim or the final audit.

Audit procedure	Interim audit	Final audit
(1)	✓	
(2)		✓
(3)		✓
(4)	✓	

67 During the interim audit, you performed internal controls testing and the results of these indicate that, to date, the control environment is strong and internal controls are operating effectively.

James has asked you to explain the factors that will determine the extent of further work on internal controls that will need to be performed at the final audit.

Which of the following should be taken into account when determining the extent of the additional work needed at the final audit?

(1) The significance of the assessed risks of material misstatement at the assertion level

(2) The specific controls that were tested during the interim period, and significant changes to them since they were tested, including changes in the information system, processes, and personnel

(3) The length of the remaining period

- [ ] 1 and 2 only
- [ ] 2 and 3 only
- [ ] 1 and 3 only
- [x] 1, 2 and 3

68 Which of the following considerations is the **MOST** important when deciding whether or not to rely on the work performed by Carlise's internal audit department?

- [ ] Whether any members of Carlise's internal audit department hold a professional qualification
- [x] Whether the work performed by the internal audit department relates to specific audit assertions over which UYE & Co have concerns
- [ ] Whether a separate Audit Committee exists
- [ ] Whether Carlise's internal audit department has a work plan which schedules the work they should perform to the end of the year

69 At his previous audit firm James had several audit clients which had an effective internal audit department. He asks you whether you would consider asking Carlise's internal audit department to provide direct assistance to your audit team.

Which **TWO** of the following statements relating to direct assistance are valid?

- ☑ Direct assistance describes the use of internal auditors to perform audit procedures under the direction, supervision and review of the external auditor
- ☐ The external auditor should only use direct assistance in relation to areas of the audit where there the assessed risk of material misstatement is high
- ☑ The external auditor should document their review of the work performed by the internal auditors
- ☐ The internal auditors will be separately liable for any material misstatements in the work they have performed

70 All work carried out by the external auditor should be documented in their working papers regardless of whether it relates to an interim or a final audit.

Which of the following is **NOT** a valid reason for producing audit documentation?

- ☑ It prevents the auditor from being sued for negligence
- ☐ It provides evidence for the basis of key conclusions
- ☐ It enables senior team members to direct, supervise and review the audit work
- ☐ It enables quality control reviews to be performed

(Total = 10 marks)

71 Sleeptight   59 mins

You are an audit senior for Mills & Co. Mills & Co were recently appointed as external auditors of Sleeptight Co for the year ending 31 March 20X0 and you are in the process of planning the audit. The previous auditors issued an unmodified audit opinion last year and access to prior year working papers has been granted.

Sleeptight's principal activity is the manufacture and sale of expensive high quality beds which are largely sold to luxury hotels and owners of holiday apartments. Each bed is crafted by hand in the company's workshop. Construction of each bed only begins once a customer order is received, as each customer will usually want their bed to have a unique feature or to be in a unique style.

The business is family run and all the shares in Sleeptight are owned by the two joint Managing Directors. The directors are two sisters, Anna and Sophie Jones and they both have a number of other business interests. As a result they only spend a few days a week working at the company and rely on the small accounts department to keep the finances in order and to keep them informed. There is no finance director but the financial controller is a qualified accountant.

Sleeptight requires customers who place an order to pay a deposit of 40% of the total order value at the time the order is placed. The beds will take four to eight weeks to build, and the remaining 60% of the order value is due within a week of the final delivery. Risks and rewards of ownership of the beds do not pass to the customer until the beds are delivered and signed for. Beds also come with a two year guarantee and the financial controller has made a provision in respect of the expected costs to be incurred in relation to beds still under guarantee.

Although the company does have some employees working in the workshop, it often uses external subcontractors to help make the beds in order to fulfil all its orders. These sub-contractors should invoice Sleeptight at the end of each month for the work they have carried out, but sometimes do not get round to it until the following month.

The company undertakes a full count of raw materials at the year end. The quantities are recorded on inventory sheets and the financial controller assigns the costs based on the cost assigned in the previous year or, if there was no cost last year, using the latest invoice. Most beds are made of oak or other durable woods and the cost of these raw materials is known to fluctuate considerably.

It is expected that work in progress will be insignificant this year, but there will be a material amount of finished goods awaiting despatch. Anna Jones will estimate the value of these finished goods and has said she will take into account the order value when doing so.

There has been steady growth in sales in recent years and, in January 20X0 Sleeptight purchased a building close to its existing workshop. Anna and Sophie plan to turn this into another workshop which should more than double its existing manufacturing capacity. The new workshop is currently undergoing extensive refurbishment in order to make it suitable for bed manufacturing.

The purchase of the new premises was funded by a bank loan repayable in monthly instalments over 12 years and has covenants attached to it. These covenants are largely profit related measures and if they are breached the bank has the option to make the remaining loan balance repayable immediately.

Required

(a)   Auditors are required to plan and perform an audit with professional scepticism, to exercise professional judgement and to comply with ethical standards.

    Required

    (i)   Explain what is meant by 'professional scepticism' and why it is so important that the auditor maintains professional scepticism throughout the audit.   **(3 marks)**

    (ii)   Define 'professional judgement' and describe two areas where professional judgement is applied when planning an audit of financial statements.   **(3 marks)**

(b)   (i)   Identify and explain **EIGHT** audit risks in respect of the financial statements of Sleeptight for the year ending 31 March 20X0. For each risk suggest a suitable audit response.   **(16 marks)**

    (ii)   Describe Mill & Co's responsibilities in relation to the physical inventory count that will take place at the year end   **(4 marks)**

(c)   The workshop currently in use is owned by the company and will be included in the financial statements at its revalued amount rather than at cost. The company has always adopted this policy for land and buildings and the valuation of the workshop is to be brought up to date at 31 March 20X0 by an external valuer.

    Required

    Describe the procedures the auditor should carry out to gain evidence over the adequacy of the value of the workshop and the related disclosures included in the financial statements.   **(4 marks)**

(Total = 30 marks)

72 Raisin

39 mins

You are an audit senior in Raisin & Co, a firm of Chartered Certified Accountants. You are temporarily assigned as audit senior to the audit of Sultana Co, a scaffolding specialist supplying the construction industry, after the senior on the engagement fell ill. The final audit of Sultana Co for the year ended 30 September 20X9 is nearing completion, and you are now reviewing the audit files and discussing the audit with the junior members of the audit team.

Sultana Co's draft financial statements show revenue of $12.5 million, net profit of $400,000, and total assets of $78 million.

The following information has come to your attention during your review of the audit files.

After the year end, Cherry Co, a major customer with whom Sultana Co has several significant contracts, announced its insolvency. Procedures to shut down the company have commenced. The administrators of Cherry Co have suggested that the company may be able to pay approximately 25% of the amounts owed to Sultana Co. A trade receivable of $300,000 is recognised on Sultana Co's statement of financial position in respect of this customer.

In addition, one of the junior members of the audit team has voiced concerns over how the audit had been managed. The junior said the following.

'I have only worked on two audits prior to being assigned the audit team of Sultana Co. I was expecting to attend a meeting at the start of the audit, where the partner and other senior members of the audit team discussed the audit, but no meeting was held. In addition, the audit manager has been away on holiday for three weeks, and left a senior in charge. However, the senior was busy with other assignments, so was not always available.

'I was given the task of auditing the goodwill which arose on an acquisition made during the year. I also worked on the audit of inventory, and attended the inventory count, which was quite complicated, as Sultana Co has a lot of work-in-progress. I tried to be as useful as possible during the count, and helped the client's staff count some of the raw materials. As I had been to the inventory count, I was asked by the audit senior to challenge the finance director regarding the adequacy of the provision against inventory, which the senior felt was significantly understated.

'Lastly, we found that we were running out of time to complete our audit procedures. The audit senior advised that we should reduce the sample sizes used in our tests as a way of saving time. He also suggested that we should select items which would be quick to audit when carrying out audit sampling.'

Required

(a)   Comment on the matters to be considered, and explain the audit evidence you should expect to find during your file review in respect of the trade receivable recognised in relation to Cherry Co.   **(6 marks)**

(b)   Evaluate the audit junior's concerns regarding the management of the audit of Sultana Co.   **(14 marks)**

(Total = 20 marks)

73 Abrahams (12/11)   39 mins

Abrahams Co develops, manufactures and sells a range of pharmaceuticals and has a wide customer base across Europe and Asia. You are the audit manager of Nate & Co and you are planning the audit of Abrahams Co whose financial year end is 31 January. You attended a planning meeting with the finance director and engagement partner and are now reviewing the meeting notes in order to produce the audit strategy and plan. Revenue for the year is forecast at $25 million.

During the year the company has spent $2.2 million on developing several new products. Some of these are in the early stages of development whilst others are nearing completion. The finance director has confirmed that all projects are likely to be successful and so he is intending to capitalise the full $2.2 million.

Once products have completed the development stage, Abrahams begins manufacturing them. At the year end it is anticipated that there will be significant levels of work in progress. In addition the company uses a standard costing method to value inventory; the standard costs are set when a product is first manufactured and are not usually updated. In order to fulfil customer orders promptly, Abrahams Co has warehouses for finished goods located across Europe and Asia; approximately one third of these are third party warehouses where Abrahams just rents space.

In September a new accounting package was introduced. This is a bespoke system developed by the information technology (IT) manager. The old and new packages were not run in parallel as it was felt that this would be too onerous for the accounting team. Two months after the system changeover the IT manager left the company; a new manager has been recruited but is not due to start work until January.

In order to fund the development of new products, Abrahams has restructured its finance and raised $1 million through issuing shares at a premium and $2.5 million through a long-term loan. There are bank covenants attached to the loan, the main one relating to a minimum level of total assets. If these covenants are breached then the loan becomes immediately repayable. The company has a policy of revaluing land and buildings, and the finance director has announced that all land and buildings will be revalued as at the year end.

The reporting timetable for audit completion of Abrahams Co is quite short, and the finance director would like to report results even earlier this year.

(a) Explain the components of audit risk and, for each component, state an example of a factor which can result in increased audit risk. **(6 marks)**

(b) Using the information provided, identify and describe **FIVE** audit risks and explain the auditor's response to each risk in planning the audit of Abrahams Co. **(10 marks)**

(c) Describe substantive procedures you should perform to obtain sufficient appropriate evidence in relation to:

    (i) Inventory held at the third party warehouses; and
    (ii) Use of standard costs for inventory valuation. **(4 marks)**

(Total = 20 marks)

74 Recorder (12/14)   39 mins

Recorder Communications Co (Recorder) is a large mobile phone company which operates a network of stores in countries across Europe. The company's year end is 30 June 20X4. You are the audit senior of Piano & Co. Recorder is a new client and you are currently planning the audit with the audit manager. You have been provided with the following planning notes from the audit partner following his meeting with the finance director.

Recorder purchases goods from a supplier in South Asia and these goods are shipped to the company's central warehouse. The goods are usually in transit for two weeks and the company correctly records the goods when received. Recorder does not undertake a year-end inventory count, but carries out monthly continuous (perpetual) inventory counts and any errors identified are adjusted in the inventory system for that month.

During the year the company introduced a bonus based on sales for its sales persons. The bonus target was based on increasing the number of customers signing up for 24-month phone line contracts. This has been successful and revenue has increased by 15%, especially in the last few months of the year. The level of receivables is considerably higher than last year and there are concerns about the creditworthiness of some customers.

Recorder has a policy of revaluing its land and buildings and this year has updated the valuations of all land buildings.

During the year the directors have each been paid a significant bonus, and they have included this within wages and salaries. Separate disclosure of the bonus is required by local legislation.

Required

(a) Describe **FIVE** audit risks, and explain the auditor's response to each risk, in planning the audit of Recorder Communications Co. **(10 marks)**

(b) Explain the audit procedures you should perform in order to place reliance on the continuous (perpetual) counts for year-end inventory. **(3 marks)**

(c) Describe substantive procedures you should perform to confirm the directors' bonus payments included in the financial statements. **(3 marks)**

The finance director of Recorder informed the audit partner that the reason for appointing Piano & Co as auditors was because they audit other mobile phone companies, including Recorder's main competitor. The finance director has asked how Piano & Co keeps information obtained during the audit confidential.

Required

(d) Explain the safeguards which your firm should implement to ensure that this conflict of interest is properly managed. **(4 marks)**

(Total = 20 marks)

75 Walters (2014 Specimen Paper)   39 mins

You are the audit senior of Holtby & Co and are planning the audit of Walters Co (Walters) for the year ended 31 December 20X4. The company produces printers and has been a client of your firm for two years; your audit manager has already had a planning meeting with the finance director. He has provided you with the following notes of his meeting and financial statement extracts.

Walters's management were disappointed with the 20X3 results and so in 20X4 undertook a number of strategies to improve the trading results. This included the introduction of a generous sales-related bonus scheme for their salesmen and a high profile advertising campaign. In addition, as market conditions are difficult for their customers, they have extended the credit period given to them.

The finance director of Walters has reviewed the inventory valuation policy and has included additional overheads incurred this year as he considers them to be production related.

The finance director has calculated a few key ratios for Walters; the gross profit margin has increased from 44.4% to 52.2% and receivables days have increased from 61 days to 71 days. He is happy with the 20X4 results and feels that they are a good reflection of the improved trading levels.

FINANCIAL STATEMENT EXTRACTS FOR YEAR ENDED 31 DECEMBER

	Draft 20X4 $m	Actual 20X3 $m
Revenue	23.0	18.0
Cost of sales	(11.0)	(10.0)
Gross profit	12.0	8.0
Operating expenses	(7.5)	(4.0)
Profit before interest and taxation	4.5	4.0
Inventory	2.1	1.6
Receivables	4.5	3.0
Cash	–	2.3
Trade payables	1.6	1.2
Overdraft	0.9	–

Required

(a)   Using the information above:

  (i)   Calculate an additional **THREE** ratios, for **BOTH** years, which would assist the audit senior in planning the audit. **(3 marks)**

  (ii) From a review of the above information and the ratios calculated, describe **SIX** audit risks and explain the auditor's response to each risk in planning the audit of Walters Co. **(12 marks)**

(b)   Describe the procedures that the auditor of Walters Co should perform in assessing whether or not the company is a going concern. **(5 marks)**

(Total = 20 marks)

76 Sycamore (6/15)   39 mins

You are the audit supervisor of Maple & Co and are currently planning the audit of an existing client, Sycamore Science Co (Sycamore), whose year end was 30 April 20X5. Sycamore is a pharmaceutical company, which manufactures and supplies a wide range of medical supplies. The draft financial statements show revenue of $35.6 million and profit before tax of $5.9 million.

Sycamore's previous finance director left the company in December 20X4 after it was discovered that he had been claiming fraudulent expenses from the company for a significant period of time. A new finance director was appointed in January 20X5 who was previously a financial controller of a bank, and she has expressed surprise that Maple & Co had not uncovered the fraud during last year's audit.

During the year Sycamore has spent $1.8 million on developing several new products. These projects are at different stages of development and the draft financial statements show the full amount of $1.8 million within intangible assets. In order to fund this development, $2.0 million was borrowed from the bank and is due for repayment over a ten-year period. The bank has attached minimum profit targets as part of the loan covenants.

The new finance director has informed the audit partner that since the year end there has been an increased number of sales returns and that in the month of May over $0.5 million of goods sold (and recognised in revenue) in April were returned.

Maple & Co attended the year-end inventory count at Sycamore's warehouse. The auditor present raised concerns that during the count there were movements of goods in and out the warehouse and this process did not seem well controlled.

During the year, a review of plant and equipment in the factory was undertaken and surplus plant was sold, resulting in a profit on disposal of $210,000.

Required

(a) State Maple & Co's responsibilities in relation to the prevention and detection of fraud and error.

(4 marks)

(b) Describe **SIX** audit risks, and explain the auditor's response to each risk, in planning the audit of Sycamore Science Co. **(12 marks)**

(c) Sycamore's new finance director has read about review engagements and is interested in the possibility of Maple & Co undertaking these in the future. However, she is unsure how these engagements differ from an external audit and how much assurance would be gained from this type of engagement.

Required

(i) Explain the purpose of review engagements and how these differ from external audits; and

(2 marks)

(ii) Describe the level of assurance provided by external audits and review engagements. **(2 marks)**

(Total = 20 marks)

77 Smoothbrush (6/10) 59 mins

Introduction and client background

You are an audit senior in Staple and Co and you are commencing the planning of the audit of Smoothbrush Paints Co ('Smoothbrush') for the year ending 31 August 20X0.

Smoothbrush is a paint manufacturer and has been trading for over 50 years. It operates from one central site which includes the production facility, warehouse and administration offices.

Smoothbrush sells all of its goods to large home improvement stores, with 60% being to one large chain store called Homewares. The company has a one year contract to be the sole supplier of paint to Homewares. It secured the contract through significantly reducing prices and offering a four-month credit period, the company's normal credit period is one month.

Goods in/purchases

In recent years, Smoothbrush has reduced the level of goods directly manufactured and instead started to import paint from South Asia. Approximately 60% is imported and 40% manufactured. Within the production facility is a large amount of old plant and equipment that is now redundant and has minimal scrap value. Purchase orders for overseas paint are made six months in advance and goods can be in transit for up to two months. Smoothbrush accounts for the inventory when it receives the goods.

To avoid the disruption of a year end inventory count, Smoothbrush has this year introduced a continuous/perpetual inventory counting system. The warehouse has been divided into 12 areas and these are each to be counted once over the year. The counting team includes a member of the internal audit department and a warehouse staff member. The following procedures have been adopted:

1. The team prints the inventory quantities and descriptions from the system and these records are then compared to the inventory physically present.

2. Any discrepancies in relation to quantities are noted on the inventory sheets, including any items not listed on the sheets but present in the warehouse area.

3. Any damaged or old items are noted and they are removed from the inventory sheets.

4. The sheets are then passed to the finance department for adjustments to be made to the records when the count has finished.

5. During the counts there will continue to be inventory movements with goods arriving and leaving the warehouse.

At the year end it is proposed that the inventory will be based on the underlying records. Traditionally Smoothbrush has maintained an inventory provision based on 1% of the inventory value, but management feels that as inventory is being reviewed more regularly it no longer needs this provision.

Finance Director

In May 20X0 Smoothbrush had a dispute with its finance director (FD) and he immediately left the company. The company has temporarily asked the financial controller to take over the role while they recruit a permanent replacement. The old FD has notified Smoothbrush that he intends to sue for unfair dismissal. The company is not proposing to make any provision or disclosures for this, as they are confident the claim has no merit.

Required

(a) Identify and explain the audit risks identified at the planning stage of the audit of Smoothbrush Paints Co.

(10 marks)

(b) Discuss the importance of assessing risks at the planning stage of an audit. **(4 marks)**

(c) List and explain suitable controls that should operate over the continuous/perpetual inventory counting system, to ensure the completeness and accuracy of the existing inventory records at Smoothbrush Paints Co.

(10 marks)

(d) Describe **THREE** substantive procedures that the auditor of Smoothbrush Paints Co should perform at the year end in confirming each of the following:

   (i) The valuation of inventory; **(3 marks)**
   (ii) The completeness of provisions or contingent liabilities. **(3 marks)**

(Total = 30 marks)

78 Aquamarine Co (Mar/Jun 16)   39 mins

You are an audit supervisor of Amethyst & Co and are currently planning the audit of your client, Aquamarine Co (Aquamarine) which manufactures elevators. Its year end is 31 July 20X6 and the forecast profit before tax is $15.2 million.

The company undertakes continuous production in its factory, therefore at the year end it is anticipated that work in progress will be approximately $950,000. In order to improve the manufacturing process, Aquamarine placed an order in April for $720,000 of new plant and machinery; one third of this order was received in May with the remainder expected to be delivered by the supplier in late July or early August.

At the beginning of the year, Aquamarine purchased a patent for $1.3 million which gives them the exclusive right to manufacture specialised elevator equipment for five years. In order to finance this purchase, Aquamarine borrowed $1.2 million from the bank which is repayable over five years.

In January 20X6 Aquamarine outsourced its payroll processing to an external service organisation, Coral Payrolls Co (Coral). Coral handles all elements of the payroll cycle and sends monthly reports to Aquamarine detailing the payroll costs. Aquamarine ran its own payroll until 31 December 20X5, at which point the records were transferred over to Coral.

The company has a policy of revaluing land and buildings and the finance director has announced that all land and buildings will be revalued at the year end. During a review of the management accounts for the month of May 20X6, you have noticed that receivables have increased significantly on the previous year end and against May 20X5.

The finance director has informed you that the company is planning to make approximately 65 employees redundant after the year end. No decision has been made as to when this will be announced, but it is likely to be prior to the year end.

Required

(a)   Define audit risk and the components of audit risk.   **(5 marks)**

(b)   Describe **SIX** audit risks, and explain the auditor's response to each risk, in planning the audit of Aquamarine Co.   **(12 marks)**

(c)   Explain the additional factors Amethyst & Co should consider during the audit in relation to Aquamarine Co's use of the payroll service organisation.   **(3 marks)**

(Total = 20 marks)

79 Kangaroo Construction Co   39 mins

You are the audit senior of Rhino & Co and you are planning the audit of Kangaroo Construction Co (Kangaroo) for the year ended 31 March 20X3. Kangaroo specialises in building houses and provides a five-year building warranty to its customers. Your audit manager has held a planning meeting with the finance director. He has provided you with the following notes of his meeting and financial statement extracts:

Kangaroo has had a difficult year; house prices have fallen and, as a result, revenue has dropped. In order to address this, management has offered significantly extended credit terms to their customers. However, demand has fallen such that there are still some completed houses in inventory where the selling price may be below cost. During the year, whilst calculating depreciation, the directors extended the useful lives of plant and machinery from three years to five years. This reduced the annual depreciation charge.

The directors need to meet a target profit before interest and taxation of $0.5 million in order to be paid their annual bonus. In addition, to try and improve profits, Kangaroo changed their main material supplier to a cheaper alternative. This has resulted in some customers claiming on their building warranties for extensive repairs. To help with operating cash flow, the directors borrowed $1 million from the bank during the year. This is due for repayment at the end of 20X3.

FINANCIAL STATEMENT EXTRACTS FOR YEAR ENDED 31 MARCH

	Draft 20X3 $m	Actual 20X2 $m
Revenue	12.5	15.0
Cost of sales	(7.0)	(8.0)
Gross profit	5.5	7.0
Operating expenses	(5.0)	(5.1)
Profit before interest and taxation	0.5	1.9
Inventory	1.9	1.4
Receivables	3.1	2.0
Cash	0.8	1.9
Trade payables	1.6	1.2
Loan	1.0	–

Required

(a)   Explain the concepts of materiality and performance materiality in accordance with ISA 320 *Materiality in planning and performing an audit.*   **(5 marks)**

(b)   Using the information above:

(i)   Calculate **FIVE** ratios, for **BOTH** years, which would assist the audit senior in planning the audit.
(5 marks)

(ii)   Using the information provided and the ratios calculated, identify and describe **FIVE** audit risks and explain the auditor's response to each risk in planning the audit of Kangaroo Construction Co.
(10 marks)

(Total = 20 marks)

80 Sunflower Stores Co   39 mins

Sunflower Stores Co (Sunflower) operates 25 food supermarkets. The company's year end is 31 December 20X2. The audit manager and partner recently attended a planning meeting with the finance director and have provided you with the planning notes below.

You are the audit senior, and this is your first year on this audit. In order to familiarise yourself with Sunflower, the audit manager has asked you to undertake some research in order to gain an understanding of Sunflower, so that you are able to assist in the planning process. He has then asked that you identify relevant audit risks from the notes below and also consider how the team should respond to these risks.

Sunflower has spent $1.6 million in refurbishing all of its supermarkets; as part of this refurbishment programme their central warehouse has been extended and a smaller warehouse, which was only occasionally used, has been disposed of at a profit. In order to finance this refurbishment, a sum of $1.5 million was borrowed from the bank. This is due to be repaid over five years.

The company will be performing a year-end inventory count at the central warehouse as well as at all 25 supermarkets on 31 December. Inventory is valued at selling price less an average profit margin as the finance director believes that this is a close approximation to cost.

Prior to 20X2, each of the supermarkets maintained their own financial records and submitted returns monthly to head office. During 20X2 all accounting records have been centralised within head office. Therefore at the beginning of the year, each supermarket's opening balances were transferred into head office's accounting records. The increased workload at head office has led to some changes in the finance department and in November 20X2 the financial controller left. His replacement will start in late December.

Required

(a)   List **FIVE** sources of information that would be of use in gaining an understanding of Sunflower Stores Co, and for each source describe what you would expect to obtain.   **(5 marks)**

(b)   Using the information provided, describe **FIVE** audit risks and explain the auditor's response to each risk in planning the audit of Sunflower Stores Co.   **(10 marks)**

(c)   The finance director of Sunflower Stores Co is considering establishing an internal audit department.

Required

Describe the factors the finance director should consider before establishing an internal audit department.
(5 marks)

(Total = 20 marks)

INTERNAL CONTROL

Questions 81–116 cover Internal controls, the subject of Part C of the BPP Study Text for F8.

Flowers Anytime (AIR 12/02) (amended)

20 mins

The following scenario relates to questions 81–85.

You are an audit manager in a medium-sized audit firm. You are currently planning the audit of Flowers Anytime (Flowers) for the year ended 31 March 20X7. Flowers, a traditional flower wholesaler, is a new audit client for your firm.

As this is the first year you are auditing Flowers, it is necessary to understand and evaluate the company's system of internal control. The audit firm's policy requires the following steps to be taken when performing first year audits:

(1)   Perform walkthrough tests
(2)   Complete flowcharts and internal control evaluation questionnaires
(3)   Revise the audit strategy and audit plan
(4)   Perform tests of control

You have obtained the following background information about your new client. When customers call the company, their orders are taken by clerks who take details of the flowers to be delivered, the address to which they are to be delivered, and the account details of the customer. The clerks input these details into the company's computer system (whilst the order is being taken) which is integrated with the company's inventory control system.

The audit junior has made the following notes on the system for the receipt, processing and recording of the orders:

(1)   All orders are recorded on pre-printed, three-part sequentially numbered order forms. One copy is kept by the sales clerk, one copy is forwarded to the warehouse for the dispatch of inventory, and one copy being is sent to the customer as evidence of the order.

(2)   The sales clerk regularly performs reviews of the standing data on the system, matching the price of flowers against an up-to-date price list.

(3)   To ensure completeness of orders, a sequence check is performed on the sales invoices manually by the sales clerk and any missing documents are investigated.

(4)   Sales invoices are posted on a weekly basis to the sales daybook and accounts receivable ledger.

81   Which of the following correctly summarises the order in which the steps required by the firm's policy for first year audits would take place?

    A   1, 2, 3, 4
    B   3, 2, 1, 4
    C   1, 2, 4, 3
  ✓ D   2, 1, 4, 3

---

82   The audit junior has asked you whether internal control questionnaires (ICQs) should be completed as well as internal control evaluation questionnaires (ICEQs).

Which of the following statements is correct in relation to ICQs and ICEQs?

    A   ICEQs determine whether controls exist which meet specific control objectives; ICQs determine whether there are controls which prevent or detect specified errors or omissions

  ✓ B   ICEQs are generally easier to apply to a variety of different systems than ICQs

    C   ICQs are likely to overlook how internal controls deal with unusual transactions; this will normally have to be recorded using ICEQs

    D   ICQs can give the impression that all controls are of equal weight; this issue is resolved by using ICEQs

83 Which of the internal control activities identified in the audit junior's notes above would satisfy the objective of preventing/detecting a material misstatement if it is operating effectively?

    A   1 only
✓ B   3 only
    C   1 and 2
    D   3 and 4

---

84 You instruct the audit junior to confirm whether the post is opened by more than one individual.

Over which of the following internal control objectives would this provide assurance?

(1)   Cash receipts are not misappropriated
(2)   All cash receipts that occurred are recorded
(3)   Cash receipts are recorded at the correct amounts in the ledger
(4)   Cash receipts are posted to the correct receivables accounts and to the general ledger

✓ A   1 only
    B   2 only
    C   3 and 4
    D   1 and 4

---

85 During the course of the audit, the audit team identified numerous deficiencies in internal control relating to the sales system. The amounts exposed to the deficiencies were high and you have concluded that it is likely that the deficiencies would result in material misstatements in the financial statements. A deficiency was also identified in the purchases system but further investigation showed this to be a minor, isolated issue.

Which of the following statements is correct regarding the deficiencies which must be included in the report to management?

significant

✓ A   The deficiencies identified in the sales system only
    B   The deficiencies identified in the purchases system only
    C   The deficiencies identified in the sales and purchases system
    D   Neither the deficiencies identified in the sales system nor the purchases system

(Total = 10 marks)

KLE Co   20 mins

The following scenario relates to questions 86–90.

You are an audit manager in the internal audit department of KLE Co, a listed retail company. The internal audit department is auditing the company's procurement system. The system operates as follows:

Ordering

KLE's ordering department consists of six members of staff: one chief buyer and five purchasing clerks.

All orders are raised on pre-numbered purchase requisition forms, and are sent to the ordering department.

In the ordering department, each requisition form is approved and signed by the chief buyer. A purchasing clerk transfers the order information onto an order form and identifies the appropriate supplier for the goods.

Part one of the two part order form is sent to the supplier and part two to the accounts department. The requisition is thrown away.

Goods received

When goods are received, the goods inwards department immediately raises a two-part pre-numbered Goods Received Note (GRN).

- Part one is sent to the ordering department, which then forwards the GRN to the accounts department

- Part two is filed in order of the reference number for the goods being ordered (obtained from the supplier's goods despatched documentation), in the goods inwards department.

KLE Co's management is concerned that a number of inefficiencies in the procurement system may be having a negative financial impact on the company. As a result, they have requested the internal audit department to carry out a Value for Money audit focused on the company's procurement practices.

86   Which of the following is **NOT** a likely effect of the deficiencies in the internal control system for ordering described above?

    A   Purchases may be made unnecessarily at unauthorised prices
    B   Subsequent queries on orders cannot be traced back to the original requisition
    C   The order forms may contain errors that are not identified
    D   Goods could be ordered twice in error or deliberately

87   Which of the following statements are valid recommendations with regards to improving the internal controls for goods received described above?

    (1)   The ordering department should match orders to GRNs and mark orders as closed once all goods have been received, to enable any outstanding orders to be chased up.

    (2)   The first copy of the GRN should be sent directly to the accounts department, without first going through the ordering department, to prevent delays in recording the purchase.

    (3)   The goods inwards department should review the goods for their condition, in order to identify and return any damaged goods.

    (4)   GRNs should be filed in date order or by purchase order number, instead of by the supplier's reference number, to ensure that they can be matched easily to orders.

    A   1 and 3
    B   1, 2 and 3
    C   1, 2 and 4
    D   1, 3 and 4

88   As part of your audit of the procurement system, you have recommended that the goods inwards department should ensure that the goods received are valid business purchases, by matching all deliveries to an authorised order form before issuing a GRN.

Which of the following would be an appropriate test of control to confirm that the control is operating effectively?

    A   For a sample of orders, check that there is a matching goods received note
    B   Check that the numerical sequence of purchase orders is complete
    C   For a sample of goods received notes check that there is an authorised purchase order
    D   Check that the numerical sequence of goods received notes is complete

89   KLE Co's management is keen to increase the range of assignments that the company's internal audit undertake.

Which of the following assignments could the internal audit department be asked to perform by management?

    A   Undertake 'mystery shopper' reviews, where they enter the store as a customer, purchase goods and rate the overall shopping experience

    B   Assist the external auditors by requesting bank confirmation letters

    C   Provide advice on the implementation of a new payroll package for the payroll department

    D   Review the company's financial statements on behalf of the board.

90   Which of the following best summarises the meaning of 'efficiency' in the context of a Value for Money audit as requested by KLE Co's management?

   A   The lowest cost at which the appropriate quantity and quality of physical, human and financial resources can be achieved   *economy*

   B   Producing the required goods and services in the shortest time possible   *1/2 efficiency -*

   C   The extent to which an activity is achieving its policy objectives   *effectiveness*

   ✓ D   The relationship between goods and services produced and the resources used to produce them

                                                                                    (Total = 10 marks)

SouthLea (2007 Pilot Paper) (amended) (CBE)   20 mins

The following scenario relates to questions 91–95.

SouthLea Co, your audit client, is a large unlisted construction company (building houses, offices and hotels) employing a large number of workers on various construction sites.

As part of planning for the audit of the financial statements for the year ended 31 December 20X6, you are reviewing the cash wages systems within the company.

The following information is available concerning the wages systems:

(i)   Hours worked are recorded using a clocking in/out system. On arriving for work and at the end of each days work, each worker enters their unique employee number on a keypad.

(ii)   Workers on each site are controlled by a foreman. The foreman has a record of all employee numbers and can issue temporary numbers for new employees.

(iii)   Any overtime is calculated by the computerised wages system and added to the standard pay.

(iv)   The two staff in the wages department make amendments to the computerised wages system in respect of employee holidays, illness, as well as setting up and maintaining all employee records.

(v)   The computerised wages system calculates deductions from gross pay, such as employee taxes, and net pay. Every month a wages clerk checks the gross pay and deductions for a sample of employees. Finally a list of net cash payments for each employee is produced.

(vi)   Cash is delivered to the wages office by secure courier.

(vii)   The two staff place cash into wages packets for each employee along with a handwritten note of gross pay, deductions and net pay. The packets are given to the foreman for distribution to the individual employees.

SouthLea's finance director has mentioned to you that an allegation of suspected fraud had been made against a member of the senior management team during the year. This is currently being investigated by the internal audit team and the finance director hopes that the audit may shed further light on the matter.

SouthLea has an internal audit department of six staff. The chief internal auditor appoints staff within the internal audit department, although the chief executive officer (CEO) is responsible for appointing the chief internal auditor. The chief internal auditor reports directly to the finance director. The chief internal auditor decides on the scope of work of the internal audit department. SouthLea does not currently have an audit committee.

91   In preparation for the audit planning meeting, the audit junior has identified a number of areas requiring audit focus.

   Based on the information regarding the wages system, which **TWO** of the following are likely to introduce the highest risk of material misstatement?

   ☐   Completeness of wages
   ☐   Accuracy of deductions from gross pay
   ☑   Cut-off of starters' and leavers' wages
   ☑   Potential fraud risk factors

92   During the previous audit, the audit team had recommended SouthLea's management to ensure that any amendments to standing data on the wages system are reviewed by an authorised manager.

Which of the following is a test of control designed to provide evidence that the recommended internal control is operating effectively?

- [ ] Review overtime lists for evidence of authorisation
- [✓] Review the log of amendments to standing data for evidence of review
- [ ] Perform a proof in total using the number of employees and average wage
- [ ] Obtain printouts of employee wage rates and compare these to HR records

93   Which of the following statements about the responsibilities of external and internal auditors with regards to fraud is **NOT** correct?

- [ ] The external auditor must maintain an attitude of professional scepticism throughout the audit, recognising the possibility that a material misstatement due to fraud could exist.
- [✓] The internal auditor must always consider the potential of management overriding controls and modify their audit procedures accordingly when performing internal audit engagements.
- [ ] It is not the responsibility of the external auditors to detect fraud within a client.
- [ ] The work of internal auditors in reviewing the company's internal control systems helps management to fulfill its responsibility for preventing and detecting fraud.

94   Which of the following recommendations are appropriate in increasing the independence of SouthLea's internal audit department?

(1)   The chief internal auditor should be appointed by the board of directors.
(2)   The chief internal auditor should report to the board of directors.
(3)   The finance director should decide on the scope of the internal audit work

- [✓] (1) and (2) only
- [ ] (1) and (3) only
- [ ] (2) and (3) only
- [ ] (1), (2) and (3)

95   You have been told by the finance director that the senior management team is looking to upgrade the company's computerised accounting system in a year's time. This is partly because the senior management team believes that due to the increasing size and complexity of the business, the company will need more robust general IT controls in the future.

Which **TWO** of the following are general IT controls?

- [✓] Full testing procedures using test data when developing computer applications
- [ ] One for one checking
- [✓] Disaster recovery procedures
- [ ] Hash totals

(Total = 10 marks)

Cherry (6/15) (amended)

The following scenario relates to questions 96–100.

Cherry Blossom Co (Cherry) manufactures custom made furniture and its year end is 30 April.

You are the audit supervisor of Poplar & Co and are developing the audit programmes for Cherry's forthcoming interim audit.

You have ascertained that Cherry purchases its raw materials from a wide range of approved suppliers. When production supervisors require raw materials, they complete a requisition form and this is submitted to the purchase ordering department. Requisition forms do not require authorisation and no reference is made to the current inventory levels of the materials being requested.

96   As part of audit planning, the audit team needs to obtain and understanding of the company's system of internal control. Peter, the audit junior, is unsure what a company's internal control comprises.

Which of the following is **NOT** a component of an entity's internal control?

A   The control environment
B   Control activities relevant to the audit
C   The selection and application of accounting policies
D   The information system relevant to financial reporting

97   Which of the following are the most likely consequences of the internal control deficiency described in the requisition system for raw materials?

(1)   Fraudulent purchases may be made, leading to funds being diverted to third parties for illegal purposes

(2)   Stock-outs may occur, resulting in the company being unable to meet orders and lost revenue

(3)   Unnecessary purchases may be made, resulting in excess obsolescent raw materials accumulating in inventory requiring to be written down

(4)   Raw materials of poor quality may be purchased, resulting in low-quality products being produced, customer goodwill being lost and going concern risks

A   1 and 3
B   2 and 3
C   1 and 4
D   2 and 4

98   While reviewing Cherry's purchases cycle, you identified that goods received notes for raw material purchases are not sequentially numbered.

Which of the following areas would you consider to be most at risk of material misstatement, as a result of this internal control deficiency?

A   Rights and obligations of inventory
B   Valuation of payables
C   Existence of inventory
D   Completeness of payables

99   You now need to gain an understanding of Cherry's non-current assets cycle.

Which of the following statements is correct regarding audit procedures concerning the non-current asset cycle?

A   The same ordering documentation may be used in the non-current assets cycle as in the purchases cycle. If this is the case, it will not be necessary to document the non-current assets cycle.

B   Because there are likely to be less capital purchases than standard purchases in the year, it may not be cost-efficient to undertake tests of controls.

C   Because the control risk around the non-current asset cycle is likely to be high, it is important to perform tests of controls.

D   The non-current assets cycle is likely to have a lower risk of material misstatement than the purchases cycle.

---

100   Cherry's internal audit department has provided you with details of the internal controls around the non-current assets cycle. The controls include the following:

- On receipt, each asset is assigned a unique serial number and this is recorded on the asset and in the non-current assets register.

Which **TWO** of the following describe the **MOST RELIABLE** audit procedures which enable the auditor to assess whether this control is operating effectively?

(1)   Select a sample of capital additions on site, agree that a serial number is recorded on the asset and confirm it is included in the non-current assets register

(2)   Select a sample of assets recorded on the non-current assets register, confirm that it includes a serial number for each asset and agree the number to the physical asset

(3)   Inspect the non-current asset register and verify that there are no duplicated serial numbers

(4)   Observe the receipt of assets to confirm that serial numbers are assigned and recorded

A   1 and 3
B   2 and 3
C   1 and 4
D   2 and 4

(Total = 10 marks)

Swan

20 mins

The following scenario relates to questions 101–105.

You are the audit senior on the interim audit of Swan Co. The company introduced a new system at the beginning of this financial year. You have discussed the new system with the sales director, and have noted the following two points in particular:

(1)   Existing and new customers input their orders into computerised orders forms on Swan Co's website. The order notes the items requested, the billing and sales addresses, the customer number (if any). The system checks whether goods are in stock and approves the order instantly if so. The order is forwarded automatically to the sales department to be prepared.

(2)   When an order is ready to send out, the sales department input the details to their system, and if it matches the order, a goods outward note is produced and the invoicing department is notified automatically. Staff have experienced multiple issues of goods outward notes not matching on the system, and have often resorted to simply printing the order and using it as a goods outward note. The printed order is then taken to the invoicing department for invoicing.

The partner has requested that you document the new system fully during the interim audit. She wants the system notes to be easy to update, and to contain an element of evaluation of the system.

101   In relation to orders received through the website which of the following control objectives is met?

    A   Goods are sold to customers with good credit ratings.
    B   The company is able to fulfil the orders.
    C   Customers do not exceed credit limits.
    D   Changes in customer data are authorised.

102   Your audit junior has identified the following possible risks arising from the use of the printed order as a goods outward note and subsequent hand delivery to the invoicing department :

    (1)   Orders are not fulfilled.
    (2)   Goods are sent out but not invoiced.
    (3)   Goods are invoiced but not sent out.
    (4)   Wrong goods are sent to customers.

Which of the above risks arise from the identified system deficiency?

    A   1 and 2
    B   2 and 3
    C   2 and 4
    D   1 and 3

103   You are reviewing the audit plan for tests of controls over invoicing, which reads:

    (1)   Observe the invoicing clerk to ensure that prices are checked to the official price list.

    (2)   Review a sample of invoices to ensure their numerical sequence.

    (3)   Review a sample of goods out notes to ensure they have been matched to sales invoices.

    (4)   Review a sample of sales invoices to verify evidence that the calculations were checked before they were sent to customers.

Which of the above procedures relate to the completeness assertion?

    A   1 and 4
    B   2 and 3
    C   1 and 3
    D   2 and 4

104   Your audit junior is seeking to understand when deficiencies in internal control would be judged to be significant and therefore should be reported to those charged with governance.

Which of the following factors would influence your judgement of whether the control deficiencies identified at Swan are significant?

    (1)   The likelihood of material misstatement resulting
    (2)   The fact that the system is new
    (3)   The number of deficiencies identified
    (4)   The fact that the deficiencies are associated with the sales system

    A   1 and 3
    B   2 and 4
    C   1 and 2
    D   3 and 4

105   In the light of the partner's request concerning documentation, you are considering different options for recording the system.

Which of the following recording methods most suits her requirements?

   √ A   A computerised ICEQ
     B   Computerised narrative notes
     C   A flow chart
     D   Copying the company's control manual

(Total = 10 marks)

106 Chuck (12/11)   59 mins

Introduction and client background

You are the audit senior of Blair & Co and your team has just completed the interim audit of Chuck Industries Co, whose year end is 31 January 20X2. You are in the process of reviewing the systems testing completed on the payroll cycle, as well as preparing the audit programmes for the final audit.

Chuck Industries Co manufactures lights and the manufacturing process is predominantly automated; however there is a workforce of 85 employees, who monitor the machines, as well as approximately 50 employees who work in sales and administration. The company manufactures 24 hours a day, seven days a week.

Below is a description of the payroll system along with deficiencies identified by the audit team.

Factory workforce

The company operates three shifts every day with employees working eight hours each. They are required to clock in and out using an employee swipe card, which identifies the employee number and links into the hours worked report produced by the computerised payroll system. Employees are paid on an hourly basis for each hour worked. There is no monitoring/supervision of the clocking in/out process and an employee was witnessed clocking in several employees using their employee swipe cards.

The payroll department calculates on a weekly basis the cash wages to be paid to the workforce, based on the hours worked report multiplied by the hourly wage rate, with appropriate tax deductions. These calculations are not checked by anyone as they are generated by the payroll system. During the year the hourly wage was increased by the Human Resources (HR) department and this was notified to the payroll department verbally.

Each Friday, the payroll department prepares the pay packets and physically hands these out to the workforce, who operate the morning and late afternoon shifts, upon production of identification. However, for the night shift workers, the pay packets are given to the factory supervisor to distribute. If any night shift employees are absent on pay day then the factory supervisor keeps these wages and returns them to the payroll department on Monday.

Sales and administration staff

The sales and administration staff are paid monthly by bank transfer. Employee numbers do fluctuate and during July two administration staff joined; however, due to staff holidays in the HR department, they delayed informing the payroll department, resulting in incorrect salaries being paid out.

Required

(a)   For the deficiencies already identified in the payroll system of Chuck Industries Co:

   (i)   Explain the possible implications of these; and
   (ii)   Suggest a recommendation to address each deficiency.   **(12 marks)**

(b)   Describe substantive procedures you should now perform to confirm the accuracy and completeness of Chuck Industries' payroll charge.   **(6 marks)**

(c)   Last week the company had a visit from the tax authorities who reviewed the wages calculations and discovered that incorrect levels of tax had been deducted by the payroll system, as the tax rates from the previous year had not been updated. The finance director has queried with the audit team why they did not identify this non-compliance with tax legislation during last year's audit.

Required

Explain the responsibilities of management and auditors of Chuck Industries Co in relation to compliance with law and regulations under ISA 250 *Consideration of laws and regulations in an audit of financial statements.* **(4 marks)**

(d) Chuck Industries has decided to outsource its sales ledger department and as a result it is making 14 employees redundant. A redundancy provision, which is material, will be included in the draft accounts.

Required

Describe substantive procedures you should perform to confirm the redundancy provision at the year end.
(5 marks)

(e) Chuck Industries is considering establishing an internal audit (IA) department next year. The finance director has asked whether the work performed by the IA department can be relied upon by Blair & Co.

Required

Explain the factors that should be considered by an external auditor before reliance can be placed on the work performed by a company's internal audit department. **(3 marks)**

(Total = 30 marks)

107 Greystone (12/10) 59 mins

Greystone Co is a retailer of ladies clothing and accessories. It operates in many countries around the world and has expanded steadily from its base in Europe. Its main market is aimed at 15 to 35 year olds and its prices are mid to low range. The company's year end was 30 September 20X0.

In the past the company has bulk ordered its clothing and accessories twice a year. However, if their goods failed to meet the key fashion trends then this resulted in significant inventory write downs. As a result of this the company has recently introduced a just in time ordering system. The fashion buyers make an assessment nine months in advance as to what the key trends are likely to be, these goods are sourced from their suppliers but only limited numbers are initially ordered.

Greystone Co has an internal audit department but at present their only role is to perform regular inventory counts at the stores.

Ordering process

Each country has a purchasing manager who decides on the initial inventory levels for each store, this is not done in conjunction with store or sales managers. These quantities are communicated to the central buying department at the head office in Europe. An ordering clerk amalgamates all country orders by specified regions of countries, such as Central Europe and North America, and passes them to the purchasing director to review and authorise.

As the goods are sold, it is the store manager's responsibility to re-order the goods through the purchasing manager; they are prompted weekly to review inventory levels as although the goods are just in time, it can still take up to four weeks for goods to be received in store.

It is not possible to order goods from other branches of stores as all ordering must be undertaken through the purchasing manager. If a customer requests an item of clothing, which is unavailable in a particular store, then the customer is provided with other branch telephone numbers or recommended to try the company website.

Goods received and Invoicing

To speed up the ordering to receipt of goods cycle, the goods are delivered directly from the suppliers to the individual stores. On receipt of goods the quantities received are checked by a sales assistant against the supplier's delivery note, and then the assistant produces a goods received note (GRN). This is done at quiet times of the day so as to maximise sales. The checked GRNs are sent to head office for matching with purchase invoices.

As purchase invoices are received they are manually matched to GRNs from the stores, this can be a very time consuming process as some suppliers may have delivered to over 500 stores. Once the invoice has been agreed then it is sent to the purchasing director for authorisation. It is at this stage that the invoice is entered onto the purchase ledger.

Required

(a) Auditors have a responsibility under ISA 265 *Communicating deficiencies in internal control to those charged with governance and management*, to communicate deficiencies in internal controls. In particular, **significant** deficiencies in internal controls must be communicated in writing to those charged with governance.

Required

Explain examples of matters the auditor should consider in determining whether a deficiency in internal controls is significant.

(5 marks)

(b) As the external auditors of Greystone Co, write a report to management in respect of the purchasing system which:

(i) Identifies and explains **FOUR** deficiencies in that system
(ii) Explains the possible implication of each deficiency
(iii) Provides a recommendation to address each deficiency.

A covering letter is required.

Note. Up to two marks will be awarded within this requirement for presentation. **(14 marks)**

(c) Describe substantive procedures the auditor should perform on the year-end trade payables of Greystone Co.

(5 marks)

(d) Describe additional assignments that the internal audit department of Greystone Co could be asked to perform by those charged with governance.

(6 marks)

(Total = 30 marks)

108 Blake (12/08) (amended)   39 mins

Introduction

Blake Co assembles specialist motor vehicles such as lorries, buses and trucks. The company owns four assembly plants to which parts are delivered and assembled into the motor vehicles.

The motor vehicles are assembled using a mix of robot and manual production lines. The 'human' workers normally work a standard eight hour day, although this is supplemented by overtime on a regular basis as Blake has a full order book. There is one shift per day; mass production and around the clock working are not possible due to the specialist nature of the motor vehicles being assembled.

Wages system – shift workers

Shift-workers arrive for work at about 7.00 am and 'clock in' using an electronic identification card. The card is scanned by the time recording system and each production shift-worker's identification number is read from their card by the scanner. The worker is then logged in as being at work. Shift-workers are paid from the time of logging in. The logging in process is not monitored as it is assumed that shift-workers would not work without first logging in on the time recording system.

Shift-workers are split into groups of about 25 employees, with each group under the supervision of a shift foreman. Each day, each group of shift-workers is allocated a specific vehicle to manufacture. At least 400 vehicles have to be manufactured each day by each work group.

If necessary, overtime is worked to complete the day's quota of vehicles. The shift foreman is not required to monitor the extent of any overtime working although the foreman does ensure workers are not taking unnecessary or prolonged breaks which would automatically increase the amount of overtime worked. Shift-workers log off at the end of each shift by re-scanning their identification card.

Payment of wages

Details of hours worked each week are sent electronically to the payroll department, where hours worked are allocated by the computerised wages system to each employee's wages records. Staff in the payroll department compare hours worked from the time recording system to the computerised wages system, and enter a code word to confirm the accuracy of transfer. The code word also acts as authorisation to calculate net wages. The code word is the name of a domestic cat belonging to the department head and is therefore generally known around the department.

Each week the computerised wages system calculates:

(i)   Gross wages, using the standard rate and overtime rates per hour for each employee,
(ii)   Statutory deductions from wages, and
(iii) Net pay.

The list of net pay for each employee is sent over Blake's internal network to the accounts department. In the accounts department, an accounts clerk ensures that employee bank details are on file. The clerk then authorises and makes payment to those employees using Blake's online banking systems. Every few weeks the financial accountant reviews the total amount of wages made to ensure that the management accounts are accurate.

Termination of employees

Occasionally, employees leave Blake. When this happens, the personnel department sends an email to the payroll department detailing the employee's termination date and any unclaimed holiday pay. The receipt of the email by the payroll department is not monitored by the personnel department.

Salaries system – shift managers

All shift managers are paid an annual salary; there are no overtime payments.

Salaries were increased in July by 3% and an annual bonus of 5% of salary was paid in November.

(a)   As the external auditors of Blake Co, write a management letter to the directors in respect of the shift-workers wages recording and payment systems which:

   (i)   Identifies and explains **FOUR** deficiencies in that system;

   (ii)   Explains the possible effect of each deficiency;

   (iii) Provides a recommendation to alleviate each deficiency. Note up to two marks will be awarded within this requirement for presentation. **(14 marks)**

(b)   List **THREE** substantive analytical procedures you should perform on the shift managers' salary system. For each procedure, state your expectation of the result of that procedure. **(6 marks)**

(Total = 20 marks)

109 Tinkerbell (6/11)   59 mins

Introduction

Tinkerbell Toys Co (Tinkerbell) is a manufacturer of children's building block toys; they have been trading for over 35 years and they sell to a wide variety of customers including large and small toy retailers across the country. The company's year end is 31 May 20X1.

The company has a large manufacturing plant, four large warehouses and a head office. Upon manufacture, the toys are stored in one of the warehouses until they are despatched to customers. The company does not have an internal audit department.

Sales ordering, goods despatched and invoicing

Each customer has a unique customer account number and this is used to enter sales orders when they are received in writing from customers. The orders are entered by an order clerk and the system automatically checks that the goods are available and that the order will not take the customer over their credit limit. For new customers, a sales manager completes a credit application; this is checked through a credit agency and a credit limit entered into the system by the credit controller. The company has a price list, which is updated twice a year. Larger customers are entitled to a discount; this is agreed by the sales director and set up within the customer master file.

Once the order is entered an acceptance is automatically sent to the customer by mail/email confirming the goods ordered and a likely despatch date. The order is then sorted by address of customer. The warehouse closest to the customer receives the order electronically and a despatch list and sequentially numbered goods despatch notes

(GDNs) are automatically generated. The warehouse team pack the goods from the despatch list and, before they are sent out, a second member of the team double checks the despatch list to the GDN, which accompanies the goods.

Once despatched, a copy of the GDN is sent to the accounts team at head office and a sequentially numbered sales invoice is raised and checked to the GDN. Periodically a computer sequence check is performed for any missing sales invoice numbers.

Fraud

During the year a material fraud was uncovered. It involved cash/cheque receipts from customers being diverted into employees' personal accounts. In order to cover up the fraud, receipts from subsequent unrelated customers would then be recorded against the earlier outstanding receivable balances and this cycle of fraud would continue.

The fraud occurred because two members of staff 'who were related' colluded. One processed cash receipts and prepared the weekly bank reconciliation; the other employee recorded customer receipts in the sales ledger. An unrelated sales ledger clerk was supposed to send out monthly customer statements but this was not performed. The bank reconciliations each had a small unreconciled amount but no-one reviewed the reconciliations after they were prepared. The fraud was only uncovered when the two employees went on holiday at the same time and it was discovered that cash receipts from different customers were being applied to older receivable balances to hide the earlier sums stolen.

Required

(a) Recommend **SIX** tests of controls the auditor would normally carry out on the sales system of Tinkerbell, and explain the objective for each test.

(12 marks)

(b) Describe substantive procedures the auditor should perform to confirm Tinkerbell's year-end receivables balance.

(8 marks)

(c) Identify and explain controls Tinkerbell should implement to reduce the risk of fraud occurring again and, for each control, describe how it would mitigate the risk.

(6 marks)

(d) Describe substantive procedures the auditor should perform to confirm Tinkerbell's revenue.

(4 marks)

(Total = 30 marks)

110 Trombone (6/14)   59 mins

Trombone Co (Trombone) operates a chain of hotels across the country. Trombone employs in excess of 250 permanent employees and its year end is 31 August 20X4. You are the audit supervisor of Viola & Co and are currently reviewing the documentation of Trombone's payroll system, detailed below, in preparation for the interim audit.

Trombone's payroll system

Permanent employees work a standard number of hours per week as specified in their employment contract. However, when the hotels are busy, staff can be requested by management to work additional shifts as overtime. This can either be paid on a monthly basis or taken as days off.

Employees record any overtime worked and days taken off on weekly overtime sheets which are sent to the payroll department. The standard hours per employee are automatically set up in the system and the overtime sheets are entered by clerks into the payroll package, which automatically calculates the gross and net pay along with relevant deductions. These calculations are not checked at all. Wages are increased by the rate of inflation each year and the clerks are responsible for updating the standing data in the payroll system.

Employees are paid on a monthly basis by bank transfer for their contracted weekly hours and for any overtime worked in the previous month. If employees choose to be paid for overtime, authorisation is required by department heads of any overtime in excess of 30% of standard hours. If employees choose instead to take days off, the payroll clerks should check back to the 'overtime worked' report; however, this report is not always checked.

The 'overtime worked' report, which details any overtime recorded by employees, is run by the payroll department weekly and emailed to department heads for authorisation. The payroll department asks department heads to only report if there are any errors recorded. Department heads are required to arrange for overtime sheets to be authorised by an alternative responsible official if they are away on annual leave; however, there are instances where this arrangement has not occurred.

The payroll package produces a list of payments per employee; this links into the bank system to produce a list of automatic payments. The finance director reviews the total list of bank transfers and compares this to the total amount to be paid per the payroll records; if any issues arise then the automatic bank transfer can be manually changed by the finance director.

Required

(a)   In respect of the payroll system of Trombone Co:

   (i)   Identify and explain **FIVE** deficiencies;

   (ii)   Recommend a control to address each of these deficiencies; and

   (iii) Describe a test of control Viola & Co should perform to assess if each of these controls is operating effectively.

   Note. The total marks will be split equally between each part.   **(15 marks)**

(b)   Explain the difference between an interim and a final audit.   **(5 marks)**

(c)   Describe substantive procedures you should perform at the final audit to confirm the completeness and accuracy of Trombone Co's payroll expense.   **(6 marks)**

Trombone deducts employment taxes from its employees' wages on a monthly basis and pays these to the local taxation authorities in the following month. At the year end the financial statements will contain an accrual for income tax payable on employment income. You will be in charge of auditing this accrual.

Required

(d)   Describe the audit procedures required in respect of the year end accrual for tax payable on employment income.   **(4 marks)**

(Total = 30 marks)

111 Fox Industries Co   59 mins

Introduction

Fox Industries Co (Fox) manufactures engineering parts. It has one operating site and a customer base spread across Europe. The company's year end was 30 April 20X3. Below is a description of the purchasing and payments system.

Purchasing system

Whenever production materials are required, the relevant department sends a requisition form to the ordering department. An order clerk raises a purchase order and contacts a number of suppliers to see which can despatch the goods first. This supplier is then chosen. The order clerk sends out the purchase order. This is not sequentially numbered and only orders above $5,000 require authorisation.

Purchase invoices are input daily by the purchase ledger clerk, who has been in the role for many years and, as an experienced team member, he does not apply any application controls over the input process. Every week the purchase day book automatically updates the purchase ledger, the purchase ledger is then posted manually to the general ledger by the purchase ledger clerk.

Payments system

Fox maintains a current account and a number of saving (deposit) accounts. The current account is reconciled weekly but the saving (deposit) accounts are only reconciled every two months.

In order to maximise their cash and bank balance, Fox has a policy of delaying payments to all suppliers for as long as possible. Suppliers are paid by a bank transfer. The finance director is given the total amount of the payments list, which he authorises and then processes the bank payments.

(a) ISA 260 *Communication with those charged with governance* provides guidance to auditors in relation to communicating with those charged with governance on matters arising from the audit of an entity's financial statements.

Required

(i) Explain why it is important that auditors communicate throughout the audit with those charged with governance; and **(2 marks)**

(ii) Describe **THREE** examples of matters that the auditors may communicate to those charged with governance. **(3 marks)**

(b) As the external auditors of Fox Industries Co, write a report to management in respect of the purchasing and payments system described above which:

(i) Identifies and explains **FOUR** deficiencies in the system;
(ii) Explains the possible implication of each deficiency; and
(iii) Provides a recommendation to address each deficiency.

A covering letter **IS** required.

Note. Up to two marks will be awarded within this requirement for presentation and the remaining marks will be split equally between each part. **(14 marks)**

(c) Identify and explain **FOUR** application controls that should be adopted by Fox Industries Co to ensure the completeness and accuracy of the input of purchase invoices. **(4 marks)**

(d) Describe substantive procedures the auditor should perform to confirm the bank and cash balance of Fox Industries Co at the year end. **(7 marks)**

(Total = 30 marks)

112 Bluesberry (12/10)   39 mins

Bluesberry hospital is located in a country where healthcare is free, as the taxpayers fund the hospitals which are owned by the government. Two years ago management reviewed all aspects of hospital operations and instigated a number of measures aimed at improving overall 'value for money' for the local community. Management have asked that you, an audit manager in the hospital's internal audit department, perform a review over the measures which have been implemented.

Bluesberry has one centralised buying department and all purchase requisition forms for medical supplies must be forwarded here. Upon receipt the buying team will research the lowest price from suppliers and a purchase order is raised. This is then passed to the purchasing director, who authorises all orders. The small buying team receive in excess of 200 forms a day.

The human resources department has had difficulties with recruiting suitably trained staff. Overtime rates have been increased to incentivise permanent staff to fill staffing gaps, this has been popular, and reliance on expensive temporary staff has been reduced. Monitoring of staff hours had been difficult but the hospital has implemented time card clocking in and out procedures and these hours are used for overtime payments as well.

The hospital has invested heavily in new surgical equipment, which although very expensive, has meant that more operations could be performed and patient recovery rates are faster. However, currently there is a shortage of appropriately trained medical staff. A capital expenditure committee has been established, made up of senior managers, and they plan and authorise any significant capital expenditure items.

Required

(a) Explain the purpose of a value for money audit. **(4 marks)**

(b) (i) Identify and explain **FOUR STRENGTHS** within Bluesberry's operating environment; and **(6 marks)**

(ii) For each strength identified, describe how Bluesberry might make further improvements to provide best value for money. **(4 marks)**

(c) Describe **TWO** substantive procedures the external auditor of Bluesberry should adopt to verify **EACH** of the following assertions in relation to an entity's property, plant and equipment:

(i) Valuation
(ii) Completeness; and
(iii) Rights and obligations.

Note. Assume that the hospital adopts International Financial Reporting Standards. **(6 marks)**

(Total = 20 marks)

113 Bronze Industries Co (Sep/Dec 15) 39 mins

You are an audit senior of Scarlet & Co and are in the process of reviewing the systems testing completed on the payroll cycle of Bronze Industries Co (Bronze), as well as preparing the audit programmes for the final audit.

Bronze operate several chemical processing factories across the country, it manufactures 24 hours a day, seven days a week and employees work a standard shift of eight hours and are paid for hours worked at an hourly rate. Factory employees are paid weekly, with approximately 80% being paid by bank transfer and 20% in cash; the different payment methods are due to employee preferences and Bronze has no plans to change these methods. The administration and sales teams are paid monthly by bank transfer.

Factory staff are each issued a sequentially numbered clock card which details their employee number and name. Employees swipe their cards at the beginning and end of the eight-hour shift and this process is not supervised. During the shift employees are entitled to a 30-minute paid break and employees do not need to clock out to access the dining area. Clock card data links into the payroll system, which automatically calculates gross and net pay along with any statutory deductions. The payroll supervisor for each payment run checks on a sample basis some of these calculations to ensure the system is operating effectively.

Bronze has a human resources department which is responsible for setting up new permanent employees and leavers. Appointments of temporary staff are made by factory production supervisors. Occasionally overtime is required of factory staff, usually to fill gaps caused by staff holidays. Overtime reports which detail the amount of overtime worked are sent out quarterly by the payroll department to production supervisors for their review.

To encourage staff to attend work on time for all shifts Bronze pays a discretionary bonus every six months to factory staff; the production supervisors determine the amounts to be paid. This is communicated in writing by the production supervisors to the payroll department and the bonus is input by a clerk into the system.

For employees paid by bank transfer, the payroll manager reviews the list of the payments and agrees to the payroll records prior to authorising the bank payment. If any changes are required, the payroll manager amends the records. For employees paid in cash, the pay packets are prepared in the payroll department and a clerk distributes them to employees; as she knows most of these individuals she does not require proof of identity.

Required

(a) Identify and explain **FIVE** internal control **STRENGTHS** in Bronze Industries Co's payroll system. **(5 marks)**

(b) Identify and explain **SIX** internal control **DEFICIENCIES** in Bronze Industries Co's payroll system and provide a **RECOMMENDATION** to address each of these deficiencies. **(12 marks)**

(c) Describe substantive **ANALYTICAL PROCEDURES** you should perform to confirm Bronze Industries Co's payroll expense. **(3 marks)**

(Total = 20 marks)

114 Lemon Quartz Co (Mar/Jun 16) 39 mins

You are an audit senior of Hessonite & Co and are in the process of reviewing the inventory system documentation for your audit client, Lemon Quartz Co (Quartz) which manufactures computer equipment. The company's factory and warehouse are based on one large site, and their year end is 30 June 2016. Quartz is planning to undertake a full inventory count at the year end of its raw materials, work in progress and finished goods and you will be attending this count. In preparation you have been reviewing the inventory count instructions for finished goods provided by Quartz.

The count will be undertaken by 15 teams of two counters from the warehouse department with Quartz's financial controller providing overall supervision. Each team of two is allocated a number of bays within the warehouse to count and they are provided with sequentially numbered inventory sheets which contain product codes and quantities extracted from the inventory records. The counters move through each allocated bay counting the inventory and confirming that it agrees with the inventory sheets. Where a discrepancy is found, they note this on the sheet.

The warehouse is large and approximately 10% of the bays have been rented out to third parties with similar operations; these are scattered throughout the warehouse. For completeness, the counters have been asked to count the inventory for all bays noting the third party inventories on separate blank inventory sheets, and the finance department will make any necessary adjustments.

Some of Quartz's finished goods are high in value and are stored in a locked area of the warehouse and all the counting teams will be given the code to access this area. There will be no despatches of inventory during the count and it is not anticipated that there will be any deliveries from suppliers.

Each area is counted once by the allocated team; the sheets are completed in ink, signed by the team and returned after each bay is counted. As no two teams are allocated the same bays, there will be no need to flag that an area has been counted. On completion of the count, the financial controller will confirm with each team that they have returned their inventory sheets.

Required

(a)   In respect of the inventory count procedures for Lemon Quartz Co:

(i)   Identify and explain **FIVE** deficiencies;

(ii)   Recommend a control to address each of these deficiencies; and

(iii)   Describe a **TEST OF CONTROL** the external auditors would perform to assess if each of these controls, if implemented, is operating effectively.

Note. The total marks will be split equally between each part.   **(15 marks)**

(b)   Quartz's finance director has asked your firm to undertake a non-audit assurance engagement later in the year. The audit junior has not been involved in such an assignment before and has asked you to explain what an assurance engagement involves.

Required

Explain the five elements of an assurance engagement.   **(5 marks)**

(Total = 20 marks)

115 Shesha Co   39 mins

Shesha Co (Shesha) is a rapidly growing company which has recently approached your firm, Smith & Co (Smith), for audit services.

The directors of Shesha Co are Kate Shelby and Fatima Shahid, who met at design college. They are innovators who developed a niche product and then starting selling it. They have no business experience. The product has proved very successful and business is growing rapidly with a number of staff involved in production.

Initially Kate and Fatima were able to oversee all aspects of the business, but with the growth in business this is not possible. The directors are keen to set up a control system to ensure that assets are safeguarded and financial records are properly maintained, now that they can no longer control everything themselves. They believe this will protect their business from fraud.

Fatima used to be in charge of sourcing all raw materials, and they have always been bought from the same supplier. However, recently the supplier has been unable to meet Shesha's demands on time, which has led to some business interruption. Shesha has therefore recently employed a purchases manager tasked with diversifying Shesha's suppliers and obtaining the best terms possible for the company.

The existing supplier invoices Fatima directly for goods and she records and pays the invoice. However, Kate and Fatima are keen to divert profits into further development and have therefore also employed an accounts controller to deal with invoicing (both sales and purchases) and maintenance of accounting records, so they can focus on development.

They have requested advice from your firm on setting up internal controls.

(a)   List and explain **SIX** limitations of internal controls   **(5 marks)**

(b)   Define segregation of duties and explain how it might operate at Shesha.   **(4 marks)**

(c)   In respect of the purchases system,

   (i)   Outline **FOUR** objectives you would expect the system have.   **(2 marks)**
   (ii)   For each objective, set out a control relevant to Shesha which would meet that objective.   **(6 marks)**

(d)   Explain the factors the partners of Smith should consider in relation to giving advice on internal controls to an audit client.   **(3 marks)**

(Total = 20 marks)

116 Oregano Co   **39 mins**

You are a member of the recently formed internal audit department of Oregano Co (Oregano). The company manufactures tinned fruit and vegetables which are supplied to large and small food retailers. Management and those charged with governance of Oregano have concerns about the effectiveness of their sales and dispatch system and have asked internal audit to document and review the system.

Sales and dispatch system

Sales orders are mainly placed through Oregano's website but some are made via telephone. Online orders are automatically checked against inventory records for availability; telephone orders, however, are checked manually by order clerks after the call. A follow-up call is usually made to customers if there is insufficient inventory. When taking telephone orders, clerks note down the details on plain paper and afterwards they complete a three part pre-printed order form. These order forms are not sequentially numbered and are sent manually to both dispatch and the accounts department.

As the company is expanding, customers are able to place online orders which will exceed their agreed credit limit by 10%. Online orders are automatically forwarded to the dispatch and accounts department.

A daily pick list is printed by the dispatch department and this is used by the warehouse team to dispatch goods. The goods are accompanied by a dispatch note and all customers are required to sign a copy of this. On return, the signed dispatch notes are given to the warehouse team to file.

The sales quantities are entered from the dispatch notes and the authorised sales prices are generated by the invoicing system. If a discount has been given, this has to be manually entered by the sales clerk onto the invoice. Due to the expansion of the company, and as there is a large number of sale invoices, extra accounts staff have been asked to help out temporarily with producing the sales invoices. Normally it is only two sales clerks who produce the sales invoices.

Required

(a)   Describe **TWO** methods for documenting the sales and dispatch system; and for each explain an advantage and a disadvantage of using this method.   **(6 marks)**

(b)   List **TWO** control objectives of Oregano Co's sales and dispatch system.   **(2 marks)**

(c)   Identify and explain **SIX** deficiencies in Oregano Co's sales and dispatch system and provide a recommendation to address each of these deficiencies.   **(12 marks)**

(Total = 20 marks)

AUDIT EVIDENCE

Questions 117–158 cover Audit evidence, the subject of Part D of the BPP Study Text for F8.

Expert (12/08) (amended)

20 mins

The following scenario relates to questions 117–121.

You are the audit manager in the firm of WSD & Co, an audit firm. You are planning the audit of Truse Co, which operates as a high street retailer and has 15 shops.

All of the shops are owned by Truse Co and have always been included in the financial statements at cost less depreciation. The shops are depreciated over 50 years. However, you know from discussions with management that the company intends to include one of the shops, the flagship store, at a revalued amount rather than cost in the current accounting period. The revalued amount is expected to be materially above the carrying value of the shop. The valuation will be based on a management estimate.

Management has explained that the reason for the revaluation is because the flagship store is located in an area where property prices have risen much more quickly compared to other shop locations. They consider the flagship store to be significantly undervalued on the statement of financial position.

Management will not depreciate the revalued amount allocated to the flagship store's building because they maintain the building to a high standard.

117 In his notes for the audit planning meeting, the audit junior made the following statements in relation to the valuation of the shops:

(1) Truse Co is allowed under IAS 16 to revalue the flagship shop while continuing to measure its three other shops at cost less depreciation.

(2) The revaluation constitutes a change in accounting policy, so we will need to consider the adequacy of the disclosures made in respect of this.

(3) The flagship store should be depreciated on its revalued amount

(4) We must confirm that all repairs and maintenance costs have been capitalised

Which **TWO** of the above statements are correct?

- A 1 and 3
- B 2 and 4
- √ C 2 and 3
- D 1 and 4

118 Which of the following assertions are relevant to the audit of tangible non-current assets?

(1) Existence
(2) Occurrence
(3) Classification
(4) Presentation

- A 1 only
- √ B 1, 3 and 4
- C 2, 3 and 4
- D 1, 2, 3 and 4

119 Which of the following procedures will provide appropriate audit evidence in respect of the completeness of non-current assets?

✓ A   For a sample of assets selected by physical inspection, agree that they are listed on the non-current assets register

B   For a sample of non-current assets listed on the non-current assets register, physically inspect the asset   *inspect existence*

C   For a sample of assets on the assets register, recalculate the net book values in accordance with the entity's accounting policies

D   For a sample of assets on the assets register, inspect relevant purchase invoices or deeds

120 At the planning meeting, it was decided that an auditor's expert should be sought in relation to the valuation of Truse Co's properties as the company has not used an independent valuer.

ISA 620 states that the nature, timing and extent of audit procedures to evaluate the work of the auditor's expert depend on the circumstances of the engagement.

Which of the following matters should the audit team **NOT** consider in determining the nature, timing and extent of these audit procedures?

A   The risk of material misstatement associated with Truse Co's properties

B   WSD & Co's experience with previous work performed by the expert

C   Whether the expert is subject to WSD & Co's quality control policies and procedures

✓ D   The existence of any interests in or relationships with Truse Co that might pose a threat to the expert's objectivity

121 The audit junior has been assigned to the audit of the bank and cash balances of Truse Co. He has noted down the audit evidence he plans to obtain in respect of the bank and cash balances:

(1)   Bank reconciliation carried out by the cashier
(2)   Bank confirmation report from Truse Co's bank
(3)   Verbal confirmation from the directors that the overdraft limit is to be increased
(4)   Cash count carried out by the audit junior himself

What is the order of reliability of the audit evidence, starting with the most reliable first?

A   4, 2, 1 and 3
B   2, 1, 4 and 3
C   4, 3, 2 and 1
D   2, 4, 1 and 3

(Total = 10 marks)

Newthorpe (CBE)   20 mins

The following scenario relates to questions 122–126.

You are an audit manager, auditing the financial statements of Newthorpe Engineering Co, a listed company, for the year ended 30 April 20X7.

Newthorpe's management has provided you with a schedule of the realisable values of the inventories. A full inventory count was carried out at 30 April 20X7.

Audit tests have confirmed that the inventory counts are accurate and there are no purchases or sales cut-off errors.

One of the company's factories was closed on 30 April 20X7. The plant and equipment and inventories were to be sold. By the time the audit work commenced in June 20X7, most of the inventory had been sold.

You have instructed the audit junior to evaluate the valuation of the inventory related to the closing factory at the year end. The audit junior has sent you a list of planned audit procedures.

On 17 March 20X7, Newthorpe's managing director was dismissed for gross misconduct. It was decided that the managing director's salary should stop from that date, and that no redundancy or compensation payments should be made.

The managing director has claimed unfair dismissal and is taking legal action against the company to obtain compensation for loss of his employment. The managing director says he has a service contract with the company which would entitle him to two years' salary at the date of dismissal. The directors believe that there is a 35% chance of the managing director succeeding in his claim.

The financial statements for the year ended 30 April 20X7 record the resignation of the director. However, they do not mention his dismissal and no provision for any damages has been included in the financial statements.

122   Which **TWO** of the following statements are true regarding the auditor's attendance at the inventory count?

☐   It is the auditor's responsibility to organise the inventory count.

☑   The auditor observes client staff to determine whether inventory count procedures are being followed.

☑   The auditor reviews procedures for identifying damaged, obsolete and slow-moving inventory.

☐   If the results of the auditors' test counts are not satisfactory, the auditor should insist that the inventory is recounted.

123   Which of the audit procedures below is **NOT** appropriate in auditing the valuation assertion for Newthorpe's inventory?

☐   Agree the selling prices of inventory sold since the year-end to sales invoices and the cash book.

☐   Assess the reasonableness of management's point estimates of realisable value of inventory that has not yet been sold by reviewing sales before the year-end, comparing the values with inventory that has been sold since the year-end and considering offers made which have not yet been finalised.

☑   For a sample of inventory sold just before and just after the year end, match dates of sales invoices/date posted to ledgers with date on related goods despatched notes.

☐   For unsold inventory, assess reasonableness of provisions for selling expenses by comparison of selling expenses with inventory sold.

124   Which of the following options correctly summarises the correct accounting treatment for the legal claim made by the managing director for unfair dismissal?

Accounting treatment	Reason
☐ Record a provision	A present obligation exists, but the outflow of economic resources is not probable.
☐ Record a provision	A possible obligation exists, depending on whether or not some uncertain future event occurs.
☑ No provision but disclose as a contingent liability	A present obligation exists, but the outflow of economic resources is not probable.
☐ No provision but disclose as a contingent liability	A possible obligation exists, depending on whether or not some uncertain future event occurs.

125 Which of the following audit procedures is likely to provide the auditor with the **MOST** reliable audit evidence regarding the legal claim?

☐ Review the minutes of the disciplinary hearing to understand whether the company has acted in accordance with employment legislation and its internal rules

☐ Review correspondence between the company and its lawyers regarding the likely outcome of the case

☐ Request a written representation from management supporting their assertion that the claim will not be successful

☑ Send an enquiry letter to Newthorpe's lawyers to obtain their view as to the probability of the claim being successful

126 The dismissal of Newthorpe's managing director has alerted you to the possibility that the company may not have complied with employment regulations. You therefore need to determine the impact that such non-compliance may have on the audit.

In accordance with ISA 250 *Consideration of laws and regulations in an audit of financial statements*, which of the following responsibilities is **CORRECT** regarding the responsibilities of the auditors of Newthorpe in relation to compliance with employment regulations?

☐ To obtain sufficient appropriate evidence regarding compliance as they have a direct effect on the financial statements

☑ To perform specific audit procedures to identify possible non-compliance

☐ The auditors do not have any responsibility as the employment regulations do not have a direct effect on the financial statements

☐ To prevent and detect all non-compliance with the regulations

(Total = 10 marks)

Tirrol (6/09) (amended) (CBE)   20 mins

The following scenario relates to questions 127–131.

Your audit firm Cal & Co has just gained a new audit client, Tirrol Co, in a tender in which Cal & Co offered competitively low audit fees. You are the manager in charge of planning the audit work. Tirrol Co's year end is 30 June 20X9 with a scheduled date to complete the audit of 15 August 20X9. The date now is 3 June 20X9.

Tirrol Co provides repair services to motor vehicles from 25 different locations. All inventory, sales and purchasing systems are computerised, with each location maintaining its own computer system. The software in each location is the same because the programs were written specifically for Tirrol Co by a reputable software house. Data from each location is amalgamated on a monthly basis at Tirrol Co's head office to produce management and financial statements.

You are currently planning your audit approach for Tirrol Co. One option being considered is to rewrite Cal & Co's audit software to interrogate the computerised inventory systems in each location of Tirrol Co (except for head office) as part of inventory valuation testing. The testing will need to take place while the system is live. You are aware that July is a major holiday period for Tirrol Co.

127 The audit junior is concerned about various circumstances of the audit, which are likely to increase audit risk. He has written to you with some suggestions.

Which **TWO** of the following suggestions are valid?

- [x] We should budget for the extra time required to document an understanding of the entity, its environment and its systems, and to verify material opening balances.

- [ ] Given the tight reporting deadline, a combined approach should be adopted on the audit, relying on tests of controls wherever possible.

- [x] We must agree a clear timetable with the client for the testing of the computerized inventory systems, setting out availability of access to the system, files and personnel required to complete testing.

- [ ] As this is our first year of audit, we should agree separate fees with the client for any additional audit procedures required. If the client refuses, we should consider withdrawing from the audit as Cal & Co would be deemed to be lowballing.

128 Which of the following are benefits of using audit software in auditing the inventory of Tirrol Co? (Select as many responses as you feel is appropriate.)

- [x] The ability to test all 25 of Tirrol Co's locations using the same audit software, resulting in time and cost savings

- [x] The ability to search all items for exceptions, thus giving greater assurance over the inventory figure

- [x] The ability to select and extract a sample of inventory data for testing, thus reducing sampling risk

- [x] The ability to test the actual computer files from the originating programme, rather than printouts from a spook or preview files, thus eliminating exporting errors

129 It has been decided that systematic sampling would be applied to the audit of Tirrol Co's inventory.

Which of the following sampling methods correctly describes systematic sampling?

- [ ] A sampling method which is a type of value-weighted selection in which sample size, selection and evaluation results in a conclusion in monetary amounts

- [x] A sampling method which involves having a constant sampling interval, the starting point for testing is determined randomly

- [ ] A sampling method in which the auditor selects a block(s) of contiguous items from within the population

- [ ] A sampling method in which the auditor selects a sample without following any particular structured technique

130 Tirrol Co's internal audit department is going to assist with the statutory audit. The chief internal auditor will provide you with documentation on the computerised inventory systems at Tirrol Co. The documentation provides details of the software and shows diagrammatically how transactions are processed through the inventory system. This documentation can be used to significantly decrease the time needed to understand the computer systems and enable audit software to be written for this year's audit.

Which of the following is **NOT** a matter the audit team should consider in determining whether or not the internal auditor's work is adequate for the purposes of the audit?

- [ ] Whether the work was properly planned, performed, supervised, reviewed and documented

- [x] Whether there are any significant threats to the objectivity of the internal auditor

- [ ] Whether sufficient appropriate evidence was obtained to allow the internal auditors to draw reasonable conclusions

- [ ] Whether the conclusions reached are appropriate in the circumstances and the reports prepared are consistent with the results of the work done

131 The audit junior has obtained the following extract of the aged inventory report:

Inventory code	Days in inventory	Original cost $	Selling price $	Costs to sell $	Carrying value $
X070003	98	12,000	20,200	2,000	12,000
X079001	127	14,500	16,000	2,500	14,500
X084000	109	18,000	26,000	3,000	23,000

What is the impact on the value of inventory if no adjustments are made to the carrying values above?

- [ ] Inventory would be overstated by $5,000
- [✓] Inventory and profit for the year would be overstated by $6,000
- [ ] Inventory would be understated by $6,200
- [ ] Inventory would be understated by $12,700

(Total = 10 marks)

Wright

20 mins

The following scenario relates to questions 132–136.

You are the audit manager in the firm of Wright & Co, a large accountancy firm with 30 offices.

It is January 20X6, and a new intake of graduates and apprentices has recently started work at the Audit department after completing their first ACCA exams. Julie, one of the new recruits, has been allocated to the audit of Wilbur Co, your audit client, for the year ended 31 December 20X5. You are responsible for providing guidance to her and have asked her to assist in the audit of trade payables and cash at bank.

Trade payables

Julie has performed a reconciliation of key trade payables balances as follows and has concluded that no further work is required:

	Balance per purchase ledger $'000	Cash in transit $'000	Goods in transit $'000	Balance per supplier statement $'000
Supplier XX1	400	–	100 (1)	500
Supplier XX2	650	50 (2)	–	700
Supplier XX3	100	–	–	100
	1,150			1,300

Notes

(1) Agreed to GRN dated 31 December 20X5
(2) Agreed to cheque posted in the cash book 30 December 20X5

Your follow up work on this identifies that:

- The goods in transit received from supplier XX1 were recognised in inventory at 31 December 20X5.
- The cheque payment to supplier XX2 appeared on the bank statement on 2 January 20X6.
- There is a nil balance on the purchase accruals account.

Cash at bank

In order to gain assurance over the company's bank balance, you asked Julie to arrange for a bank confirmation letter to be sent to Wilbur Co's bank.

Julie has also prepared a bank reconciliation. This shows a significant number of lodgements which were recorded in the cash book on 31 December 20X5. You are concerned that the cash book may have been kept open to include remittances actually received after the year end.

132 Julie has approached you with the following query:

'I know that as auditors, we have to collect audit evidence in order to support our audit opinion. But how can we tell how much audit evidence we need to get?'

Which of the below factors influence the auditor's judgement regarding the sufficiency of the evidence obtained?

(1) The materiality of the account
(2) The size of the account
(3) The source and quality of the evidence available
(4) The amount of time allocated to the audit

A 1 and 3
B 2 and 4
C 2 and 3
D 1 and 4

133 Which of the in-transit items included in the supplier statement reconciliations indicate that there is a cut-off problem?

(1) Cash-in-transit
(2) Goods-in-transit

A 1 only
B 2 only
C 1 and 2
D Neither 1 nor 2

134 What further evidence, if any, is required in relation to the balance due to XX3 to determine if trade payables is understated?

A A review of post year-end purchase orders from supplier XX3
B A confirmation request must be sent to supplier XX3
C No further evidence is required
D A review of credit notes issued by Wilbur Co should be performed

135 Which of the following summarises the steps Julie should take in preparing the bank confirmation letter you have requested?

A Written on the audit firm's headed paper; information requested to be sent directly to the auditor
B Written on the client's headed paper; information requested to be sent directly to the auditor
C Written on the audit firm's headed paper; information requested to be sent directly to the client
D Written on the client's headed paper; information requested to be sent directly to the client

136 Which of the following pieces of audit evidence would provide the most reliable audit evidence that the lodgements recorded on 31 December 20X5 do not relate to amounts received after the period end?

A Bank statement showing the lodgements cleared by the bank
B The date on the cheque paid by the supplier
C The date on the remittance advice
D The bank's date stamp on the paying-in slip

(Total = 10 marks)

Lodestar

The following scenario relates to questions 137–141.

You are an audit senior of Beacon & Co and are currently conducting the audit of Lodestar Co (Lodestar) for the year ended 30 September 20X1. You are reviewing the work of your audit assistant.

Trade receivables

Your audit assistant has carried out a direct confirmation (a receivables circularisation) on trade receivables at Lodestar. She selected the ten largest balances, representing 85% of the sales ledger at year end, including two items that were individually material. Seven customers agreed the sales ledger balance, two replied noting discrepancies which she has followed up and one has not replied.

The audit working papers contain the following work in respect of the two balances with discrepancies.

Customer	Balance per sales ledger $	Balance per customer confirmation $	Comments
Polaris Co	23,400	19,250	Balance is payment sent out on 30 September, agreed to cash book 2 October.
Sirius Co	45,000	39,000	Balancing item is credit requested for goods customer claims were defective in February. Production manager confirms no credit will be issued.

Allowance for doubtful accounts

The company has an accounting policy of creating an allowance for doubtful accounts at 2% of year end sales ledger balance.

137 You are analysing the sample selection with regard to the direct confirmation.

Which of the following statements in relation to the sample selection is **TRUE**?

A The sample is appropriate and, at 85% of the balance, gives good assurance about the overall balance.

B As 15% of the ledger balance has not been sampled, the sample is inappropriate.

√ C The sample selection does not address the risk of understatement as it has focused on the ten largest balances.

D The sample should have been stratified to provide a representative sample.

138 The audit assistant has identified further procedures to be carried out in respect of the customer who has not responded to the circularisation request as follows.

(1) Send out a follow up request.
(2) Inspect the sales invoices in the customer account at year end.
(3) Ask the credit controller whether the customer exists.
(4) Reconcile cash receipts after date with pre-year end invoices in the customer account.

Which of these procedures would provide audit evidence of the **EXISTENCE** of this receivable?

A 1, 2 and 3
√ B 1, 2 and 4
C 3 and 4
D 1 and 2

139   You are reviewing the work carried out on the disputed balances.

What is the misstatement arising from the above issues and the resultant impact on current assets?

A   Trade receivables should be $10,150 lower, current assets are overstated.
✓ B   Trade receivables should be $6,000 lower, current assets are overstated.
C   Trade receivables should be $4,150 lower, no net effect on current assets as balance is in cash.
D   Trade receivables should be S10,150 higher, current assets are understated.

---

140   Your audit assistant has heard that auditing accounting estimates can be problematic and has asked you to explain why this is the case.

Which of the following statements concerning auditing accounting estimates is **INCORRECT**?

A   It can be difficult to obtain evidence concerning accounting estimates as management use judgement in their estimation.

B   Accounting estimates are high risk as they can be subject to management bias.

C   Auditors can formulate a point estimate to compare to management's estimate.

✓ D   Auditors should use their own estimate in the financial statements, as auditor generated evidence is more conclusive than management generated evidence.

---

141   The audit junior has suggested the following tests could be carried out to test the allowance for doubtful accounts:

(1)   Review cash receipts after year-end
(2)   Review an aged debt analysis of the sales ledger
(3)   Ask the credit controller what debts are considered to be doubtful.
(4)   Review sales invoices relating to overdue accounts.

Which of the following correctly ranks these tests in terms of their appropriateness to the **VALUATION** assertion (most appropriate being listed first)?

A   1, 2, 3, 4
B   2, 4, 3, 1
C   1, 2, 4, 3
D   3, 2, 1, 4

(Total = 10 marks)

Porthos

20 mins

The following scenario relates to questions 142–146.

Porthos, a limited liability company, is a retailer of sports equipment, specialising in racquet sports such as tennis, squash and badminton. The company purchases equipment from a variety of different suppliers and then re-sells this online. Customers place their orders directly on the company website. The ordering/sales software automatically verifies the order details, customer address and credit card information prior to orders being verified and goods despatched.

Once the order has been verified the system produces a pre-numbered picking note. The order is then picked in the warehouse and a goods despatched note (GDN) is produced. A copy of this is scanned in to the system and a sequentially numbered invoice is automatically produced and sent to the customer.

You are the audit senior working on the audit of Porthos for the year ended 31 December 20X7.

As the sales system is highly automated the audit manager has decided that CAATs should be used where possible in the audit of the sales account. You identified the key steps to be taken in planning the application of CAATs, as follows:

(1)   Define the types of transactions to be tested
(2)   Set the objective of the CAAT application
(3)   Define the procedures to be performed on the data
(4)   Determine the content and accessibility of the entity's files

The manager has also decided that test data would be used to test the input of details into the ordering system. You identified the following test data which could be used:

(i)   Orders for unusually large quantities
(ii) Orders with fields left blank
(iii) Orders with invalid inventory codes
(iv) Orders with complete and valid details

In addition to the sales income generated from the sale of sports equipment Porthos also earns a small amount of rental income by renting out surplus warehouse space to a local company. The rental agreement shows that the annual rent from 1 March 20X5 was $24,000, increased from $21,600 per annum.

142   Which of the following identifies the correct order in which the steps to be taken in planning the application of CAATS should be performed?

A   2, 4, 1, 3
B   1, 4, 2, 3
C   2, 1, 3, 4
D   4, 2, 3, 1

143   Which of the test data identified by the audit junior should be used to confirm the completeness and accuracy of input into the sales system?

A   ii only
B   ii and iii only
C   i, ii and iii only
D   i, ii, iii and iv

144   Which of the following procedures would provide evidence that sales cut-off for Porthos has been applied correctly?

A   For a sample of sales invoices issued before 31 December 20X5 check that there is a matching GDN dated before 31 December 20X5

B   For a sample of sales invoices issued before 31 December 20X5 check that there is a matching GDN dated after 31 December 20X5

C   For a sample of picking notes issued before 31 December 20X5 confirm that there is a matching GDN dated before 31 December 20X5

D   For a sample of picking notes issued before 31 December 20X5 confirm that there is a matching GDN dated after 31 December 20X5

145   As part of substantive audit procedures, you perform a sequence check on the sales invoice numbers issued by Porthos over the year.

What is the purpose of the sequence check you have performed on the sales invoice numbers?

A   To give assurance that cut-off has been applied accurately
B   To give assurance over the occurrence of the sales transactions recorded
C   To provide audit evidence over the completeness of the recording of sales
D   To provide audit evidence that the sales figure has been calculated accurately

146   You are using a proof in total calculation to assess the accuracy of the rental income.

Which of the following correctly shows the calculation which would be used?

A $24,000 × 12/12
B $21,600 × 12/12
C   (21,600 × 2/12) + (24,000 × 10/12)
D   (21,600 × 10/12) + (24,000 × 2/12)

(Total = 10 marks)

147 Redburn (12/09)

Redburn Co, a publisher and producer of books of poetry, has been a client of your firm of Chartered Certified Accountants for a number of years. The manager in overall charge of the audit has been discussing the audit plan with the audit team, of which you are a member, prior to commencement of the work. The audit manager has informed the team, among other things, that there has been a growing interest in poetry generally and that the company has acquired a reputation for publishing poets who are still relatively unknown.

During your audit you determine:

(i) Contracts with the poets state that they are given a royalty of 10% on sales. Free copies of the books are provided to the poets and to some organisations such as copyright libraries and to others, such as reviewers and university lecturers. No royalties are given on these free copies.

(ii) The computerised customer master file contains a code indicating whether a despatch is to earn a royalty for the author. This code is shown on the sales invoice and despatch note when they are prepared.

(iii) A computerised royalties file is held, all entries therein bearing the invoice number and date.

(iv) The company keeps detailed statistics of sales made, including trends of monthly sales by type of customer, and of colleges where its books are recommended as part of course material, based on reports from sales staff.

(v) Bookshops have the right to return books which are not selling well, but about 10% of these are slightly damaged when returned. The company keeps similar records of returns as it does for sales.

Required

(a) Explain the importance of audit planning and state **TWO** matters that would be included in an audit plan.

(6 marks)

(b) Describe **TWO** procedures used to ensure that the sales statistics kept by the company may be relied upon.

(4 marks)

(c) Describe **THREE** substantive tests you should perform to ensure that the royalties charge is accurate and complete, stating the objective of each test.

(6 marks)

(d) A material figure in the statement of financial position of Redburn Co is the amount attributed to inventory of books.

Required

State **TWO** inherent risks that may affect the inventory figure and suggest **ONE** control to mitigate each risk.

(4 marks)

(e) The management of Redburn Co has told you that inventory is correctly valued at the lower of cost and net realisable value. You have already satisfied yourself that cost is correctly determined.

Required

(i) Define net realisable value;

(2 marks)

(ii) State and explain the purpose of **FOUR** procedures that you should use to ensure that net realisable value of the inventory is at or above cost.

(8 marks)

(Total = 30 marks)

148 Lily (12/12)

Lily Window Glass Co (Lily) is a glass manufacturer, which operates from a large production facility, where it undertakes continuous production 24 hours a day, seven days a week. Also on this site are two warehouses, where the company's raw materials and finished goods are stored. Lily's year end is 31 December.

Lily is finalising the arrangements for the year-end inventory count, which is to be undertaken on 31 December 20X2. The finished windows are stored within 20 aisles of the first warehouse. The second warehouse is for large piles of raw materials, such as sand, used in the manufacture of glass. The following arrangements have been made for the inventory count:

The warehouse manager will supervise the count as he is most familiar with the inventory. There will be ten teams of counters and each team will contain two members of staff, one from the finance and one from the manufacturing department. None of the warehouse staff, other than the manager, will be involved in the count.

Each team will count an aisle of finished goods by counting up and then down each aisle. As this process is systematic, it is not felt that the team will need to flag areas once counted. Once the team has finished counting an aisle, they will hand in their sheets and be given a set for another aisle of the warehouse. In addition to the above, to assist with the inventory counting, there will be two teams of counters from the internal audit department and they will perform inventory counts.

The count sheets are sequentially numbered, and the product codes and descriptions are printed on them but no quantities. If the counters identify any inventory which is not on their sheets, then they are to enter the item on a separate sheet, which is not numbered. Once all counting is complete, the sequence of the sheets is checked and any additional sheets are also handed in at this stage. All sheets are completed in ink.

Any damaged goods identified by the counters will be too heavy to move to a central location, hence they are to be left where they are but the counter is to make a note on the inventory sheets detailing the level of damage.

As Lily undertakes continuous production, there will continue to be movements of raw materials and finished goods in and out of the warehouse during the count. These will be kept to a minimum where possible.

The level of work-in-progress in the manufacturing plant is to be assessed by the warehouse manager. It is likely that this will be an immaterial balance. In addition, the raw materials quantities are to be approximated by measuring the height and width of the raw material piles. In the past this task has been undertaken by a specialist; however, the warehouse manager feels confident that he can perform this task.

Required

(a) For the inventory count arrangements of Lily Window Glass Co:

   (i)   Identify and explain **SIX** deficiencies; and
   (ii) Provide a recommendation to address each deficiency.

   The total marks will be split equally between each part.   **(12 marks)**

You are the audit senior of Daffodil & Co and are responsible for the audit of inventory for Lily. You will be attending the year-end inventory count on 31 December 20X2.

In addition, your manager wishes to utilise computer-assisted audit techniques for the first time for controls and substantive testing in auditing Lily Window Glass Co's inventory.

Required

(b) Describe the procedures to be undertaken by the auditor **DURING** the inventory count of Lily Window Glass Co in order to gain sufficient appropriate audit evidence.   **(6 marks)**

(c) For the audit of the inventory cycle and year-end inventory balance of Lily Window Glass Co:

   (i)   Describe **FOUR** audit procedures that could be carried out using computer-assisted audit techniques (CAATS);

   (ii) Explain the potential advantages of using CAATs; and

   (iii) Explain the potential disadvantages of using CAATs.

   The total marks will be split equally between each part.   **(12 marks)**

                                                                                        (Total = 30 marks)

149 Springfield Nurseries (AIR Pilot Paper) (amended) 59 mins

Your firm is the auditor of Springfield Nurseries, a company operating three large garden centres which sell plants, shrubs and trees, garden furniture and gardening equipment (such as lawnmowers and sprinklers) to the public.

Non-current assets

You are involved in the audit of the company's non-current assets for the year ended 31 December 20X8. The main categories of non-current assets are as follows:

(i)   Land and buildings (all of which are owned outright by the company, none of which are leased)
(ii)   Computers (on which an integrated inventory control and sales system is operated)
(iii)   A number of large and small motor vehicles, mostly used for the delivery of inventory to customers
(iv)   Equipment for packaging and pricing products.

The depreciation rates used are as follows:

(i)   Buildings   5% each year on cost
(ii)   Computers and motor vehicles   20% each year on the reducing balance basis
(iii)   Equipment   15% each year on cost

Year-end inventory

Although an inventory control system is operated and up-to-date inventory records are maintained, the year end inventory quantities that are used in determining the year-end inventory value are arrived at by carrying out full inventory counts at each of the garden centres. The same set of inventory count instructions are provided at each centre and an extract from these is shown below:

(1)   The inventory count will be supervised by the inventory controller for the site and will take place on 1 January 20X9. The count will commence at 6:00am. The centre will be closed on the day of the count. No sales of inventory will take place on 1 January 20X9, but transfer of inventory between garden centres is permitted in order to distribute it to where it will be needed most when the centres are re-opened.

(2)   Staff allocated to the count (one member of staff per count area) will be provided with inventory counting sheets that are produced by the computerised system showing the quantity per the system. These will be distributed and re-collected by the site inventory controller. Where the amount observed is different to the amount on the sheet, it should be crossed out and the new quantity written down.

(3)   The inventory controller will then carry out one test count in each area that has been counted. Where an error is found, the area will be re-counted.

(4)   The quantity for any inventory that looks damaged or unsaleable should be crossed out and allocated a quantity of zero.

(5)   Once all the sheets have been collected up and test counts completed, the inventory controller will manually update the computerised system to reflect the counted quantities. Once the system is updated the count sheets can be discarded.

Auditors must obtain sufficient appropriate audit evidence to issue an audit opinion on the financial statements. In order to gain that evidence, auditors may use a combination of tests of controls and substantive procedures.

Required

(a)   Explain what is meant by:

    (i)   A test of control
    (ii)   A substantive procedure

    and give one example of each that may be used when auditing the completeness of revenue.   **(4 marks)**

(b)   List and explain the main financial statements assertions tested for in the audit of non-current assets.

    (5 marks)

(c)   List the sources of evidence available to you to verify the ownership and cost of the land and buildings.

    (2 marks)

(d)   Describe the audit procedures you would perform to check the appropriateness of the depreciation rates on each of the three categories of non-current asset. **(5 marks)**

(e)   Identify and explain **SEVEN** deficiencies in the inventory counting system highlighted by the extract from Springfield's instructions for inventory counting. For each deficiency suggest how it could be overcome.

(14 marks)

(Total = 30 marks)

150 Westra Co   59 mins

Westra Co assembles mobile telephones in a large factory. Each telephone contains up to 100 different parts, with each part being obtained from one of 50 authorised suppliers.

Like many companies, Westra's accounting systems are partly manual and partly computerised. In overview the systems include:

(i)   Design software

(ii)   A computerised database of suppliers (bespoke system written in-house at Westra)

(iii)   A manual system for recording goods inwards and transferring information to the accounts department

(iv)   A computerised payables ledger maintained in the accounts department (purchased off-the-shelf and used with no program amendments)

(v)   Online payment to suppliers, also in the accounts department

(vi)   A computerised nominal ledger which is updated by the payables ledger

Mobile telephones are assembled in batches of 10,000 to 50,000 telephones. When a batch is scheduled for production, a list of parts is produced by the design software and sent, electronically, to the ordering department. Staff in the ordering department use this list to place orders with authorised suppliers. Orders can only be sent to suppliers on the suppliers' database. Orders are sent using electronic data interchange (EDI) and confirmed by each supplier using the same system. The list of parts and orders are retained on the computer in an 'orders placed' file, which is kept in date sequence.

Parts are delivered to the goods inwards department at Westra. All deliveries are checked against the orders placed file before being accepted. A hand-written pre-numbered goods received note (GRN) is raised in the goods inwards department showing details of the goods received with a cross-reference to the date of the order. The top copy of the GRN is sent to the accounts department and the second copy retained in the goods inwards department. The orders placed file is updated with the GRN number to show that the parts have been received.

Paper invoices are sent by all suppliers following dispatch of goods. Invoices are sent to the accounts department, where they are stamped with a unique ascending number. Invoice details are matched to the GRN, which is then attached to the invoice. Invoice details are then entered into the computerised payables ledger. The invoice is signed by the accounts clerk to confirm entry into the payables ledger. Invoices are then retained in a temporary file in number order while awaiting payment.

After 30 days, the payables ledger automatically generates a computerised list of payments to be made, which is sent electronically to the chief accountant. The chief accountant compares this list to the invoices, signs each invoice to indicate approval for payment, and then forwards the electronic payments list to the accounts assistant. The assistant uses online banking to pay the suppliers. The electronic payments list is filed in month order on the computer.

Required

(a)   Describe the substantive audit procedures you should perform to confirm the assertions of completeness, occurrence and cut-off for purchases in the financial statements of Westra Co. For each procedure, explain the purpose of that procedure. **(12 marks)**

(b)   Describe the audit procedures you should perform on the trade payables balance in Westra Co's financial statements. For each procedure, explain the purpose of that procedure. **(8 marks)**

(c)   Describe the internal controls that should be in place over the standing data on the trade payables master file in Westra Co's computer system. **(5 marks)**

(d) Discuss the extent to which computer-assisted audit techniques might be used in your audit of purchases and payables at Westra Co.

(5 marks)

(Total = 30 marks)

151 Panda

39 mins

Panda Co manufactures chemicals and has a factory and four offsite storage locations for finished goods. Panda Co's year end was 30 April 20X3. The final audit is almost complete and the financial statements and auditor's report are due to be signed next week. Revenue for the year is $55 million and profit before taxation is $5.6 million.

The following two events have occurred subsequent to the year end. No amendments or disclosures have been made in the financial statements.

Event 1 – Defective chemicals

Panda Co undertakes extensive quality control checks prior to the despatch of any chemicals. Testing on 3 May 20X3 found that a batch of chemicals produced in April was defective. The cost of this batch was $0.85 million. In its current condition it can be sold at a scrap value of $0.1 million. The costs of correcting the defect are too significant for Panda Co's management to consider this an alternative option.

Event 2 – Explosion

An explosion occurred at the smallest of the four offsite storage locations on 20 May 20X3. This resulted in some damage to inventory and property, plant and equipment. Panda Co's management have investigated the cause of the explosion and believe that they are unlikely to be able to claim on their insurance. Management of Panda Co has estimated that the value of damaged inventory and property, plant and equipment was $0.9 million and it now has no scrap value.

Required

(a) Explain the five elements of an assurance engagement. *CREST*

(5 marks)

(b) For each of the two events above:

(i) Explain whether the financial statements require amendment; and

(ii) Describe audit procedures that should be performed in order to form a conclusion on any required amendment.

Note. The total marks will be split equally between each event.

(12 marks)

(c) The directors do not wish to make any amendments or disclosures to the financial statements for the explosion (Event 2).

Required

Explain the impact on the auditor's report should this issue remain unresolved.

(3 marks)

(Total = 20 marks)

152 Rose (12/12)

39 mins

Rose Leisure Club Co (Rose) operates a chain of health and fitness clubs. Its year end was 31 October 20X2. You are the audit manager and the year-end audit is due to commence shortly. The following three matters have been brought to your attention.

(i) **Trade payables and accruals**

Rose's finance director has notified you that an error occurred in the closing of the purchase ledger at the year end. Rather than it closing on 1 November, it accidentally closed one week earlier on 25 October. All purchase invoices received between 25 October and the year end have been posted to the 20X3 year-end purchase ledger.

(6 marks)

(ii)   **Receivables**

Rose's trade receivables have historically been low as most members pay monthly in advance. However, during the year a number of companies have taken up group memberships at Rose and hence the receivables balance is now material. The audit senior has undertaken a receivables circularisation for the balances at the year end; however, there are a number who have not responded and a number of responses with differences.   **(5 marks)**

(iii)   **Reorganisation**

The company recently announced its plans to reorganise its health and fitness clubs. This will involve closing some clubs for refurbishment, retraining some existing staff and disposing of some surplus assets. These plans were agreed at a board meeting in October and announced to their shareholders on 29 October. Rose is proposing to make a reorganisation provision in the financial statements.   **(4 marks)**

Required

(a)   Identify and explain each of the **FIVE** fundamental principles contained within ACCA's Code of Ethics and Conduct.   **(5 marks)**

(b)   Describe substantive procedures you would perform to obtain sufficient and appropriate audit evidence in relation to the above three matters.

Note. The mark allocation is shown against each of the three matters above.

(Total = 20 marks)

153 Donald (6/11)   39 mins

Donald Co operates an airline business. The company's year end is 31 July 20X1.

You are the audit senior and you have started planning the audit. Your manager has asked you to have a meeting with the client and to identify any relevant audit risks so that the audit plan can be completed. From your meeting you ascertain the following:

In order to expand their flight network, Donald Co will need to acquire more airplanes; they have placed orders for another six planes at an estimated total cost of $20m and the company is not sure whether these planes will be received by the year end. In addition the company has spent an estimated $15m on refurbishing their existing planes. In order to fund the expansion Donald Co has applied for a loan of $25m. It has yet to hear from the bank as to whether it will lend them the money.

The company receives bookings from travel agents as well as directly via their website. The travel agents are given a 90-day credit period to pay Donald Co, however, due to difficult trading conditions a number of the receivables are struggling to pay. The website was launched in 20X0 and has consistently encountered difficulties with customer complaints that tickets have been booked and paid for online but Donald Co has no record of them and hence has sold the seat to another customer.

Donald Co used to sell tickets via a large call centre located near to their head office. However, in May they closed it down and made the large workforce redundant.

Required

(a)   The auditor has a responsibility to design audit procedures to obtain sufficient and appropriate evidence. There are various audit procedures for obtaining evidence, such as external confirmation.

Required

Apart from external confirmation:

(i)   State and explain **FIVE** procedures for obtaining evidence and;
(ii)   For each procedure, describe an example relevant to the audit of purchases and other expenses.

(10 marks)

(b)   Using the information provided, describe **FIVE** audit risks and explain the auditor's response to each risk in planning the audit of Donald Co.   **(10 marks)**

(Total = 20 marks)

154 Rocks Forever (AIR 12/05) (amended)

39 mins

You are the audit manager in the firm of DeCe & Co, an audit firm with ten national offices. You are planning the audit of Rocks Forever, one of your clients.

Rocks Forever purchases diamond jewellery from three manufacturers. The jewellery is then sold from Rocks Forever's four shops. This is the only client your firm has in the diamond industry.

They have also said they will not depreciate the revalued amount allocated to the store's building because they maintain the building to a high standard.

You are planning to attend the physical inventory count for Rocks Forever. Inventory is the largest account on the statement of financial position with each of the four shops holding material amounts. Due to the high value of the inventory, all shops will be visited and test counts performed.

With the permission of the directors of Rocks Forever, you have employed UJ, a firm of specialist diamond valuers who will also be in attendance. UJ will verify that the jewellery is, in fact, made from diamonds and that the jewellery is saleable with respect to current trends in fashion. UJ will also suggest, on a sample basis, the value of specific items of jewellery.

Counting will be carried out by shop staff in teams of two using pre-numbered count sheets.

Required

(a) Briefly describe the main risks associated with inventory in a company such as Rocks Forever. **(3 marks)**

(b) Describe **FOUR** audit procedures that should be used in obtaining evidence in relation to the inventory count of inventory held in the shops. For each procedure, explain the reason for the procedure. **(8 marks)**

(c) Explain the factors you should consider when placing reliance on the work of UJ. **(5 marks)**

(d) Describe the audit procedures you should perform to ensure that jewellery inventory is valued correctly. **(4 marks)**

(Total = 20 marks)

155 Andromeda Industries Co (Sep/Dec 15)

39 mins

Andromeda Industries Co (Andromeda) develops and manufactures a wide range of fast moving consumer goods. The company's year end is 31 December 2015 and the forecast profit before tax is $8.3 million. You are the audit manager of Neptune & Co and the year-end audit is due to commence in January. The following information has been gathered during the planning process:

Inventory count

Andromeda's raw materials and finished goods inventory are stored in 12 warehouses across the country. Each of these warehouses is expected to contain material levels of inventory at the year end. It is expected that there will be no significant work in progress held at any of the sites. Each count will be supervised by a member of Andromeda's internal audit department and the counts will all take place on 31 December, when all movements of goods in and out of the warehouses will cease.

Research and development

Andromeda spends over $2 million annually on developing new product lines. This year it incurred expenditure on five projects, all of which are at different stages of development. Once they meet the recognition criteria under IAS 38 *Intangible Assets* for development expenditure, Andromeda includes the costs incurred within intangible assets. Once production commences, the intangible assets are amortised on a straight line basis over five years.

Required

(a) Explain **FOUR** factors which influence the reliability of audit evidence. **(4 marks)**

(b) Describe audit procedures you would perform during the audit of Andromeda Industries Co:

    (i) **BEFORE** and **DURING** the inventory counts; and **(8 marks)**

    (ii) In relation to research and development expenditure. **(4 marks)**

(c)   During the audit, the team discovers that one of the five development projects, valued at $980,000 and included within intangible assets, does not meet the criteria for capitalisation. The finance director does not intend to change the accounting treatment adopted as she considers this an immaterial amount.

Required

Discuss the issue and describe the impact on the auditor's report, if any, if the issue remains unresolved.

(4 marks)

(Total = 20 marks)

156 Squash Co   39 mins

Squash Co (Squash) is a client of your firm. You have been assigned to the following audit areas.

(i)   Payables

Squash has a history of financing short term working capital by delaying paying suppliers. During the year two major suppliers withdrew credit from Squash and have started payment on delivery terms. This has had a difficult effect on Squash's cash flow situation. Having met the terms for several months by extending credit with other suppliers further, the purchase director is negotiating with the suppliers to reinstate credit terms.   **(5 marks)**

(ii)   Intangible assets

During the year, Squash obtained a patent from a competitor. The directors have discussed the accounting treatment with your firm and you are satisfied that it is appropriate to treat this as an intangible asset. As they purchased the patent at what they believe to be below market value, the directors wish to carry it at its fair value which they estimate to be substantially above the cost price. They have estimated that the useful life of the patent is 20 years.   **(4 marks)**

(iii)   Directors' emoluments

Under local legislation, Squash must publish details of the payments made to directors during the year in the financial statements, broken down into details of salary, bonuses and other payments.   **(5 marks)**

Required

(a)   Identify and explain the assertions which present the most audit risk in the audit of these three issues at Squash.   **(6 marks)**

(b)   Describe substantive procedures you would perform to obtain sufficient and appropriate audit evidence in relation to the three matters.

Note. The mark allocation for part (b) is shown against each of the three matters above.

(Total = 20 marks)

157 Traffic Lights   39 mins

Traffic Lights (TL) is a small local charity providing play facilities to families coping with disabilities within the family. Your firm, Amber & Co (Amber), has been the auditor of the charity for a number of years. The charity is required to receive audits to qualify for local authority grants, although it is a small charity.

TL operates a number of 'play rooms' in several towns in Wellshire. The play rooms are staffed by volunteers and operates in premises that have been donated to the charity. There is no charge for attending the play rooms, but pre-registered attendees may make a donation per visit should they wish to. The vast majority of play equipment has also been donated to TL, with some items being purchased by the charity after specific money raising appeals for those particular items.

TL's income comes from the following sources:

•   Donations by families for play sessions, which are placed into a locked donations tin at time of play. These donations are counted at the end of business on a Monday, noted in a cash book and banked on a Tuesday morning by a volunteer.

- Donations by local businesses and individuals, which are sent by cheque to the trustees at the registered office or paid directly by bank transfer.

- Legacies, which are usually paid direct to the charity's bank by the legal advisors handling the legator's estate.

- Local authority grants, which the charity reapplies for annually, and which are paid by direct transfer in January if the application is successful.

The charity has limited controls. The operation of the controls is dependent on the volunteers and the trustees (who are also volunteers). In the past your firm has judged the systems to be working effectively, but inherently limited due to the use of volunteers and the fact that cash is only banked weekly. The firm has therefore usually taken a substantive approach to the audit.

Given that most assets have been donated to the charity, TL has an accounting policy to value assets at 'value to the charity', which equates to fair value in accordance with IAS 16. Assets are depreciated over their useful lives of:

- Property   50 years
- Play equipment   10 years

Donated assets are recorded in a donated assets register. Purchased assets are recorded in a purchased asset register.

(a)   Discuss the extent to which Amber will be able to use substantive analytical procedures in the audit of TL.

(3 marks)

(b)   Describe substantive procedures the auditor could perform to obtain sufficient and appropriate audit evidence in relation to the valuation of:

   (i)   Property   **(4 marks)**
   (ii)   Play equipment   **(5 marks)**

(c)   Describe substantive procedures the auditor could perform to obtain sufficient and appropriate audit evidence in relation to:

   (i)   Legacies   **(2 marks)**
   (ii)   Donations   **(6 marks)**

(Total = 20 marks)

158 Hawthorn Enterprises Co   39 mins

Hawthorn Enterprises Co (Hawthorn) manufactures and distributes fashion clothing to retail stores. Its year end was 31 March 20X5. You are the audit manager and the year-end audit is due to commence shortly. The following three matters have been brought to your attention.

(i)   **Supplier statement reconciliations**

   Hawthorn receives monthly statements from its main suppliers and although these have been retained, none have been reconciled to the payables ledger as at 31 March 20X5. The engagement partner has asked the audit senior to recommend the procedures to be performed on supplier statements.   **(3 marks)**

(ii)   **Bank reconciliation**

   During last year's audit of Hawthorn's bank and cash, significant cut off errors were discovered with a number of post year-end cheques being processed prior to the year end to reduce payables. The finance director has assured the audit engagement partner that this error has not occurred again this year and that the bank reconciliation has been carefully prepared. The audit engagement partner has asked that the bank reconciliation is comprehensively audited.   **(4 marks)**

(iii)   **Receivables**

   Hawthorn's receivables ledger has increased considerably during the year, and the year-end balance is $2.3 million compared to $1.4 million last year. The finance director of Hawthorn has requested that a receivables circularisation is not carried out as a number of their customers complained last year about the inconvenience involved in responding. The engagement partner has agreed to this request, and tasked you with identifying alternative procedures to confirm the existence and valuation of receivables.   **(5 marks)**

Required

(a) (i) Identify and explain **FOUR** financial statement assertions relevant to classes of transactions and events for the year under audit; and

(ii) For each identified assertion, describe a substantive procedure relevant to the audit of **REVENUE**.

(8 marks)

(b) Describe substantive procedures you would perform to obtain sufficient and appropriate audit evidence in relation to the above three matters.

Note. The mark allocation is shown against each of the three matters above.   (Total = 20 marks)

REVIEW AND REPORTING

Questions 159–198 cover Review and reporting, the subject of Part E of the BPP Study Text for F8.

Chestnut (6/15) (amended) (CBE)

20 mins

The following scenario relates to questions 159–163.

You are the audit manager of Chestnut & Co and are reviewing the key issues identified in the files of two audit clients.

The first audit client is Palm Industries Co (Palm), a listed company. Palm's year end was 31 March 20X5 and the draft financial statements show revenue of $28.2m, receivables of $5.6m and profit before tax of $4.8m. The fieldwork stage for this audit has been completed.

A customer of Palm owed an amount of $350,000 at the year end. Testing of receivables in April highlighted that no amounts had been paid to Palm from this customer as they were disputing the quality of certain goods received from Palm. The finance director is confident the issue will be resolved and no allowance for receivables was made with regards to this balance.

The second audit client is Ash Trading Co (Ash). Ash is a new client of Chestnut & Co, its year end was 31 January 20X5 and the firm was only appointed auditors in February 20X5, as the previous auditors were suddenly unable to undertake the audit. The fieldwork stage for this audit is currently ongoing.

The inventory count at Ash's warehouse was undertaken on 31 January 20X5 and was overseen by the company's internal audit department. Neither Chestnut & Co nor the previous auditors attended the count. Detailed inventory records were maintained but it was not possible to undertake another full inventory count subsequent to the year end.

The draft financial statements show a profit before tax of $2.4 million, revenue of $10.1 million and inventory of $510,000.

159 Which **TWO** of the following audit procedures should be performed in order to form a conclusion on whether an amendment is required in Palm's 20X5 financial statements in respect of the disputed balance?

☑ Review whether any payments have subsequently been made by this customer since the audit fieldwork was completed

☐ Match the total of the aged receivables' listing to the sales ledger control account

☐ Vouch the balance owed by the customer at the year end to sales invoices

☑ Review the latest customer correspondence with regards to an assessment of the likelihood of the customer making payment

160 The auditor's report for Palm is due to be signed in the next week or so. You have concluded that the disputed balance is likely to be irrecoverable, but the directors have not made any changes to the financial statements in respect of this.

Which of the following options correctly summarises the impact on the auditor's report for Palm if the issue remains unresolved?

☐ Unmodified with key audit matters section
☐ Disclaimer of opinion
☑ Qualified 'except for'
☐ Adverse opinion

161 Which of the following correctly summarises the effect of the issue relating to the inventory count of Ash at the year end?

	Material	Financial statement impact
☐	No	Current assets are understated
☐	No	Gross profit may be understated
☐	Yes	Opening inventory may be materially misstated
☑	Yes	Gross profit may be overstated

162 The audit engagement partner for Ash has requested that additional audit procedures be performed in order to conclude on the level of adjustment needed in relation to the above inventory issue.

Which **TWO** of the following audit procedures should be performed in order to form a conclusion as to whether Ash's 20X5 financial statements require amendment?

☐ Obtain a copy of the aged inventory report and use computer assisted audit techniques to verify the accuracy of the report. Discuss the valuation of slow moving inventory with the production director.

☑ Review the internal auditors' reports of the inventory count to identify the level of adjustments made to the records, in order to assess the reasonableness of relying on the inventory records for the purpose of the year end audit.

☑ Perform test counts of inventory in the warehouse and compare these first to the inventory records, and then from inventory records to the warehouse, in order to assess the reasonableness of the inventory records maintained by Ash.

☐ Review Ash's sales order book for February, March and April 20X5 to estimate the level of inventory that will need to be produced in the new accounting period to fulfil customer demand.

163 Alternative procedures performed as Chestnut & Co were unable to attend the inventory count of Ash did not provide sufficient appropriate audit evidence regarding the inventory balance in the statement of financial position.

From the options below indicate the audit opinion which would be given in these circumstances and the appropriate disclosure in the auditor's report.

	Audit opinion		Disclosure in the auditor's report
☑	Qualified	☑	Basis for qualified opinion
☐	Disclaimer	☐	Basis for disclaimer of opinion
☐	Qualified	☐	Key audit matters section
☐	Disclaimer	☐	Emphasis of matter

(Total = 10 marks)

Humphries (12/11) (amended)   20 mins

The following scenario relates to questions 164–168.

Humphries Co, your audit client, operates a chain of food wholesalers across the country and its year end was 30 September 20X1. The final audit is nearly complete and it is proposed that the financial statements and auditor's report will be signed on 13 December. Revenue for the year is $78 million and profit before taxation is $7.5 million.

The following information comes to light:

Humphries Co has three warehouses; following extensive rain on 20 November, rain and river water flooded the warehouse located in Bass. All of the inventory in the warehouse was damaged and has been disposed of. The insurance company has been contacted. No amendments or disclosures have been made in the financial statements.

A customer of Humphries Co has been experiencing cash flow problems and its year-end balance is $0.3m. The company has just become aware that its customer is experiencing significant going concern difficulties. The management of Humphries believes that as the company has been trading for many years, they will receive some, if not full, payment from the customer; hence they have not adjusted the receivable balance.

A key supplier of Humphries Co is suing them for breach of contract. The lawsuit was filed prior to the year end, and the sum claimed by them is $1 million. This has been disclosed as a contingent liability in the notes to the financial statements.

Correspondence has just arrived from the supplier indicating that they are willing to settle the case for a payment by Humphries Co of $0.6 million. It is likely that the company will agree to this.

164   Which of the following audit procedures would identify subsequent events occurring up to the date of the auditor's report?

   (1)   Enquire of management whether there have been any unusual accounting adjustments

   (2)   Enquire of management whether there have been any issues of shares/debentures, or changes in business structure

   (3)   Review management procedures for identifying subsequent events to ensure that such events are identified

   (4)   Obtain written representation that all subsequent events requiring adjustment or disclosure have been adjusted or disclosed

   A   1 and 2
   B   1 and 3
   C   1, 3 and 4
  ✓ D   1, 2, 3 and 4

165   Which of the following statements correctly describe the likely impact that the flooding of the warehouse will have on Humphries' financial statements for the year ended 30 September 20X1?

   (1)   Inventory should be written down, because the flood damage is an adjusting event

   (2)   Inventory should not be written down, because the damage is not an adjusting event

   (3)   If a material amount of inventory is uninsured, it may be necessary to disclose the event and an estimate of the financial losses

   (4)   If insurance proceeds are more likely than not to be received, a contingent asset should be recognised

   A   1 only
   B   2 only
   C   1 and 4
  ✓ D   2 and 3

166   Which of the following audit procedures should be performed in order to form a conclusion on the amendment required to Humphries' 20X1 financial statements in respect of the $0.3m owed by the customer experiencing financial difficulties?

   (1)   Reviewing the post year-end period for payments received from the customer in respect of the year end debt

   (2)   Reviewing correspondence with the customer to assess the likelihood of Humphries recovering the $0.3m

   (3)   Writing to the customer to request confirmation of the amount owed to Humphries at the year end

   (4)   Ask management to produce a revised cash flow forecast covering at least 12 months after the year end

  ✓ A   1 and 2
   B   2 and 3
   C   1 and 4
   D   3 and 4

167 Which of the following options correctly summarises the impact on the auditor's report if the financial statements are not revised in the light of the new information regarding the lawsuit for breach of contract?

A   Unmodified
B   Unmodified with emphasis of matter
✓C   Qualified 'except for'
D   Adverse opinion

168 It is now 13 December 20X1. The auditor's report has been signed. The financial statements are due to be issued on 25 December 20X1.

Which of the following statements correctly describes the auditor's responsibility in relation to subsequent events occurring between now and 25 December?

A   The auditor must design procedures to obtain sufficient appropriate audit evidence that all events up to that date that may require adjustment or disclosure have been identified

B   The auditor must perform procedures on matters examined during the audit, which may be susceptible to change after the year-end.

C   The auditor has no obligation to perform procedures, or make enquiries regarding the financial statements. Any subsequent events should be noted and considered in the next period's audit.

✓D   If the auditor becomes aware of a fact that, had it been known to the auditor at the date of the auditor's report, may have caused the auditor to amend the auditor's report, the auditor shall discuss the need for any adjustments with management.

(Total = 10 marks)

Minnie (6/11) (amended) (CBE)   20 mins

The following scenario relates to questions 169–173.

You are the audit manager of Daffy & Co and you are briefing your team on the approach to adopt in undertaking the review and finalisation stage of the audit of the financial statements for the year ended 31 December 20X7.

During the audit of Minnie Co, an uncorrected misstatement was identified with regards to a property balance which was revalued during the year. The revaluation was carried out by an independent expert valuer and incorrect assumptions were provided to the valuer. The audit team's audit procedures have determined that the property is overvalued by $600,000.

The following additional issues have also arisen during the course of the audit of Minnie Co.

(i)   Depreciation has been calculated on the total of land and buildings. In previous years it has only been charged on buildings. Total depreciation is $2.5m and the element charged to land only is $0.7m.

(ii) Minnie Co's main competitor has filed a lawsuit for $1m against them alleging a breach of copyright; this case is ongoing and will not be resolved prior to the auditor's report being signed. You have concluded that the outcome of the lawsuit is uncertain. The matter is disclosed as a contingent liability.

Profit before tax for the year ended 31 December 20X7 is $10m.

169 Which **TWO** of the following statements correctly describe the auditor's responsibility in relation to misstatements?

☐   The auditor must accumulate misstatements over the course of the audit unless they are immaterial.

✓   As part of their completion procedures, auditors shall consider whether the aggregate of uncorrected misstatements in the financial statements is material

✓   In deciding whether the uncorrected misstatements are material, the auditor shall consider the size and nature of the misstatements

☐   The auditor is required to consider misstatements relating to transactions and account balances, but not misstatements related to qualitative disclosures

170 Which of the following steps should you take first in relation to the uncorrected misstatement in respect of the revalued property?

☐ Accumulate the misstatement along with other uncorrected misstatements in a schedule of unadjusted audit differences. If the aggregate is material, ask the directors to correct the misstatements.

☑ Ask the directors to correct the specific misstatement, explaining that it is material to the financial statements.

☐ Speak to the expert valuer to assess the methodology used in performing the valuation.

☐ Modify the audit opinion, because the misstatement is material.

---

171 Which of the following correctly summarises the effect of the depreciation charged on land and buildings on the financial statements?

	Material	Financial statement impact
☐	No	Profit is understated
☐	No	Assets are overstated
☑	Yes	Profit is understated
☐	Yes	Assets are overstated

---

172 You have concluded that knowledge of the litigation is not fundamental to understanding the financial statements.

In the light of this, indicate the audit opinion which would be given and how the matter would be disclosed in the auditor's report.

	Audit opinion		Disclosure in the auditor's report
☐	Disclaimer	☐	Material uncertainty related to going concern
☑	Unmodified	☐	Basis for adverse opinion
☐	Qualified	☑	No related disclosure
☐	Adverse	☐	Basis for qualified opinion

---

173 Having commenced audit fieldwork on Minnie Co on 1 February 20X8, the audit was completed on 20 February 20X8. The auditor's report is due to be signed on 5 March 20X8. Minnie's board plans to issue the financial statements on 30 April 20X8.

Indicate on the timeline below which date would be the most appropriate date for the directors to sign the written representation letter.

1 February 20X8	20 February 20X8	5 March 20X8	30 April 20X8
☐	☐	☑	☐

(Total = 10 marks)

Greenfields (12/10) (amended)

20 mins

The following scenario relates to questions 174–178.

Greenfields Co specialises in manufacturing equipment which can help to reduce toxic emissions in the production of chemicals. The company has grown rapidly over the past eight years and this is due partly to the warranties that the company gives to its customers. It guarantees its products for five years and if problems arise in this period it undertakes to fix them, or provide a replacement product.

You are the manager responsible for the audit of Greenfields and you are performing the final review stage of the audit and have come across the following issues.

Receivable balance owing from Yellowmix Co

Greenfields has a material receivable balance owing from its customer, Yellowmix Co. During the year-end audit, your team reviewed the ageing of this balance and found that no payments had been received from Yellowmix for over six months, and Greenfields would not allow this balance to be circularised. Instead management has assured your team that they will provide a written representation confirming that the balance is recoverable.

Warranty provision

The warranty provision included within the statement of financial position is material. The audit team has performed testing over the calculations and assumptions which are consistent with prior years. The team has requested a written representation from management confirming the basis and amount of the provision are reasonable. Management has yet to confirm acceptance of this representation.

Other information

You have reviewed a financial summary which is to be included in the annual report and have found that the details are inconsistent with the financial statements. Your investigations have shown that the error is in the summary and not the financial statements.

174 Assuming you received the written representations as described above for both the receivables balance and the warranty provision, in respect of which balances is the auditor most likely to conclude that sufficient appropriate evidence has been obtained?

- A   Receivables balance only
- ✓ B   Warranty provision only
- C   Receivables balance and warranty provision
- D   Neither the receivables balance nor the warranty provision

175 Which of the following audit procedures could the audit team carry out to obtain independent evidence relating to the recoverability of the debt from Yellowmix?

- (1)   Review correspondence with Yellowmix regarding the late payment
- (2)   Trace a sample of goods despatched notes for Yellowmix to sales invoices
- (3)   Trace the entries in Yellowmix's account in the receivables ledger to invoices and remittances
- (4)   Perform a review of post year-end cash receipts

- A   1 and 2
- ✓ B   1 and 4
- C   2 and 3
- D   2 and 4

176 Management has now stated that it is not prepared to confirm that the basis and amount of the warranty provision are reasonable.

In accordance with ISA 580 *Written representations* which of the following actions must you take?

- (1)   Discuss with management why they have refused to provide the representations requested
- (2)   Re-asses the integrity of management and consider the implications for any other representations
- (3)   Seek legal advice
- (4)   Resign as auditors

- ✓ A   1 and 2
- B   3 and 4
- C   1 and 3
- D   2 and 4

177　You have discussed the matter with management but they are still not prepared to provide the representations you have requested.

What type of modified opinion would be issued and what would be the basis for this modification?

	Audit opinion	Reason
A	Qualified	Material misstatement
B	Disclaimer	Inability to obtain sufficient appropriate evidence
C	Adverse	Material misstatement
✓ D	Qualified	Inability to obtain sufficient appropriate evidence

178　You have notified the directors of the error in the summary financial statements.

Which of the following correctly summarises the impact on the auditor's report if the directors do not correct this error?

	Audit opinion	Disclosure
A	Modified	Other Information section stating that there is nothing to report
B	Modified	Other Information section would not be required as there is nothing to report
✓ C	Unmodified	Other Information section including a description of the uncorrected misstatement
D	Unmodified	Other Matter paragraph including a description of the uncorrected misstatement

(Total = 10 marks)

Strawberry (6/12) (amended)　　　　20 mins

The following scenario relates to questions 179–183.

You are the audit manager of Kiwi & Co. Your client is Strawberry Kitchen Designs Co (Strawberry), who is a kitchen manufacturer. The company's year end is 30 April 20X2.

Strawberry has had a challenging year. Grape Co, a major customer of Strawberry who owes $0.6m is experiencing financial difficulties. However the balance is included within the financial statements. The sales director has recently left Strawberry and has yet to be replaced. As a result Strawberry has struggled to win any new business in the last six months.

The monthly cash flow has shown a net cash outflow for the last two months of the financial year and is forecast as negative for the forthcoming financial year

You have performed some analytical procedures on the draft financial statements and have calculated the following ratios:

	20X2 Draft	20X1 Actual
Inventory turnover days	95	97
Receivables days	65	49
Payables days	120	86

Due to its poor cash flow, Strawberry missed a loan repayment and, as a result of this breach in the loan covenants, the bank has asked that the loan of $4.8m be repaid in full within six months.

179 Which of the following are potential indicators that Strawberry is not a going concern?

    (1)   The breach of the loan covenants
    (2)   The departure of the sales director
    (3)   The fall in inventory turnover days
    (4)   The negative cash flow figures

    A   1, 2 and 3
    B   2, 3 and 4
    C   1, 3 and 4
✓ D   1, 2 and 4

180 You are reviewing the management's assessment of Strawberry's ability to continue as a going concern.

What period must management's assessment cover?

    A   At least 12 months from the date of the auditor's report
✓ B   At least 12 months from the date of the financial statements
    C   A maximum of 12 months from the date of the auditor's report
    D   A maximum of 12 months from the date of the financial statements

181 You are concerned that the debt due from Grape Co may not be recoverable and believe that this would have a significant effect on the viability of Strawberry.

Which of the following would provide you with the most reliable evidence regarding the recoverability of this debt?

    A   A management representation confirming its recoverability

    B   The response from the customer to your circularisation performed earlier in the audit confirming the amount owed

✓ C   Identification during your subsequent events review of a cash receipt for the full amount

    D   Correspondence between Strawberry's lawyer and Grape Co's lawyers confirming that the amount will be paid

182 You have raised your concerns with management regarding the ability of Strawberry to repay the $0.6m loan in six months. The directors have assured you that this will be possible as they have a contingency plan.

Which of the following courses of action by the directors would provide you with the most assurance that Strawberry will be able to meet this commitment?

    A   Plans to dispose of a property valued at $5.2m in August 20X2
    B   The reopening of negotiations regarding the terms of the loan with the current provider
    C   Plans to substantially cut production costs by moving production to Asia
✓ D   Agreement by an alternative financial institution to lend Strawberry $4.8m in September 20X2

183 You have concluded that Strawberry is not a going concern.

If the directors refuse to amend the financial statements which of the following correctly describes the impact on the auditor's report?

	Audit opinion	Explanation of circumstances
✓ A	Adverse opinion	Basis for adverse opinion
B	Qualified opinion	Basis for qualified opinion
C	Adverse opinion	Material Uncertainty Related to Going Concern section
D	Qualified opinion	Material Uncertainty Related to Going Concern section

qualified but not pervasive

(Total = 10 marks)

Clarinet (6/14) (amended)

20 mins

The following scenario relates to questions 184–188.

Clarinet Co (Clarinet) is a computer hardware specialist and has been trading for over five years. The company is funded partly through overdrafts and loans and also by several large shareholders; the year end is 30 April 20X4.

Clarinet has experienced significant growth in previous years; however, in the current year a new competitor, Drums Design Co (Drums), has entered the market and through competitive pricing has gained considerable market share from Clarinet including one of its largest customers. Clarinet is looking to develop new products to differentiate itself from the rest of its competitors. It has approached its shareholders to finance this development; however, they declined to invest further in Clarinet. Clarinet's loan is long term and it has met all repayments on time. The overdraft has increased significantly over the year and the directors have informed you that the overdraft facility is due for renewal next month and they believe it will be renewed.

The directors have produced a cash flow forecast which shows a significantly strengthening position over the coming 12 months. They are confident with the new products being developed, and in light of their trading history of significant growth, believe it is unnecessary to make any disclosures in the financial statements regarding going concern.

At the year end, Clarinet received notification from one of its customers that the hardware installed by Clarinet for the customers' online ordering system has not been operating correctly. As a result, the customer has lost significant revenue and has informed Clarinet that they intend to take legal action against them for loss of earnings. Clarinet has investigated the problem post year end and discovered that other work-in-progress is similarly affected and inventory should be written down by $375,000. The finance director believes that as this misstatement was identified after the year end, it can be amended in the 2015 financial statements. Draft financial statements for the year ended 30 April 20X4 showed profit after tax of $2.5m.

184 Which of the following correctly summarises whether the uncorrected misstatement of inventory is material and its impact on the 20X4 financial statements?

	Material	Adjust in 20X4 financial statements
A	No	No
B	No	Yes
√C	Yes	Yes
D	Yes	No

185 Which of the following factors are indicators that may cast doubt on Clarinet's ability to continue as a going concern?

(1) The entry of the new competitor reducing Clarinet's market share ✓
(2) The significant increase in the overdraft ✓
(3) The company has a long term loan
(4) The reluctance of the shareholders to provide further investment in Clarinet

A	1, 2 and 3
√B	1, 2 and 4
C	1, 3 and 4
D	2, 3 and 4

186 As part of your assessment of going concern you have reviewed the cash flow forecast. This is based on the assumption of significant increases in revenue.

Which of the following procedures would provide the most reliable evidence regarding the validity of this assumption?

A	Email correspondence between the sales director and potential new customers
B	A review of board minutes showing details of new customers won
√C	A review of post year-end sales and the order book
D	Discussions with management regarding their plans for obtaining new business

187 You have concluded that circumstances exist which cast significant doubt on Clarinet's ability to continue as a going concern.

Which of the following must you include in your communication with those charged with governance in accordance with ISA 570 *Going concern*?

(1) Whether the circumstances you have identified constitute a material uncertainty

(2) Whether the use of the going concern basis of accounting is appropriate in the preparation and presentation of the financial statements

(3) The adequacy of the related disclosures

(4) The period of time your assessment has covered if less than 12 months from the date of the financial statements

✓ A   1, 2 and 3
B   1, 2 and 4
C   1, 3 and 4
D   2, 3 and 4

188 The auditors have been informed that Clarinet's bankers will not make a decision on the overdraft facility until after the auditor's report is completed. The directors have now agreed to include some going concern disclosures and you believe these disclosures are adequate.

Which of the following correctly summarises the impact on the auditor's report of Clarinet if the auditor believes the company is a going concern but that this is subject to a material uncertainty?

	Opinion	Disclosure
A	Modified	Key Audit Matters
✓ B	Unmodified	Material Uncertainty Related to Going Concern
C	Unmodified	Key Audit Matters
D	Modified	Material Uncertainty Related to Going Concern

(Total = 10 marks)

Czech & Dawson   20 mins

The following scenario relates to questions 189–193.

You are the audit manager of Savage & Co. It is a busy time of year for you as you have several on-going audit clients at the moment and you are in the process of dealing with a number of outstanding issues and queries from members of your audit teams.

Czech Co (Czech)

Czech is a pharmaceutical company. The fieldwork has been completed and you are currently reviewing the audit file. The audit senior is not sure how to deal with the following issue.

Czech has incurred $2.1m and development expenditure of $3.2m during the year, all of which has been capitalised as an intangible asset. Profit before tax is $26.3m.

Dawson Co (Dawson)

The fieldwork on this audit is also complete with the exception of the following issue which the audit senior has been unable to deal with.

Dawson's computerised wages program is backed up daily, however for a period of two months the wages records and back-ups have been corrupted, and therefore cannot be accessed. Wages and salaries for these two months are $1.1m. Profit before tax is $10m.

189   You have just received a phone call from one particular audit senior who is unsure about the steps to take in relation to uncorrected misstatements.

Which of the following statements correctly describe the auditor's responsibility in respect of misstatements?

A   ISA 450 *Evaluation of misstatements identified during the audit* states that the auditor only has a responsibility to accumulate material misstatements identified during the audit

B   Where misstatements are not material the auditor should request that management to correct the misstatements in the following accounting period

C   If management refuses to correct some or all of the misstatements, the auditor should consider the implications of this for their audit opinion

D   A written representation should be requested from management to confirm whether they believe that the effects of the unadjusted misstatements are immaterial, both individually and in aggregate, to the financial statements as a whole

190   Which of the following audit procedures should be performed in order to form a conclusion on whether an amendment is required to Czech's financial statements in respect of the research and development expenditure?

(1)   Discuss the requirements of IAS 38 *Intangible assets* with the directors in order to determine whether they understand the required accounting treatment of research and development expenditure

(2)   Obtain a breakdown of the $5.3m capitalised as an intangible asset and agree to supporting documentation to determine the nature of the projects to which the expenditure relates

(3)   Review minutes of Board meetings to determine whether the expenditure was authorised

(4)   Visit the laboratory where the current research is being undertaken and to confirm occurrence of the research expenditure

A   1 and 2
B   1 and 4
C   2 and 3
D   3 and 4

191   Which of the following options correctly summarises the impact on the auditor's report for Czech if the issue remains unresolved?

A   Unmodified opinion with key audit matters paragraph
B   Qualified opinion with key audit matters paragraph explaining the issue
C   Qualified opinion
D   Adverse opinion

192   Which of the following correctly summarises the effect of the issue relating to the wages balance in the financial statements of Dawson?

	Material	Financial statement impact
A	No	Liabilities to tax authorities may be understated
B	No	Profit may be overstated
C	Yes	Wages may be materially misstated
D	Yes	Proper accounting records have not been kept

193   Based on the above information which of the following options correctly summarises the impact of the wages and salaries issue on the auditor's report for Dawson?

	Audit opinion	Disclosure in the auditor's report
A	Qualified	Basis for qualified opinion
B	Disclaimer	Basis for disclaimer of opinion
C	Qualified	Key audit matters section
D	Qualified	Emphasis of matter

(Total = 10 marks)

Medimade (CBE)

The following scenario relates to questions 194–198.

Medimade Co is an established pharmaceutical company that has for many years generated 90% of its revenue through the sale of two specific cold and flu remedies. Medimade has lately seen a real growth in the level of competition that it faces in its market and demand for its products has significantly declined.

You are the audit manager responsible for the audit of Medimade's financial statements for the year ended 31 March 20X7.

In addition to recruiting staff, Medimade also needed to invest $2m in plant and machinery. The company wanted to borrow this sum but was unable to agree suitable terms with the bank; therefore it used its overdraft facility, which carried a higher interest rate. Consequently, some of Medimade's suppliers have been paid much later than usual and hence some of them have withdrawn credit terms meaning the company must pay cash on delivery.

194 Which **TWO** of the following statements are correct with regards to the going concern basis of accounting?

- [✓] The going concern basis of accounting is used when the entity will be able to continue in business for the foreseeable future
- [ ] The foreseeable future is defined for accounting purposes as 36 months from the company's reporting date.
- [✓] The going concern basis of accounting assumes that the entity will be able to realise its assets and discharge its liabilities in the normal course of business
- [ ] Financial statements that are prepared on a going concern basis assert that the company intends to liquidate its operations.

195 Which **TWO** of the following statements describe the most direct impact the withdrawal of supplier credit has on Medimade's use of the going concern basis of accounting?

- [✓] Medimade now has to pay cash on delivery and this adds further cash flow strain imposed by the overdraft
- [✓] Some suppliers may end their relationship with Medimade, preventing the company from producing its products, thus further reducing sales
- [ ] Medimade will have to seek alternative suppliers, who may not meet Medimade's quality control standards
- [ ] The bank may impose strict covenants on the overdraft, restricting the way Medimade can conduct its future operations

196 It is May 20X7. The directors have informed you that the bank overdraft facility is due for renewal next month, after the auditor's report is signed. They are confident that it will be renewed.

Which of the following audit procedures would be most effective in assessing whether or not Medimade is a going concern?

- [ ] Agree current overdraft level to bank letter
- [ ] Obtain confirmation from the bank that the overdraft facility will be renewed
- [ ] Obtain written representation from management that they consider the going concern assumption to be appropriate
- [✓] Review board minutes for meetings held after the year end for evidence which indicate further financial difficulties or evidence of alternative sources of finance

197 The directors have now agreed to include going concern disclosures, while continuing to use the going concern basis of accounting.

You agree with Medimade's management that the going concern basis of accounting is appropriate under the circumstances. You have reviewed the draft disclosures and believe they are correct and adequate.

Indicate which form of audit opinion would be appropriate and how the going concern issue would be disclosed in the auditor's report.

Audit opinion

☐ Disclaimer

☑ Unmodified opinion

☐ Qualified opinion

☐ Adverse opinion

Disclosure in the auditor's report

☑ Describe the nature of the going concern uncertainty in the Material Uncertainty Related to Going Concern section

☐ Describe the nature of the going concern uncertainty in the Key Audit Matters section

☐ Describe the nature of the going concern uncertainty in the Basis for Adverse Opinion section

☐ Describe the nature of the going concern uncertainty in the Basis for Qualified Opinion section

198 The audit is completed. The auditor's report and the financial statements have been signed but not yet issued.

The finance director of Medimade has just informed the audit team that he has been informed by the bank that the overdraft facility will not be renewed. Medimade currently does not have any other source of finance.

What actions, if any, should you now take in order to meet the auditor's responsibilities under ISA 560 *Subsequent events*?

☐ No actions required as the auditor's report and financial statements have already been signed

☑ Discuss with management about their plans for the company and determine whether the 20X7 financial statements should now be prepared on a break-up basis. If yes, request management to adjust the financial statements, audit the adjustments and provide a new auditor's report

☐ Discuss with management about their plans for the company and determine whether disclosures should be revised in the 20X7 financial statements. If yes, request management to revise the disclosures and redraft the auditor's report to refer to the revised disclosures

☐ Request that management adjust for this event in the 20X8 financial statements, as it occurred in the year ending 31 March 20X8

(Total = 10 marks)

Answers

BJM Co

1   A   The external audit is carried out by external auditors, who are independent of the company so that they can provide an independent opinion on whether the company's financial statements are prepared, in all material respects, in accordance with an applicable financial reporting framework. The principal aim of the audit is not in relation to the control system in place or to identify other areas of deficiency, although deficiencies and recommendations may be suggested by the external auditors as a by-product of the external audit in a report to management at the conclusion of the audit.

2   B   ISA 250 distinguishes between regulations which have a direct effect on the financial statements (in the sense of directly affecting the determination of balances), and those which do not have a direct effect but can still have a material effect (such as an operating licence).

           The hygiene regulations do not have a direct effect but they may have a material effect. The external auditor must therefore perform audit procedures to help identify any non-compliance which might have a material effect on the financial statements, ie any breaches of the hygiene regulations that could result in material fines or restaurant closures.

3   C   This review engagement is an example of an assurance engagement. There are five elements to an assurance engagement: criteria, report, evidence, subject matter and three-party relationship (CREST) (IFAC, 2016).

4   D   A review engagement, such as a review of compliance with hygiene regulations, is an assurance engagement where the practitioner carries out limited procedures on BJM's internal controls relating to hygiene compliance.

           As the procedures are limited, the practitioner will gain only enough evidence to provide a negative expression of opinion. This means the practitioner gives assurance that nothing has come to his or her attention which indicates that BJM's internal controls relating to hygiene compliance are not, in all material respects, compliant with national regulation.

5   C   The fees from the review engagement are likely to be very lucrative, so there is a risk that YHT & Co will not seek adjustments during the external audit process for fear of upsetting the Board of BJM and losing the review engagement work.

           The provision of non-audit services to unlisted audit clients is not specifically prohibited. While YHT & Co should be alert to self-review threats, in this case it seems unlikely: the scenario states that the review engagement does not include the provision of accounting advice or the preparation of figures in the financial statements. A firm is not required to turn down work when a 15% limit is exceeded. Where fee income from a listed audit client is expected to exceed 15% of the audit firm's total fee revenue, this fact should be disclosed to those charged with governance and a separate review may be required (ACCA Code of Ethics and Conduct: para. 290.217). However, the 15% fee cap is not a major concern to YHT in this instance because BJM is unlisted.

Conoy

6   The correct answers are:

    The chief internal auditor should not be part of the audit committee. Establishing an audit committee will mean that there is a specialist group of individuals which is responsible for monitoring high quality internal controls

    The audit committee should be formed of independent non-executive directors, and so the remaining shareholders should not be appointed to the audit committee.

    Although the existence of an audit committee may result in a more efficient external audit there is no direct link between the existence of the audit committee and the audit fee.

7   The correct answer is:

Appointing the external auditor

The audit committee will make recommendations regarding whether the external auditor is re-appointed or whether an alternative audit firm should be used. However, the external auditor is actually appointed by the shareholders at a general meeting of the company.

8   The correct answers are:

The position of the internal audit department will be strengthened within the organisation

The effectiveness of the internal audit department will be improved as the audit committee will monitor and review its performance on a regular basis

Conoy's internal audit department is currently poorly supported and reports directly to the Board, which does not understand its reports. Establishing an audit committee will strengthen the position of the internal audit department by providing a greater degree of independence from management. The audit committee will also monitor and review the effectiveness of internal audit.. The audit committee should report to the board as it undertakes tasks on behalf of the board, as opposed to the board reporting to the audit committee. Although the audit committee provides an independent channel of communication between the external auditor and the Board, it is not involved in planning the external audit in any way.

9   The correct answer is:

The audit committee will have at least one member who has relevant financial experience, so that they can monitor the integrity of the financial statements

Conoy's finance director has left and had not yet been replaced. It appears that no-one else has appropriate financial reporting knowledge required by Conoy. The audit committee should contain at least one member who has financial experience so that they can monitor the integrity of the financial statements. This may give the bank the confidence they need before they lend Conoy the money.

Guaranteeing the loan or standing in as interim finance director are not acceptable options, as that will impair the independence of the audit committee.

Substantiating evidence for information used in financial reporting is a function of internal audit, not the audit committee.

10   The correct answer is:

The audit committee will support RWG & Co's viewpoint in the event of any disputes with the management of Conoy

The audit committee will be an impartial platform for the external auditors to raise issues they have not been able to resolve with Conoy's management. However, RWG & Co cannot assume that the audit committee will always support its viewpoint.

Stark

11   B   Including Mr Day's daughter, Zoe, is unusual but should not raise any significant risks to the audit.

The gift of the balloon flight represents a self-interest threat.

The tax fee represents a self-interest threat as Ali & Co will want to save as much tax as possible in order to charge as high a tax fee as possible. There is also an intimidation threat created by the request as the finance director may make Ali & Co feel that it has to accept the method of calculating tax fees in order to keep Stark as a tax client.

The fact that Stark expects Ali & Co to represent it in a dispute with the tax authorities creates an advocacy threat to audit independence.

12   C   Gifts and hospitality should only be accepted where the value is trivial and inconsequential. In this case it is likely that the value of the gift is too high, so the balloon flight should be declined.

13	D	Stark is a public interest entity, so the audit engagement partner should only remain on the audit team for a maximum of seven years before being rotated. It would also be beneficial for an independent review partner to be appointed but Mr Day should not take on this role as, following rotation, he should have no involvement with the audit client for a 'cooling off' period of two years (ACCA Code of Ethics and Conduct; para. 290.149).
14	C	This is the process by which the IAASB develops new standards.
15	C	There is no blanket prohibition on disclosure, nor is there any general right of the police or taxation authorities to demand information. Auditors have an implied contractual duty of confidentiality. There is no statutory duty of confidentiality.

Tangerine Tech Co

16	B	The board as a whole should take on the responsibility for liaising with shareholders, not just the chairman. (The board should state in the annual report the steps they have taken to ensure that the members of the board, and in particular the non-executive directors, develop an understanding of the views of the major shareholders about the company). (FRC UK Corporate Governance Code: Section E)
		As the chairman and one of the NEDs are former executive directors they were previously employed by the company and as a result this raises questions about their independence. Independent non-executive directors should be appointed to the board of Tangerine.
		Tangerine is not required to have an internal audit function (however where there is no internal audit function, the audit committee is required annually to consider the need for one).
17	A	The directors should be subject to re-election by the shareholders at regular intervals, not exceeding three years. They are re-elected by the shareholders, not the chairman. They do not have to be re-appointed annually (unless a FTSE 350 company in the UK) (FRC UK Corporate Governance Code: s. B.7.1).
		There should be an appropriate balance of executives and NEDs to ensure that the board makes the correct objective decisions. At least half of the board should be comprised of NEDs. (FRC UK Corporate Governance Code: s. B.1.2)
18	B	The audit committee is supposed to be made up of independent NEDs. The chairman should cease to undertake the role of chair of the audit committee. (For smaller companies the chairman can sit on the audit committee provided that he is an independent non-executive. This is not the case for Tangerine).
		All four members of the audit committee were previously involved in sales and production related roles. At least one member of the audit committee should have recent and relevant financial experience. (FRC UK Corporate Governance Code: s. C.3.1)
19	D	The directors are responsible for implementing and monitoring the company's system of internal control. An annual assessment of internal control should be conducted to confirm that the board has considered all significant aspects of internal control. The directors should report on its review as part of the annual report. (FRC UK Corporate Governance Code: s. C.2.3)
20	B	The board is responsible for a company's internal control. The establishment of an internal audit function is one of the practical ways in which the board can meet its responsibility to monitor and review internal controls. However, as with all key decisions, costs versus benefits will be assessed too.
		The directors are responsible for the prevention and detection of fraud. Whilst the internal audit function may assist the directors in this, the directors retain the ultimate responsibility.

LV Fones

21 The correct answer is:

Self-interest: 1, 3 and 4

Self-review: 2 only

The audit team have previously been offered a 10% discount on luxury phones from LV Fones (LV) which will potentially have a high value. As only goods with a trivial and inconsequential value can be received, if the same discount is again offered, it will constitute a self-interest threat.

The fee income from LV is 16% of Jones & Co's total fees. If, after accounting for non-recurring fees such as the secondment, it remains at this percentage of total fees on a recurring basis there is likely to be a self-interest threat because of undue dependence on this client.

The overdue fees (20% of the total fee) may be perceived as a loan which is prohibited, but may also create a self-interest threat. This is because Jones & Co may be less robust than they should be when it disagrees with management out of fear they may not recover the fees.

The audit senior probably prepared a significant proportion of the records to be audited; this creates a self-review threat as he will review his own work during the audit.

22 The correct answer is:

Threats: Familiarity and self-interest

Safeguards: Rotation of audit partner

The partner and finance director of LV have been on holiday together and appear to have a longstanding close relationship. This results in a familiarity and self-interest threat. Both are senior in their respective organisation and any onlooker would perceive independence to be threatened. The audit firm does not need to resign but the partner should no longer be involved in the audit.

23 The correct answer is: Unless the value of the discount is trivial and inconsequential to the audit team members, the offer should be declined.

ACCA Code of Ethics and Conduct states that unless the value of a gift is trivial and inconsequential it should be declined. 10% of the value of a smart-phone is unlikely to be trivial and inconsequential. (ACCA Code of Ethics and Conduct: s. 290.225)

24 The correct answer is: 2 and 3

For the audit of a public interest entity (which includes listed companies), where total fees from the client exceed more than 15% of the firm's total fees for two consecutive years, the auditor must disclose this to those charged with governance and arrange for a review to be conducted (either pre-issuance or post-issuance). Provided these mandatory safeguards are applied the firm is not required to resign from the audit. (ACCA Code of Ethics and Conduct: s. 290.217)

25 The correct answer is:

	Service can be provided	Service cannot be provided
Design and implementation of IT systems over financial reporting		X
Assistance with preparation of tax return	X	
Accounting services		X
Recruiting service for the position of credit controller	X	

In general terms audit firms can provide other services provided that the firm does not assume a management responsibility. The provision of certain services are deemed to create such a threat to independence that safeguards will not be adequate to reduce this to an acceptable level. Additional restrictions will apply to LV as it is a public interest entity. The provision of IT services re accounting systems and accounting services cannot be made to LV, as these services have a direct impact on the financial statements that would be audited. (ACCA Code of Ethics and Conduct: s. 290.201) Assistance with preparation of a tax return would be allowed as it is generally based on historical information. (ACCA Code of Ethics and Conduct: s. 290.179) Provision of the recruitment service would be possible in this instance as the role is for a credit controller. The recruitment of senior management would be prohibited. (ACCA Code of Ethics and Conduct: s. 290.210)

Orange

26 The correct answer is: 1 only

This represents an advocacy threat as this may be interpreted as the audit firm promoting investment in Orange Financial Co.

Current & Co would like to conduct other assignments for Orange Financials Co.

This gives rise to a potential self-interest threat as the total fees generated from this client may form a substantial proportion of the fees of the firm which may have an impact on the firm's objectivity.

Current & Co have been asked to produce the financial statements of Orange Financials Co.

This represents a possible self-review threat as Currant & Co would be both preparing and auditing the same information.

The assistant finance director of Orange Financials Co has joined Currant & Co as a partner and it has been suggested that he should be the independent review partner.

This represents a self-review threat as the same individual would be responsible for reviewing the audit of financial statements which he has been involved in preparing.

27 The correct answers are: intimidation and self-interest

This gives rise to an intimidation threat as the audit team may feel under pressure not to perform a thorough audit in order to comply with this request. There is also a self-interest threat as Currant & Co will be keen to win the additional work.

28 The correct answers are: (1) Not accepted (2) Not accepted

As the value of the hospitality is unlikely to be inconsequential no safeguards would be adequate to reduce the threat to an acceptable level. The offer of the weekend away should be declined politely.

If the loan had been made at normal commercial rates then the senior would be able to accept without any consequences for independence.

In this case as the terms are preferential the loan must be declined.

29 The correct answer is: Total fees from Orange Financials make up more than 15% of Currant Co's total fees for the second consecutive year

The mandatory safeguards apply to public interest entity audits therefore would be applied to the audit Orange Financials when it is listed.

30 The correct answer is:

	True	False
The audit committee should be made up of independent non-executive directors	X	
The audit committee normally appoints the external auditors at the AGM		X
The audit committee monitors and reviews the internal audit function	X	
The audit committee sets out the scope of the external auditor's work		X

The audit committee makes recommendations about the appointment of external auditors but the shareholders are responsible for appointing them at the AGM.

The scope of the external auditor's work is determined by the audit engagement partner on the basis of the requirements of auditing standards. The scope of the audit may be discussed with the audit committee but the audit committee do not set out the scope of the work as the audit must be an independent exercise.

SGCC

31 The correct answer is:

SGCC should appoint a new Chief Executive Officer or board chairman

Corporate governance codes indicate that there should be a clear division of responsibilities between running the board of directors and running the company's business so that no individual has unfettered powers of decision.

32 The correct answer is:

SGCC should appoint three new non-executive directors to the board

Corporate governance codes indicate that the Board should have a balance of executive and non-executive directors. SGCC currently has five executive and two non-executive directors and should therefore appoint a further three non-executive directors in order to balance the Board.

33 The correct answers are:

Once SGCC has an audit committee and an internal audit department, the head of the internal audit department should report to the audit committee

SGCC should not rely on the external audit to inform them of deficiencies in internal controls

SGCC should establish an Audit Committee with at least three non-executive directors.

Listed companies should review the need for an internal audit department at least annually. They are not automatically required to have an internal audit department.

34 The correct answer is:

Taking responsibility for the implementation of a new sales ledger system

The internal audit function is a review and monitoring function. It should not take operational responsibility for any part of the accounting or information systems.

35 The correct answer is:

Consideration	Employed	Outsourced
(1)		X
(2)		X
(3)		X
(4)	X	

Where the internal audit department is outsourced to an external firm, SGCC is likely to benefit from specialist industry skills and will benefit from the greater flexibility in staffing numbers as the team can be modified depending on the workload at a particular point in time. SGCC will also be shielded from the direct costs of training staff. However, if the staff are employed by SGCC, this increases the skills held within the business and therefore increases the value of the work-force which is an asset of the company.

Bridgford

36   The correct answer is:

Audit strategy	Detailed audit plan
(1) and (4)	(2) and (3)

The audit strategy includes areas such as identifying the characteristics of the engagement; the reporting objectives, timing and nature of communications, knowledge gained from previous audits and during the preliminary risk assessments and the nature, timing and extent of resources in terms of using appropriate personnel.

The availability of the client's data and staff (including internal audit) and the potential for using CAATs are included in the characteristics of the engagement.

The auditor will take the overall audit strategy and convert it into a more detailed audit plan. This will include the allocation of work to audit team members and the audit procedures to be undertaken for each area of the financial statements.

37   The correct answer is:

Performance materiality refers to the amounts set by the auditor at higher than the materiality level for particular classes of transactions, account balances or disclosures where the materiality level might otherwise mean that such items are not tested.

The auditor sets performance materiality at amount which is lower than the materiality level for the financial statements as a whole. This is so that the impact of misstatements for particular classes of transactions, account balances or disclosures will be considered even if they are not material to the financial statements as a whole. (ISA 320: paras. 10–11)

38   The correct answer is:

Perform a trend analysis on current year and prior year monthly revenue, to identify whether revenue is overstated as a result of fraud or error

An overstatement of revenue would result in a reduction, not an increase in receivables' days.

39   The correct answer is:

Valuation of receivables

The audit risk relates to the concern about receivables taking 127 days to settle their invoices rather than the permitted 90 days (three month credit terms), and that some customers are refusing to pay for products due to the reliability issues encountered. This means that receivables may be overstated and therefore the valuation of receivables is a concern.

Despite the worsening working capital position indicated by the increase in receivables days, on its own it is unlikely to give rise to doubts over Bridgford's going concern status.

40   The correct answer is:

Review sales prices of inventory sold after the year end to identify inventory where cost exceeds net realisable value.

The risk which has been identified relates to inventory quantities. Whilst the comparison of cost and net realisable value is a valid audit test it provides evidence regarding the valuation of inventory rather than quantity. The other three procedures would provide evidence regarding the operation of the system used to record the number of units of inventory held.

EuKaRe

41   The correct answer is:

Inherent risk

Inherent risk is the risk that an item will be misstated due to the characteristics of that item. High levels of income in the form of cash increase the risk that income may be misstated either in error or deliberately. In addition there may be no other independent source to show what the income should be. For example in this instance there would not be any formal record to support the majority of the takings (eg invoice or receipt) collected in the buckets.

Control risk is the risk that controls will not prevent or detect misstatements.

Detection risk is the risk that audit procedures will not detect material misstatements.

Business risk is the risk that the business will not achieve its objectives and is not an element of audit risk.

42   The correct answer is:

The risk assessment will enable the audit senior to produce an accurate budget for the audit assignment

Whilst an audit firm is a commercial and profit making organisation, ISA 315 is not concerned with the auditor's budget but rather with ensuring that the auditor has a sufficient understanding of the business so that they can select appropriate audit procedures, in order to minimise the risk of undetected material misstatements.

43   The correct answer is:

Obtain a breakdown of the income recorded from the cash that was collected in buckets, and vouch a sample of entries back to the volunteer in order to determine which volunteer collected the relevant donations

This will provide evidence of the occurrence of income, but the key risk here is completeness of income.

44   The correct answer is:

The auditor is responsible for obtaining reasonable assurance that the financial statements are free from material misstatement whether caused by fraud or error. (ISA 240: para. 5)

The directors, or rather here the trustees, are ultimately responsible for the prevention and detection of fraud and error within EuKaRe. The auditor needs to obtain reasonable assurance that the financial statements are not materially misstated due to fraud or error.

45   The correct answers are:

EuKaRe's finance department relies on volunteers who may not have accounts experience.
Understaffing in the finance department at certain times is due to the ad hoc nature of volunteer working hours.

The fact that EuKaRe has a detailed constitution which explains how the charity's income can be spent is a positive influence on the control environment, as it indicates that there is a benchmark in place against which the suitability of EuKaRe's expenditure can be measured.

The fact that the income of EuKaRe is primarily cash increases inherent risk but does not automatically mean that the control environment is weak.

South

46	B	ISA 315 requires auditors to use analytical procedures and inquiry when obtaining an understanding of South and its environment. They should also use observation and inspection. (ISA 315: para. 6)
47	C	The main aim of planning is not to ensure the audit is completed within budget restraints but that it is carried out in an effective manner as described by the other statements. (ISA 300: para. 2)
48	C	The audit risk relates to the concern that South may have capitalised costs which are revenue in nature. As such the appropriate response is to review the invoices which have been capitalized not just for their amount but also to determine the nature of the expense to which the invoice relates.
49	D	The audit risk relates to the concern that the system may not be reliable, that not all invoices have been recorded and that staff may not be familiar with the system. All of the responses are therefore valid with the exception of response (2). This involves vouching the revenue per the system back to till receipts. Given that one concern is that revenue is understated, testing should be from the till receipts to the system to ensure that all sales have been recorded.
50	B	The concern over deficiencies in South's internal controls is a valid concern, but the review of legal correspondence is unlikely to be an appropriate response to this as the auditor would need to review internal controls. The impact on the reputation of South is also a valid concern as it could have implications for the viability of the company but again it is unlikely that information specifically relating to this would be available in the legal correspondence reviewed.

Mason

51	C	There is a risk that the revenue for the annual fees is not properly recognised in the period to which it relates, leading to revenue (and deferred income) being materially misstated in the financial statements. Revenue should be recognised according to the accounting period in which the related performance obligations of the contract are met.
52	C	The auditor should obtain a breakdown of the capitalised costs and vouch them back to invoices to determine whether they relate to a capital or revenue expense. They can then determine whether they have been recognised appropriately in accordance with IAS 16 *Property, plant and equipment*.
53	B	The key risk here is going concern. It is possible that the company will lose one of only four customers. In addition a bank loan is being renegotiated and it is expected that costs will increase. This may threaten Mason's ability to continue as a going concern.
54	C	All of the responses are valid with the exception of contacting the customer directly
55	D	Specialist equipment has been removed from the aircraft and is now included in inventory. Inventory should be valued at the lower of cost and net realisable value, not at amortised cost. The fact that the equipment has been replaced suggests that its net realisable value is lower than its cost. This may mean that inventory is overstated in the financial statements.

Severn

56	C	Overall level of materiality to be used in the audit.
		The materiality level used is included in the audit plan, not the audit tender document. The proposed fee is a critical part of the tender, as is a description of the firm and the key personnel to be associated with Severn.
		While there will be limits associated with what other services can be offered to Severn (as it is a listed entity), it would still be appropriate for the firm to list the services they offer, tailored to areas where it might be possible to offer services, as this might be a critical factor for Severn.

57   A   1 and 2

These two issues are important when tendering for any audit, but particularly in this case, where Severn would represent a major client, and therefore self-interest issues might apply (for instance, the firm might consider it would become over-reliant on the fee).

In addition, given the significance of Severn to Rivers, it is particularly important to consider whether the firm has the resources (eg number of audit staff available at the appropriate time of year) to provide this audit service.

While the existence of preconditions of audit is an essential part of accepting an audit, in this instance, the firm has already identified that the company applies an applicable financial reporting framework, acknowledges its responsibilities and is prepared to confirm this in writing, so this is of less significance to consider prior to tendering in this circumstance.

While the issue of access to working papers might influence the audit approach in the first year and hence impact on budgeting and fee-setting, it is not a reason not to tender, so again, less important to consider than items 1 and 2.

58   C   A reply from the outgoing auditors stating that they declined to seek reappointment to the audit of Severn Co due to a disagreement over accounting policies.

This would imply a lack of integrity on the part of the director who asserted the firm had not been re-elected due to familiarity issues. Disagreement over accounting policies suggests the opposite of familiarity risk, which was the reason the company gave the firm for the change in auditors. It also raises the threat of possible future intimidation, if there may be disagreements concerning accounting policy. It is even possible that the company has deliberately asked a relatively small firm to tender in order to have more sway over them.

It is not necessary to have an engagement letter set up prior to acceptance, although this should be dealt with soon after acceptance.

Although the ACCA Code of Ethics and Conduct contains a 15% benchmark in relation to fees from one audit client, it recommends safeguards which could be implemented to mitigate the threat, and the firm could actively seek other clients to replace the lost client and hence lower the proportion represented by Severn. (ACCA Code of Ethics and Conduct: s. 290.217)

Similarly, although the apparent lack of resources in March is an issue, it is an issue that the firm may be able to work around, by negotiating different audit timetables with other clients, or by coming to a different arrangement with Severn Co. It is not a reason to automatically decline.

59   D   1 and 2

Items 3 and 4 may be included in an engagement letter, but they are not mandatory elements according to ISA 210 (which items 1 and 2 are). (ISA 210: para. 10)

60   A   Obtain references concerning the directors.

This should have been done before the engagement was accepted. The other matters should all be attended to before audit planning/fieldwork is carried out.

Although the firm will have obtained a limited understanding of the entity to enable an appropriate tender process, this will be carried out more extensively at this stage prior to audit planning.

Goofy Co

61   B   The management of both Goofy and Mickey should be informed and their consent obtained.

Separate audit teams should be used including audit partners and independent review partners.

Confidentiality agreements should be signed by NAB & Co's staff, not by the client.

62   C   The long association of the audit engagement partner with Goofy represents a familiarity threat as she may not maintain professional scepticism and objectivity. Similarly the audit engagement partner's daughter being employed by Goofy is also a familiarity threat, although there would not be a

need for additional safeguards as a warehouse manager is unlikely to influence the financial statements.

A self-interest threat arises from the financial interest in Goofy which the audit engagement partner's daughter will receive if she is awarded a bonus. As an immediate family member of the partner this creates an indirect interest in a client which is not permitted by the ACCA (ACCA Code of Ethics and Conduct: s. 290.104).

A bonus relating to the audit being completed three weeks earlier than last year creates a self-interest threat, as there is a danger NAB & Co will be less thorough in order to achieve the deadline and not risk losing the client as a result of not meeting it.

63   D   NAB & Co should contact the existing auditor before accepting nomination, in order to find out whether there are any reasons behind Mickey's decision to change its auditors about which NAB & Co should be aware. Once this is done, client screening must be performed.

Ensuring that the existing auditor's resignation has been properly conducted and issuing an engagement letter are procedures which should be taken after accepting nomination.

64   D   Although management are responsible for the prevention and detection of fraud this is not one of the matters included in the agreement obtained by the auditors to establish that the preconditions of an audit exist.

65   C   In accordance with ISA 210 *Agreeing the terms of audit engagements* the expected form and content of any reports must be included (ISA 210.10(e)). The other items may be included but there is no requirement to do so.

Carlise

66   The correct answer is:

Audit procedures	Interim audit	Final audit
(1)	X	
(2)		X
(3)		X
(4)	X	

Audit procedures performed during an interim audit are likely to include analytical procedures, tests of controls, updating risk assessments and substantive testing of transactions which have occurred during the first part of the year.

When it comes to the final audit a trial balance or draft set of financial statements will be available, so detailed substantive testing of year end balances will be conducted. This is in addition to completing the tests of controls and substantive procedures started during the interim audit.

67   The correct answer is:

1, 2 and 3

All of the factors should be taken in to account.

68   The correct answer is:

Whether the work performed by the internal audit department relates to specific audit assertions over which UYE & Co have concerns

Where the external auditor plans to rely on the work of the internal audit department, they must ensure that the internal auditors work has been performed to a good standard. However most important is the requirement that the work performed by the internal audit department must be relevant to the evidence the external auditor is trying to gather.

69   The correct answers are:

Direct assistance describes the use of internal auditors to perform audit procedures under the direction, supervision and review of the external auditor. (ISA 620: para. 14)

The external auditor should document their review of the work performed by the internal auditors.

The external auditor is likely to be less inclined to use direct assistance where the assessed risk of material misstatement is high, as this increases audit risk. The auditor must take full responsibility for their audit opinion regardless of whether they rely on the work of others.

70   The correct answer is:

It prevents the auditor from being sued for negligence.

Audit documentation in itself does not prevent the auditor from being sued, but would provide evidence in court to support the work which had been performed.

71 Sleeptight

Text references. Chapters 6 and 13.

Top tips. This 30 mark case study style question contains a mixture of knowledge-based questions and questions requiring application to a long scenario.

Part (a) requires you to recall your knowledge of professional scepticism and judgement. In part (ii), notice that your examples of areas to apply professional judgement should be limited to the planning stage.

Part (b)(i) worth 16 marks contains a common requirement where you are asked to explain audit risks and then suggest appropriate responses. Audit risks will be related to potential material misstatements of the financial statements and this should be in the forefront of your mind throughout when you are answering this part of the question. When you are explaining your risk you should therefore state how the financial statements are affected.

Responses are the auditor's responses, not management responses. These will therefore be procedures or actions the auditor will carry out to mitigate the risks.

In part (b)(ii) you should have realised that the auditor must attend the inventory count and is required to perform certain procedures specified by ISA 501.

In part (d), although you would assess the reliability of the expert, don't forget there are also other important procedures such as reviewing the disclosures and the revaluation adjustments.

Easy marks. In part (a), easy marks are available for explaining professional scepticism and defining professional judgement.

Marking scheme

			Marks
(a)	(i)	Professional scepticism 1 mark per valid point up to a maximum of	
	(ii)	Professional judgement 1 mark per valid point up to a maximum of	3
			3
(b)	(i)	Risks and responses 1 mark per well explained risk (maximum of 8) and 1 mark for each valid response (maximum of 8) up to a total maximum of	
	(ii)	Inventory count attendance 1 mark per valid point up to a maximum of	16
			4
(c)		Audit procedures for value of property and disclosure Up to 1 mark per procedure to a maximum of	4
		Maximum marks	30

(a) (i) **Professional scepticism**

Professional scepticism is an attitude that includes having a questioning mind, being alert to conditions which may indicate possible misstatement due to error or fraud, and subjecting audit evidence to a critical assessment rather than just taking it at face value. (ISA 200: para. 13(l))

It is important that professional scepticism is maintained throughout the audit to reduce the risks of overlooking unusual transactions, of over-generalising when drawing conclusions, and of using inappropriate assumptions in determining the nature, timing and extent of audit procedures and evaluating the results of them.

Professional scepticism is necessary to the critical assessment of audit evidence. This includes questioning contradictory audit evidence and the reliability of documents and responses from management and those charged with governance.

(ii) **Professional judgement**

Professional judgement is the application of relevant training, knowledge and experience in making informed decisions about the appropriate courses of action in the circumstances of the audit engagement. The auditor must exercise professional judgement when planning an audit of financial statements. (ISA 200: para. 13(k))

Professional judgement will be required in many areas when planning. For example the determination of materiality for the financial statements as a whole and performance materiality levels will require professional judgement.

Professional judgement will also be required when deciding on the nature, timing and extent of audit procedures.

(b) (i)

Audit risk	Response(s)
The firm has recently been appointed as auditor. There is a lack of cumulative knowledge and understanding of the business, which may result in a failure to identify events and transactions which impact on the financial statements. Furthermore, opening balances may be misstated.	Adopt procedures to ensure opening balances are properly brought forward and corresponding amounts are correctly classified and disclosed. Review previous auditor's working papers and consider performing additional substantive procedures on opening balances.
The directors only work part time at Sleeptight and there is no finance director. This may promote a weak control environment, resulting in undetected errors or frauds.	The controls will need to be documented and evaluated. If these are weak the level of substantive testing will need to be increased accordingly.
The requirement for customers to pay 40% on ordering and the remainder following delivery could result in revenue recorded before it should be, if the deposit is recorded as a sale and not deferred until delivery. This would result in revenue being overstated. Alternatively, revenue could be understated if the final payment were only recognised when it is received, rather than on delivery of the bed.	Enquire of management the point at which revenue is actually recognised, and review the system of accounting for deposits to ensure they are not included in revenue until goods delivered and signed for. For a sample of transactions within eight weeks of the year end, ensure the revenue recorded is only in respect of beds delivered to customers in the same period and ensure they have been signed for.
The two-year guarantee on the beds gives rise to a provision, the measurement of which involves a high degree judgement, and therefore carries a risk of misstatement. This	Establish the basis of the amount provided for and assumptions made by the financial controller. Re-perform any calculations and establish the level of

Audit risk	Response(s)
risk is increased by the fact the loan covenants are profit-related and there is an incentive to manipulate areas of the financial statements based on judgements.	warranty costs in the year, and compare with the previous provision. Review the level of repair costs incurred post year-end and use these to assess the reasonableness of the provision.
Contractors are required to invoice at the end of each month but often there is delay in receiving these. There is therefore a risk the company will not accrue for costs, resulting in incomplete liabilities and understatement of expenses.	Review invoices and payments to contractors after the year end, and if they relate to work undertaken before the year end, ensure they are included as accruals.
The current year raw materials costs for materials also in inventory last year are based on prices at least a year old. They should be based on the actual cost or reasonable average cost. Given that prices fluctuate the value of year end raw materials may be over or undervalued due to price rises/decreases occurring during the year.	For a sample of materials to include the cost of wood, compare material costs to actual prices on invoices. Investigate and resolve any significant differences and evaluate the potential impact on the inventory value in the financial statements.
The finished goods value is to be estimated by Anna Jones, who appears to be basing her estimate on order value rather that applying the IAS 2 rule that goods should be valued at the lower of cost and NRV (IAS 2: para. 9). This could result in inventory being overstated in the financial statements.	For beds awaiting despatch, establish the lower of cost and NRV and compare with the figures provided by Anna Jones. Investigate any differences evaluate the potential impact on the inventory value in the financial statements.
The new workshop is undergoing refurbishment that could result in inappropriate treatment of capital or non capital items, potentially misstating non-current assets, or repair costs in the statement of profit or loss. Again, this risk is increased by the fact the loan covenants are profit related and there is an incentive to manipulate areas of the financial statements based on judgements.	Obtain a breakdown of the related costs and establish which are included as non-current assets and which are treated as repair costs. Review the nature of items included in non-current assets to ensure only capital items included and review repairs to ensure no capital items are included.
The new premises purchase was funded by a bank loan which may not be classified correctly between current and non-current liabilities, or may not be properly presented or disclosed as required by IFRSs.	Reperform the calculation of the split between current and non-current liabilities and ensure the loan is properly presented and terms are disclosed as required by IFRSs.
There is a risk the company may fail to comply with the loan covenants, resulting in the loan being recalled. This could then possibly lead to going concern issues.	Obtain and review (or re-perform) covenant calculations to identify any breaches. If there are any, the likelihood of the bank demanding repayment will need to be assessed, along with the potential impact on the company. The need to avoid breaching the covenants reinforces the audit team's need to maintain professional scepticism in areas that could be manipulated.

(**Note.** Only eight risks and eight related responses were needed to gain 16 marks.)

(ii)   ISA 501 *Audit evidence – specific considerations for selected items* sets out the responsibilities of auditors in relation to the physical inventory count. It states that where inventory is material, auditors shall obtain sufficient appropriate audit evidence regarding its existence and condition by attending the physical inventory count. (ISA 501: para. 4(a))

At the count attendance, Mills & Co will need to evaluate management's instructions and procedures for recording and controlling the result of the physical inventory count.

They must also observe the performance of the count procedures to assess whether they are properly carried out.

In addition Mills & Co should inspect the inventory to verify that it exists and look for evidence of damaged or obsolete inventory. They will also perform test counts to assess the accuracy of the counts carried out by the company.

Mills & Co are also required by ISA 501 to perform audit procedures over the entity's final inventory records to determine whether they accurately reflect the count results. (ISA 501: para. 4(b))

(c)   **Procedures in relation to property valuation and related disclosures**

Obtain a copy of the valuer's report and consider the reliability of the valuation after taking account of:

- The basis of valuation
- Independence/objectivity
- Qualifications
- Experience
- Reputation of the valuer

Compare the valuation with the value of other similar properties in the locality and investigate any significant difference.

Reperform the calculation of the revaluation adjustments and ensure the correct accounting treatment has been applied.

Inspect notes to the financial statements to ensure appropriate disclosures have been made in accordance with IFRSs.

72 Raisin

Study text reference. Chapters 4 and 18.

Top Tips. The scenario gives you the figures to calculate materiality in a fairly obvious way (by stating that the 'draft financial statements show revenue of $12.5m, net profit of $400,000, and total assets of $78m'). This is almost always a hint that you're going to have to calculate materiality at some point in your answer, and the opportunity to do so comes up straight away in part (a)'s requirement for 'matters to consider' in relation to audit evidence. These are easy marks, so to make sure you get them, calculate materiality, and then apply it to the scenario by stating whether or not the matter in question is actually material.

Note, also, that you're asked to explain audit evidence that you should expect to find during your file review.

There were plenty of points in the scenario that you should have picked up on for your answer to part (b). Quality control is a new addition to the F8 syllabus, so it's likely to appear in the exams. Make sure you are familiar with this topic. You should have been looking to pass this part of question well – but without exceeding the time allocation for it!

Easy marks. The calculation of materiality in part (a) offers easy marks.

Marks

(a) **Trade receivable**

Generally 1 mark per matter/evidence point:

Matters

- Correct calculation and assessment of materiality (max 1½ marks)
- Receivable impaired
- Consider any inventory in relation to Cherry Co
- Qualification re material misstatement

Evidence

- Initial correspondence with administrators of Cherry Co
- Confirmation with the administrators
- Agreement to receivables ledger
- Recalculations of impairment losses
- Review of inventory schedules

Maximum   6

(b) **Quality control matters**

Up to 2 marks for each point evaluated from ideas list

- No audit planning meeting – lack of direction
- Absence of manager and senior – lack of supervision
- Junior assigned difficult audit work (goodwill and WIP)
- Junior helped out with inventory count – lack of understanding/supervision
- Junior asked to challenge FD – inappropriate delegation
- Audit running out of time – poor planning?
- Changed sample size – inappropriate response to time pressure
- Changed item selected in sample – inappropriate response to time pressure

Maximum   14

Total   **20**

(a) **Trade receivable**

Materiality for whole receivable

Materiality on revenue: $\dfrac{\$30,000}{\$12.5m} = 2.4\%$

Materiality on net profit: $\dfrac{\$300,000}{\$400,000} = 75\%$

Materiality on total assets: $\dfrac{\$300,000}{\$78m} = {<}1\%$

The receivable is not material to the statement of financial position. It would, however, be material to the statement of profit or loss if an impairment loss were recognised in relation to it.

Accounting treatment

IFRS 9 *Financial instruments* requires receivables to be recognised at fair value (IFRS 9: para. 5.1.1). The fair value of the Cherry Co receivable is the 25% that the administrators suggest it may be able to pay, ie $75,000. $225,000 should therefore be recognised as an impairment loss in the statement of profit or loss.

Calculating materiality for the impairment loss:

Materiality on revenue: $\dfrac{\$225{,}000}{\$12.5m} = 1.8\%$

Materiality on net profit: $\dfrac{\$225{,}000}{\$400{,}000} = 56\%$

This is clearly material to profit for the year.

Inventory

As Cherry Co is a customer, it is possible that Sultana Co is holding inventory or work in progress that was ordered by Cherry Co. Raisin & Co needs to ascertain whether this is the case, and if so whether the inventory can in fact be sold. If it cannot be, then it may be impaired and should be written down, recognising the loss in profit for the year.

Audit opinion

If Sultana Co does not amend its financial statements, the audit opinion will be modified due to a material misstatement. This would probably be an 'except for' qualification as the misstatement is material but not pervasive.

Audit evidence

- External documentation confirming the insolvency of Cherry Co and the possible repayment of only 25% of the receivable

- Confirmation from the administrator of the 25% to be paid, including an indication of when this is likely to happen

- Agreement of the amount owed from the receivables listing to the ledger

- Review of inventory documentation, and evidence of enquiries made of management, regarding the value and the potential recoverability of any inventory relating to contracts with Cherry Co

- Calculations regarding the amount to be recognised as an impairment loss

(b) **Selection of engagement staff**

The fact that the junior had only worked on two audits before this is not a problem. However, it is important that they be given work appropriate to their level of skill and experience. This does not appear to have happened here, as detailed below.

No audit planning meeting

The audit planning meeting, led by the partner, is a crucial part of the audit. It is the best way of giving the team an understanding of the client, and should discuss both the overall strategy and the detailed audit plan, perhaps going into difficulties that have been experienced in previous years and which could come up again. The discussion should focus on what individual members of the team need to do. This is particularly important for less experienced and junior members of the team.

Audit manager away

The manager should not have given the senior responsibility for the audit while they were away on holiday for three weeks. It is important that an audit is properly supervised, and it may have been more appropriate for another manager to take responsibility for the audit.

Senior busy

Not only is there a question mark over whether they have the experience to manage the audit, but the senior was also busy with other assignments and thus unable to devote sufficient time to this one. It is very important that someone is available to supervise junior members of the audit team. This is not happening here.

It is also possible that the lack of attention paid by both the manager and the senior has led to the misstatements in respect of the trade receivables not being picked up by the audit team.

Junior auditing goodwill and inventory

Goodwill is a complex accounting area to audit, and should not be given to a junior to do. The same can be said of inventory and in particular work-in-progress. A junior is very unlikely to have developed the judgement needed to audit these areas. This seems to be the case here, as shown by the junior's error at the inventory-take (see below).

Inventory count

The junior helped the client's staff to count raw materials at the inventory count, when they should instead have been observing that the client's staff were counting them correctly and in accordance with the count procedures. This would seem to imply that the junior had not been properly briefed on their responsibilities at the inventory count, as this is a basic error.

It is likely that more audit evidence will be needed to be done on inventory as a result of this error.

Junior asked to challenge FD

It is not appropriate for a junior to be asked to challenge a client's finance director regarding an accounting issue that they are unlikely to understand fully. This should have been done by either the audit manager or the partner, as they would be in a position to understand the technical issues involved, and would carry sufficient authority with the client to make the challenge effective.

Running out of time to complete procedures

Pressure of time is an important contributor to audit risk. Audit time budgets should allow staff enough time to complete the audit to the required quality. It is also possible that the lack of supervision of the audit team's work has led to the audit being conducted inefficiently, with inadequate monitoring of progress and discussion of issues as they arise.

Reduction of sample sizes

It is clearly unacceptable to reduce sample sizes as a way of saving time. The sample sizes detailed in the audit plan should have been designed to gather sufficient appropriate audit evidence. Reducing the sample size beneath this point increases detection risk, and the risk of the auditor giving the wrong opinion.

Basis of sample selection

Selecting a sample on the basis of the ease of finding evidence for an item, is not an appropriate basis. Indeed, this might actively increase detection risk as it means by definition that those items for which evidence is not readily available, or might not even exist, are not tested.

Conclusion

The litany of failures above suggests that this engagement has not been adequately supervised, and that the audit work performed is inadequate in some areas. A detailed review should be performed so that any other shortcomings can be addressed.

Doubt is also cast over the sufficiency of the firm's quality control procedures. This matter should be referred to the relevant partner for consideration.

73 Abrahams

Text references. Chapters 6 and 13.

Top tips. The first requirement in part (a) was straightforward and you should have been able to explain each component (inherent risk, control risk and detection risk) in turn. Note that the definition of audit risk itself was not required. The example of a factor which would **increase** audit risk in relation to each component required more thought as often auditors think of how to **reduce** these risks. However if you know what decreases the risk, it is not difficult to work out what increases it. For example, increasing sample sizes can decrease detection risk, so not selecting an appropriate sample size will increase it. There are a number of factors to choose from in each case, but only one example was required for each – so only give one and then move on.

Part (b) tested the important area of identifying and responding to audit risks. It should be clear from your answer how each risk impacts on a financial statement assertion or area, since this is the nature of an audit risk. If there is no clear link the chances are you have identified a business risk that may not be a relevant audit risk. Your response should be clear and include a specific action rather a general response of, for example, 'do more work on this area'.

Part (c) asks for substantive procedures in relation to gaining evidence over two specific aspects of inventory (inventory held by a third party and standard costs used in the inventory valuation). In (ii) there is always a danger that standard costs are not updated enough to take account of movements in actual costs so your tests should focus on this, for example comparing standard costs with actual costs per invoices or wages records.

Easy marks. Easy marks were available in (a) for explaining the components of audit risk.

Examination Team's comments. Part (a) was knowledge based and candidates performed well.

Part (b) for 10 marks required a description of five audit risks and responses for Abrahams. Many candidates performed inadequately on this part of the question. As stated in previous examiner's reports, audit risk is a key element of the Audit & Assurance syllabus and candidates must understand audit risk. The main area where candidates continue to go wrong is that they did not actually understand what audit risk relates to. Hence they provided answers which considered the risks the business would face or 'business risks', which are outside the scope of the syllabus.

Part (c) was answered unsatisfactorily by most candidates, especially (cii) on standard costs. Candidates seemed to see 'inventory valuation' in the requirement and so produced generic tests for verifying that inventory should be at the lower of cost and NRV. This was not what the question required. Candidates did not seem to understand that standard costing was an acceptable option for calculating the cost of inventory and hence they needed to test how close an approximation to actual cost standard cost was.

Marking scheme

		Marks
(a)	Up to 1 mark for each component of audit risk (if just a component is given without an explanation then just give 0.5) and up to 1 mark for each example of factor which increases risk.	
	Inherent risk	
	Control risk	
	Detection risk	6
(b)	Up to 1 mark per well explained risk and up to 1 mark for each well explained response. Overall max of 5 for risks and 5 for responses.	
	Development expenditure treatment	
	Standard costing for valuation of inventory	
	Expert possibly required in verifying work in progress	
	Third party inventory locations	
	New accounting system introduced in the year	
	Lack of support by IT staff on new system may result in errors in accounting system	
	New finance obtained; loans and equity finance treatment	
	Loan covenants and risk of going concern problems	
	Revaluation of land and buildings	
	Reduced reporting timetable	10
(c)	1 mark per well explained procedure, maximum of 2 marks for each of (i) and (ii)	
	(i) Third party locations	
	Letter requesting direct confirmation	
	Attend inventory count	
	Review other auditor reports and documentation	2
	(ii) Standard costing	
	Discuss with management basis of standard costs	
	Review variances	
	Breakdown of standard costs and agree to actual costs	2
		20

(a) Audit risk is made up of the following components:

Inherent risk is the susceptibility of an assertion about a class of transaction, account balance or disclosure to a misstatement that could be material either individually or when aggregated with other misstatements, before consideration of any related controls. (ISA 200: para. n(i))

Factors which may increase inherent risk include:

- Changes in the nature of the industry the company operates in
- A high degree of regulation over certain areas of the business
- Going concern issues and loss of significant customers
- Expanding into new territories
- Events or transactions that involve significant accounting estimates
- Developing new products or services, or moving into new lines of business
- The application of new accounting standards
- Accounting measurements that involve complex processes
- Pending litigation and contingent liabilities

Control risk is the risk that a misstatement, that could occur in an assertion about a class of transaction, account balance or disclosure and that could be material, either individually or when aggregated with other misstatements, will not be prevented, or detected and corrected on a timely basis by the entity's internal control. (ISA 200: para. n(ii))

The following factors may increase control risk:

- Changes in key personnel such as the departure of key management
- A lack of personnel with appropriate accounting skills
- Deficiencies in internal control
- Changes in the IT environment
- Installation of significant new IT systems related to financial reporting

Detection risk is the risk that the procedures performed by the auditor to reduce audit risk to an acceptably low level will not detect a misstatement that exists and that could be material, either individually or when aggregated with other misstatements. (ISA 200: para. 13(e))

Detection risk is affected by sampling and non-sampling risk. Factors which may result in an increase include:

- Poor planning
- Inappropriate assignment of personnel to the engagement team
- Failing to apply professional scepticism
- Inadequate supervision and review of the audit work performed
- Incorrect sample sizes
- Incorrect sampling techniques performed

(**Note.** Only one example of a factor increasing the relevant risk was needed for each component.)

(b) **Audit risks and responses**

Audit risk	Response
Abraham's finance director intends to capitalise the $2.2 million of development expenditure incurred. This material amount should only be capitalised if the related product can generate future profits as set out in IAS 38 *Intangible assets* (IAS 38: para. 57). There is a risk at least some of the expenditure does not meet the criteria. This will mean assets and profits are overstated.	An analysis showing developments costs in relation to each product should be obtained and reviewed. Testing should be carried out to ensure the technical and commercial feasibility of each product and where it can't be proven that future economic benefits will result from the product developed, the related costs should be expensed.

Audit risk	Response
At the year end it is anticipated that there will be significant levels of work in progress, likely to constitute a material balance. The pharmaceuticals production process is likely to be complex and the audit team may not be sufficiently qualified to assess the quantity and value of work in progress. Therefore they be unable to gain sufficient evidence over a material area of the financial statements.	Nate & Co should assess their ability to gain the required level of evidence and if it is not sufficient, they should approach an independent expert to value the work in progress. This should be arranged after obtaining consent from Abrahams' management and in time for the year-end inventory count.
Abrahams use standard costing to value inventory and under IAS 2 *Inventories* the standard cost method may be used for convenience, but only if the results approximate actual cost. However, standard costs have not been updated since the product was first manufactured, leading to a risk that standard costs are out of date. If they are, this could mean inventory is over or under valued in the statement of financial position.	Standard costs used for inventory valuation should be compared to actual cost for an appropriate sample of inventory items. Any significant variations should be discussed with management to gain evidence that the valuation is reasonable and inventory is fairly stated.
Approximately one-third of the warehouses storing finished goods for Abrahams belong to third parties. Sufficient and appropriate audit evidence will need to be obtained to confirm the quantities of inventory held in these locations in order to verify existence and completeness.	Additional procedures, including attending inventory counts at third party warehouses, will be required to ensure that inventory quantities have been confirmed across all locations.
In September a new accounting package was introduced. The fact the two systems were not run in parallel increases the risk that errors occurring during the changeover were not highlighted, and all areas of the financial statements could potentially be affected.	The new system will need to be fully documented by the audit team including relevant controls. Testing should be performed to ensure the closing data on the old system was correctly transferred as the opening data on the new system, and that transactions have not been duplicated on both systems and therefore include twice.
The IT manager who developed the bespoke system left the company two months after the changeover and his replacement is not due to start until just before the year end. Without an IT manager's support in the interim, errors may occur and may not be picked up due to a lack of knowledge or experience of the system. This could potentially result in misstatements in many areas of the financial statements.	This audit team will need to ascertain from the finance director how this risk of misstatement is being mitigated. During the audit the audit team should remain alert throughout the audit for evidence of errors, particularly when testing transactions occurring between September and January.
$1 million of equity finance and $2.5 million of long-term loans has been raised during the year. The accounting treatment and disclosure of these can be complex with the equity finance to be allocated correctly between share capital and share premium, and the loan to be properly presented as a non-current liability. Disclosures need to be sufficient to comply with IFRSs.	The audit team must ensure the split of the equity finance is correct and that total financing proceeds of $3.5 million were received. Disclosures relating to the equity and loan finance should be reviewed to ensure compliance with relevant IFRSs.

Audit risk	Response
The loan has covenants attached to it. If these are breached then the loan would be repayable straight away and would need to be classified as a current liability, potentially resulting in a net current liability position on the statement of financial position. If the company did not have sufficient cash available to repay the loan balance the going concern status of the company could be threatened.	Obtain and review (or re-perform) covenant calculations to identify any breaches. If there are any the likelihood of the bank demanding repayment will need to be assessed and the potential impact on the company. The need to avoid breaching the covenants reinforces the audit team's need to maintain professional scepticism in areas that could be manipulated.
The finance director has announced that all land and buildings will be revalued as at the year end. The revaluation surplus or deficit is likely to be material and if the revaluation is not carried out and recorded in accordance with IAS 16 *Property, plant and equipment*, non-current assets may be under or over-valued.	Review the reasonableness of the valuation and assess the competence, experience and independence of the individual performing the valuation. The surplus/deficit should be recalculated to ensure that land and buildings are included at a reasonable amount in the statement of financial position.
The already short reporting timetable for Abrahams is likely to be reduced. This could increase detection risk because there is pressure on the team to obtain sufficient and appropriate evidence in a shorter time scale, which could adversely influence judgement on the size of samples and the extent of work needed.	If it is confirmed with the finance director that the time available at the final audit is to be reduced then the ability of the team to gather sufficient appropriate evidence should be assessed. If it is not realistically possible to perform all the required work at a final audit then an interim audit should take place in late December or early January to reduce the level of work to be done at the final audit.

(**Note.** Only five risks and five related responses were required.)

(c) (i) **Substantive procedures for inventory held at third party warehouses**

- Attend any inventory count at the third party warehouses to review the controls in operation, to ensure the completeness and existence of inventory and to perform any necessary test counts.

- Request direct written confirmation of quantities of inventory balances held at year end from the third party warehouse providers and request confirmation of any damaged or slow moving goods.

- Review any available reports by the auditors of the third parties owning the warehouses in relation to the adequacy of controls over inventory.

- Inspect any documentation relating to third party inventory.

(ii) **Substantive procedures to confirm standard costs used for inventory valuation**

- Obtain an analysis of the standard costs used in inventory valuation and compare them with the costs shown on actual invoices or in wages records to see if they are reasonable

- Analyse the variances between standard and actual costs and discuss the reason for these with management and the action taken in respect of any variances.

- Discuss with management how standard costs are formulated and applied to the inventory valuation, and the procedures in place to ensure these are updated to account for movements in actual cost when necessary.

74 Recorder

Text references. Chapters 6, 7 and 16.

Top tips. This question is packed with several requirements, both scenario-based and knowledge-based. In part (b), you must link your answer to audit risk in order to score marks. Be as specific as possible in describing the impact each fact would have on the financial statements and on the audit. Likewise, when describing auditor's responses, be as specific as possible: whenever you can, use the audit procedures that you would have memorised using the 'AEIOU' mnemonic.

Easy marks. You should have found part (d) straightforward.

Examination Team's comments. As in previous diets, in part (b) some candidates tended to only identify facts from the scenario such as 'Recorder purchases goods from a supplier in South Asia and the goods are in transit for two weeks' but failed to describe how this could impact audit risk; this would only have scored ½ marks. To gain 1 mark the point needed to be developed to also explain that this could result in issues over the completeness of inventory.

More so than in previous diets, candidates disappointingly provided business risks rather than audit risks with answers such as stock outs due to the two week transit period and possible damage to inventory during transit. As a result these candidates then provided responses related to how management should address these business risks rather than how the auditor should respond. This meant that out of a potential 2 marks per point, candidates would only score ½ marks for the identification of the issue from the scenario.

Additionally, many candidates performed poorly with regards to the auditor's responses. Many candidates gave business advice, such as changing the salesmen's bonus structure or provided vague responses such as perform detailed substantive testing or maintain professional scepticism. Responses which start with 'ensure that......' are unlikely to score marks as they usually fail to explain exactly how the auditor will address the audit risk. Audit responses need to be practical and should relate to the approach (ie what testing) the auditor will adopt to assess whether the balance is materially misstated or not.

Part (c) for 3 marks required substantive procedures for confirming the directors' bonus payment made during the year. Candidates' performance was disappointing.

Unfortunately, many candidates focussed on the authorisation of the bonus; this is not a substantive procedure and would not have scored any marks. A significant minority thought that the directors' bonus was based on sales which was not the case. The scenario stated that salesmen's bonuses were based on sales, hence candidates either confused these two items or failed to read the scenario properly. They then looked to recalculate the bonus based on sales levels which was not appropriate in the circumstances.

A number of vague procedures were suggested such as obtaining written representations or reading board minutes without explaining what for. Analytical procedures were suggested; however they were unlikely to be valid procedures as bonuses by their very nature tend to vary each year.

Marking scheme

		Marks
(a)	Up to 1 mark per well described risk and up to 1 mark for each well explained response. Overall maximum of 5 marks for risks and 5 marks for responses.	
	New client leading to increased detection risk	
	Cut-off of goods in transit	
	Continuous (perpetual) inventory counts	
	Sales cut-off	
	Overstatement of receivables	
	Valuation of land and buildings	
	Directors' bonus remuneration	10

(b)   Up to 1 mark per well explained procedure

Attend one of the continuous (perpetual) inventory counts to review whether the controls are adequate

Review the schedule of counts to confirm completeness of all inventory lines

Review the adjustments made to the inventory records to gain an understanding of the level of differences arising

If significant differences, discuss with management how they will ensure that year-end inventory will not be under or overstated

Attend the inventory count at the year end to undertake test counts to confirm the completeness and existence of inventory

3

(c)   Up to 1 mark per well described procedure

Cast schedule of directors' remuneration including the bonus paid

Agree the individual bonus payments to the payroll records

Confirm the amount of each bonus paid by agreeing to the cash book and bank statements

Review the board minutes to confirm whether any additional bonus payments relating to this year have been agreed

Obtain written representation from management

Review disclosures and assess whether these are in compliance with local legislation

3

(d)   Up to 1 mark per well explained safeguard.

Notify Recorder Communications Co and its competitor

Advise seek independent advice

Separate engagement teams

Procedures prevent access to information

Clear guidelines on security and confidentiality

Confidentiality agreements

Monitoring of safeguards

4
──
20

(a)   **Audit risks and auditor's response to each risk**

Audit risk	Auditor's response
Increased **detection risk** due to the fact that Recorder is a new client.	Ensure that the audit team is made up of suitably **experienced staff**. Ensure that **sufficient time** is allocated to obtain an understanding of Recorder's business and assess the entity's risks of material misstatement.
Increased risk of material misstatement around **cut-off of inventory, purchases and payables** as a result of purchased goods taking two weeks to arrive at the company's central warehouse.	Perform detailed cut-off testing of goods in transit around the year end to ensure that cut-off has been correctly applied.
Increased risk of material misstatement related to the **completeness, existence and valuation of inventory** under the perpetual inventory system, if all inventory is not counted at least once a year.	Review the inventory count instructions and perform audit procedures to determine whether all inventory is counted at least once a year. Assess the adequacy of internal controls around inventory records to determine whether the inventory records can be relied upon.

Audit risk	Auditor's response
Increased risk of material misstatements due to **sales cut-off**, as a result of the sales-based bonus scheme encouraging sales staff to maximise their current year bonus.	Increase sales cut-off testing, and perform additional audit procedures on post year-end cancellations to identify cut-off errors.
Increased risk of **over-valuation of receivables**, highlighted by the considerable increase of the receivables balance compared to the prior year, and concerns about the creditworthiness of some customers.	Perform extended testing of post-year end cash payments and review the aged receivables ledger. Consider the adequacy of the allowance for receivables.
Risk of material misstatements relating to the **valuation of land and buildings**, if recent revaluations do not comply with IAS 16.	Obtain an understanding of the revaluation process through discussions with management, and review the process for compliance with IAS 16. Review the disclosures of the revaluation in the financial statements for compliance with IAS 16.
Non-compliance with local legislation concerning the **disclosure of directors' remuneration**, currently included within wages and salaries.	Discuss the matter with management. Review disclosures required by local legislation in the financial statements to gain assurance over compliance.

(b) **Audit procedures where continuous (perpetual) counts for year-end inventory is used**

- Agree the total on the inventory listing to the continuous inventory records, using CAATs, to check for accuracy

- Attend at least one of the continuous inventory counts: observe the count and review the inventory count instructions to confirm that the procedures are as rigorous as those for a year-end inventory count.

- Review the schedule of counts undertaken/to be undertaken during the year to confirm whether all inventory lines have been counted (or are due to be counted).

- Review corrections to the inventory records to determine the amount of corrections made and the reason for the corrections. Confirm whether the corrections have been authorised by a manager.

- Where significant differences arise, enquire of management the actions they will take to ensure that the valuation of inventory is accurate.

(c) **Substantive procedures for directors' bonus payments**

- Cast the addition of the schedule of director's bonus payments and ensure the totals are in agreement with the disclosure in the financial statements.

- Compare the bonuses with both the previous year's bonuses and with expectations, taking into account the knowledge obtained during the audit (for example, whether the performance targets, if any, have been met).

- Agree the bonus payments to payroll records for the individual directors and agree the amounts paid on the bank statements to the payroll records.

- Review board meeting minutes and meetings of any remuneration committee for evidence of any bonuses not disclosed.

- Review the cash book for any unusual transactions which suggest undisclosed directors' emoluments.

- Review the disclosure of directors' bonuses and consider whether they are in accordance with applicable accounting standards and local legislation.

BPP
LEARNING MEDIA

(d)   **Conflicts of interest**

- Both Recorder Communications Co and its competitor should be notified that Piano & Co would be acting as auditors for each company and, if necessary, consent obtained.

- Advising one or both clients to seek additional independent advice.

- The use of separate engagement teams, with different engagement partners and team members; once an employee has worked on one audit, such as Recorder Communications Co, then they would be prevented from being on the audit of the competitor for a period of time. This separation of teams is known as building a 'Chinese wall'.

- Procedures to prevent access to information, for example, strict physical separation of both teams, confidential and secure data filing.

- Clear guidelines for members of each engagement team on issues of security and confidentiality. These guidelines could be included within the audit engagement letters.

- Potentially the use of confidentiality agreements signed by employees and partners of the firm.

- Regular monitoring of the application of the above safeguards by a senior individual in Piano & Co not involved in either audit.

75 Walters

Text references. Chapters 7 and 18.

Top tips. In part (a), make sure you read the requirement carefully and calculate the required number of ratios. The risks and the auditor's response to each risk need to be clearly explained: the ratios must be linked to the audit risks, and specific audit procedures should be stated. Again, you will not be awarded marks for vague responses such as 'check cut-off is appropriate.'

Easy marks. Part (a)(i) should not pose a problem, and part (b) also contains easy marks.

			Marks
(a)	(i)	½ mark per ratio calculation per year	
		Operating margin	
		Inventory days	
		Payable days	
		Current ratio	
		Quick ratio	3
	(ii)	Up to 1 mark per well explained audit risk, maximum of 6 marks for risks and up to 1 mark per audit response, maximum of 6 marks for responses	
		Management manipulation of results	
		Sales cut-off	
		Revenue growth	
		Misclassification of costs between cost of sales and operating	
		Inventory valuation	
		Receivables valuation	
		Going concern risk	12

(b) 1 mark per well explained point – If the procedure does not clearly explain how this will help the auditor to consider going concern then a ½ mark only should be awarded:

Review cash flow forecasts
Review bank agreements, breach of key ratios
Review post year-end sales and order book
Review suppliers correspondence
Inquire of lawyers for any litigation
Subsequent events
Board minutes
Management accounts
Consider additional disclosures under IAS 1
Written representation

$\dfrac{5}{20}$

(a) (i) **Additional ratios**

		20X4	20X3
Operating margin	PBT/Revenue	4.5/23 = 19.6%	4/18 = 22.2%
Inventory days	Inventories/COS × 365 days	2.1/11 × 365 = 70 days	1.6/10 × 365 = 58 days
Payable days	Payables/COS × 365 days	1.6/11 × 365 = 53 days	1.2/10 × 365 = 44 days
Current ratio	Current assets/Current liabilities	6.6/2.5 = 2.6	6.9/1.2 = 5.8
Quick ratio	(Current assets – inventories)/Current liabilities	(6.6 – 2.1)/2.5 = 1.8	(6.9 – 1.6)/1.2 = 4.4

(**Note.** Only three ratios were required.)

(ii) **Audit risks and responses:**

Audit risk	Audit response
Management were disappointed with the 20X3 results and are under pressure to improve the trading results in 20X4. There is a risk that management have a greater incentive to manipulate the results by adopting a more aggressive approach in relation to accounting estimates (ie provisions).	The audit team will need to remain alert to the risk of creative accounting throughout the audit. It is important that they exercise professional scepticism and evaluate any assumptions made by management in auditing accounting estimates. Current year balances should be compared to the prior year to highlight any unusual trends.
A generous sales-related bonus scheme has been introduced for the company's salesmen. This increases the risk of misstatements arising from sales cut-off as the sales staff seek to maximise their bonus.	Increased sales cut-off testing will be required. Post year-end sales returns should be reviewed, as they may provide evidence of incorrect cut-off.

Audit risk	Audit response
Revenue has grown by 28%, while cost of sales has only increased by 10%. The gross profit margin has increased significantly. Although the bonus scheme and the advertising campaign may explain the growth in revenue, the fact that the cost of sales has seen a corresponding increase need to be investigated.	Inquiries should be made of management regarding the reason why cost of sales has not increased in line with sales. Substantive procedures should be performed on an increased sample of costs, with an aim to identify any costs omitted or misclassified.
Although the gross margin has increased from 44.4% to 52.2%, the operating margin has decreased from 22.2% to 19.6%. This trend is unusual. While the bonus scheme and advertising campaign could account for some of the increase in operating expenses, there is a possibility that costs may have been misclassified from cost of sales to operating expenses.	The classification of costs between cost of sales and operating expenses will be compared with the prior year to ensure consistency. A detailed breakdown of operating expenses and cost of sales should be reviewed for evidence of misclassification. The main components of costs of sales and operating expenses should be identified and compared to the prior year. Any unusual trends (for example, significant costs in the prior year not present in the current year, and vice versa) should be discussed with management.
The inventory valuation policy has been changed, with additional overheads to be included within inventory. Inventory days have increased from 58 to 70 days. There is a risk that inventory is overvalued.	The change in the inventory valuation policy should be discussed with management. The additional overheads included should be reviewed, to confirm that they are related to production. Detailed cost and net realisable value testing should be performed and the aged inventory report should be reviewed to assess whether a write-down is required.
Receivables days have increased from 61 to 71 days and management have extended the credit period given to customers. This leads to an increased risk of unrecoverable receivables.	Extended post year end cash receipts testing and a review of the aged receivables ledger should be performed to assess the need for any write-offs or provision.
The current ratio and quick ratio have both decreased significantly. In addition, the company's positive cash balance of $2.3m in 20X3 has become an overdraft of $0.9m. Taken together with the growth in revenue and the increase in operating expenses, this may indicate overtrading. A going concern risk should be considered.	Detailed going concern testing to be performed during the audit. Cash flow forecasts covering at least 12 months from the year end should be reviewed, and the assumptions discussed with management.

(b)   **Going concern procedures**

- Obtain Walters' cash flow forecast and review the cash payments and receipts. Assess the assumptions for reasonableness and discuss the findings with management to understand if the company will have sufficient cash flows.

- Review any current agreements with the bank to determine whether any covenants in relation to the overdraft have been breached.

- Read minutes of the meetings of shareholders, the board of directors and important committees for reference to financing difficulties and for evidence of any future financing plans.

- Review the company's post year-end sales and order book to assess the levels of trade. Evaluate whether the revenue figures in the cash flow forecast are reasonable.

- Review post year-end correspondence with suppliers to identify any restriction in credit that may not be reflected in the cash flow forecasts.

- Inquire of the lawyers of Walters as to the existence of litigation and claims.

- Perform audit tests in relation to subsequent events to identify any items that might indicate or mitigate the risk of going concern not being appropriate.

- Review post year end management accounts to assess if it is in line with cash flow forecast.

- Consider whether any additional disclosures as required by IAS 1 *Presentation of financial statements* in relation to material uncertainties over going concern should be made in the financial statements.

- Confirm the existence, legality and enforceability of arrangements to provide or maintain financial support with related and third parties and assess the financial ability of such parties to provide additional funds.

- Consider Walter's position concerning any unfulfilled customer orders.

- Obtain a written representation confirming the director's view that Walters is a going concern.

Note. Only five procedures were required.

76 Sycamore

Text references. Chapters 1 and 6.

Top tips. In part (b), make sure that you explain both the audit risk and the auditor's response to the risk. Using a two-column format can help. Make sure that you discuss audit risks – the risks which have an impact on the financial statements – only. Talking about business risks in general will not get you marks!

Easy marks. Parts (a) and (c) both offer easy marks. If you know the material well, you should score good marks there.

Marking scheme

		Marks
(a)	Up to 1 mark per point.	
	• Per ISA 240 – obtain reasonable assurance that the financial statements are free from material misstatement, whether caused by fraud or error	
	• Identify and assess the risks of material misstatement due to fraud	
	• Obtain sufficient appropriate audit evidence	
	• Respond appropriately to fraud or suspected fraud identified during the audit	
	• Maintain professional scepticism throughout the audit	
	• Discussion within the engagement team	4
(b)	Up to 1 mark per well described risk and up to 1 mark for each well explained response. Overall max of 6 marks for risks and 6 marks for responses.	
	• Fraud of previous finance director	
	• Competence of new finance director	
	• Treatment of capitalised development expenditure	
	• New loan finance obtained	
	• Completeness of finance costs	
	• Loan covenants	
	• Post year-end sales returns	
	• Goods in and out during the inventory count	
	• Profit on disposal of plant and equipment	12

(c) (i) Up to 1 mark per well explained valid point.

- Description of review engagements
- Difference to external audit

2

(ii) Up to 1 mark per well described valid point.

- Level of assurance of external audit
- Level of assurance of review engagements

2

20

(a) Fraud responsibility

Maple & Co must conduct an audit in accordance with ISA 240 *The Auditor's responsibilities relating to fraud in an audit of financial statements* and are responsible for obtaining reasonable assurance that the financial statements taken as a whole are free from material misstatement, whether caused by fraud or error. (ISA 240: para. 5)

In order to fulfil this responsibility, Maple & Co is required to identify and assess the risks of material misstatement of the financial statements due to fraud. (ISA 240: para. 10(a))

They need to obtain sufficient appropriate audit evidence regarding the assessed risks of material misstatement due to fraud, through designing and implementing appropriate responses. In addition, Maple & Co must respond appropriately to fraud or suspected fraud identified during the audit. (ISA 240: para. 10(b) & (c))

When obtaining reasonable assurance, Maple & Co is responsible for maintaining professional scepticism throughout the audit, considering the potential for management override of controls and recognising the fact that audit procedures which are effective in detecting error may not be effective in detecting fraud. (ISA 240: para.12)

To ensure that the whole engagement team is aware of the risks and responsibilities for fraud and error, ISAs require that a discussion is held within the team. For members not present at the meeting, Sycamore's audit engagement partner should determine which matters are to be communicated to them. (ISA 240: para. 15)

(b) Audit risks and auditors' responses

Audit risks

Sycamore's previous finance director left in December after it was discovered that he had been committing fraud with regards to expenses claimed.

There is a risk that he may have undertaken other fraudulent transactions; these would need to be written off in the statement of profit or loss. If these have not been uncovered, the financial statements could include errors.

The new finance director was appointed in January 2015 and was previously a financial controller of a bank. Sycamore is a pharmaceutical company which is very different to a bank; there is a risk that the new finance director is not sufficiently competent to prepare the financial statements, leading to errors.

During the year, Sycamore has spent $1.8 million on developing new products; these are at different stages and the total amount has been capitalised as an intangible asset.

However, in order to be capitalised it must meet all of the criteria under IAS 38 *Intangible assets*. There is a risk that some projects may not reach final development stage and hence should be expensed rather than capitalised. Intangible assets and profit could be overstated.

Sycamore has borrowed $2.0 million from the bank via a ten-year loan. This loan needs to be correctly split between current and non-current liabilities in order to ensure correct disclosure.

Also as the level of debt has increased, there should be additional finance costs. There is a risk that this has been omitted from the statement of profit or loss, leading to understated finance costs and overstated profit.

The loan has a minimum profit target covenant. If this is breached, the loan would be instantly repayable and would be classified as a current liability.

If the company does not have sufficient cash flow to meet this loan repayment, then there could be going concern implications. In addition, there is a risk of manipulation of profit to ensure that covenants are met.

There have been a significant number of sales returns made subsequent to the year end. As these relate to pre year-end sales, they should be removed from revenue in the draft financial statements and the inventory reinstated. If the sales returns have not been correctly recorded, then revenue will be overstated and inventory understated.

During Sycamore's year-end inventory count there were movements of goods in and out. If these goods in transit were not carefully controlled, then goods could have been omitted or counted twice. This would result in inventory being under or overstated.

Surplus plant and equipment was sold during the year, resulting in a profit on disposal of $210,000. As there is a minimum profit loan covenant, there is a risk that this profit on disposal may not have been correctly calculated, resulting in overstated profits.

In addition, significant profits or losses on disposal are an indication that the depreciation policy of plant and equipment may not be appropriate. Therefore depreciation may be overstated.

Auditors' responses

Discuss with the new finance director what procedures they have adopted to identify any further frauds by the previous finance director.

In addition, the team should maintain their professional scepticism and be alert to the risk of further fraud and errors.

During the audit, careful attention should be applied to any changes in accounting policies and in particular any key judgemental decisions made by the finance director.

A breakdown of the development expenditure should be reviewed and tested in detail to ensure that only projects which meet the capitalisation criteria are included as an intangible asset, with the balance being expensed.

During the audit, the team would need to confirm that the $2 million loan finance was received. In addition, the split between current and non-current liabilities and the disclosures for this loan should be reviewed in detail to ensure compliance with relevant accounting standards.

The finance costs should be recalculated and any increase agreed to the loan documentation for confirmation of interest rates and cashbook and bank statements to confirm the amount was paid and is not therefore a year-end payable.

Review the covenant calculations prepared by Sycamore and identify whether any defaults have occurred; if so, determine the effect on the company.

The team should maintain their professional scepticism and be alert to the risk that profit has been overstated to ensure compliance with the covenant.

Review a sample of the post year-end sales returns and confirm if they relate to pre year-end sales that were recognised in revenue, that the revenue has been reversed and the inventory included in the year-end ledgers.

In addition, the reason for the increased level of returns should be discussed with management. This will help to assess if there are underlying issues with the net realisable value of inventory.

During the final audit, the goods received notes and goods despatched notes received during the inventory count should be reviewed and followed through into the inventory count records as correctly included or not.

Recalculate the profit and loss on disposal calculations and agree all items to supporting documentation.

Discuss the depreciation policy for plant and equipment with the finance director to assess its reasonableness.

(c) (i) **Review engagements**

Review engagements are often undertaken as an alternative to an audit, and involve a practitioner reviewing financial data, such as six-monthly figures. This would involve the practitioner undertaking procedures to state whether anything has come to their attention which causes the practitioner to believe that the financial data is not in accordance with the financial reporting framework.

A review engagement differs to an external audit in that the procedures undertaken are not nearly as comprehensive as those in an audit, with procedures such as analytical review and enquiry used extensively. In addition, the practitioner does not need to comply with ISAs as these only relate to external audits.

(ii) **Levels of assurance**

The level of assurance provided by audit and review engagements is as follows (ISAE 3000: para. 12):

External audit – A high but not absolute level of assurance is provided, this is known as reasonable assurance. This provides comfort that the financial statements present fairly in all material respects (or are true and fair) and are free of material misstatements.

Review engagements – where an opinion is being provided, the practitioner gathers sufficient evidence to be satisfied that the subject matter is plausible; in this case limited assurance is given whereby the practitioner confirms that nothing has come to their attention which indicates that the subject matter contains material misstatements.

77 Smoothbrush

Text references. Chapter 6, 13 and 16.

Top tips. Maintaining focus is essential on a long 30 mark question such as this one. A common theme throughout this question is the risk of answering the question you hoped would come up, rather than the question actually being asked.

In part (a), just because you see the words 'audit risks' it doesn't mean you should straight away start describing the audit risk model. You are asked to **identify and explain** (two mini-requirements) audit risks for the actual audit client described in the question. Therefore you need to work methodically through the scenario, pick out a suitable number of risks and explain each of them to gain as many of the 10 marks as you can.

For example, new systems such as the new inventory system in the scenario always carry the risk they may have not been properly implemented and could impact on year end inventory balances. Limit your answer to audit risks only; that is, only those that relate to the audit of the financial statements.

Part (b) is a discussion question. You should know why assessing risks at the planning stage is important, in order to focus audit work on important areas and help ensure the audit is performed efficiently and effectively.

Part (c) has two mini-requirements: First to list and secondly to explain suitable controls. Make sure you do both. Also limit your answer to controls over the assertions specified in the question. Commit to memory the fact you want controls over completeness and accuracy only, otherwise you may find yourself listing and explaining controls over all assertions, many of which will be gaining no marks.

In part (d), even though you have just answered a question on controls, you need to switch your mindset to substantive procedures, and be careful not to mix these up with tests of control. Also, you are now looking at valuation of inventory only in part (i), so substantive tests will be concentrated on looking at the different aspects of valuation. Inventory is valued at the lower of cost and NRV, so you need to make sure NRV is above cost by reviewing post year end sales and test that unit costs are in agreement with supporting documents such as purchase invoices. You also need to ensure any damaged items are correctly valued. These thought processes should help you identify appropriate tests. Part (ii) focuses on provisions/contingent liabilities and a different assertion, completeness. You should have picked up on the possible need for a provision as a result of the FD's dismissal and suggested specific procedures in respect of this matter.

Easy marks. Part (b) is a relatively straightforward requirement that does not require application to the scenario. A good knowledge of the importance of risk assessment will enable you to gain the majority of the marks on this part. In part (d) you should be familiar with the standard tests over valuation of inventory.

Examination Team's comments. Many candidates performed inadequately on part (a) of the question. Audit risk is a key element of the Audit & Assurance syllabus and candidates must understand audit risk. A number of candidates wasted valuable time by describing the audit risk model. This generated no marks as it was not part of the requirement. Candidates are reminded that they must answer the question asked as opposed to the one they wish had been asked. The main area where candidates lost marks is that they did not actually understand what audit risk relates to. Hence they provided answers which considered the risks the business would face or 'business risks,' which are outside the scope of the syllabus.

Part (b) for 4 marks required a discussion of the importance of assessing risk at the planning stage of an audit. This was well answered by the majority of candidates with many identifying that assessing risk would lead to an effective audit with the focus of testing being on high risk areas only.

Part (c) for 10 marks required an identification and explanation of controls over the continuous/perpetual inventory counting system in order to ensure completeness and accuracy of the inventory records. This question proved to be challenging for a number of candidates and there were some unsatisfactory answers. Many identified controls, such as 'the inventory team should be independent of the warehouse staff' but failed to then explain these controls, this would have restricted their marks to ½ mark per control as opposed to the 1½ marks available for an identification and explanation.

Part (d) for 6 marks required three substantive procedures each to confirm the valuation of inventory and the completeness of provisions or contingent liabilities. Performance was mixed for this question; candidates were generally able to provide adequate substantive procedures for provisions or contingent liabilities. The requirement to consider valuation of inventory, which is a topic which is regularly examined, was on the whole inadequately answered. Candidates seemed to ignore the requirement to consider valuation and often structured their answers with headings such as existence or rights and obligations. Clearly many failed to read the question properly.

Marking scheme

Marks

(a)   1/2 mark for each identification of risk and up to 1 per description of the risk
  - Sole supplier to Homewares, NRV of inventory
  - Recoverability of receivable as credit period extended
  - Valuation of plant and equipment
  - Cut-off
  - New system
  - Inventory provision
  - Provision/contingent liability
  - Inherent risk increased
  - Perpetual inventory counts

10

(b)   Up to 1 mark per valid point
  - ISA 315 requirement (1/2 mark only for ISA ref)
  - Early identification of material errors
  - Understand entity
  - Identification of unusual transactions/balances
  - Develop strategy
  - Efficient audit
  - Most appropriate team
  - Reduce risk incorrect opinion
  - Understanding fraud, money laundering
  - Assess risk going concern

4

BPP
LEARNING MEDIA

(c)   1/2 mark for each identification of a control and up to 1 mark per well explained description of the control
- Team independent of warehouse
- Timetable of counts
- Inventory movements stopped
- No pre-printed quantities on count sheets
- Second independent team
- Direction of counting floor to records
- Damaged/obsolete goods to specific area
- Records updated by authorised person   10

(d)   Up to 1 mark per substantive procedure
  (i)   Inventory:
- Cost to purchase invoice
- NRV to sales invoice
- Manufactured items to invoices/time sheets/production overheads
- Review aged inventory reports
- Compare aged items to 1% provision
- Total level of adjustment over year
- Follow up items noted at inventory count
- Inventory days   Max 3
- Gross margin
  (ii)   Provisions:
- Discuss with management
- Review correspondence with FD
- Write to lawyers
- Review board minutes
- Obtain written representation
    Marks awarded for tests for additional provisions and contingent liabilities   Max 3
    Total marks   **30**

(a)   **Identified risks at the planning stage**

Identified risk	Explanation
Extending the credit period to Homewares results in irrecoverable receivables and liquidity problems	A four month credit period may result in debts up to three months older than under previous credit terms. These older balances may ultimately become irrecoverable or resultant cash flow problems may impact on the gong concern status of the company.
Inventory may be overvalued because Smoothbrush sells the majority of its goods at reduced prices.	Inventory should be stated at the lower of cost and net realisable value (NRV) in accordance with IAS 2 (IAS 2: para. 9). Selling prices are heavily discounted for goods sold to Homewares, and the NRV of some inventory items may be below cost but with no adjustment having been made to write down inventory.
Plant and equipment is overvalued in the financial statements (FS)	Per IAS 16 (IAS 16: para. 63) and IAS 36 (IAS 36: para. 9), plant and equipment should be included in the FS at the lower of its carrying value and recoverable amount. The redundant plant and equipment at the production facility will probably need to be valued at scrap value, but may be included at a higher value of cost less depreciation.

Identified risk	Explanation
Cut-off treatment of purchases and inventory may not be correct	Smoothbrush records its inventory when received for imported goods from South Asia but the fact that paint can be in transit for up to two months means it is possible that a liability and purchase are recognised pre year end, but without a corresponding inventory entry being made. All entries should be made in the same period, the correct period being that in which the risks and rewards of ownership pass to Smoothbrush.
The new inventory system was inadequately implemented resulting in misstated inventory balances.	Smoothbrush introduced a continuous/perpetual inventory counting system in the year to be used for recording year end inventory. If any stage of the system implementation was flawed, then inventory in the financial statements could be misstated.
Inventory is overstated because inventory that is obsolete or damaged is no longer provided for.	Previously Smoothbrush maintained an inventory provision of 1%. Presumably there was a rationale for this provision (audited in the past). The regular reviews may not be sufficient to replace the previous rational and without a provision, inventory may be overvalued.
Provisions or contingent liability disclosures may not be complete.	The company's finance director (FD) intends to sue Smoothbrush for unfair dismissal following his pre-year end departure, and the company does not intend to make any provision/disclosures in respect of this. Under IAS 37, the approach taken by management is only permitted if the likelihood of paying out is remote. If there is a present obligation, a probable outflow of resources to settle the obligation and a reliable estimate can be made of the obligation, then a provision should be recognised (IAS 37: para. 14). If the obligation is only possible, a contingent liability should be disclosed (IAS 37: para. 86).

Top tip: There are other risks you could have identified and explained, such as the risks arising if the inventory counts are not complete and accurate, but only seven were needed to gain full marks.

(b) **Importance of assessing risks at the planning stage**

ISA 315 says that the auditor 'shall identify and assess the risks of material misstatement at the financial statement level and at the assertion level for classes of transactions and related disclosures, and account balances and related disclosures'. (ISA 315: para. 25)

It is very important that auditors carry out this risk assessment at the planning stage because:

- It helps the auditor gain an understanding of the entity for audit purposes

- It helps the auditor focus on the most important areas of the financial statements (where material misstatements are more likely), therefore increasing efficiency

- The risk assessment will form the basis of the audit strategy and the more detailed audit plan

- Once the risks have been assessed, audit team members of sufficient skill and experience can be allocated to maximise the chance of those risks being addressed.

Top tip: Other valid points could have been made here, such as risk assessment as aiding in assessing going concern and the assessment of fraud risks. However stating the ISA 315 requirement along with four valid points relating to the importance of risk assessment would have gained full marks on this question.

(c) **Controls over inventory system: completeness and accuracy**

Suitable Controls	Explanation
An inventory count team independent of the warehouse team is used.	There should be segregation of duties between those who have day-to-day responsibility for inventory and those who are checking it to help prevent fraud and error. The current team including a member of warehouse staff is inadequate and two internal auditors should be used if possible.
Pre-printed inventory sheets are used stating code/descriptions, but without quantities.	Using sheets with quantities already filled in means counters could potentially agree the current quantities to avoid counting and save time. The lack of quantities forces a count to be undertaken in each case.
Damaged/obsolete goods are moved to a designated area for inspection, but left on the sheets. They are provided against if necessary.	Rather than removing damaged/obsolete items from the sheet (and losing the audit trail), they should be written down or provided against to ensure that they are included at the lower of cost and NRV. A member of the finance team should make the assessment as to what needs writing down.
Movements of inventory are not allowed into or out of the area being counted during inventory counts.	Allowing movements in and out of inventory during counts could result in double counting, or inventory not being counted at all. Therefore such movements should be stopped during the count.
A sample of independent checks of the counts carried out by a separate team. Items to be checked are determined after the first count has been completed.	By counting a sample of inventory lines again this should help to ensure completeness and accuracy of the counts, and act as an incentive for the first team to carry out counts more accurately initially.
As a separate exercise after the counts of items on the sheets, teams check a sample of items that are physically present are correctly included on the sheets.	A count performed from the records to the warehouse will only test for existence or overstatement of inventory line quantities. Testing for completeness requires a different approach where inventory in the warehouse is compared to the records to identify goods physically present but not recorded.
Inventory count sheets are compared to the inventory records after the count. Where adjustments are needed, the reason for them is investigated and they are processed on a timely basis by appropriate personnel.	Only authorised individuals should be able to amend the records in which year end inventory will be based. On a periodic basis, senior finance team members should review the types and levels of adjustments for indications of fraud.

Top tip: You may have come up with other valid controls here. As long as they meet the control objective for the assertions specified in the question, and are adequately explained, you will have gained marks for these. Other valid controls include the monitoring of timetabling of the counts to ensure all areas are covered at least once a year.

(d) **Substantive procedures to confirm:**

(i) **Valuation of inventory**

Verify the cost of imported paint and materials to produce manufactured paint to supplier invoice costs (for a statistical sample).

Confirm that the recorded inventory costs do not exceed the NRV by comparing the costs with the value of paint sales made after the year end.

Review aged inventory reports and investigate older items to ensure they are valued at the lower of NRV or are already provided against.

(ii) **Completeness of provisions/contingent liabilities**

Discuss with management the reason for not providing for or disclosing a potential payment to the director for unfair dismissal and corroborate the responses with documentary evidence where possible.

Review correspondence with the old financial director and the company's lawyers to help assess the likelihood of a claim being successful and to try and assess whether a reliable estimate of any potential payment is possible.

Obtain written representations from directors confirming that they believe a potential liability is only a remote probability, and that is the reason for including no provision or disclosure on the matter.

Top tips: There are a number of other procedures you may have come up with for (d) (i) and (ii), but only three of each were required.

For (i) other procedures include following up on damaged items identified at inventory counts, verifying labour costs for manufactured items against timesheets, confirming production overhead allocation is appropriate, and analytical procedures such as reviewing inventory days against the previous year's or comparing gross margin with that of the previous year.

In (ii) you may have suggested writing to the company's lawyers in respect of the unfair dismissal claim and reviewing board minutes for details to support managements' assessment of the claim.

---

78 Aquamarine Co

Text references. Chapters 6 and 11

Top tips. For part (b) of the question it is important that you describe the audit risks clearly. A common mistake in this type of question is to simply identify a risk factor from the question eg the company carries out continuous production. This is a risk factor ie something about the way in which the business operates that increases audit risk. The risk itself is the potential issue that this causes. For example in this case the risk would be the difficulty this would create for establishing the cut off point for WIP which could result in under or overstatement of inventory. Notice that to score well you must both identify the risk factor and then explain the associated risk. The examination team's comments below give helpful advice about the way in which the audit risk should be explained. Part (b) then asks for the auditor's response at the planning stage. Essentially you are being asked what you would plan to do to address the risks identified. This is probably the more demanding part of the question as you have to tailor your points to the risks you have identified. Think carefully about how you respond though as general statements will score few marks and check that the action you are suggesting links to the risk. For example if you have identified that cut-off is an issue make sure that the procedures you have suggested would provide evidence regarding this assertion.

Take care with timing. Part (c) is for only 3 marks but it is important that you attempt all parts of the question. Although you may be able to use your knowledge of ISA 402 to help you, you must tailor your answer to the scenario.

Easy marks. Part (a) should represent easy marks as you should be familiar with the concept of audit risk and its components.

Examination team's comments. The scenario contained more issues than were required to be discussed, a significant minority identified more issues than necessary, often combining risks into one point. This approach sometimes resulted in a lack of detail in the risk and also led to unfocused auditor responses. In addition a large number of candidates did not explain how each issue could result in an audit risk or impact on the financial statements and therefore were not awarded the explanation ½ mark. To explain audit risk candidates need to state the area of the financial statements impacted with an assertion (eg cut off, valuation etc) or, a reference to under/over/misstated, or, a reference to inherent, control or detection risk. Misstated was only awarded if it was clear that the balance could be either over or understated. In addition, many candidates misunderstood the implication of payroll being outsourced, failing to understand that there was increased detection risk with regards to access to outsourced records and the risk of data being incorrectly transferred to the service organisation.

The provision of relevant auditor's responses continues to be a poorly attempted area and candidates are once again reminded to ensure that this area of the syllabus is adequately studied and practised. While an auditor's response does not have to be a detailed audit procedure, rather an approach the audit team will take to address the identified risk, the responses given were sometimes either too weak eg 'discuss with management' or, did not address the issue due to a failure to understand the risk (eg response to a possible understated provision, an incorrect response was to 'undertake going concern testing').

In comparison to recent exam sessions, it was disappointing that a significant minority of candidates discussed business risks and therefore concentrated their responses on what management should do rather than the auditor (eg in relation to the plant and machinery ordered pre year end, an inappropriate response was that the auditor should contact the supplier to ensure the delivery was on time.

Further it was pleasing to note that many candidates presented their answers well using a two-column approach with audit risk in one column and the related response in the other column.

Marking scheme

		Marks
(a)	Up to 1 mark for each definition of audit risk and its components (if just a component is given without an explanation then just give ½ marks).	
	• Audit risk (max of 2 marks)	
	• Inherent risk	
	• Control risk	
	• Detection risk	5
(b)	Up to 1 mark per well described risk and up to 1 mark for each well explained response. Overall maximum of 6 marks for risks and 6 marks for responses.	
	• Work in progress	
	• Existence of plant and machinery ordered	
	• Valuation of intangible asset	
	• New loan finance obtained	
	• Completeness of finance costs	
	• Use of service organisation	
	• Transfer of data to service organisation	
	• Valuation of land and buildings	
	• Overvaluation of receivables	
	• Redundancy provision	12
(c)	Up to 1 mark per well explained point.	
	• Gain an understanding of the services being provided	
	• Assess the design and implementation of internal controls over Aquamarine's payroll at Coral	
	• Visit Coral and undertake tests of controls	
	• Contact Coral's auditors to request either a type 1 or type 2 report	
	• No reference in auditor's report of use of information from Coral's auditors	3
		20

(a) **Audit risk and its components**

Audit risk is the risk that the auditor expresses an inappropriate audit opinion when the financial statements are materially misstated. Audit risk is a function of two main components, being the risk of material misstatement and detection risk. Risk of material misstatement is made up of a further two components, inherent risk and control risk.

Inherent risk is the susceptibility of an assertion about a class of transaction, account balance or disclosure to a misstatement which could be material, either individually or when aggregated with other misstatements, before consideration of any related controls.

Control risk is the risk that a misstatement which could occur in an assertion about a class of transaction, account balance or disclosure and which could be material, either individually or when aggregated with other misstatements, will not be prevented, or detected and corrected, on a timely basis by the entity's internal control.

Detection risk is the risk that the procedures performed by the auditor to reduce audit risk to an acceptably low level will not detect a misstatement which exists and which could be material, either individually or when aggregated with other misstatements. Detection risk is affected by sampling and non-sampling risk.

(b) **Audit risks and auditors' responses**

Audit risks	Auditors' responses
Aquamarine Co (Aquamarine) under takes continuous production and the work in progress balance at the year end is likely to be material. As production will not cease, the exact cut-off of the work in progress will need to be assessed. If the cut-off is not correctly calculated, the inventory valuation may be under or over stated.	The auditor should discuss with management the process they will undertake to assess the cut-off point for work in progress at the year end. This process should be reviewed by the auditor while attending the year-end inventory count. In addition, consideration should be given as to whether an independent expert is required to value the work in progress. If so, this will need to be arranged with consent from management and in time for the year-end count.
Aquamarine has ordered $720,000 of plant and machinery, two-thirds of which may not have been received by the year end. Only assets which physically exist at the year end should be included in property, plant and equipment. If items not yet delivered have been capitalised, PPE will be overstated. Consideration will also need to be given to depreciation and when this should commence. If depreciation is not appropriately charged when the asset is available for use, this may result in assets and profit being over or understated.	Discuss with management as to whether the remaining plant and machinery ordered have arrived; if so, physically verify a sample of these assets to ensure existence and ensure only appropriate assets are recorded in the non-current asset register at the year end. Determine if the asset received is in use at the year end by physical observation and if so, if depreciation has commenced at an appropriate point.
A patent has been purchased for $1.3 million, and this enables Aquamarine to manufacture specialised elevator equipment for the next five years. In accordance with IAS 38 *Intangible assets*, this should be included as an intangible asset and amortised over its five-year life. If management has not correctly accounted for the patent, intangible assets and profits could be overstated.	The audit team will need to agree the purchase price to supporting documentation and to confirm the useful life is five years. The amortisation charge should be recalculated in order to ensure the accuracy of the charge and that the intangible is correctly valued at the year end.

Audit risks	Auditors' responses
The company has borrowed $1.2 million from the bank via a five-year loan. This loan needs to be correctly split between current and non-current liabilities in order to ensure correct disclosure.	During the audit, the team would need to confirm that the $1.2 million loan finance was received. In addition, the split between current and non-current liabilities and the disclosures for this loan should be reviewed in detail to ensure compliance with relevant accounting standards. Details of security should be agreed to the bank confirmation letter.
Also, as the level of debt has increased, there should be additional finance costs. There is a risk that this has been omitted from the statement of profit or loss leading to understated finance costs and overstated profit.	The finance costs should be recalculated and any increase agreed to the loan documentation for confirmation of interest rates. Interest payments should be agreed to the cash book and bank statements to confirm the amount was paid and is not therefore a year-end payable.
During the year Aquamarine outsourced its payroll processing to an external service organisation. A detection risk arises as to whether sufficient and appropriate evidence is available at Aquamarine to confirm the completeness and accuracy of controls over payroll. If not, another auditor may be required to undertake testing at the service organisation.	Discuss with management the extent of records maintained at Aquamarine and any monitoring of controls undertaken by management over the payroll charge. Consideration should be given to contacting the service organisation's auditor to confirm the level of controls in place.
The payroll processing transferred to Coral Payrolls Co from 1 January. If any errors occurred during the transfer process, these could result in the payroll charge and related employment tax liabilities being under/overstated.	Discuss with management the transfer process undertaken and any controls put in place to ensure the completeness and accuracy of the data. Where possible, undertake tests of controls to confirm the effectiveness of the transfer controls. In addition, perform substantive testing on the transfer of information from the old to the new system.
The land and buildings are to be revalued at the year end; it is likely that the revaluation surplus/deficit will be material. The revaluation needs to be carried out and recorded in accordance with IAS 16 *Property, plant and equipment*, otherwise non-current assets may be incorrectly valued.	Discuss with management the process adopted for undertaking the valuation, including whether the whole class of assets was revalued and if the valuation was undertaken by an expert. This process should be reviewed for compliance with IAS 16.
Receivables for the year to date are considerably higher than the prior year. If this continues to the year end, there is a risk that some receivables may be overvalued as they are not recoverable.	Discuss with management the reasons for the increase in receivables and management's process for identifying potential irrecoverable debt. Test controls surrounding management's credit control processes. Extended post year-end cash receipts testing and a review of the aged receivables ledger to be performed to assess valuation. Also consider the adequacy of any allowance for receivables.

Audit risks	Auditors' responses
Aquamarine is planning to make approximately 65 employees redundant after the year end. The timing of this announcement has not been confirmed; if it is announced to the staff before the year end, then under IAS 37 *Provisions, contingent liabilities and contingent assets* a redundancy provision will be required at the year end. Failure to provide will result in an understatement of provisions and expenses.	Discuss with management the status of the redundancy announcement; if before the year end, review supporting documentation to confirm the timing. In addition, review the basis of and recalculate the redundancy provision.

(c) **Payroll service organisations**

Additional factors Amethyst & Co should consider in relation to Aquamarine's use of the service organisation, Coral Payrolls Co (Coral) include:

- The audit team should gain an understanding of the services being provided by Coral, including the materiality of payroll and the basis of the outsourcing contract.

- They will need to assess the design and implementation of internal controls over Aquamarine's payroll at Coral.

- The team may wish to visit Coral and undertake tests of controls to confirm the operating effectiveness of the controls.

- If this is not possible, Amethyst & Co should contact Coral's auditors to request either a type 1 (report on description and design of controls) or type 2 report (on description, design and operating effectiveness of controls).

- Amethyst & Co is responsible for obtaining sufficient and appropriate evidence, therefore no reference may be made in the auditor's report regarding the use of information from Coral's auditors.

79 Kangaroo Construction Co

Text reference. Materiality and performance materiality are covered in Chapter 6. Audit risk and analytical procedures are also covered in Chapter 6.

Top tips. This is a typical scenario-based exam question on audit risk, with a knowledge element. It is important to go through the scenario carefully, line by line, so that you can identify the risk factors as you will need to explain how they may impact on the financial statements in part (b)(ii). This part also requires you to describe the auditor's responses to the identified audit risks – vague answers here will not score well. For example, it is not sufficient to say 'Discuss with management'. Your answer needs to be more detailed and explain how you, as auditor, are going to undertake audit work to address the risk. This part of the question is best answered in a columnar format so that you can link the audit risks with the appropriate responses and give your answer more structure. Make sure you make reference to the ratios you calculated in part (b)(i) of the question.

Easy marks. Part (a) is a knowledge-based part for five marks on materiality and performance materiality. Provided you are comfortable with the definitions of these terms, this part should pose no problems. Part (b)(i) asks you to calculate five ratios for **both** years and again, this is a relatively straightforward part of the question – you should be able to score maximum marks here. Note the requirement for the number of ratios you need to calculate and the fact that you need to calculate each ratio for both financial years.

Marks

(a)   Up to 1 mark per well explained point:

- Materiality for financial statements as a whole and also performance materiality levels
- Definition of materiality
- Amount or nature of misstatements, or both
- 5% profit before tax or 1% revenue or total expenses
- Judgement, needs of users and level of risk
- Small errors aggregated
- Performance materiality

5

(b)   (i)   ½ mark per ratio calculation per year.

- Gross margin
- Operating margin
- Inventory days
- Inventory turnover
- Receivable days
- Payable days
- Current ratio
- Quick ratio

5

(ii)   Up to 1 mark per well described audit risk and up to 1 mark per well explained audit response

- Receivables valuation
- Inventory valuation
- Depreciation of plant and machinery
- Management manipulation of profit to reach bonus targets
- Completeness of warranty provision
- Disclosure of bank loan of £1 million
- Going concern risk

<u>10</u>
<u>20</u>

(a)   **Materiality and performance materiality**

Materiality is not specifically defined in ISA 320 *Materiality in planning and performing an audit* but it does state that misstatements are material if they could reasonably be expected to influence the economic decisions of users (either individually or in aggregate) (ISA 320: para. 2). ISA 320 also states that judgements about materiality are affected by the size and/or nature of a misstatement (ISA 320: para. 6). Auditors set their own materiality levels, based on their judgement of risk. During audit planning, the auditor will set materiality for the financial statements as a whole and this involves the exercise of professional judgement. Benchmarks and percentages are often used to calculate a materiality level for the financial statements as a whole, eg 5% of profit before tax or 1–2% of total assets, but ultimately, the level of materiality set is down to the auditor's professional judgement, and may be revised during the course of the audit.

The auditor also has to set performance materiality, which is lower than materiality for the financial statements as a whole. Performance materiality is defined in ISA 320 as the amount or amounts set by the auditor at less than materiality for the financial statements as a whole to reduce to an appropriately low level the probability that the aggregate of uncorrected and undetected misstatements exceeds materiality for the financial statements as a whole (ISA 320: para. 9).

(b) (i) **Ratios**

Ratio	20X3	20X2
Gross profit margin (gross profit/sales × 100)	5.5/12.5 × 100 = 44%	7.0/15.0 × 100 = 47%
Operating margin (profit before interest and taxation/sales × 100)	0.5/12.5 × 100 = 4%	1.9/15 × 100 = 13%
Inventory turnover (cost of sales/inventory)	7/1.9 = 3.7	8/1.4 = 5.7
Inventory days (inventory/cost of sales × 365)	1.9/7 × 365 = 99 days	1.4/8 × 365 = 64 days
Receivables days (receivables/sales × 365)	3.1/12.5 × 365 = 91 days	2/15 × 365 = 49 days
Payables days (payables/cost of sales × 365)	1.6/7 × 365 = 83 days	1.2/8 × 365 = 55 days
Current ratio (current assets/current liabilities)	(1.9 + 3.1 + 0.8)/(1.6 + 1.0) = 2.2	(1.4 + 2.0 + 1.9)/1.2 = 4.4
Quick ratio (current assets except inventory/current liabilities)	(3.1 + 0.8)/(1.6 + 1.0) = 1.5	(2.0 + 1.9)/1.2 = 3.3

(**Note.** Only five ratios were required.)

(ii) **Audit risk and responses**

Audit risk	Auditor's response
The company offers a five year building warranty on its houses. During the year, as a result of switching to a cheaper supplier, some customers have claimed on their guarantees. There is a risk that the warranty provision is understated in the financial statements.	As this is a judgemental area, the auditors need to discuss the basis of calculating the provision with the directors and assess the reasonableness of any assumptions made. They should also review a sample of guarantees claimed during the year and vouch amounts to repairs invoices. They should review the level of claims made in the year and assess whether the provision needs revising in light of this.
The company has had a difficult year due to a fall in house prices. Gross profit margin has fallen by 3% and operating margin has fallen significantly from 13% to 4%. In addition, the company has had to take out a loan of $1m during the year to help with operating cash flow. Payables days have also increased from 55 days to 83 days, indicating that the company is having problems paying suppliers. The current and quick ratios have also fallen significantly from the prior year. There is therefore a risk that the company may not be a going concern.	The auditors must discuss with directors whether they believe that the company is still a going concern in light of the results of the ratio analysis, and review cash flow forecasts and budgets for the forthcoming year.

Audit risk	Auditor's response
Receivables days have increased from 49 days to 91 days as a result of the directors increasing the credit terms offered to customers. There is a risk that the receivables' balance at year-end is materially misstated as customers may not be able to pay.	The auditors should carry out post year end testing and cut-off testing on receivables' balances to verify the accuracy of the year-end balance. The auditors should also review the aged receivables listing to identify any balances that need writing off.
There is a risk that inventory is overstated in the financial statements as there may be some houses whose selling price is less than cost. Inventory days have also increased from 64 days to 99 days, and inventory turnover has fallen from 5.7 to 3.7. Inventory should be valued at the lower of cost and net realisable value.	Detailed audit work on inventory should be carried out as this is likely to be a material balance. An auditor's expert may need to be used to independently verify the value of inventory at the year end.
There is a risk that revenue and costs have been deliberately misstated in the financial statements in order for the directors to meet the target profit before interest and taxation figure of $0.5m so as to get their bonuses (window dressing). This is also indicated by the fact that the directors have changed the useful economic life of plant and machinery from three to five years to reduce the depreciation charge for the year and hence inflate the profit figure to attain the minimum target figure.	The auditors need to maintain professional scepticism throughout the audit and carry out detailed cut-off testing on revenue and expenses to confirm that the figures are correctly stated.
There is a risk that the depreciation charge for the year is understated and non-current assets on the statement of financial position are overstated as the directors have amended the useful economic life of plant and machinery from three to five years.	The auditors should discuss the change and the reasons for it with the directors and assess whether it is reasonable or not. They should also examine a sample of plant and machinery assets to assess whether the change is appropriate.
The company has taken out a loan of $1m from the bank which is repayable within a year. There is a risk that this loan has been incorrectly disclosed in the financial statements. It should be disclosed as a current liability as it is repayable within a year.	The auditors should review the terms of the loan agreement to verify the repayment date and the amount borrowed. They should review the draft financial statements to confirm the correct disclosure of the loan.

(**Note**. Only **five** audit risks were required.)

80 Sunflower Stores Co

Text references. Chapters 5 and 6

Top tips. This question tests risk assessment both in terms of gaining an understanding of a client and in relation to identifying and responding to specific audit risks.

In (a) you should make sure you both identify information sources and describe what you expect to obtain.

Part (b) is a common requirement for F8 and on these questions a tabular approach will help to show the examination team you have addressed both the risk and the response. To adequately describe a risk you need to show how it impacts on a financial statement assertion or area. Your responses to risks should be clear and include a full explanation of any relevant procedure or action. Your responses should be responses of the auditor, not those of management.

Part (c) requires you to put yourself in the finance director's shoes and come up with the factors to consider before establishing an internal audit department. Cost will always be a factor for a finance director, as will the role any potential internal audit department will play.

Easy marks. In part (a) you should have found it relatively easy to generate sources of information.

		Marks
(a)	½ mark for source of documentation and ½ mark for information expect to obtain, max of 2½ marks for sources and 2½ marks for information expect.	
	Prior year audit file	
	Prior year financial statements	
	Accounting systems notes	
	Discussions with management	
	Permanent audit file	
	Current year budgets and management accounts	
	Sunflower's website	
	Prior year report to management	
	Financial statements of competitors	5
(b)	Up to 1 mark per well explained risk and up to 1 mark for each well explained response. Overall max of 5 marks for risks and 5 marks for responses.	
	Treatment of $1.6m refurbishment expenditure	
	Disposal of warehouse	
	Bank loan of $1.5m	
	Attendance at year-end inventory counts	
	Inventory valuation	
	Transfer of opening balances from supermarkets to head office	
	Increased inherent risk of errors in finance department and new financial controller	10
(c)	Up to 1 mark per well described point	
	Costs versus benefits of establishing an internal audit (IA) department	
	Size and complexity of Sunflower should be considered	
	The role of any IA department should be considered	
	Whether existing managers/employees can undertake the roles required	
	Whether the control environment has a history of control deficiencies	
	Whether the possibility of fraud is high	5
		20

(a) **Information sources**

Information source	Expect to obtain:
Permanent audit file	Information on matters of continuing importance for the company and the audit team, such as governing documents, share certificates and ongoing contractual agreements.
Prior year audit file	An awareness of issues arising in the prior year audit and the implications for the current year audit, especially the risk assessment where issues in the prior year suggest a particular area is more susceptible to misstatements.

Information source	Expect to obtain:
Prior year financial statements	Information on the historic performance of the entity and its accounting policies. Last year's financial statements can help the auditor form expectations for the purposes of performing analytical procedures.
Systems notes/Internal control questionnaires	Information on how each of the key accounting systems is designed, how it operates and how robust the internal controls are.
Company website	Information on recent developments or press activity which could impact on the risk assessment.
Financial statements or financial information relating to competitors	Information from which the auditor can develop expectations when undertaking preliminary analytical procedures and undertaking the risk assessment.
Company budgets	A reference point for expected performance which can be compared with actual performance.
Prior year report to management	Information on deficiencies identified last year and auditor recommendations. If the deficiencies are unresolved this will impact on the risk assessment.
Discussions with management	Information in relation to any important issues arising or changes to the company during the period under review.

Note. Only five sources were required.

(b)   **Audit risks and responses**

Audit risk	Response
The $1.6m spent on refurbishing may have been incorrectly analysed between non-current assets and repairs. There is therefore a risk that non-current assets and expenses are misstated.	Obtain and review an analysis of the costs, tracing to invoices and other supporting documents to establish the nature of the expenditure. Then accounting entries should be reviewed to ensure revenue expenditure has been charged to the statement of profit or loss and capital expenditure is included in non-current assets.
The five year loan of $1.5m from the bank may have been incorrectly analysed between current and non-current liabilities.	The allocation of the loan between current and non-current liabilities and the related disclosures for the loan should be reviewed to assess whether it is presented in accordance with IFRSs.
If Sunflower has given the bank a charge over its assets as security for the loan, the related financial statement disclosures may be incomplete or inadequate.	The loan agreement should be obtained and reviewed for evidence that security has been given. A bank confirmation should be obtained including details of any security. Financial statement disclosures relating to security should be reviewed to ensure they are complete and in accordance with IFRSs.
The warehouse disposed of during the year may have been incorrectly accounted for resulting in a potential overstatement of non-current assets and the related profit on disposal.	The non-current asset register should be reviewed to ensure that the asset has been removed. Disposal proceeds should be agreed to bank statements and the profit on disposal should be recalculated.

Audit risk	Response
Due to Sunflower conducting numerous inventory counts simultaneously on 31 December it may not be possible to attend all counts. As a result there is a risk sufficient appropriate audit evidence may not be gained over inventory in the financial statements.	A sample of sites should be visited with those holding material inventory, including the warehouse, prioritised. Supermarkets with a history of inventory count issues should also be visited.
Sunflower's inventory valuation policy is selling price less average profit margin. Although IAS 2 *Inventories* allows this as an inventory valuation method it is only permitted if it proves a close approximation to cost (IAS 2: paras. 21–22). If this is not the case, inventory could be under or overvalued.	Valuation testing should include a comparison of the cost of inventory with the selling price less margin to assess if the method used does result in a close approximation to cost. The actual NRV (rather than anticipated selling price) for some items should be tested to ensure it does not fall below recorded values.
Transfer of opening balances to head office may not have been performed completely and accurately. If the opening balances are misstated, for some statement of financial position accounts (such as non-current assets) the closing balances may also be misstated.	Enquire of management how the data was transferred, what controls were in place and which procedures were performed to confirm the transfer was complete and accurate. Review the journal(s) made to transfer the opening balances and compare with the prior year financial statements to ensure they were as expected.
The increased workload for the finance department has forced the financial controller to leave and his replacement will not start until late December. The increased workload increases the risk of staff making errors. In addition the new financial controller's lack of experience of Sunflower's systems and accounting records may mean he or she is more likely to produce financial statements with misstatements or incorrect disclosures. In addition audit queries may be less likely to be resolved.	Sample sizes and the level of substantive procedures may need to be increased in light of the increased inherent risk of overworked staff and an inexperienced financial controller. A request that the finance director be available to answer audit questions should be made in anticipation that the new financial controller may not be able to resolve audit issues relating to events during the year. The audit team should remain alert to the possibility of errors.

Note. Only five risks and five related responses were required.

(c) **Factors to be considered before establishing an internal audit department**

Before establishing an internal audit department the finance director would consider:

(i) *The costs of establishing an internal audit department*

These are likely to be significant and should be weighted against the benefits and future cost savings.

(ii) *The size and complexity of Sunflower*

As Sunflower has numerous supermarkets, a central warehouse and a head office, its size and complexity could benefit from an IA department.

(iii) *The effectiveness of the current control environment and past experience of control deficiencies*

The less effective the controls in the organisation, the greater the need for an internal audit department.

(iv) *The role of the proposed internal audit department*

The finance director needs to establish the nature of the assignments to be carried out by internal audit. These could be compliance based reviews, control reviews, or observing controls and test counting at the inventory counts.

(v) *The ability of current employees in current roles carry out proposed internal audit assignments*

It may be that the relevant expertise and time exists within the organisation already to fulfil the objectives that would be set for an internal audit department.

(vi) *The susceptibility of the business to fraud*

The more susceptible the business is to fraud the greater the need for an internal audit department (eg to review relevant controls and assist in fraud investigations). Supermarkets collect large sums of cash so Sunflower is likely to be relatively susceptible and will need robust controls to prevent fraud. These controls will need to be monitored.

Flowers Anytime

81 D The first step should be to document the system of internal control – this is done using the flowchart and internal control evaluation questionnaire. The second step should be to confirm our understanding of the system – this is done with a walk-through test. Tests of control are then performed to obtain audit evidence about the effectiveness of the design and operation of internal controls. Finally, if controls testing reveal any deficiencies in internal controls that have not been previously identified, the audit strategy and the audit plan should be revised as required.

82 B In Option A, the descriptions of ICQs and ICEQs are reversed. Neither ICQs nor ICEQs are likely to capture how internal controls deal with unusual transactions: narrative notes are needed to do this. Both ICQs and ICEQs give the impression that all controls are of equal importance. The significance of each control would only be highlighted in narrative notes.

83 B A sequence check of the invoices is an effective control, be it carried out manually or electronically. Order forms should have four, not three parts. No copy of the order is sent to accounts receivables clerk – as a result, the recording of receivables may be incomplete or delayed, and outstanding balances may remain uncollected. The sales clerk should not be reviewing the standing data himself – this review should be performed by an independent, senior member of staff. Sales invoices should be posted automatically to the sales daybook and the accounts receivables ledger immediately after the order is taken.

84 A This simply reduces the risk that cash will be misappropriated. It does not provide any assurance that subsequent recording will be complete or accurate.

85 A ISA 265 *Communicating deficiencies in internal control to those charged with governance and management* requires the auditor to communicate significant deficiencies in internal control (ISA 265: paras. 5&6). The fact that the amounts exposed to the deficiencies in the sales system were high and it is likely that the deficiencies would result in material misstatements in the financial statements are indicators that the deficiencies are significant (ISA 265: para. A6).

KLE Co

86 A The fact that the ordering clerk transfers information from the order requisition to the order form without any subsequent approval increases the risk that errors on the order form go unnoticed. The fact that the order requisition is thrown away means that any subsequent queries cannot be traced back to the original order. The fact that the ordering department does not retain copies of the order forms means that orders may be duplicated, either in error or deliberately. The chief buyer authorises the order requisitions and determines the appropriate supplier, so the risk of purchases being made at unauthorised prices is reduced.

87 D It is important that the ordering department receives a copy of the GRN, so that they can monitor which orders are closed and which remain outstanding. To ensure efficiency and to avoid delays, a three-part GRN could be used – one for the ordering department, one for the goods inward department and one for the accounts department.

88 C The direction of the test is important here. The sample is taken from goods received notes as these represent deliveries. The auditor can then check that each delivery is supported by a valid order. If the sample is chosen from purchase orders (Option A) the test would confirm whether orders have been fulfilled. Options B and D are tests of controls regarding completeness of accounting information.

89 A Bank confirmations should always be carried out by the auditor. Providing advice on the implementation of a new payroll system would impair the internal auditors' independence. Reviewing the financial statements on behalf of the board is the responsibility of the audit committee, not internal audit.

90 D A Value for Money focuses on three Es: Economy, Efficiency and Effectiveness. Option A describes economy. Option C describes effectiveness. Option B only describes one aspect of efficiency.

SouthLea

91 The correct answers are:

Cut-off of starters' and leavers' wages

Potential fraud risk factors

The facts that the foreman is authorised to issue new employee numbers, and the two wages clerks are responsible for setting up employee records, make it more likely for bogus employees to be set up on the system than for bona fide employees to be omitted. This is likely to give rise to questions around the occurrence of wages, not their completeness. The fact that a wages clerk reviews the calculations for the deductions from gross pay should reduce the risk of computerised errors.

92 The correct answer is:

Review the log of amendments to standing data for evidence of review

Reviewing overtime lists for evidence of authorisation is a test of control over the authorisation of wages. The other two procedures can identify unauthorised amendments to standing data, but they are substantive procedures.

93 The correct answer is:

The internal auditor must always consider the potential of management overriding controls and modify their audit procedures accordingly when performing internal audit engagements.

The need to consider the potential of management override applies mainly to the external auditors. The external auditor's objective is to conclude whether the financial statements are free from material misstatement, whether from error or fraud. Audit procedures that are effective in detecting error may not be appropriate in detecting fraud due to the nature of fraud.

94 The correct answer is:

(1) and (2) only

In the absence of the audit committee the work of the internal audit department should be directed by the board. The scope being set by the finance director reduces independence.

95 The correct answers are:

Full testing procedures using test data when developing computer applications

Disaster recovery procedures

One for one checking and hash totals are application controls.

Cherry

96 C The selection and application of accounting policies is one of the areas in which the auditor is required to gain an understanding, as part of the auditor's risk assessment procedures. It is not a component of internal control. The other components of internal control are the risk assessment process and monitoring of controls.

97	B	The fact that raw materials are being ordered without reviewing inventory levels, both stock-outs and excess obsolescent inventory are likely. The lack of authorisation means that fraudulent purchases could be made, but there is an approved supplier list and money-laundering risks seem far-fetched. Likewise, poorer quality goods may be order but the approved supplier list does act as a control here – and going concern risks are irrelevant.
98	D	The fact that GRNs are not sequentially numbered means that GRNs may be omitted from accounting records and it would be difficult to trace the unrecorded GRNs. As a result, the risk is that payables (and inventory) is understated.
99	B	It is likely that the number of capital purchases in the year will be less than the number of standard purchases in the year. If the invoices are not segregated, it may not be cost-efficient to test the controls over this area, in which case substantive testing would have to be undertaken. Although controls around the non-current assets cycle will probably resemble those around the purchases cycle, the auditor should still understand how the company's system records capital invoices. The risk of material misstatement in relation to the non-current assets cycle is high, because orders are likely to be of a less routine nature, larger amounts may be involved, and there may be an incentive to account creatively for tax or other purposes.
100	A	The direction of the test is important here. If the sample of serial numbers were taken from the non-current assets register, the physical assets which were not assigned serial numbers and/or were not recorded would not be identified. Reviewing the non-current register to identify duplicate serial numbers will identify instances when the serial numbers assigned were not unique, making it difficult to trace the related assets. Observation is a valid audit procedure, but it provides a weak form of audit evidence, since it does not assure the auditor that the control would be operated when the auditor is not there to observe it.

Swan

101	B	The company is able to fulfil the orders.
		It is a deficiency in the system that the other three objectives do not appear to be met.
102	C	2 and 4
		This is because there is a risk that the printed orders will not be invoiced properly as they may be lost or overlooked (being outside the electronic system), hence 2. In addition, if the reason the GRN details do not match is that they have been fulfilled incorrectly (rather than due to simple typographical errors), the staff member may assume it is a typing issue and simply print the order, but not double check the goods properly against it, hence 4. In this situation, a customer might be sent 50 goods rather than the ordered 5, but only be invoiced for 5, as the invoice is generated from the order.
		This issue should not cause goods to be invoiced without being sent out, as invoices are generated from goods out notes or orders being used as goods out notes.
		It should also not cause orders not to be fulfilled, as the issue arises when the order has been processed, so the order has not been overlooked.
103	B	2 and 3
		1 and 4 relate to accuracy
104	A	1 and 3
		The likelihood of material misstatement occurring is a key factor in determining whether the deficiency is significant. The number of deficiencies is a factor, as deficiencies may become significant if there is a significant combination of deficiencies.
		A control deficiency does not increase in significance simply due to the area of business it relates to, but may become significant if there is a risk of fraud. There is no more significant risk of fraud in the sales system than in other systems, for example, the purchases system or payroll system, so the business area is not a critical factor.

Similarly, a deficiency is a deficiency regardless of whether the related control is new or not. In fact, an old deficiency might be more significant than a new one, say if it had been previously reported and not acted on.

105   A   A computerised ICEQ

This is the only option that has the element of evaluation that the partner requires. The fact that it is computerised should also influence how easy it is to update, therefore addressing her second issue.

106 Chuck

Text references. Chapters 6, 10, 11, 16 and 19

Top tips. As always in the long 30 mark questions you should make sure you keep to time for each individual part and the question as a whole. In part (a) you should notice you are given the deficiency and need to explain the implications and suggest recommendations. Therefore a two column tabular approach will be appropriate, one column for implications and one for recommendations. You will find that if you properly explain the implication the deficiency itself will be evident. There is no need to describe the deficiency – no marks are available for the deficiencies, although you could have listed them briefly as headings to help structure your answer. The marks are awarded for implications and recommendations, not identification of the deficiencies already given.

In (b) keep your answers focused on substantive procedures, not tests of control. Also your procedures should remain relevant to the assertions stated in the question – completeness and accuracy of the payroll charge. Don't forget simple procedures such as casting the payroll records since this will also help to confirm accuracy and completeness.

Part (c) was on the auditor's responsibility in relation to laws and regulations. Remember the auditor's opinion will be on the financial statements, so the auditor's responsibility will be focussed on those laws and regulations that could have a material effect on the financial statements, whether direct or indirect. There are a number of substantive procedures you could have suggested in (d) in respect of the redundancy provision, but the most you could gain is four marks so it is important you did not carry on stating more than four procedures and risk exceeding your time allocation of eight minutes. Part (e) was relatively straightforward in relation to reliance on internal audit as long as you knew the four key factors of objectivity, technical competence, due professional care and communication.

Easy marks. These were available in parts (d) and (e), but all in all it was possible to score well in every part of this question.

Examination Team's comments. In part (a) the scenario contained an abundance of deficiencies and so on the whole candidates were able to easily identify enough points. A small minority of candidates provided implications and recommendations for general deficiencies which were not specified within the scenario; these points would not have gained credit as the question requirement clearly stated that points needed to be raised for the deficiencies identified in the scenario. A significant proportion of candidates wasted time by writing out the deficiencies from the scenario; there were no marks available for deficiencies, only for the implications and recommendations.

Performance was mixed in part (b). As noted in previous examiner's reports candidates are often confused with the differences between tests of controls and substantive tests. The requirement verb was to 'describe' therefore sufficient detail was required to score the 1 mark available per test.

Part (c) was answered unsatisfactorily by most candidates. Most candidates focused on management's responsibility for preparing financial statements and implementing controls and auditors' responsibility to provide a true and fair opinion. These points are not related to laws and regulations. Part (d) was answered unsatisfactorily by many candidates. Candidates must tailor their knowledge to the scenario in order to pick up application marks and those candidates who performed well were able to produce detailed procedures which related to the scenario. In relation to the popular answer of obtaining written representations this procedure needs to be phrased with sufficient detail to obtain credit. 'Obtain a written representation from management' would not have scored any marks as it does not specify what the representation is for. Candidates performed well on part (e), with many attaining full marks.

Marks

(a)   Up to 1 mark per well explained implication and up to 1 mark for each well
      explained recommendation
      Multiple employees can be clocked in
      Weaker control environment
      Unauthorised overtime hours
      Payroll system errors not identified
      Payroll increases to be agreed by the board
      Written notification of pay increases to payroll department
      Night shift wages susceptible to risk of theft
      Factory supervisor not independent
      Absent night shift employees' pay not secure over weekend
      Joiners/leavers notified on timely basis   12

(b)   Up to 1 mark per substantive procedure
      Agree wages and salaries per payroll to trial balance
      Cast payroll records
      Recalculate gross and net pay
      Recalculate statutory deductions, agree relevant to current year rates
      Compare total payroll to prior year
      Review monthly payroll to prior year and budget
      Proof in total of payroll
      Verify joiners/leavers and recalculate first/last pay
      Agree salaries paid per payroll to bank transfer list and cashbook
      Agree total cash withdrawn from bank equates to wages paid and surplus
      cash banked
      Agree tax liabilities to payroll and post year-end cashbook
      Agree the individual wages and salaries as per the payroll to the personnel
      records and records of hours worked per clocking in cards   6

(c)   Up to 1 mark per valid point
      Management responsibility to comply with law and regulations
      Auditors not responsible for preventing non-compliance
      Auditors – reasonable assurance financial statements free from material error
      Law and regulations – Direct effect responsibility
      Law and regulations – Indirect effect responsibility
      Remain alert/Professional scepticism   4

(d)   Up to 1 mark per substantive procedure
      Discuss with directors whether formal announcement made of redundancies
      Review supporting documentation to confirm present obligation
      Review board minutes to confirm payment probable
      Cast breakdown of redundancy provision
      Recalculate provision and agree components of calculation to supporting
      documentation
      Review post-year-end period to compare actual payments to amounts
      provided
      Written representations to confirm completeness
      Review disclosures for compliance with IAS 37 *Provisions, contingent
      liabilities and contingent assets*   5

(e)   Up to 1 mark per well explained point
       Objectivity – independence, status and to whom report
       Technical Competence – qualifications and experience
       Due professional care – properly planned and performed
       Communication – between internal and external auditors

$\dfrac{3}{30}$

(a)   **Chuck Industries – payroll system implications and recommendations**

Implication	Recommendation
Lack of monitoring of clocking in:	
The lack of monitoring of the clocking in/out process allows other employees to clock in colleagues resulting in a payroll cost in excess of that expected for the actual hours worked.	Clocking in and out should be monitored by a supervisor of an appropriate level.
The lack of supervision over clocking in and out also gives employees the opportunity to delay clocking out (or to clock in before starting work) to increase their overtime, leading to invalid payroll costs being incurred.	Payment of overtime hours should only be made on authorisation by a supervisor who has reviewed the overtime hours for reasonableness and compared them to production volumes and observed working patterns.
The absence of clocking in/out monitoring may result in a weak control environment as it promotes an attitude where it is acceptable to override controls.	Formal communications should be made on the importance and purpose of the company's policies and procedures in relation to clocking in and out, and the importance of adhering to company controls in general.
Payroll calculations not reviewed:	
Since payroll calculations are not checked and the system is entirely trusted, any errors made as a result of standing or underlying data being incorrect or occurring during payroll processing would not be discovered. Overpayments or underpayments (and incorrect payroll costs) may result and lead to losses or disgruntled employees.	A payroll supervisor should periodically recalculate the net pay based on the gross pay and expected deductions, then compare the result with the computer generated figures for a sample of employees. The review should be evidenced by a signature and wages should not be paid until this signed review is completed.
Verbal notification of pay increases:	
HR have authorised a pay increase. This indicates a lack of authorisation at board level and could lead to invalid increases in employee wages (eg for HR personnel's friends or relatives).	HR should be required to gain written board authorisation for any proposed wage increase before passing this to Payroll.
Payroll have accepted verbal instruction from HR as sufficient authority to increase wages. This could contribute to invalid increases in employee wages.	Payroll should be informed only to action a wage increase on receipt of written authorisation approved by the board.

Implication	Recommendation
Factory supervisor distribution of wages:	
The factory supervisor is trusted with substantial cash sums in advance of distribution of wages to the night shift. This cash is susceptible to theft and loss while not with employees or securely stored.	Payroll officials should be available for certain hours during the night shift to distribute wages.
The factory supervisor keeps absent employee's wages over the weekend before handing back to payroll and this further increases the risk of loss or theft of cash wages.	Any amounts not paid out on Fridays should be kept by payroll in a safe or other secure means until Monday when the employee can collect from Payroll.
The supervisor entrusted with the wages is not independent and may take it upon him/herself to reallocate the wages as he/she deems necessary.	The supervisor should not be responsible for distribution of cash wages. Payroll should distribute these and should consider the proposal of operating for at least part of the night shift.
Poor communication of joiners/leavers:	
The lack of procedures in place to ensure timely notification of joiners/leavers means leavers may still be paid in error and joiners may not be paid on time. The payroll records will not reflect accurate wages costs at least temporarily.	HR staff duties and responsibilities should be reallocated when staff are ill or on holiday, including the responsibility of immediate communication of new joiners/leavers to payroll. In addition new joiner forms showing start date should be completed and authorised and passed to payroll so they are aware of the need to update the payroll records.

(**Note.** Only six well explained implications and six related recommendations were required.)

(b) **Substantive procedures – Payroll cost**

- Compare the total payroll expense to the previous year and investigate any significant variances.

- Review monthly payroll charges and compare this to the prior year monthly charges and to budgets. Discuss significant variances with management.

- Reconcile the total wages and salaries expense per the payroll records to the cost in the financial statements and investigate any differences.

- Agree amounts owed to the tax authorities to the payroll records and with the amount subsequently paid and clearing the bank statement post year-end to ensure completeness.

- Cast a sample of payroll records to confirm completeness and accuracy of the payroll expense.

- Recalculate the gross and net pay for a sample of employees and agree to the payroll to confirm accuracy.

- Re-calculate statutory deductions to confirm whether the correct deductions are included within the payroll expense.

- Perform a proof in total of total factory workforce wages by taking last year's expense, dividing by last year's average employee numbers to arrive at an average wage and multiplying by current year average employee numbers (the calculation should also incorporate the pay increase). Compare this estimate of the current year charge with the actual wages cost in the financial statements and investigate significant differences.

- Agree the start or leaving date to supporting documentation for a sample of joiners and leavers, and recalculate their first or last pay packet to ensure it was accurately calculated and properly recorded.

- Agree the total net salaries paid on the payroll records to the bank transfer listing of payments for sales and administrative staff, and to the cashbook for weekly paid employees.

- Agree the total cash withdrawn for wage payments equates to the weekly wages paid plus any left over cash subsequently banked to confirm completeness and accuracy.

- Agree individual wages and salaries per the payroll to the personnel records and records of hours worked per the swipe card system.

(**Note.** Only six procedures were needed to gain full marks.)

(c)   **Responsibilities – Laws and regulations**

It is Chuck Enterprises management that have a responsibility to ensure that the entity complies with the relevant laws and regulations. It is not the auditor's responsibility to prevent or detect non-compliance with laws and regulations.

The auditor's responsibility is to obtain reasonable assurance that the financial statements are free from material misstatement, and in this respect, the auditor must take into account the legal and regulatory framework within which the entity operates.

ISA 250 *Consideration of laws and regulations in an audit of financial statements* distinguishes the auditor's responsibilities in relation to compliance with two different categories of laws and regulations:

- Those that have a direct effect on the determination of material amounts and disclosures in the financial statements

- Those that do not have a direct effect on the determination of material amounts and disclosures in the financial statements but where compliance may be fundamental to the operating aspects, ability to continue in business, or to avoid material penalties. (ISA 250: para. 6)

For the first category, the auditor's responsibility is to obtain sufficient appropriate audit evidence about compliance with those laws and regulations. For the second category, the auditor's responsibility is to undertake specified audit procedures to help identify non-compliance with laws and regulations that may have a material effect on the financial statements. (ISA 250: para. 7)

Blair & Co must also maintain professional scepticism and be alert to the possibility that other audit procedures may bring instances of identified or suspected non-compliance with laws and regulations. (ISA 250: para. 8)

(d)   **Substantive procedures – Redundancy provision**

- Obtain an analysis of the redundancy calculations (cost by employee) and cast it to ensure completeness.

- Obtain written representation from management confirming the completeness of the provision.

- In order to establish that a present obligation exists at the year end, ask the directors whether they formally announced their intention to make the sales ledger department redundant during the year.

- If the redundancies have been announced pre-year end, review any documentation corroborating that the decision has in fact been formally announced.

- Review the board minutes to assess the probability the redundancy payments will be paid.

- Recalculate the redundancy provision to confirm completeness and agree components of the calculation to supporting documents.

- Confirm whether any redundancy payments have been made post year end and compare any amounts paid to amounts provided to assess the adequacy of the provision.

- Review the disclosure of the redundancy provision to ensure it complies with IAS 37 *Provisions, contingent liabilities and contingent assets.*

(**Note.** Only five procedures were needed to gain full marks.)

(e)   **Factors to consider – Reliance on work performed by internal audit**

The following important criteria will be considered by the external auditors when determining if the work of internal auditors is likely to be adequate.

Extent to which its objectivity is supported

The auditor must consider the extent to which the internal audit function's objectivity is supported by its organisational status, relevant policies and procedures. Considerations include to whom internal auditors' reports, any conflicting responsibilities, any constraints or restrictions, whether those charged with governance oversee employment decisions regarding internal auditors and whether management acts on recommendations made.

Level of technical competence

The auditor must consider whether internal auditors are members of relevant professional bodies, have adequate technical training and proficiency and whether there are established policies for hiring and training.

Whether a systematic and disciplined approach is taken

The auditor must also consider whether internal audit activities are systematically and properly planned, supervised, reviewed and documented; and whether suitable audit manuals, work programs and internal audit documentation exist. The auditor must also consider whether the function has appropriate quality control procedures in place.

107 Greystone

Text reference. Chapters 5, 9, 10, 16 and 19.

Top tips. Part (a) is a standalone requirement which asks for an explanation of matters to be considered when determining whether a deficiency is significant. So, assuming a deficiency has been identified, what would make it a significant one? Remember that a significant deficiency is one that the auditor judges to be of sufficient importance to merit the attention of those charged with governance (TCWG) – so even if you couldn't remember the factors listed in the ISA, you could have tried to think of what sort of factors will influence the need to report to TCWG and which might not.

In Part (b), you don't want miss out on the two marks for the presentation of your answer, so make sure you include a suitable covering letter with your report to management. As you look through a scenario such as this, you should be alive to any clue you are given that there is a deficiency in a particular area. For example, here there is a lot of potential for running out of inventory where you have a four week wait for orders to arrive. In the absence of a robust control, you should be able to pick up that the current ordering system is not up to the job and suggest viable improvements, such as setting minimum re-order levels.

Part (c) is a relatively straightforward requirement if you know your trade payables substantive procedures. Remember to focus on year end trade payable procedures and only include substantive procedures, not tests of controls.

For part (d) you may well be familiar with the sorts of assignments internal audit carry out. You should always bear the scenario in mind though and prioritise your suggestions according to how well they fit the scenario.

Easy marks. You should be very comfortable with substantive procedures over trade payables, making (c) relatively straightforward.

Examination Team's comments. Part (a) was unrelated to the Greystone Co scenario and hence tested candidates' knowledge as opposed to application skills. This question related to ISA 265 *Communicating deficiencies in internal control to those charged with governance and management*, and candidates performed inadequately on this part of the question. The main reason for this is that candidates failed to read the question properly or did not understand what the requirement entailed. The question asked for matters which would mean internal control deficiencies were significant enough to warrant reporting to those charged with governance. The question was not asking for examples of significant internal control deficiencies, however this is what a majority of candidates gave.

Part (b) was answered well by the vast majority of candidates with some scoring full marks. The scenario was quite detailed and hence there were many possible deficiencies which could gain credit. Where candidates did not score well this was mainly due to a failure to explain the deficiency and/or the implication in sufficient detail.

Many candidates failed to score the full 2 marks available for presentation as they did not produce a covering letter. A significant minority just gave the deficiencies, implications and recommendations without any letter at all; this may be due to a failure to read the question properly. Also even when a letter was produced this was often not completed.

The question asked for four deficiencies, implications and recommendations, however many candidates provided much more than the required four points. It was not uncommon to see answers which had six or seven points. Whilst it is understandable that candidates wish to ensure that they gain credit for four relevant points, this approach can lead to time pressure and subsequent questions can suffer.

Part (c) was answered satisfactorily for many candidates. The most common mistake made by some candidates was to confuse payables and purchases and hence provide substantive tests for purchases such as 'agree purchase invoices to goods received notes'. The requirement verb was to 'describe' therefore sufficient detail was required to score the 1 mark available per test. Candidates are reminded that substantive procedures is a core topic area and they must be able to produce relevant detailed procedures. Answers such as 'discuss with management to confirm ownership of payables' is far too vague to gain credit as there is no explanation of what would be discussed and also how such a discussion could even confirm ownership.

Part (d) required candidates to use their knowledge of internal audit assignments and apply it to a retailer scenario. On the whole candidates performed satisfactorily on this question. However some candidates restricted their answers to assignments the auditors would perform in light of the control deficiencies identified in part (b) of their answer. This meant that their answers lacked the sufficient breadth of points required to score well.

Marking scheme

Marks

(a) Up to 1 mark per valid point
Likelihood of deficiencies leading to errors
Risk of fraud
Subjectivity and complexity
Financial statement amounts
Volume of activity
Importance of the controls
Cause and frequency of exceptions
Interaction with other deficiencies   5

(b) Up to 1 mark per well explained deficiency, up to 1 mark per implication
and up to 1 mark per recommendation. If not well explained 0.5 marks
for each.
2 marks for presentation, 1 for address and intro, 1 for conclusion
Purchasing manager orders goods without consulting store
Purchase order reviewed in aggregate by purchasing director
Store managers re-order goods
No inter-branch transfer system
Deliveries accepted without proper checks
Sales assistants produce the goods received note
Goods received but not checked to purchase orders
Manual matching of goods received notes to invoice
Purchase invoice logged late   14

(c) Up to 1 mark per well explained substantive procedure
Agree purchase ledger to general and financial statements
Review payable to prior year
Calculate trade payables
After date payments review
After date invoices/credit notes review
Supplier statement reviews

Payables circularisation
Goods received not invoiced
Cut-off testing
Debit balances review
Disclosure within current liabilities

5

(d)   Up to 1 mark per well-explained point
Cash controls testing
Mystery shopper
Financial/operational controls
Fraud investigations
IT systems review
Value for money review
Regulatory compliance

6

30

(a)   ISA 265 includes examples of matters to consider when determining whether a deficiency in internal control is a significant deficiency. These include (ISA 265: para. A6):

- The likelihood of the deficiencies resulting in material misstatements in the financial statements in the future

- The importance of the controls to the financial reporting process

- The susceptibility to loss or fraud of the related asset or liability

- The interaction of the deficiency with other deficiencies in internal control

- The amounts exposed to the deficiencies

> **Top tips.** In (a) you could have included the following factors:
> - The cause and frequency of the exceptions identified as a result of the deficiencies
> - The volume of activity that has occurred or could occur
> - The subjectivity and complexity of determining estimated amounts
>
> However, only five were needed to pick up all of the available marks.

(b)

ABC & Co
Certified Accountants
29 High Street

The Board of Directors
Greystone Co
15 Low Street

8 December 20X0

Members of the board,

Financial statements for the year ended 30 September 20X0

We set out in this letter deficiencies in the purchases system which arose as a result of our review of the accounting systems and procedures operated by your company during our recent audit. The matters dealt with in this letter came to our notice during the conduct of our normal audit procedures which are designed primarily for the purpose of expressing our opinion on the financial statements.

Determination of inventory levels

(i)   *Deficiency*
        The purchasing manager determines store inventory levels without consulting those who are best place to judge the local market; the store or sales managers.

(ii) *Implication*
Certain clothes and accessories may be initially over-ordered and may need to be sold at reduced prices. This may also result in overvalued inventory (if held at cost) in the management accounts and ultimately the financial statements. Also some inventory may not be ordered in enough volume to meet demand and the reputation of Greystone may suffer.

(iii) *Recommendation*
The purchasing manager should consult (in a meeting or by conference call) the store managers and a joint decision should be made on the initial inventory levels to be ordered for clothes/accessories.

Re-ordering

(i) *Deficiency*
Store managers are responsible for re-ordering through the purchases manager and it can take four weeks for goods to be received.

(ii) *Implication*
The reliance is on Store managers to be proactive and order four weeks before a potential stock out. Without prompting they may order too late and inventory may run out for a period of up to four weeks, resulting in lost revenue.

(iii) *Recommendation*
Realistic re-order levels should be established in the inventory system. When inventory is down to the pre-determined level, the purchasing manager should be prompted to raise a purchase order (for example the system may generate an automatic re-order request which is emailed to the purchasing manager).

Internal ordering

(i) *Deficiency*
Stores can not transfer goods between each other to meet demand. Customers are directed to try other stores/the website when an item of clothing is sold out.

(ii) *Implication*
Revenue is lost because the system is inconvenient for the customer, who may not follow up at other stores, but may have purchased if the goods were transferred to their local store. Additionally the perceived lack of customer service may damage the store's reputation.

(iii) *Recommendation*
An internal ordering system should be set up which allows for the transfer of goods between stores. In particular, stores with very low inventory levels should be able to obtain excess inventories from those with high levels to meet demand while goods are re-ordered.

Checking of goods received

(i) *Deficiency*
Goods received are not checked against purchase orders.

(ii) *Implication*
Goods which were not ordered in the first place could be received. Once received, it may be difficult to return these goods and they may need to be paid for. In any case there is a potential unnecessary administrative cost. Additionally, some goods ordered may not be received leading to insufficient inventory levels and potential lost revenue.

(iii) *Recommendation*
A copy of authorised orders should be kept at the relevant store and checked against GRNs. If all details are correct, the order should be marked completed and sent to head office. The purchasing clerk should review the purchase orders at regular intervals for incomplete items and investigate why these are not completed.

This letter has been produced for the sole use of your company. It must not be disclosed to a third party, or quoted or referred to, without our written consent. No responsibility is assumed by us to any other person.

We should like to take this opportunity of thanking your staff for their co-operation and assistance during the course of our audit.

Yours faithfully

ABC & Co

Top tips. The answer to (b) includes four well explained deficiencies, implications and recommendations as four were needed to gain 12 marks. Together with the 2 marks available for presentation, this would be enough for the full 14 marks.

Please note however, there were a number of alternative deficiencies/implications/recommendations you may have identified, including those shown in the table below:

(i) Deficiency	(ii) Implication	(iii) Recommendation
The purchase orders reviewed and authorised by the purchasing director are aggregated by region.	The lack of detail does not allow the purchasing director to make an informed assessment of the buying policies and they may be unsuitable for specific markets within regions.	A country by country review of orders should be carried out by the purchasing director. Where appropriate, discussions should take place between the purchasing director and local purchasing managers before authorisation of orders.
Quality of goods is not checked by sales assistants, only quantity.	Poor quality clothes are accepted and may not be saleable (also inventory may be temporarily overvalued).	Goods should be checked on arrival for quantity and quality prior to acceptance.
Purchase invoices and GRNs are manually matched, which is time consuming.	The manual process of such a high volume of documents is prone to human error. Invalid invoices may be processed as a result.	A purchasing system should be adopted which allows for logging of GRNs against original invoices, and then electronic/automatic matching of invoices against GRNs. A regular review by the purchasing clerk should then be focused on unmatched items.
A purchase invoice is not put on the system until it is ready for authorisation by the purchasing director	The purchase ledger will not have all invoices posted, understating liabilities. Also payables may be paid late.	Invoices not matched should be filed separately, as should those not posted. These should be reviewed at period ends and accrued for to ensure completeness of payables.

(c) **Substantive procedures for year-end trade payables**

- Obtain a trade payables purchase ledger listing and agree the total to the general ledger and the figure for trade payables included in the financial statements.
- Compare the list of trade payables with the previous year's to identify any potentially significant omissions
- Compare the payables turnover and payables days to the previous year and industry data
- Reconcile a sample of payables balances with supplier statements and investigate differences which could indicate a significant misstatement.
- Review the cash book entries or the bank statements after the end of the year for payments which could indicate the existence of unrecorded trade payables.

(d) **Additional assignments for internal audit**

Testing of controls over cash

Retail stores have a significant amount of cash at each shop and need robust controls over the cash receipts process. Internal audit could test the design and operation of these controls at each store on a periodic basis. They could also conduct cash counts at the same time they carry out inventory counts.

Fraud investigations

A retailer such as Greystone with large sums of cash and desirable, easily moveable, inventory is more susceptible to fraud than many other businesses. Internal audit assignments may therefore include reviewing the fraud risk areas and suggesting controls to mitigate these risks. Where fraud is uncovered, internal audit could also investigate these instances of fraud.

Value for money review

Internal audit could undertake value for money audits examine the economy, efficiency and effectiveness of activities and systems, such as the just in time ordering system recently introduced.

Overall review of financial/operational controls

Internal audit could undertake reviews of central controls at head office, making recommendations to management over, for example the sales, purchases and payroll systems.

Review of information technology (IT) systems

Greystone may have complex computer systems linking tills in the stores to head office. If internal audit has an IT specialist, they could be asked to perform a review over the computer controls for this system or other computer systems.

Compliance with laws and regulations

Like all businesses, Greystone will be subject to law and regulation, which will vary depending on the part of the world a store is operating in. The internal audit department could review compliance with these laws and regulations.

108 Blake

Marking scheme

		Marks
(a)	Management letter – 1 mark for each deficiency, 1 for each possible effect and 1 for each recommendation = 3 marks × 4 sets of points = 12 marks	
	Logging in process not monitored	
	Overtime not authorised	
	Poor password control (cat's name)	
	Transfer total wages not checked	
	Employees leaving details sent on email	
	Other valid points	
	4 points × 3 marks each =	12
	Letter format	1
	Introduction and conclusion to letter	1
	Maximum marks	**14**
(b)	1 mark for each valid procedure and 1 for expectation of result of procedure = 2 marks for each procedure	
	Total salary cost	
	Average salary	
	List of payments each month	
	Other valid points	
	Maximum marks	**6**
	Total marks	**20**

(a) **Wages system management letter**

ABC & Co
Certified Accountants
29 High Street

The Board of Directors
Blake Co.
10 Low Street

December 20X8

Members of the board,

Deficiencies in internal control

We set out in this letter deficiencies in the wages system which arose as a result of our review of the accounting systems and procedures operated by your company during our recent audit. The matters dealt with in this letter came to our notice during the conduct of our normal audit procedures which are designed primarily for the purpose of expressing our opinion on the financial statements.

Deficiency	Consequence of deficiency	Recommendation
Shift workers can log in and out just by using their electronic identification cards.	Workers can be paid even if they are not working because the time recording system logs them in and out when their cards are scanned and they are paid from and to this time.	The shift manager should agree the number of workers with the computer records at the start and end of the shift.
Overtime is not authorised appropriately or monitored.	Workers could be paid at overtime rates when they are not actually working and could collude with the shift foreman for extra overtime without actually working it.	All requests for overtime must be authorised by the shift manager. Overtime costs should also be monitored regularly.
The code word for the time recording system is generally known within the department.	Unauthorised individuals could log onto the system and enter extra hours so that they are paid more than they should be. Fictitious employees could also be set up on the system.	The code word should be changed immediately to one containing random letters and numbers. The system should be set up so that the code word has to be changed on a regular basis, such as every six weeks.
Payments into workers' bank accounts are made by one member of accounts staff, without any authorisation.	Unauthorised payments into workers' and fictitious bank accounts could be made.	The payroll should be authorised by the Finance Director or another senior manager prior to payments being made.
Review of wages payments is done every few weeks by the financial accountant, seemingly on an ad hoc basis.	There is no regular monitoring of wages by senior management.	The Finance Director should review payroll costs on a weekly basis so that he can assess whether they are reasonable and any unusual amounts can be investigated.

This letter has been produced for the sole use of your company. It must not be disclosed to a third party, or quoted or referred to, without our written consent. No responsibility is assumed by us to any other person.

We should like to take this opportunity of thanking your staff for their co-operation and assistance during the course of our audit.

Yours faithfully

ABC & Co

(**Note.** Only four deficiencies, consequences and recommendations were required.)

Substantive analytical procedures

    (i)   Perform a proof in total of the salaries charge for the year using the prior year charge and increasing it for the pay increase and taking account of any starters or leavers in the period.

        The figures should be comparable with the exception of the salary increase and any starters or leavers in the year.

    (ii)   Perform a comparison of the annual charge to the prior year and to the budgeted figure. Where the variance is significant, investigate further to ascertain why.

        The figures should be comparable with the exception of the salary increase of 3%.

    (iii) Review monthly salaries month by month.

        The figures should be about the same each month, except for July and November when the pay rise and annual bonus were paid respectively. Any starters or leavers would also be reflected in the relevant month.

109 Tinkerbell

Text reference. Chapters 9, 10 and 14.

Top tips. Read the examination team's comments below carefully in relation to part (a). You must be able to differentiate between a test of control and a substantive procedure or you risk losing a high proportion of marks on some questions. A test of control must provide evidence that a control is operating effectively (or otherwise).

Parts (b) and (d) were relatively straightforward and you should have been able to come up with enough procedures to gain the majority of marks. You should use the scenario to help you to generate tests, for example identifying procedures in relation to the discounts offered to large customers.

Part (c) could be answered in a tabular format to help address both mini requirements – (1) identify and explain controls, (2) describe how the risk of fraud is mitigated. The description of the 'teeming and lading' fraud uncovered in the year pointed out the current lack of controls, so this could form the basis of your controls which should fill the gap. For example customer statements were not sent out and this is one of the reasons the fraud was not uncovered before, so making sure that they are sent out in the future is a valid control.

Easy marks. These are available in parts (b) and (d) where you are asked for substantive procedures in relation to receivables and revenue.

Examination Team's comments. In part (a) most candidates performed inadequately. The main problems encountered were that candidates struggled to differentiate between tests of control and substantive tests and hence often provided long lists of substantive procedures, which scored no marks. In addition a significant minority of candidates did not read the question carefully, and instead of providing tests of controls, gave control procedures management should adopt. The approach candidates should have taken was to firstly identify from the scenario the controls present for Tinkerbell, they then should have considered how these controls could be confirmed by the auditor. In addition candidates' explanations of tests were vague such as; 'check that credit limits are set for all new customers.' This procedure does not explain how the auditor would actually confirm that the control for new customer credit limits operates effectively. Tests that start with 'check' are unlikely to score many marks as they do not explain how the auditor would actually check the control. Future candidates should practice generating tests; both substantive and tests of controls, which do not start with the word 'check'.

The second part of this requirement was to explain the objective of the test of control provided. Again, this was not answered well. A common answer was to state that the objective was 'to ensure that the control is operating effectively.' This was far too vague. Instead, candidates should have considered the aim of the specific control being tested. Therefore the objective of a test over credit limits is 'to ensure that orders are not accepted for poor credit risks'.

As noted in previous examiner's reports candidates are often confused with the differences between tests of controls and substantive tests. Candidates must ensure that they understand when tests of controls are required and when substantive procedures are needed. They need to learn the difference between them and should practice questions requiring the generation of both types of procedures. A significant number of candidates presented their answers in a columnar format and this seemed to help them to produce concise and relevant answers.

Part (b) for 8 marks required substantive procedures the auditor should perform on year-end receivables. This was answered well by many candidates. Candidates were able to provide variety in their procedures including both tests of detail and analytical review tests.

The most common mistakes made by some candidates were providing tests of control rather than substantive procedures, providing substantive procedures for revenue rather than receivables, not generating enough tests for 8 marks and describing the process for a receivables circularisation at length (this was not part of the question requirement.)

Part (c) for 6 marks required identification and explanation of controls that Tinkerbell should adopt to reduce the risk of fraud occurring again, as well as an explanation of how this control would mitigate the fraud risk. This question was answered well by most candidates, with some scoring full marks.

The scenario provided details of a 'teeming and lading fraud' which had occurred during the year and candidates needed to think practically about how Tinkerbell could reduce the risk of this occurring again. However, candidates' performance on the second requirement to describe how the control would mitigate the risk of fraud occurring again was mixed.

The main problem was that answers were not specific enough, frequently vague answers such as 'this will reduce the risk of fraud and error occurring' were given.

Part (d) for 4 marks required substantive procedures the auditor should perform on Tinkerbell's revenue. This requirement was not answered well. Some candidates confused this requirement with that of 1b, which required receivables tests, and so provided the same tests from 1b again. In addition a significant number of candidates provided procedures to confirm bank and cash rather than revenue.

Those candidates who performed well were able to provide a good mixture of analytical procedures such as, 'compare revenue to prior year or to budget' and 'review monthly sales against prior year' and also detailed tests such as confirming cut-off of sales.

Marking scheme

Marks

(a) Up to 1 mark per well explained point and up to 1 mark for each objective
Process order for fictitious order
Sales order over credit limit
Inspect credit applications
Agree prices used to relevant price list
Confirm discounts used on invoices agree to customer master file
Attempt to process a discount for a small customer
Inspect orders to confirm order acceptance generated
Observe sales order clerk processing orders to see if acceptance generated
Observe goods despatch process
Agree goods despatch notes (GDN) to invoices
Sequence checks over invoices   12

(b) Up to 1 mark per well explained procedure
Trade receivables circularisation, follow up any non-replies
Review the after date cash receipts
Calculate average receivable days
Reconciliation of sales ledger control account
Cut-off testing of GDN

Aged receivables report to identify any slow moving balances

Review customer correspondence to assess whether there are any invoices in dispute

Review board minutes

Review post year-end credit notes

Review for any credit balances

Agree to GDN and sales order to ensure existence

8

(c) Up to 1 mark per well explained control and up to 1 mark for how it mitigates risk

Relatives not permitted to work in the same department

Cash receipts processed by two members of staff

Monthly customer statements sent

Bank reconciliations reviewed by responsible official

Rotation of duties within finance department

Sales ledger control account reconciliation regularly performed

Consider establishing an internal audit department

6

(d) Up to 1 mark per well explained procedure

Analytical review over revenue compared to budget and prior year

Analytical review of major categories of toy sales compared to prior year

Gross margin review

Recalculate discounts allowed for larger customers

Recalculate sales tax

Follow order to goods despatched note to sales invoice to sales ledger

Sales cut-off

Review post year-end credit notes

$\underline{4}$

$\underline{30}$

(a) **Tinkerbell – Tests of control and test objectives for the sales cycle**

Test of control	Test objective
Enter an order for a fictitious customer account number and ensure the system does not accept it.	To ensure that orders are only accepted and processed for valid customers.
Inspect a sample of processed credit applications from the credit agency and ensure the same credit limit appears in the sales system.	To ensure that goods are only supplied to customers with acceptable credit ratings.
For a sample of invoices, agree that current prices have been used by comparing them with prices shown on the current price list.	To ensure that goods are only sold at authorised prices.
For a sample of invoices showing discounts, agree the discount terms back to the customer master file information.	To ensure that sales discounts are only provided to those customers the sales director has authorised.
For a sample of orders ensure that an order acceptance email or letter was generated.	To ensure that all orders are recorded completely and accurately.
Visit a warehouse and observe whether all goods are double checked against the GDN and despatch list before sending out.	To ensure that goods are despatched correctly to customers and are of an adequate quality.

Top tips: Six tests of controls and six objectives such as those shown above were enough to gain the 12 marks available. However other valid tests and objectives you may have come with are shown below.

Test of control	Test objective
With the client's permission, attempt to enter a sales order which will take a customer over the agreed credit limit and ensure the order is rejected as expected.	To ensure that goods are not supplied to poor credit risks.
Attempt to process an order with a sales discount for a customer not normally entitled to discounts to assess the application controls.	To ensure that sales discounts are only provided to valid customers.
Observe the sales order clerk processing orders and look for proof that the order acceptance is automatically generated (eg email in sent folder)	To ensure that all orders are recorded completely and accurately.
Inspect a sample of GDNs and agree that a valid sales invoice has been correctly raised.	To ensure that all goods despatched are correctly invoiced.
Review the latest report from the computer sequence check of sales invoices for omissions and establish the action taken in respect of any omissions found.	To ensure completeness of income for goods despatched.

(b) **Substantive procedures to confirm Tinkerbell's year-end receivables balance**

- Circularise trade receivables for a representative sample of the year-end balances. If authorised by Tinkerbell's management, send an e-mail or reminder letter to follow up non-responses.

- Review cash receipts after the year-end in respect of pre year-end receivable balances to establish if anything is still outstanding. Where amounts are unpaid investigate whether an allowance is needed.

- Review the reconciliation of the receivables ledger control account (sales ledger control account) to the list of receivables (sales ledger) balances and investigate unusual reconciling items.

- Review the aged receivables report to identify any old balances and discuss the probability of recovery with the credit controller to assess the need for an allowance.

- Calculate average receivable days and compare this to prior year and expectations, investigating any significant differences.

- Select a sample of goods despatched notes just before and just after the year end to ensure the related invoices are recorded in the correct accounting period.

- Review a sample of credit notes raised after the year end to identify any that relate to pre year-end transactions and confirm that they have not been included in receivables.

- Review the aged receivables ledger for any credit balances and inquire of management whether these should be reclassified as payables.

> **Top tips**: Eight substantive procedures like the ones shown above were enough to gain the 8 marks available. However other valid procedures you may have come with are shown below.

- For slow moving/aged balances, review customer correspondence files to assess whether there are any invoices in dispute which require an allowance.

- Review board minutes to assess whether there are any material disputed receivables.

- Select a sample of year-end receivable balances and agree back to a valid GDN and sales order to ensure existence.

(c) **Controls to reduce the risk of fraud reoccurring and explanation of how the risk is mitigated**

Control	Explanation of how risk is mitigated by control
Related members of staff should not be allowed to work in the same department where they can seek to override segregation of duty controls.	The risk of related staff colluding and being able to commit a fraud without easily being discovered will be reduced.
Customer statements should be sent out each month to all customers. The receivables ledger supervisor should check that all customers have been sent statements.	Customers receiving statements may notice anomalies in the allocation of payments (either timing or amount) and may alert the company of these anomalies. This may draw attention to the sort of fraud that occurred at Tinkerbell (known as 'teeming and lading').
Bank reconciliations should be reviewed regularly by an appropriate level of management who is not involved in its preparation. Unreconciled amounts should be investigated and resolved at the time of review.	Any compensating material balances netted off to a small difference on the bank reconciliation will be discovered quickly, increasing the probability of uncovering fraud on a timely basis.

Top tips: Three controls such as those shown above along with three explanations were enough to gain the 6 marks available. However other valid controls and explanations are given below.

Control	Explanation of how risk is mitigated by control
Two members of staff should process cash receipts	This would mean another collusion would be necessary (on top of the one that has already occurred) to steal cash receipts. This therefore reduces the risk of re-occurrence.
Staff within the finance department should rotate duties on a regular basis.	Rotation will act as a deterrent to fraud. This is because staff will be less likely to commit fraudulent activities due to an increased risk of the next person to be rotated to their position uncovering any wrongdoing.
The receivables ledger should be reconciled to the receivables ledger control account on at least a monthly basis. The reconciliation should be reviewed by a responsible official and anomalies investigated.	This will increase the chance of discovering errors in the receivable balances and help to create a strong control environment likely to deter fraud.
Management should consider establishing an internal audit department to assess and monitor the effectiveness of controls, identify any deficiencies, and carry out specific fraud investigations.	The presence of an internal audit department would help to deter employees committing fraud and identification of fraud would be more likely due to ongoing monitoring of internal controls.

(d) **Substantive procedures to confirm Tinkerbell's revenue**

- Compare the total revenue with that reported in previous years and the revenue budgeted, and investigate any significant fluctuations.

- For a sample of customer orders, trace the details to the related despatch notes and sales invoices and ensure there is a sale recorded in respect of each (to test the completeness of revenue).

- For a sample of sales invoices for larger customers, recalculate the discounts allowed to ensure that these are accurate.

- Select a sample of despatch notes in the month immediately before and month immediately after the year end. Trace these through to the related sales invoices and resultant accounting entries to ensure each sale was recorded in the appropriate period.

> **Top tips**: Four procedures such as those shown above would have been sufficient to gain full marks on this part of the question. However other procedures are given below.

- Obtain an analysis of sales by major categories of toys manufactured and compare this to the prior year breakdown and discuss any unusual movements with management.

- Calculate the gross profit margin for Tinkerbell for the year and compare this to the previous year and expectations. Investigate any significant fluctuations.

- Recalculate the sales tax for a sample of invoices and ensure that the sales tax has been correctly applied to the sales invoice.

- Select a sample of credit notes issued after the year end and trace these through to the related sales invoices to ensure sales returns were recorded in the proper period.

110 Trombone

Text references. Chapters 7, 9 and 10.

Top tips. Part (a) asks you to identify deficiencies in the control system for payroll, to recommend improvements and to describe a relevant test of control. Make sure that your answer addresses all three requirements. A tabular format is a particularly useful way of presenting your answer.

Part (c) tests you knowledge of the difference between an interim audit and a final audit. You should find this relatively straightforward.

Easy marks. Easy marks can be found in part (b).

Examination Team's comments. The first two parts of part (a) were answered satisfactorily by candidates, however the tests of controls proved challenging for many.

The requirement for tests of controls was answered unsatisfactorily. Many candidates are still confusing substantive procedures and test of controls. A significant number of candidates suggested substantive procedures such as 'recalculating gross and net pay calculations', rather than a test of control which might be to 'review evidence of the recalculation of payroll'. Candidates need to review their understanding of these different types of audit procedures and ensure that they appreciate that substantive tests focus on the number within the financial statements whereas test of controls are verifying if client procedures are operating.

In many instances candidates focused on re-performing the control rather than testing it had operated. Observation of a control was commonly suggested by candidates, however in many cases this is not an effective way of testing that a control has operated throughout the year. Part (c) was answered very poorly by a significant number of candidates, demonstrating a worrying lack of knowledge about substantive procedures and tests of controls. This is an important area which needs to be addressed.

Part (b) was generally answered well by candidates. A minority of candidates incorrectly suggested that planning procedures would be undertaken at the interim audit and that they were undertaken by internal auditors. Also a significant minority confused this requirement with a comparison of internal and external audit roles. Candidates must remember to read the question carefully and think and plan before writing to ensure that they answer the question asked.

Marks

(a) **Internal control deficiencies, recommendations and tests of control**

Up to 1 mark per well explained deficiency, up to 1 mark for each well explained recommendation and up to 1 mark for each well described test of control.

Overall maximum of 5 marks each for deficiencies, controls and tests of control.

Payroll calculations not checked

Payroll clerks update standing data for wages increases

Authorisation of overtime sheets only undertaken if overtime exceeds 30% of standard hours

Time off as payment for overtime not checked to overtime worked report

Review of overtime worked reports by department heads

Authorisation of overtime sheets when department heads on annual leave

Finance director only reviews totals of payroll records and payments list

Maximum marks 15

(b) **Final audit and interim audit**

Up to 1 mark per well explained point, maximum of 3 marks each for interim and final audit, overall maximum of 5 marks.

Interim audit

Final audit 5

(c) Up to 1 mark per well described substantive procedure.

Agree wages and salaries per payroll to trial balance

Cast payroll records

Recalculate gross and net pay

Recalculate statutory deductions

Compare total payroll to prior year

Review monthly payroll to prior year and budget

Proof in total of payroll and agree to the financial statements

Verify joiners/leavers and recalculate first/last pay

Agree wages and salaries paid per payroll to bank transfer list and cashbook

Agree the individual wages and salaries as per the payroll to the personnel records

Agree sample of weekly overtime sheets to overtime payment in payroll records 6

(d) Up to 1 mark per well described procedure.

Agree to the payroll records to confirm the accuracy of the accrual

Re-perform the calculation of the accrual

Agree the subsequent payment to the post year-end cash book and bank statements

Review any correspondence with tax authorities to assess whether there are any additional outstanding payments due, if so, agree they are included in the year end accrual

Review disclosures and assess whether these are adequate and in compliance 4

Maximum marks 30

(a)

Deficiencies	Recommended controls	Test of control
The gross and net pay automatically calculated by the payroll package are not checked at all. The lack of checking increases the risk that errors being accumulated without being detected. This could lead to wages being over- or understated. Additional wages may be paid as a result. Statutory deductions may be over- or under-paid, giving rise to compliance issues. There is also likely to be a loss of employee goodwill.	A senior member of the payroll department should reperform a sample of the gross and net pay calculations. Any discrepancies should be investigated. The automatic gross and net pay calculations must be reviewed and approved before payments are made.	Obtain the recalculations performed by the senior payroll reviewer for evidence that the automatic calculations have been reviewed. Review a sample of the gross and net pay calculations generated by the payroll system for evidence that they have been approved and signed off.
The clerks update the standing data to reflect the increase of wages each year. The apparent lack of authorisation to changes in standing data increases the risk of errors, leading to the over- or understatement of wages, and the incorrect payment of wages. This also increases the risk of fraud, as the clerks have the ability to make unauthorised changes to standing data.	Payroll clerks should not be allowed to make standing data changes. Changes to the standing data to reflect the annual wage increase should be made by a senior member of the payroll department. These changes should be checked by another responsible official to identify any errors or inconsistencies.	Observe a payroll clerk attempting to make changes to payroll standing data, to determine whether the system rejects the changes. Review the log of changes made to the standing data for evidence that they were made by a senior member of the payroll department. Review the log of changes made to the standing data for evidence that they have been reviewed by another responsible official.
Only payment for overtime in excess of 30% of the standard hours are authorised by department heads. This increases the risk of employees claiming for overtime not worked, leading to additional payroll costs.	All overtime hours worked, whether in lieu of pay or holidays, must be authorised by the relevant department head. The authorisation should be evidenced by signatures.	Review a sample of the weekly overtime sheets for evidence of signature by the head of the department concerned.
The payroll clerks do not always check the overtime worked report before employees take time off in lieu of overtime worked. This increases the risk of employees taking unauthorised leave, leading, again, to wages being paid for days which have not been worked.	Payroll clerks must agree holidays taken in lieu to the overtime report, and record that this has been done. Where inconsistencies are identified, the payroll clerks should notify the relevant department head.	Review a sample of holidays taken in lieu of overtime to verify whether the payroll clerk has agreed the time taken in lieu to the overtime report.

Deficiencies	Recommended controls	Test of control
The overtime worked report is emailed by the payroll department to department heads, who report only by exception if errors are identified. *The authorisation of overtime sheets by an alternative responsible official while the department heads are on leave does not always occur.* The fact that the department heads only report by exception can cause the payroll department to mistakenly assume that the overtime report is correct when it is not – leading to the payment of incorrect overtime. The lack of holiday cover for the authorisation of overtime can lead to overtime pay being delayed, resulting in the loss of employee goodwill.	Departments should be required to respond to the payroll department regarding each overtime worked report, regardless of whether it is correct. The department heads should be reminded of the procedures with regards to holiday cover. No payment should be made until the report has been authorised by the relevant official. The payroll department should monitor the authorisation of the overtime worked report and follow up with each relevant head where no response has been received.	For a sample of overtime worked reports, inspect the responses received from each department head. For a sample of overtime payments, compare the dates on which authorisation has been received with the dates on which overtime payment is made, to confirm that payment is only made after authorisation has been obtained. Make enquiries of payroll clerks regarding the process of obtaining authorisation for overtime sheets while the department heads are on leave.
The finance director reviews the total list of bank transfers and compares this to the total payable per the payroll records. This process does not prevent employees to be omitted from the payroll. There is equally a risk of fictitious employees, or employees who have left the company, appearing on payroll. As a result, fraudulent payments could be made.	The finance director should agree a sample of the employees on the payroll records to the payment list, and vice versa, to ensure that payments are complete, and made only to bona fide employees. These checks should be evidenced by the finance director's signature.	Inspect payments lists for evidence that the finance director has agreed a sample of payees to the payroll records, and vice versa.

(b)   The differences between an interim and a final audit can be summarised as follows:

	When it occurs	Purpose	Procedures performed
Interim audit	During the period of review	To carry out procedures that would be difficult to perform at the year-end because of time constraints. No statutory requirement to perform interim audit.	• Inherent risk assessment and gaining an understanding of the entity • Documenting and evaluating the entity's system of internal control • Carrying out tests of control on the company's internal controls to ensure they are operating as expected • Performing substantive testing of profit or loss transactions/balances to gain evidence that the books and records are a reliable basis for the preparation of financial statements • Identification of issues that may have an impact on work to take place at the final audit

Final audit	After the year end	To express an audit opinion on the financial statements covering the entire period being audited. The performance of the final audit is a statutory requirement.	Substantive procedures involving verification of statement of financial position balances and amounts in the statement of profit or loss • Obtaining third party confirmations • Analytical procedures relating to figures in the financial statements • Subsequent events review • Agreeing the financial statements to the accounting records • Examining adjustments made during the process of preparing the financial statements • Consideration of the going concern status of the entity • Performing tests to ensure that the conclusions formed at the interim audit are still valid • Obtaining written representations

(c) **Payroll substantive procedures**

- Agree the total wages and salaries expense per the payroll system to the trial balance, investigate any differences.

- Cast a sample of payroll records to confirm completeness and accuracy of the payroll expense.

- For a sample of employees, recalculate the gross and net pay and agree to the payroll records to confirm accuracy.

- Re-perform the calculation of statutory deductions to confirm whether correct deductions for this year have been made in the payroll.

- Compare the total payroll expense to the prior year and investigate any significant differences.

- Review monthly payroll charges, compare this to the prior year and budgets and discuss with management for any significant variances.

- Perform a proof in total of total wages and salaries, incorporating joiners and leavers and the annual pay increase. Compare this to the actual wages and salaries in the financial statements and investigate any significant differences.

- Select a sample of joiners and leavers, agree their start/leaving date to supporting documentation, recalculate that their first/last pay packet was accurately calculated and recorded.

- Agree the total net pay per the payroll records to the bank transfer listing of payments and to the cashbook.

- Agree the individual wages and salaries per the payroll to the personnel records for a sample.

- Select a sample of weekly overtime sheets and trace to overtime payment in payroll records to confirm completeness of overtime paid.

(d) **Accrual for income tax payable on employment income**

Procedures the auditor should adopt in respect of auditing this accrual include:

- Agree the year-end income tax payable accrual to the payroll records to confirm accuracy.

- Re-perform the calculation of the accrual to confirm accuracy.

- Agree the subsequent payment to the post year-end cash book and bank statements to confirm completeness.

- Review any correspondence with tax authorities to assess whether there are any additional outstanding payments due; if so, agree they are included in the year-end accrual.

- Review any disclosures made of the income tax accrual and assess whether these are in compliance with accounting standards and legislation.

111 Fox Industries Co

Text reference. ISA 260 is covered in Chapter 3. Controls over the purchasing system are discussed in Chapter 10. Reports to management are covered in Chapter 19. Application controls can be found in Chapter 9. Substantive audit procedures relating to bank and cash are set out in Chapter 15.

Top tips. The requirements for this question are typical for question 16 of the F8 paper, with the scenario being about control deficiencies within a particular system. There is a lot to do in this question, so there is a risk of over-running on the time. Make sure you stick to time for each part of the question and move on to the next requirement once the time is up.

Part (b) should be presented in a tabular format for the deficiencies, impacts and recommendations but do note the requirement for a covering letter – this is relatively unusual for this type of question. Note also that there are two presentation marks available, so make sure your covering letter is addressed and dated appropriately and that you use a ruler for the table and headings. These two marks could be the difference between passing and failing. You must ensure that you identify deficiencies from both the purchases system and the payments system – go through the scenario line-by-line and make notes on areas where there are weaknesses. Your recommendations need to be sufficiently detailed and useful to the organisation. Imagine that you are drafting a real report to management to a real client. Saying things like 'Discuss with management' or 'Reconciliations' will not score many marks.

Part (c) is on application controls. This is a notorious area of weakness for F8 students. Make sure you know the difference between application and general IT controls and that the controls you describe are relevant to the scenario in the question.

Easy marks. Part (a) on ISA 260 is knowledge-based for five marks and relatively straightforward. Part (d) asks for substantive procedures for bank and cash. This is worth seven marks and provided your procedures are adequately detailed, you should be able to score well here.

			Marks
(a)	(i)	Up to 1 mark per well explained point	
		• Assists the auditor and those charged with governance in understanding matters related to the audit	
		• Obtains information relevant to the audit	
		• Helps those charged with governance in fulfilling their responsibility to oversee the financial reporting process	2
	(ii)	Up to 1 mark for each example matter to be communicated to those charged with governance	3
(b)		Up to 1 mark per well explained deficiency, implication and recommendation. If not well explained then just give ½ mark for each. Overall maximum of 4 marks each for deficiencies, implications and recommendations. 2 marks for presentation: 1 for address and intro and 1 for conclusion.	
		• No approved suppliers list	
		• Purchase orders not sequentially numbered	
		• Orders below $5,000 are not authorised by a responsible official	
		• No application controls over input of purchase invoices	
		• Purchase ledger manually posted to general ledger	
		• Saving (deposit) bank accounts only reconciled every two months	

- Payments to suppliers delayed
- Finance director only reviews the total of the payment list prior to payment authorising   14

(c)   Up to 1 mark per well explained application control

- Document counts
- Control totals
- One for one checking
- Review of output to expected value
- Check digits
- Range checks
- Existence checks   4

(d)   Up to 1 mark per substantive procedure

- Check additions of bank reconciliation
- Obtain bank confirmation letter
- Bank balance to statement/bank confirmation
- Cash book balance to cash book
- Outstanding lodgements
- Unpresented cheques review
- Old cheques write back
- Agree all balances on bank confirmation
- Unusual items/window dressing
- Security/legal right set-off
- Review reconciliations for saving (deposit) accounts
- Cash counts for significant cash balances
- Review disclosure of bank and cash in financial statements $\frac{7}{30}$

(a)   **ISA 260 requirements**

(i)   It is important that auditors communicate throughout the audit with those charged with governance for the following reasons (ISA 260: para. 4):

- It assists the auditor and those charged with governance to understand audit-related matters in context and allows them to develop a constructive working relationship.

- It allows the auditor to obtain information relevant to the audit.

- It assists those charged with governance to fulfil their responsibility to oversee the financial reporting process, thus reducing the risks of material misstatement in the financial statements.

(ii)   Examples of matters that the auditors may communicate with those charged with governance ISA 260: paras. 14–17):

- The auditor's responsibilities in relation to the audit of the financial statements, including that the auditor is responsible for forming and expressing an opinion on the financial statements and that the audit does not relieve management or those charged with governance of their responsibilities

- The planned scope and timing of the audit

- Significant deficiencies in internal control

- The auditor's views about significant qualitative aspects of the entity's accounting practices, including accounting policies, accounting estimates and financial statement disclosures

- Significant difficulties encountered during the audit

- Significant matters arising from the audit that were discussed or subject to correspondence with management

- Written representations requested by the auditor

- Other matters that, in the auditor's professional judgement, are significant to the oversight of the financial reporting process

- For listed entities, a statement that the engagement team and others in the firm, the firm, and network firms have complied with relevant ethical requirements regarding independence, any relationships between the firm and entity that might affect independence, and safeguards applied to eliminate identified threats to independence or reduce them to an acceptable level

(Note. Only three matters were required.)

(b)   **Purchasing and payments system**

ABC Auditors
Any Street
Any Town
AB1 2YZ
1 June 20X3

Board of Directors
Fox Industries Ltd
Trading Estate
Any Town
AB1 3DE

To the Board of Directors, Fox Industries Ltd,

Financial statements for the year ended 30 April 20X3

Please find enclosed in an Appendix to this letter the report to management detailing deficiencies in internal control found within the purchases and payments system during our recent external audit. This details only the significant deficiencies identified during our audit. If more extensive procedures on internal control had been carried out, we might have identified and reported more deficiencies.

This report to management is solely for the use of Fox Industries Co. It must not be disclosed to a third party, or quoted or referred to, without our consent. No responsibility is assumed by us to any other person.

Yours faithfully,

ABC Auditors

Appendix

Deficiency	Implication	Recommendation
Purchase orders are not reviewed by a second person before the order is sent out unless the amount is greater than $5,000.	Orders can be made for unauthorised goods up to a value of $5,000.	All orders should be reviewed before the order is placed and signed off and dated as authorised by a more senior team member. Delegated levels of authority should be in place.
The purchase order clerk chooses the supplier based on the supplier who can deliver the goods fastest.	Goods of poor quality could be ordered or a higher price may be paid for goods from particular suppliers.	An approved suppliers list should be in place so that the company knows exactly who the supplier is and how much the goods cost.
Purchase orders are not sequentially numbered.	Purchase orders can be lost and there is no way of keeping track of unfulfilled orders.	Purchase orders should be sequentially numbered and multi-part. Order forms should be filed in sequential order and reviewed on a weekly basis to flag any unfulfilled orders for chasing up.

Deficiency	Implication	Recommendation
Purchase invoices are not matched back to the purchase order before being input onto the system.	Invoices for incorrect amounts and incorrect goods may be entered onto the system and paid for.	Purchase invoices should be matched back to the purchase order to ensure they tally up before being input onto the system. A copy of the order should be attached to the invoice and filed away.
The purchase ledger clerk does not use any application controls over the input of purchase invoices to the ledger.	The lack of application controls increases the risk of errors being made during the input of invoices to the ledger. This could result in misstatements in the financial statements and also errors in amounts paid to suppliers and a consequent loss of goodwill.	There should be some application controls in place over the input of invoices to the system, such as control totals and document totals.
The purchase ledger clerk posts the purchase ledger to the general ledger manually.	Errors may be made during the posting process as it is done manually.	The system should be set up so that the purchase ledger is posted automatically to the general ledger. A reconciliation between the two should be performed each week by the purchase ledger clerk and this should be signed off and dated as reviewed by the finance director.
Deposit accounts are not reconciled on a timely basis, only every two months.	Unreconciled differences may go unnoticed for a long period of time. The length of time between reconciliations may also increase the risk of fraud being perpetrated by employees.	Deposit accounts should be reconciled at the same time as the current account. All reconciliations should be signed off and dated to evidence review by a more senior person, with all differences fully investigated and resolved on a timely basis.
Payment to suppliers is delayed for as long as possible.	Prompt payment discounts are not taken advantage of and suppliers may not look favourably on the company if it takes too long to pay and therefore may refuse credit later on, if the company is viewed as unreliable.	Suppliers should be paid as soon as possible to take advantage of early settlement discounts and to promote and maintain good relations with suppliers.
The finance director authorises the total amount of the payment list, without a review of the detail.	Unauthorised amounts may be missed as the finance director does not see the detail of the payments on the list. This opens the company up to the risk of fraud and error.	The finance director should review the detailed list of payments and query any amounts and supplier names that appear erroneous or suspicious. The review should be evidenced by the finance director's signature and date.

(Note. Only four deficiencies were required.)

(c) **Application controls**

Daily reconciliation between purchase ledger and general ledger by the purchase ledger clerk, which should be reviewed and signed and dated as reviewed by the finance director

Control totals agreeing the amount per purchase day book, purchase ledger and general ledger totals

Agreement of amounts on purchase invoices back to the purchase orders

Document counts of the number of invoices entered onto the system

One-for-one checking of output from the system against the original invoices to ensure completeness and accuracy of input

Programmes to check data fields which could include digit verification on reference numbers, reasonableness checks, existence checks on supplier names, character checks in reference numbers

(Note. Only four application controls were required.)

(d)   **Substantive procedures on bank and cash balances**

- Send out a standard bank confirmation letter to each bank where the company holds bank accounts to confirm the year-end balance.

- Review the year-end reconciliation of the bank balance per the general ledger against the bank balance per the bank letter.

- Reperform the arithmetic of the bank reconciliation for each bank account held.

- Trace cheques shown as outstanding from the bank reconciliation to the cash book prior to the year-end and to the after-date bank statements and obtain explanations for any large or unusual items not cleared at the time of the audit.

- Compare cash book(s) and bank statements in detail for the last month of the year, and match items outstanding at the reconciliation date to bank statements.

- Review the bank reconciliation previous to the year-end bank reconciliation and test whether all items are cleared in the last period or taken forward to the year-end bank reconciliation.

- Obtain satisfactory explanations for all items in the cash book for which there are no corresponding entries in the bank statement and vice versa by discussion with finance staff.

- Verify contra items appearing in the cash books or bank statements with original entry.

- Verify by inspecting paying-in slips that uncleared bankings are paid in prior to the year-end.

- Examine all lodgements in respect of which payment has been refused by the bank; ensure that they are cleared on representation or that other appropriate steps have been taken to effect recovery of the amount due.

- Verify balances per the cash book according to the bank reconciliation by inspecting cash book, bank statements and general ledger.

- Verify the bank balances with the reply to standard bank letter and with the bank statements.

- Inspect the cash book and bank statements before and after the year-end for exceptional entries or transfers which have a material effect on the balance shown to be in-hand.

- Identify whether any accounts are secured on the assets of the company by discussion with management.

- Consider whether there is a legal right of set-off of overdrafts against positive bank balances.

- Determine whether the bank accounts are subject to any restrictions by inquiries with management.

- Count year-end cash balances and match to cash records such as the petty cash book.

- Obtain certificates of cash in hand from responsible officers.

- Review draft financial statements to confirm that all amounts and relevant disclosures relating to cash and bank have been correctly stated.

(Note. Assuming there is one mark per audit procedure, you would need to have seven well-explained audit procedures in your answer to score the full seven marks available.)

112 Bluesberry

Marking scheme

		Marks
(a)	Up to 1 mark per valid point	
	Explanation of value for money audit	
	Economy – description	
	Efficiency – description	
	Effectiveness – description	4
(b)	0.5 marks for identification and up to 1 mark for explanation of each well explained strength and up to 1 mark per improvement. If not well explained 0.5 marks for each, but overall maximum of 4 points.	
	Internal audit department	
	Centralised buying department buys from lowest cost supplier	
	Authorisation of all purchase orders by purchasing director	
	Reduction in use of temporary staff	
	Employee clocking in cards to monitor hours worked	
	New surgical equipment leading to better recovery rates	
	Capital expenditure committee	10

(c)   Up to 1 mark per substantive procedure
       Valuation (i)
       Review depreciation policies for reasonableness
       Recalculate the depreciation charge
       Proof in total calculation of depreciation
       For revalued assets, consider reasonableness of valuer
       For revalued assets, agree the revalued amounts to valuation report
       Surgical equipment additions - vouch the cost to invoice   2

       Completeness (ii)
       Reconcile PPE schedule to general ledger
       Physical inspection of assets
       Reconciliation of non-current asset register to the general ledger
       Review the repairs and maintenance expense account   2

       Rights and obligations (iii)
       Verify ownership of property via inspection of title deeds
       Additions agree to purchase invoices to verify invoice relates to entity
       Review any new lease agreements
       Inspect vehicle registration documents   2
       Total for (c)   6
                                                                                          20

(a)   **Purpose of a value for money (VFM) audit**

       VFM focuses on the best combination of services for the lowest level of resources. The purpose of a VFM
       audit is to examine the **economy**, **efficiency** and **effectiveness** of the activity or process in question.

       •   **Economy**: Attaining the appropriate quantity and quality of physical, human and financial resources
            (inputs) at lowest cost.
       •   **Efficiency**: The relationship between goods or services produced (outputs) and the resources used to
            produce them.
       •   **Effectiveness**: Concerned with how well an activity is achieving its policy objectives or other intended
            effects.

(b)

Strength (i)	Improvement (ii)
The buying department researches the lowest price from suppliers before raising a purchase order. This helps with economy of the process, attaining resources at the lowest cost.	In order to also ensure the goods are of the required quality, an approved list of suppliers could be built up, with purchases only being permitted from those suppliers on the list.
Overtime rates have been increased and this has incentivised staff to fill staffing gaps. As a result the hospital has saved money by decreasing the level of expensive temporary staff. Additionally, the permanent staff may be more effective as they are familiar with the hospitals systems and the level of patient care expected at Bluesberry.	The increased hours will affect overall efficiency given that the same staff are now carrying out extended shifts, as overtime rates are higher than basic rates, even though overtime cost appears to be lower than temporary staff. There is also an increased risk of mistakes due to tiredness which could have adverse effects on the reputation of the hospital. Ideally the hospital should recruit enough permanent staff of the required level to fill shifts without then working overtime.

Strength (i)	Improvement (ii)
The hospital has implemented time card clocking in to ensure employees are only paid for those hours worked. It also provides a means for recording hours worked which is valuable management information. Before this there would have been no definitive record of actual hours worked.	The system appears to allow payable overtime to accumulate simply because an employee clocks out late, even if there is no staff gap to fill. The system should be set to automatically clock out after the normal number of shift hours. Staff will then need to clock back in for their overtime if they have an authorised shift. Overtime hours each month should be reviewed by the department head for consistency with agreed extra shifts.
A capital expenditure committee of senior managers has been set up to authorise significant capital expenditure items. This will help prevent cash out flows for unnecessary assets, or assets not budgeted for.	In a hospital there will be very expensive equipment purchases, such as the recently acquired new surgical equipment. It is better that these are authorised at board level rather than by senior managers. An authorisation policy should be drawn up setting out the different levels of authorisation needed (the highest being at board level) depending on the amount of expenditure for capital items.

> **Top tips.** You were only asked for four strengths and related improvements. Others you may have come up with in place of those given in the answer above are:

Strength (i)	Improvement (ii)
The hospital has an internal audit department monitoring the internal control environment and advising on value for money.	The remit of internal audit could be extended to advising on implementation.
Orders are authorised by a purchasing director to help ensure expenditure incurred is necessary expenditure.	The volume of forms (200 per day) will no doubt take valuable time away from the director which could be used on more pressing matters. Orders below a certain monetary level should be authorised by the next level (down) of management. Orders over the specified monetary value should still be reserved for purchase director authorisation.
New surgical equipment purchased has improved the rate of operations and patient recovery rates. This is an improvement in the effectiveness of the hospital.	The equipment is not used as efficiently as it could be due to lack of trained medical staff. The hospital should look at providing targeted training for existing medical staff and look to recruit staff that have the appropriate skills.

(c) **Substantive procedures – property, plant and equipment (non-current assets)**

   (i) *Valuation*

- Review depreciation rates applied in relation to asset lives, past experience of profits and losses on disposals, and consistency with prior years and disclosed accounting policies.

- If assets have been revalued, consider:
    - Experience and independence of valuer
    - Scope of the valuer's work
    - Methods and assumptions used
    - Whether valuation bases are in line with IFRSs

   (ii) *Completeness*

- Compare non-current assets in the general ledger with the non-current assets register and obtain explanations for differences.

- For a sample of assets which physically exist agree that they are recorded in the non-current asset register.

(iii)   *Rights and obligations*

- Verify title to land and buildings by inspection of:
    - Title deeds
    - Land registry certificates
    - Leases

- Examine documents of title for other assets (including purchase invoices, contracts, hire purchase or lease agreements).

Top tips. Only two substantive procedures were needed for each assertion. You may have come up with alternative procedures including:

Valuation

- Recalculate the depreciation charge for a sample of assets and agree the charges to the asset register

- Perform a depreciation proof in total taking into account timing of additions/disposals and investigate any differences.

- Agree the cost of a sample of additions of surgical equipment to purchase invoices

Completeness

- Reconcile the schedule of non-current assets with the general ledger
- Review the repairs and maintenance expense account in the SOCI for capital items

Rights and obligations

- Review new lease agreements to ensure properly classified as finance lease or an operating lease in accordance with IFRSs.

- Inspect vehicle registration documents (eg Ambulances) to confirm ownership of motor vehicles.

---

113 Bronze Industries Co

Text references. Chapters 10 and 11

Top tips. Part (a) asks for strengths in the payroll system. This requirement is less common than the identification of weaknesses but you should be prepared to comment on either. As with weaknesses the key here is to have a good understanding of the controls that you would expect to see in a payroll system. Work through the information systematically bearing in mind that you have been asked for five strengths only.

Part (b) essentially has three parts. You need to identify the deficiency, explain it and then make a recommendation to address it. It is important not to miss out the explanation step ie what is the possible effect/consequence of the weakness. The use of columns to present your answer would be helpful here.

Part (c) tests your understanding of substantive analytical procedures. Note that a proof in total calculation is particularly effective for payroll.

Easy marks. There are no easy marks as such in this question however you should feel confident that you know how to approach (b) as this is a very common requirement.

Examination team's comments. Candidates were able to confidently identify internal control deficiencies from the scenario, however some candidates did not clearly explain the deficiency in terms of how it affects the business. The scenario in the exam will always contain more issues than required to be discussed and it was therefore encouraging that candidates generally applied effective exam technique and focused on providing well explained answers which identified the required number of issues as noted in the question.

A minority of candidates, rather than evaluating controls just formed a point of view as to how well the company was controlling it's operations, and, also included more 'social' factors such as 'the motivational effect of having/not having a bonus system in force in a company' which was not required and does not answer the question.

Recommendations to address control weaknesses were on the whole well explained. Most candidates were able to provide good recommendations to address the deficiencies. However, occasionally some of the recommendations did not clearly address the specific control weakness and candidates are again reminded to ensure that their recommendation is specifically tailored to the requirements of the scenario.

Marking scheme

Marks

(a) Up to 1 mark each per well explained strength. If not well explained, then just give ½ mark for each, overall maximum of 5 marks for 5 points.
- Sequentially numbered clock cards
- Automatic calculations of gross, net pay and deductions
- Sample of calculations double checked
- Separate human resources and payroll department
- Bonus communicated in writing to payroll
- List of bank payments agreed in detail to payroll records

5

(b) Up to 1 mark each per well explained deficiency and recommendation. If not well explained, then just give ½ mark for each. Overall maximum of 6 marks each for deficiencies and recommendations.
- Clock in/out process unsupervised
- Employee breaks not monitored
- Temporary staff are not appointed by human resources department
- Overtime report reviewed after payment
- Authorisation of discretionary bonus
- No input checks over entry of bonus into payroll
- Payroll manager reviews the bank transfer listing prior to payment and can change payroll records
- No identity checks prior to cash wages pay out

12

(c) Up to 1 mark per well described procedure, overall maximum of 3 marks.
- Compare total payroll expense to the prior year and investigate any significant differences
- Review monthly payroll charges, compare to the prior year, budgets, discuss with management
- Compare overtime pay as a percentage of factory normal hours against prior year, investigate any significant differences
- Perform a proof in total of total wages and salaries, compare to actual, and investigate any significant differences

$\frac{3}{20}$

(a) **Bronze Industries Co (Bronze) payroll system internal control strengths**

Strengths in Bronze's payroll system are as follows:

- Factory staff are each issued a sequentially numbered clock card which details their employee number and name. This should ensure that employees are only paid for hours they have worked and that the payroll records record completely all employees, as any gaps in the sequence would be identified.

- The payroll system automatically calculates gross and net pay along with any statutory deductions. This should reduce the risk of employees' wages and statutory deductions being incorrect as there is a reduced risk of errors occurring.

- A sample of the calculations made by the automated system is checked by the payroll supervisor to ensure the system is operating effectively; this tests the automated controls within the system.

- Bronze has a human resources department which is responsible for setting up new permanent employees and leavers. Having a segregation of roles between human resources and payroll departments reduces the risk of fictitious employees being set up and also being paid.

- The discretionary bonus is communicated in writing to the payroll department. As this is in writing rather than verbal, this reduces the risk of the bonus being recorded at an incorrect amount in the payroll records.

- For employees paid by bank transfer, the list of the payments is reviewed in detail and agreed to the payroll records prior to authorising the bank payment. This reduces the risk of fraudulent payments being made through the creation of fictitious employees and other employees being omitted from the payment run.

(b) **Bronze payroll system deficiencies and controls**

Deficiencies	Controls
Employees swipe their cards at the beginning and end of the eight-hour shift; this process is not supervised. This could result in a number of employees being swiped in as present when they are not. This will result in a substantially increased payroll cost for Bronze.	The clocking in and out process should be supervised by a responsible official to prevent one individual clocking in multiple employees. A supervisor should undertake a random check of employees by reviewing who has logged in with a swipe card and confirming visually that the employee is present.
Employees are entitled to a 30-minute paid break and do not need to clock out to access the dining area. Employees could be taking excessive breaks resulting in a decrease in productivity and increased payroll costs.	Employees should be allocated set break times and there should be a supervisor present to ensure that employees only take the breaks they are entitled to.
Although there is a human resources department, appointments of temporary staff are made by factory production supervisors. The supervisor could appoint unsuitable employees and may not carry out all the required procedures for new joiners. This could result in these temporary employees not receiving the correct pay and relevant statutory deductions.	All appointment of staff, whether temporary or permanent, should only be made by the human resources department.
Overtime reports which detail the amount of overtime worked are sent out quarterly by the payroll department to production supervisors for review. These reports are reviewed after the payments have been made which could result in unauthorised overtime or amounts being paid incorrectly and Bronze's payroll cost increasing.	All overtime should be authorised by a responsible official prior to the payment being processed by the payroll department. This authorisation should be evidenced in writing.
Production supervisors determine the amount of the discretionary bonus to be paid to employees. Production supervisors are not senior enough to determine this as they could pay extra bonuses to friends or family members.	The bonus should be determined by a more senior individual, such as the production director, and this should be communicated in writing to the payroll department.
The bonus is input by a clerk into the payroll system. There is no indication that this input process is reviewed. This could result in input errors or the clerk could fraudulently change the amounts leading to incorrect bonus payments.	Once the clerk has input the bonus amounts, all entries should be double checked against the written confirmation from the production director by another member of the team to identify any amounts entered incorrectly.

Deficiencies	Controls
The payroll manager reviews the bank transfer listing prior to authorising the payments and also amends the payroll records for any changes required. There is a lack of segregation of duties as it is the payroll team which processes the amounts and the payroll manager who authorises payments. The manager could fraudulently increase the amounts to be paid to certain employees, process this payment as well as amend the records.	The payroll manager should not be able to process changes to the payroll system as well as authorise payments. The authorisation of the bank transfer listing should be undertaken by an individual outside the payroll department, such as the finance director.
A payroll clerk distributes cash pay packets to employees without requesting proof of identity. Even if most employees are known to the clerk, there is a risk that without identity checks wages could be paid to incorrect employees.	The payroll clerks should be informed that all cash wages can only be paid upon sight of the employee's clock card and photographic identification as this confirms proof of identity.

(c) **Substantive analytical procedures to confirm payroll expense**

- Compare the total payroll expense to the prior year and investigate any significant differences.

- Review monthly payroll charges, compare this to the prior year and budgets and discuss with management any significant variances.

- Compare overtime pay as a percentage of factory normal hours pay to investigate whether it is at a similar level to the prior year and within an acceptable range. Investigate any significant differences.

- Perform a proof in total of total wages and salaries, incorporating joiners and leavers and any pay increase. Compare this to the actual wages and salaries in the financial statements and investigate any significant differences.

114 Lemon Quartz Co

Text references. Chapter 10

Top tips. The key to a good answer to part (a) is to adopt a sensible structure. In this instance the question lends itself to a 3-column approach. This will ensure that each aspect of the requirement is dealt with. Notice that the questions specifies the number of deficiencies you should identify (five) so make sure that you do not waste time by addressing more points than necessary. Notice that you are asked to identify and **explain** deficiencies. You must include the explanation to score well. Make sure that you are clear on the difference between a test of control and a substantive procedure. Requirement a (iii) asks for tests of control. Remember that these are audit procedures designed to evaluate the operating effectiveness of controls as opposed to substantive procedures whose purpose is to identify material misstatements.

Easy marks. Part (b) should have represented easy marks as there was no application of knowledge required.

Examination team's comments. Internal controls questions remain a highly examinable area and in common with prior sittings, performance in the internal control question in June 2016 was mixed.

Candidates were able to identify the control deficiency from the scenario however some candidates did not clearly explain the implication of the deficiency. Additionally some candidates did not understand or incorrectly identified deficiencies eg renting space in warehouse to third parties or completing inventory count sheets in ink.

The scenario in the exam contained more issues than was required to be discussed and it was therefore pleasing that candidates generally only identified the required number of issues noted in the question.

Most candidates were able to provides good recommendations to address the deficiencies. However some of the recommendations were either poorly described, did not clearly address the specific control weakness identified or were impractical suggestions.

The tests of controls that the auditor could perform were often not well explained by candidates (eg 'ensure the bays are flagged' without saying how the auditor would ensure this or just using the word 'check' or 'observe', did not address the controls identified or were substantive audit procedures rather than tests of control.

It was pleasing to note that many candidates presented their answers well using a three-column approach with internal control deficiencies in one column, the related recommendation in the other and the related test of control in the third column.

Marking scheme

Marks

(a) Up to 1 mark per well explained deficiency, up to 1 mark for each well explained recommendation and up to 1 mark for each well described test of control. Overall maximum of 5 marks each for deficiencies, controls and tests of control.

- Warehouse employees undertaking the count
- Inventory counting sheets contain quantities per records
- No clear division of roles within counting teams
- Third-party inventory included in the count
- Access to high value finished goods
- Each location counted once only
- No flagging of bays once counted
- No sequence checks of inventory sheets
15

(b) Up to 1 mark per well explained element.
- Intended user, responsible party, practitioner
- Subject matter
- Suitable criteria
- Appropriate evidence
- Assurance report
5
20

(a) **Deficiencies, controls and test of controls**

Deficiencies (i)	Controls (ii)	Test of controls (iii)
The count will be undertaken by teams of warehouse staff. There should be a segregation of roles between those who have day-to-day responsibility for inventory and those who are checking it. If the same team are responsible for maintaining and checking inventory, then errors and fraud could be hidden.	The counting teams should be independent of the warehouse; hence members of alternative departments should undertake the counting rather than the warehouse staff.	Attend the year-end count and enquire of the counting teams which department they normally work in. Inspect the updated inventory count instructions to verify that they have been communicated to members of staff outside the warehouse department.
The inventory sheets contain quantities as per the inventory records. There is a risk that the counting teams may simply agree with the pre-printed quantities rather than counting the balances correctly, resulting in significant errors in inventory.	The count sheets should be sequentially numbered and contain product codes and descriptions but no quantities.	Inspect a sample of the counting sheets being used by the counting teams to verify that only the inventory product codes and description are pre-printed on them.

Deficiencies (i)	Controls (ii)	Test of controls (iii)
There are 15 teams of counters, each team having two members of staff. However, there is no clear division of responsibilities within the team. Therefore, both members of staff could count together rather than checking each other's count; and errors in their count may not be identified.	Each team should be informed that both members are required to count their assigned inventory separately. Therefore, one member counts and the second member also undertakes a count and then records the inventory on the count sheets correctly. In addition, the financial controller supervising the count should undertake some sample checks of inventory counted by each team.	Observe the counting teams to assess if they are counting together or if one counts and the other then double checks the quantities counted. Review the records of the sample checks undertaken by the supervisor of the inventory count.
Inventory owned by third parties is also being counted by the teams with adjustments being made by the finance team to split these goods out later. There does not appear to be a method for counters to identify which items are third party inventory. There is a risk that these goods may not be correctly removed from the inventory count sheets, resulting in inventory being overstated.	All inventories belonging to third parties should be moved to one location. This area should be clearly marked and excluded from the counting process.	Enquire of the count supervisor where the third party inventory is to be stored, confirm through inspection of the counting sheets that these bays are not included on any pre-printed forms.
High value inventory which is normally stored in a secure location will be accessible by all team members as they will be given the access code. This significantly increases the risk of theft as any member of the counting team could subsequently access these goods.	The high value inventory should be kept in the locked area of the warehouse. Senior members of the team should be allocated to count these goods, and they should be given the access code to enter the area. Upon completion of the count the access code should be changed.	Attempt to access the area where the high value inventory is stored; this should not be possible without the access code. At the year-end visit attempt to access with the code which was supplied during the inventory count.
Each bay of the warehouse is counted once only. If inventory is only checked once, then counting errors may arise resulting in under or overstated inventory.	Once all inventories have been counted once, each area should be recounted by a different team. Any differences on the first count should be promptly notified to the count supervisor and a third count undertaken if necessary. If a full second count would be too time-consuming for the company, then sample checks on the inventory counted should be undertaken by a different counting team.	Observe the counting team undertake second counts of all areas; confirm that different teams undertake this process.

Deficiencies (i)	Controls (ii)	Test of controls (iii)
Once areas are counted, the teams are not marking the bays as completed. Therefore there is the risk that some areas of the warehouse could be double counted or missed out.	All bays should be flagged as completed, once the inventory has been counted. In addition, the count supervisor should check at the end of the count that all of the bays with Quartz's inventory have been flagged as completed.	Physically confirm that the completed bays of the warehouse have been flagged to indicate that the goods have been counted. At the end of the count, review any bays containing Quartz's goods which have not been flagged.
The inventory sheets are sequentially numbered and at the end of the count they are given to the count supervisor who confirms with each team that they have returned all sheets. However, no sequence check of the sheets is per formed. If sheets are missing, then the inventory records could be understated.	After the counting has finished, each team should return all of their sequentially numbered sheets and the supervisor should check the sequence of all sheets at the end of the count.	Review the sequence of the inventory sheets for any gaps in the sequence and obtain an explanation from the count supervisor.

(b)   **Elements of an assurance engagement**

In accordance with ISAE 3000 *Assurance engagements other than audits or reviews of historical financial information*, an assurance engagement will require a three-party relationship comprising of:

- The intended user who is the person who requires the assurance report.

- The responsible party, which is the organisation responsible for preparing the subject matter to be reviewed.

- The practitioner (i.e. an accountant) who is the professional who will review the subject matter and provide the assurance.

A second element which is required for an assurance engagement is suitable subject matter. The subject matter is the data which the responsible party has prepared and which requires verification. Thirdly this subject matter is then evaluated or assessed against suitable criteria in order for it to be assessed and an opinion provided.

Fourth, the practitioner must ensure that they have gathered sufficient appropriate evidence in order to give the required level of assurance. Last, an assurance report provides the opinion which is given by the practitioner to the intended user.

115 Shesha Co

Study Text reference: Chapters 9 and 10

Tops tips: This question is testing your understanding of control objectives and procedures specific to the purchases system, as well as general control issues. You must make sure that your answers in part (c) are specific to Shesha's circumstances, noting, for instance, what staff are available to take part in controls. Part (d) is a small requirement asking you to consider the self-review issues that arise from giving advice on internal controls to an audit client , and safeguards that could be put into place.

Easy marks: Easy marks are available for a definition (of segregation of duties) in part (b), the limitations of internal control in part (a) and the safeguards relating to self-review in part (d).

Marks

(a) ½ mark for identifying and further ½ mark for explaining each limitation
of internal control   5

(b) 1 mark for definition of segregation of duties
1 mark for each explanatory point concerning application at Shesha   4

(c) (i) Objectives
½ mark per valid objective of the purchases system   2

(ii) Procedures
½ mark for each valid control procedure, with up to another 1
mark for
applicability to Shesha and explanation of how it meets control
objective   6

(d) 1 mark per valid point
- Risk of self-review
- Management responsibility
- Different staff members
- Quality control review
- Clarification in engagement letter re auditor's responsibilities
  re controls   3
                                                                           ___
                                                                            20

(a) **Limitations of internal control**

- The costs of control not outweighing their benefits. This is where a company does not implement the most effective controls because it is too expensive for them to do so.

- The potential for human error. Most controls are operated by humans and it is possible that they will be operated incorrectly, causing them not to be effective.

- Collusion between employees. Most control systems use a degree of 'segregation of duties' so that mistakes made by one person are picked up by another. However, if staff work together to commit fraud then this checking control is nullified.

- The possibility of controls being bypassed or overridden by management. Management may override controls for efficiency purposes and hence risk errors occurring. This can particularly be a problem in small companies with strong owner-manager presence, such as Shesha.

- Controls being designed to cope with routine and not non-routine transactions. Controls can only be effective in relation to events that the people designing them have anticipated (that is, routine transactions). In order to handle unusual transactions, staff might have to bypass controls and hence risk errors occurring.

(b) **Segregation of duties**

Segregation implies a number of people being involved in the accounting process. This makes it more difficult for fraudulent transactions to be processed (since a number of people would have to collude in the fraud), and it is also more difficult for accidental errors to be processed (since the more people are involved, the more checking there can be).

Segregation should take place in various ways:

- Segregation of function. The key functions that should be segregated are the carrying out of a transaction, recording that transaction in the accounting records and maintaining custody of assets that arise from the transaction. For example, at Shesha, the purchase manager could make the purchase, the accounts controller could record the purchase and other staff involved in production will maintain custody of the items purchased.

- The various steps in carrying out the transaction should also be segregated. Again, at Shesha, the purchase manager may raise an order, related goods received by the production team and related invoice paid for by the accounts controller.

- The carrying out of various accounting operations should be segregated. For example, the same staff should not record transactions and carry out the reconciliations at the period end. This may be more difficult to achieve at Shesha as the accounts department appears at present to only consist of one person. The firm will have to note this as a limitation of Shesha's system.

(c) **Purchases system at Shesha**

(i) **Objectives**

To ensure that:

- Purchases are obtained from appropriate suppliers at the best price for the company
- Recorded purchases represent goods and services received
- All purchase transactions that occurred have been recorded
- Recorded purchases represent liabilities of the entity
- Purchase transactions are recorded correctly in the purchase system
- Purchase transactions are recorded in the correct accounting period

(**Tutor's note:** You were only required to give four objectives).

(ii) **Procedures**

(**Tutor's note:** You are only required to give one procedure per objective. This answer gives more to show you the breadth of possible answers you could have given.)

(1) Purchases are obtained from appropriate suppliers at the best price for the company

- In consultation with the new purchasing manager, Kate and Fatima should set up an authorised supplier list to ensure the company is obtain appropriate pricing and supply terms.

- The accounts controller should note supplier terms to ensure that payments are made such as to ensure available discounts (eg for prompt payment) are received.

- Fatima and Kate should approve purchases made off the approved supplier list (for example, orders made to take advantages of particular special offers etc).

(2) Recorded purchases represent goods and services received

- Fatima should authorise orders proposed by the purchasing manager to ensure that goods ordered are for business purposes.

- There should be segregation in the ordering system: the purchasing manager should place orders, the accounts controller should record them and Kate or Fatima should authorise payments, to ensure that no one individual can process false invoices.

- Production staff should check goods received to an order authorised by Fatima to ensure that goods have been appropriately ordered.

(3) All purchase transactions that have occurred have been recorded

- The accounts controller should match supplier invoices with authorised orders and goods received notes.

- The accounts controller should routinely review unmatched goods received notes to identify why an invoice has not been recorded in relation to that purchase.

- The accounts controller should regularly reconcile supplier statements with the purchase ledger.

(4) Recorded purchases represent liabilities of the entity

- The accounts controller should match invoices received with goods received notes to ensure that the liability is genuine.

(5) Purchase transactions are recorded correctly in the purchase system

- The accounts controller should check the additions on supplier invoices before entering them on the purchase ledger to ensure the cost is accurate.
- The accounts controller should regularly reconcile the purchase ledger and the nominal ledger.

(6) Purchase transactions are recorded in the correct accounting period

- The production team should forward goods received notes to the accounts controller daily to ensure liabilities are processed in the correct period.
- The accounts controller should record purchase invoices promptly upon receipt.
- The accounts controller should review unmatched goods received notes and chase invoices from suppliers if necessary.

(d) **Factors to consider**

There is a threat of self-review if Smith gives business advice on internal controls systems as, during the audit, they will be reviewing whether the internal control system they advised on is capable of producing suitable financial records and preventing or detecting and correcting material misstatements. There is a threat that they would not undertake this review objectively, due to trust in their initial advice.

There is also a threat of management responsibility, as it is management's responsibility to design and implement internal controls. The firm's involvement should be limited to advice, and no individual at the firm should take responsibility for designing the internal controls at Shesha.

As Shesha is not a public interest entity, the firm is not prevented from providing them with business advice, which is often a by-product of audit services. However, the audit firm must bear in mind the threats and ensure they are safeguarded against. Safeguards that could be implemented against this threat are:

- Using a different staff members on the audit than those who provided advice to Shesha
- Carrying out a pre-issuance review on the audit of Shesha by an independent partner within the firm prior to issuing the auditor's report.

Another issue to consider is the need to clarify the firm's audit responsibility in relation to internal control and a confirmation that an audit does not provide assurance on the effectiveness of internal control, although the firm will report noted deficiencies in internal controls to management and directors. This could be done through discussion and also in the audit engagement letter.

116 Oregano Co

Text references. Chapters 9 and 10.

Top tips. This scenario-based question tests your applied knowledge of internal controls.

Part (a) is knowledge-based so should be straightforward. Note that only two methods are required.

Part (b) asks for control objectives. This can be answered independently of the scenario, but your answer here should help to inform your answer for part (c).

In part (c), keep your answer in a tabular format and make sure your answer is related to the scenario.

Easy marks. Part (a) and (b) should both yield easy marks.

Marks

(a) Up to 1 mark each for a description of a method, up to 1 mark each for an advantage, up to 1 mark each for a disadvantage. Overall max of 2 marks each for methods, advantages and disadvantages.
- Narrative notes
- Questionnaires
- Flowcharts

6

(b) 1 mark for each control objective, overall maximum of 2 points.
- To ensure orders are only accepted if goods are available to be processed for customers
- To ensure all orders are recorded completely and accurately
- To ensure goods are not supplied to poor credit risks
- To ensure goods are dispatched for all orders on a timely basis
- To ensure goods are dispatched correctly to customers and are of an adequate quality
- To ensure all goods dispatched are correctly invoiced
- To ensure completeness of income for goods dispatched
- To ensure sales discounts are only provided to valid customers

2

(c) Up to 1 mark per well explained deficiency and up to 1 mark for each control. Overall max of 6 marks for deficiencies and 6 marks for controls.
- Inventory not checked when order taken
- Orders not completed on pre-printed order forms
- Order forms not sequentially numbered
- Credit limits being exceeded
- Goods dispatched not agreed to order to check quantity and quality
- Signed dispatch notes not being sent to accounts department
- Sales invoices being raised by inexperienced staff
- Sales discounts manually entered by sales clerks 12

12
20

(a) **Documenting the sales and dispatch system**

Narrative notes are written descriptions of the system, describing how the system processes each transaction, and the controls that operate at each stage.

Advantages

- Simple to record

- No training required to document and understand; easily understood by all members of the internal audit team

Disadvantages

- Cumbersome, especially if the sales and dispatch system is complex
- Not easily updated from year on year if it is not computerised
- More difficult for users to quickly identify internal control deficiencies

Flowcharts are graphical illustrations of the physical flow of information through the sales and dispatch system.

Advantages

- After some experience, they can be prepared quickly

- Information is prepared in standard form, so it is easy to follow. Deficiencies in internal control can also be quickly identified

- Ensures that the system is recorded in its entirety; any loose ends are easily identified

Disadvantages

- While appropriate for standard systems, unusual transactions cannot be captured without the use of additional narrative
- Time-consuming to amend as redrawing is required

Questionnaires comprise a list of standard questions. Internal control questionnaires (ICQs) determine whether desirable controls are present, while internal control evaluation questionnaires (ICEQs) assess whether specific errors (or frauds) are possible at each stage of the sales and dispatch cycle.

Advantages

- If drafted thoroughly, they can ensure that all controls are considered
- Quick and easy to prepare
- Easy to use and control
- ICEQs are effective in identifying internal control deficiencies

Disadvantages

- Questionnaires are only as good as their author: drafted vaguely, the questions could be misunderstood, and if questions are incomplete, important controls could be missed
- Unusual controls may be missed
- It would be easy for staff members to overstate the level of controls
- Gives the false impression that all controls are of equal weight; in reality, certain controls may be more fundamental than others.

(b) **Control objectives**

Occurrence and existence

- To ensure that one person is not responsible for taking orders, recording sales and receiving payment
- To ensure that recorded sales transactions represent goods provided
- To ensure that goods are only supplied to customers with good credit ratings
- To ensure that goods are provided at authorised prices and on authorised terms
- To ensure that customers are encouraged to pay promptly

Completeness

- To ensure that all revenue relating to goods dispatched is recorded
- To ensure that all goods sold are correctly invoiced

Accuracy

- To ensure that all sales and adjustments are correctly journalised, summarised and posted to the correct accounts

Cut-off

- To ensure that transactions have been recorded in the correct period

Classification

- To ensure that all transactions are properly classified in accounts

(c) **Control deficiencies**

Deficiencies	Recommendations
Telephone orders are checked manually after an order has been placed.	Orders should not be confirmed before the availability of the product has been checked.
This creates a risk of goods for which orders have been placed being unavailable, leading to unfulfilled orders. This gives rise to dissatisfaction from customers and has a negative impact on the company's reputation.	To ensure that orders are fulfilled consistently, telephone orders and online orders should ideally be processed through the same system, with automatic notifications to the customer who has placed the order once product availability has been checked.

Deficiencies	Recommendations
Order forms for telephone orders are completed after an order has been placed. This increases the risk that information on the order forms is incorrect or incomplete, leading to errors in fulfilling the order.	All order forms should be completed at the time the order is placed. For telephone orders, the order clerk should confirm with the customer that all details are correct.
The order forms used for telephone orders are not sequentially numbered. This increases the risk that order forms are lost in transit, leading to unfulfilled orders and reputational damage.	All order forms should be sequentially numbered.
The same order clerk takes the orders, checks the order forms and sends the order forms onto the accounts and dispatch departments. The lack of segregation of duties increases the risk of error and fraud.	Each telephone order taken should be cross-checked by another order clerk. The check should be evidenced by signature.
Customers are able to exceed their agreed credit limit by 10% when they place their orders online. This increases the risk that customers with bad credit histories are accepted, leading to slow-moving or bad debts.	The online ordering system should be modified to reject orders which would cause credit limits to be exceeded. Customers' credit limits should be assessed on a regular basis by a responsible official. Credit limits could be extended for customers with good credit histories.
Goods do not appear to be checked to the original order before dispatch. This increases the risk of errors in fulfilling the order.	Order forms for goods on the pick list should be printed on a daily basis. Goods should be checked to the order forms before being dispatched.
The signed dispatch notes are not sent to the accounts department. This could result in delays in invoicing, leading to loss of revenue.	Copies of the signed dispatch notes should be forwarded to the accounts department once the goods have been delivered. Invoices should be raised based on the dispatch notes in a timely manner, and the dispatch notes filed by the accounts team along with evidence that the related invoices have been processed.
Discounts are manually entered by the sales clerk onto the invoice. This creates the risk of discounts being omitted by error. More importantly, the lack of authorisation process increases the risk of unauthorised discounts being given, leading to loss of revenue.	Discounts should be approved by a responsible official. The authorised discount levels should be recorded automatically in the customer master file, so that they appear on the invoices without manual input. The invoicing system should be modified to prevent the manual processing of discounts.
Extra accounts staff have been allocated to produce the sales invoices. The extra staff's lack of experience and training increases the risk of errors on the invoices, resulting in customers being over- or under-charged.	Only sales clerks with the appropriate experience should be allowed to produce sales invoices. Oregano could consider recruiting and training permanent staff with the appropriate experience.

Expert

117 C IAS 16 permits non-current assets to be revalued (IAS 16: para. 31). However, if an item of property, plant and equipment is revalued, the entire class of property, plant and equipment to which that asset belongs must be revalued (IAS 16: para. 36). Truse Co is therefore entitled to revalue the shop, but they will also need to revalue all of the other shops if it is to comply with IAS 16.

The revaluation does constitute a change of accounting policy, so disclosures do need to be reviewed.

Under IAS 16, all non-current assets used by the entity should be depreciated, even if the fair value is in excess of the carrying amount. Repair and maintenance does not negate the need to depreciate the shop over its useful life. (IAS 16: para. 50)

Repairs and maintenance costs should be expensed as incurred, not capitalised.

118 B Existence, classification and presentation are all assertions related to tangible non-current assets. Completeness and accuracy, valuation and allocation are also relevant assertions (ISA 315: para. A124 (b)). Occurrence relates to classes of transactions and events recorded in profit or loss. (ISA 315: para. A124 (a))

119 A Physically inspecting assets listed in the non-current assets register tests for existence. Recalculating net book values tests for accuracy, valuation and allocation. Inspecting relevant purchase invoices or deeds tests for rights and obligations.

120 D The existence of threats to the expert's objectivity should be considered as part of determining the competence, capability and objectivity of the auditor's expert (ISA 620: para. 9). However, it is not a matter to be considered when the auditor determines the overall nature, timing and extent of the audit procedures required to evaluate the auditor's expert and the auditor's expert's work.

Besides the three matters listed in A, B and C, the auditor should also consider the nature of the matter to which the auditor's expert's work relates (ie the nature of Truse Co's properties) and the significance of the auditor's expert's work in the context of the audit (this depends, in part, on the materiality of the property account).

121 D Third party evidence is the most reliable, followed by auditor-generated evidence. Client-generated evidence is deemed to be less reliable – more so when the evidence is verbal.

Newthorpe

122 The correct answers are:

The auditor observes client staff to determine whether inventory count procedures are being followed.

The auditor reviews procedures for identifying damaged, obsolete and slow-moving inventory.

Management is responsible for organising the inventory count, not the auditor. If the results of the auditor's test counts are not satisfactory, the auditor can request that inventory is recounted, but the auditor cannot insist on a recount. However, if management refuses the auditor's request then the auditor will need to consider the implications of this on the auditor's report.

123 The correct answer is:

For a sample of inventory sold just before and just after the year end, match dates of sales invoices/date posted to ledgers with date on related goods despatched notes.

All of the suggested audit procedures test the valuation assumption, except for matching the dates of sales invoices with the dates on the related goods despatched notes, which is an audit procedure around cut-off.

124 The correct answer is:

Accounting treatment	Reason
No provision but disclose as a contingent liability	A present obligation exists, but the outflow of economic resources is not probable.

Management believe that there is a 35% chance of the claim succeeding. For an event to be 'probable,' it should be more likely than not to occur (ie a 50% probability) (IAS 37: para. 14). In this case, the outflow of economic resources is therefore not probable, so a provision should not be recognised. A present obligation (not a possible obligation) exists, since the former managing director has sued Newthorpe for unfair dismissal. It is because the likelihood of him succeeding in his claim is not probable that the claim should be treated as a contingent liability instead of a provision.

125 The correct answer is:

Send an enquiry letter to Newthorpe's lawyers to obtain their view as to the probability of the claim being successful

Independent third party audit evidence is generally considered to be more reliable than client-generated or auditor-generated audit evidence. Although all the procedures are valid, only the written confirmation from Newthorpe's lawyers provides an expert, third party confirmation on the likelihood of the claim being successful. It is also sent directly to the auditor rather than to the client.

126 To perform specific procedures to identify possible non-compliance

ISA 250 distinguishes between laws and regulations which have a direct effect and those which have an indirect effect on the financial statements (ISA 250: para. 6). For those which do not have a direct effect on the financial statements the auditor must undertake specified audit procedures to help identify non-compliance with laws and regulations that may have a material effect on the financial statements. (ISA 250: para. 10)

Tirrol

127 The correct answers are:

We should budget for the extra time required to document an understanding of the entity, its environment and its systems, and to verify material opening balances.

We must agree a clear timetable with the client for the testing of the computerized inventory systems, setting out availability of access to the system, files and personnel required to complete testing.

As this is Cal & Co's first year of auditing Tirrol Co, additional time should be budgeted for documenting an understanding of the entity and for verifying the opening balances. Because Cal & Co's audit software has to be rewritten and the testing is taking place on a live basis, it is particularly important to plan our CAATs procedures carefully.

The ACCA's Code of Ethics and Conduct does not prohibit lowballing as such stating that 'a professional accountant in public practice may quote whatever fee is deemed appropriate' (ACCA Code of Ethics and Conduct: s. 240.1), so withdrawing from the audit engagement on this basis is disproportionate. However, the firm should be able to demonstrate that appropriate time and qualified staff are assigned to the audit, and that all applicable standards are being adhered to (ACCA Code of Ethics and Conduct: s. 240.2). It may not be appropriate to adopt a combined approach if control risk is deemed to be high. The appropriate audit approach should be determined by the risk assessment, not by time or fee constraints.

128 The correct answers are:

The ability to test all 25 of Tirrol Co's locations using the same audit software, resulting in time and cost savings

The ability to search all items for exceptions, thus giving greater assurance over the inventory figure

The ability to select and extract a sample of inventory data for testing, thus reducing sampling risk

The ability to test the actual computer files from the originating programme, rather than printouts from a spook or preview files, thus eliminating exporting errors

All of the options are valid benefits associated with the use of audit software.

129 The correct answer is:

A sampling method which involves having a constant sampling interval, the starting point for testing is determined randomly.

The first option describes monetary unit sampling. The third option is an example of block selection. The fourth option describes haphazard sampling.

130 The correct answer is:

Whether there are any significant threats to the objectivity of the internal auditor.

The objectivity of the internal auditor should be considered in determining whether or not the work of the internal auditors can be used in the first place. It is not part of evaluating the work itself.

131 The correct answer is:

Inventory and profit for the year would be overstated by $6,000.

Inventory should be measured at the lower of cost and net realisable value (IAS 2: para. 9). Net realisable value is defined by IAS 2 as estimated selling price less estimated costs necessary to make the sale (IAS 2: para. 6). In this case, inventory should be written down by $6,000 and the write-down expense charged to profit or loss.

Wright

132 A   Material items will require more evidence to support them than immaterial items, which might be tested by comparative analytical review only. If the evidence is of high quality, then less may be required than if it were of poorer quality. Time and budget constraints should never influence the auditor's judgement regarding the sufficiency of audit evidence. The size of the account is considered in determining materiality (ie materiality may be determined as 5% of profit before tax), but the auditor's judgement regarding the sufficiency of audit evidence depends on the level of audit risks associated with each account. The operating effectiveness of the company's internal control systems will also influence this judgement.

133 B   The goods were received before the year end and have been recognised in inventory. A liability should therefore be recognised in the current accounting period. Although the cheque cleared the bank account after the year end it was issued before the year end and there is nothing to suggest that it has been deliberately held back. The cash-in-transit is therefore a legitimate reconciling item.

134 C   As the supplier statement balance agrees with that on the purchase ledger no further work is required in respect of this account.

Purchase orders made after the year end would not have any effect on current year liabilities.

As a supplier statement is available there would be no need to ask for a direct confirmation of the balance from supplier XX3.

Credit notes issued by Wilbur Co would potentially affect receivables not payables balances.

135 A   The bank confirmation letter must be sent identifiably by the auditor, and responses should be provided directly to the auditor. This is to prevent the information being distorted by any lack of objectivity, or tampering by client management.

136 D   The bank's stamp on the paying in slip is the most reliable as it is third party evidence and shows the date the lodgements were actually paid in to the bank.

The bank statement would be a useful source of evidence but there may be delay between the paying-in date and the date that the balance is cleared by the banking system. Therefore the bank statement date is not necessarily an accurate reflection of when the lodgement was made. There may also be a delay between the date on the cheques/remittance advice and the date it is actually received by Wilbur Co.

Lodestar

137 C   The sample selection does not address the risk of understatement as it has focused on the ten largest balances.

Option A is incorrect as the sample is not appropriate. In order to test **completeness**, the sample selection for a receivables circularisation should consider incorporating nil balances and balances written off in the year to ensure that the balance is not understated. (Hence Option C is correct.)

Option B is incorrect as the nature of sampling means that a % of the balance will not be sampled, but conclusions can still be drawn.

Option D is incorrect as it is stratification is not required (although it may be helpful) and would not necessarily give a 'representative' sample, due to the risks discussed above in relation to Option A.

138 B   1, 2 and 4

Appropriateness refers to relevance and reliability. All the procedures are relevant to the assertion, but only some of them are reliable. Simply asking the credit controller if the client exists is not reliable, as it gives oral evidence generated by management and does not add value to the sales ledger.

Sending out a follow up request gives the auditor a chance of obtaining evidence direct from a third party, which would be considered very reliable.

Reviewing cash receipts after date gives indirect evidence from a third party, as if someone is paying the debt, it implies it existed in the first place.

Reviewing the sales invoices is auditor generated evidence that the sale was generated in the first place. It based on relatively weak internally generated evidence (the invoices) but as it involves auditor analysis (for example, whether the relevant invoices appear in numerical sequence with other genuine invoices and have associated goods outwards notes) it adds a degree of reliability. This evidence would not be sufficient on its own but it might corroborate other evidence.

139 B   Trade receivables should be £6,000 lower, current assets are overstated.

The difference caused by the payment by the customer does not require adjustment. The auditor has verified that the payment was received by Lodestar on 2 October, which is consistent with the third party evidence that it was sent out on 30 September. As far as Lodestar is concerned, the debt was genuine at 30 September and there is good evidence about its existence and valuation provided by the subsequent payment.

The customer is disputing an invoice and declaring its intention not to accept the debt. Regardless of management's intention to dispute this credit request, that suggests that the **valuation** of the debt is inappropriate (as the customer is only prepared to pay £0 in effect for that invoice), even if the **existence** of the debt can be proved. The invoice should be written off, hence receivables and current assets are overstated by £6,000.

140 D   Auditors should use their own estimate in the financial statements, as auditor generated evidence is more conclusive than management generated evidence.

Auditors do not prepare the financial statements, management do. It is inappropriate to suggest that the auditors should prepare a figure for the financial statements (and this might cause an ethical threat of self-review). Auditor generated evidence is considered reliable, so if the auditors did make an estimate which was significantly different from management's, this would be evidence that the allowance was misstated. The auditor will have to bear in mind the risk of management bias in making an estimate, and it is true that it can be difficult to obtain evidence relating to management judgement (particularly in this case if no events occur to 'prove' the debt is doubtful, such as the customer going into liquidation, or management writing the debt off – which they are likely to want to defer in case the debt is eventually paid).

| 141 | A | 1, 2, 3, 4 |

The assertion being tested is **valuation**

(1) Gives indirect third party evidence that the valuation of the debt is appropriate (ie in proving that some debts have not been paid)

(2) Gives auditor generated evidence of the age of some debt and therefore the fact that its valuation is likely to be in doubt (otherwise it would have been paid before)

(3) Gives management evidence relating to the valuation of the debt, which might give the auditor insight into issues they might otherwise be unaware of, such as conversations with customers about when debts are to be paid

(4) Gives very little evidence about current valuation, as it only shows what the value was at the time the invoice was sent, and is of low reliability anyway, as it is internally generated.

Porthos

| 142 | A | The steps should be undertaken in this order. The objective of the CAAT procedures should be determined first and foremost. The accessibility of the data files must be considered before the scope and nature of the procedures are determined. |

| 143 | D | Testing orders for unusually large quantities identifies whether any reject controls requiring special authorisation for large orders are effective. Testing orders with fields left blank determines whether controls are in place to prevent orders being placed that can't be fulfilled due to missing information (ie incomplete delivery address). Testing orders with invalid inventory codes identifies whether controls are in place to ensure that the correct goods are despatched. Finally, orders with correct and complete details should be accepted by the system. This will allow the auditor to inspect the order confirmation to determine whether the order details are transferred accurately into the despatch system. |

| 144 | A | Sales cut-off will have been correctly applied where goods are despatched and recognised as sales in the same accounting period. Therefore all GDNs relating to goods despatched before 31 December 20X5 should be matched by a sales invoice also dated before 31 December 20X5. |

The fact that goods are picked and despatched in the same accounting period does not provide evidence that sales have been recognised in the correct accounting period. Therefore options C & D are not relevant.

| 145 | C | Sequence checks on sales invoices provide evidence on the completeness of sales. |

| 146 | C | The rent recognised in the year should reflect that earned in the period. For January and February this will be based on an annual income of $21,600. For the remaining 10 months this would be based on the increased rental. The proof in total should be calculated on the same basis. |

147 Redburn

Text references. Chapters 7, 8 and 13.

Top tips. Part (a) is largely knowledge based and you should know why planning is important and the matters included in an audit plan from your studies. Remember, only two matters are required, so don't state more than you are asked for. Because there are only two marks allocated to audit plan matters, four points are needed to demonstrate the importance of planning to gain full marks.

Do not be fazed by part (b) just because the procedures are not in respect of information in the accounting records. Here the sales statistics are potentially a useful analytical review tool as they provide monthly trends, but before the auditor can use this information, he or she must confirm the integrity of this data. Therefore you needed to describe procedures which achieve this objective.

Part (c) requires a description of three substantive tests and asks you to state the associated objectives. Using a tabular approach will help you maintain focus when answering this question. Part (d) also lends itself to a tabular approach.

Part (e)(ii) is quite tricky. Although stating the procedures is straightforward, you must add sufficient explanation to gain full marks. Because there are eight marks available you will need to include sufficient detail in respect of each of the general procedures.

Easy marks. You should be able to obtain the majority of the marks in part (a), which can be answered from a basic knowledge of audit planning. There are also easy marks available in part (e)(i) for defining net realisable value.

Examination Team's comments. Most candidates performed well on part (a) of the question. Part (b) presented difficulties for almost all of the candidates and was inadequately answered. It would appear that many did not understand what was required of them and they failed to understand what the sales statistics were. The company was keeping records of sales made by month and by type of customer and colleges. The auditor could place reliance on these and perhaps use them for analytical review purposes, but would have needed to test their reliability first.

Part (c) proved to be challenging for a large number of candidates and there were some disappointing answers. Many provided procedures which tested sales income as opposed to royalty charges. Procedures such as 'agreeing sales invoices to the customer master files' were common, but these do not consider how to gain comfort over royalties. In addition the question asked for substantive procedures, but many candidates gave tests of control. Candidates need to understand the difference between a substantive procedure and a test of control.

Answers to part (d) were mixed. A significant proportion of candidates were able to provide inherent risks such as damaged goods, theft and slow moving books. However it was unsatisfactory to see the level of general risks given such as 'inventory may be overstated' with no explanation as to how it might be overstated such as it is 'overvalued due to the goods being damaged'.

Candidates were also required to suggest controls to mitigate each risk. There was a significant minority who misread the question and thought that substantive procedures were required as opposed to controls that management might adopt.

In part (e), it was pleasing to see that a significant proportion of candidates could clearly provide the definition of NRV from IAS 2 *Inventories*. However there were a large number of candidates who did not understand what NRV was. The second part of this question was not answered well. Perhaps due to the misunderstandings over what NRV involved, many candidates could not provide any relevant procedures.

Marking scheme

		Marks

(a)   Audit planning

Up to 1 mark for any of the following, but maximum 4.

Important areas of the audit
Potential problems
Effective and efficient audit
Selection of engagement team members and assignment of work
Direction, supervision and review
Coordination of work   4

Two matters

Up to 1 mark for relevant matters, but maximum 2.

Risk assessment generally
Assessment of control environment
Decision to test controls
Scope of substantive testing
Procedures to comply with ISAs   2
Maximum marks   6

(b)   Sales statistics

Up to 1 mark each for each relevant procedure, but maximum 4.

Reconcile to recorded sales
Compare trends
Discuss with management
Customer codes
Reports from sales staff
Maximum marks   4

(c)   Substantive tests on royalties

Up to 1 mark for description of test and up to 1 mark for
stating objective, but maximum 6.

Compare royalties with sales income
Compare budgeted and actual royalties
Review sales statistics
Check whether royalties due and correctly calculated
Agree royalty payments to supporting documentation
Check cut-off
Compare expected and actual royalties
Maximum marks   6

(d)   Inventory risks

Up to 1 mark for each identified risk and up to 1 mark for
mitigating control, but maximum 4.

Deterioration/Unsaleable – lack of demand or defective
Theft likely
Poor inventory counting
Poor cut-off
Sale or return
Maximum marks   4

(e)   (i)   Define net realisable value

½ mark for reference to IAS 2 and 1/2 mark for
each element of definition.

IAS 2
Selling price
Less estimated costs to completion
Less estimated costs to make the sale
Maximum marks   2

         (ii)   Four procedures

Up to 1 mark for stating procedure and up to 1 further
mark for explanation, but maximum 8.

On sales price
On costs to completion
On selling and distribution cost
Discussion with management
Maximum marks   8

                                                                                                          <u>10</u>
                                                                                                          <u>30</u>

(a) **The importance of audit planning**

ISA 300 *Planning an audit of financial statements* covers the general planning process. This requires the auditor to plan the audit so that the engagement is performed in an effective and efficient manner. Proper audit planning can (ISA 300: para. 2):

- Help the auditor devote appropriate attention to important areas of the audit
- Help the auditor identify and resolve potential problems on a timely basis
- Assist in the selection of appropriate team members and assignment of work to them
- Facilitate the direction, supervision and review of work.

> **Top tips.** You could also have validly stated that planning helps the auditor to properly organise and manage the audit so it is performed in an effective manner, and that it assists in the coordination of work done by experts.

Matters included in the audit plan

Two matters that would be included in an audit plan are as follows (ISA 300: para. 9):

- A description of the nature, timing and extent of planned risk assessment procedures
- A description of the nature, timing and extent of planned further audit procedures at the assertion level.

> **Top tips.** There are a number of other matters that would be included, but only two were required. Other matters you might have come up with include:
>
> - Assessment of inherent and control risk and an understanding and assessment of the control environment
> - Whether the auditor will undertake controls or substantive testing or a combination of both (along with details of how this was decided)
> - Other planned procedures required to be carried out to comply with ISAs.

(b) **Procedures used to ensure the sales statistics may be relied upon**

- Perform a reconciliation of the sales figures in the sales statistics to the sales recorded in the accounting system.
- Inquire of management how they use the sales statistics, and whether they form the basis of management decisions (if the statistics play an important part in decision making, management have an incentive to ensure it is accurately compiled).

> **Top tips.** Other valid procedures include:
>
> - Comparing trends in the current year with previous years to ensure they appear reasonable
> - Verifying customer codes on the customer master file are properly input to make sure the customer type is properly identified.
> - Reviewing reports from sales staff to ensure information on university take-up of books is accurate.

(c) **Substantive tests to ensure the royalties charge is accurate and complete**

Substantive test	Objective of test
Compare actual royalties with the budgeted figures for royalties and investigate significant differences by obtaining explanations from management and obtaining corroborative evidence.	To assure the auditor that actual royalties are in line with management expectations, and there is a valid reason for any variances.

Substantive test	Objective of test
Consider whether the royalties charge represents a reasonable proportion of stated sales income and obtain explanations from management if this is not the case.	To satisfy the auditor the royalties charge appears reasonable when compared to stated sales income.
Select a sample of sales entries and verify whether royalties had been correctly recorded in respect of these sales (that is, if they are due, a royalty charge is recorded at 10% of the sales value).	To provide the auditor with evidence on the completeness and accuracy of the royalties charge, and to confirm that royalties were due on despatches.

Top tips. You could have validly stated other procedures and related objectives, but only three of each was required. Other procedures which could have been included are set out below.

Agree a sample of royalty payments to supporting sales and despatch documentation, ensuring that despatches are to individuals/organisations attracting royalties.	To prove that royalty payments have come from a sale and despatch that royalties should have been paid on.
Select sales for an appropriate number of days before and after the year end and verify against despatch notes.	To check that the proper cut-off treatment has been applied and only royalties on sales on or before the year end are included.
Review the sales statistics to establish which despatches attract royalties.	To provide evidence the royalties charge was based on reliable information (as proved in (b)).
Using the sales data on monthly sales by customer type, calculate expected level of royalties paid by multiplying the sales by 10%. Compare with actual royalties and investigate significant differences by seeking explanations from management and obtaining corroborative evidence.	To gain evidence over the completeness and accuracy of royalties paid.

(d) **Inherent risks and mitigating controls**

Inherent risks that may affect Redburn Co's inventory and mitigating controls are set out below:

Inherent risk	Mitigating control
There may be insufficient demand for books of relatively unknown poets and therefore books may not be saleable.	A record should be kept of inventory movements on a line by line basis to identify slow moving book titles.
There is a risk that the poetry books will deteriorate over time.	Books should be stored in dry conditions and materials should be sourced which do not deteriorate in the short term.

Top tips. Other valid inherent risks and related mitigating controls which could have been stated include those given below (but only two were required).

Books are damaged or defective and therefore not saleable.	Active inspection at inventory counts to identify books in poor condition.
Books are relatively small removable items and therefore susceptible to theft.	Books should be stored in a secure location, preferably with CCTV if this is cost effective.

Books held on sale and return but still in the return period are not included within inventory.	A separate record of books on sale on return should be maintained, reviewed and compared with inventory records to ensure all books still owned by Redburn Co are included.
Inventory counts are not properly carried out.	Independent and experienced counters should be used during inventory counts. Clear counting instructions should be issued and counters should count in pairs using numbered sheets, with one individual counting and the other checking.
Movements in and out of inventory near the year end cause incorrect cut off treatment.	Movement of books in and out is prohibited during the inventory count.

(e)   **Net realisable value (NRV)**

(i)   **Definition of NRV**

IAS 2 *Inventories* defines NRV as 'the estimated selling price in the ordinary course of business, less the estimated costs of completion and the estimated costs necessary to make the sale' (IAS 2: para. 6).

(ii)   **Procedures**

Procedures appropriate to assess that NRV is at or above cost are as follows:

(1)   Develop an estimate of (or obtain actual) sales prices and proceeds in respect of inventory held at the year end. This is done to provide the sales price for the NRV calculation and should involve the following:

  •   Inspecting post year end sales invoices to obtain actual sales prices for year end inventory

  •   If there are no sales of the inventory line being tested, obtain management's estimated sales price. The auditor should assess the reasonableness of this, for example by inspecting current price lists or looking at the sales reports from sales staff.

  •   Having identified slow moving or damaged items from the sales reports and results of inventory counts, the auditor should ensure that these are assigned a nil value.

(2)   Establish an estimate of costs to completion (to include in the NRV calculation). This will involve the following:

  •   The books may be complete, but if not (for example the books are unbound) the auditor must determine the cost to completion using actual post year end cost records or budgeted costs. Any further costs for returned books to make them saleable should also be taken into account.

(3)   Determine directly attributable selling, distribution and marketing costs (to form part of the NRV calculation).

  •   Estimate these costs for the books being tested and whether any apportionment of costs to inventory lines is reasonable (for example apportionment by weight or size for distribution costs).

(4)   Combine the three elements above (1 less 2 and 3) to arrive at NRV and compare with the cost. Discuss your findings and estimates with management and other informed staff to gain comfort that conclusions are reasonable.

148 Lily

Marking scheme

		Marks
(a)	Up to 1 mark per well explained deficiency and up to 1 mark per recommendation. If not well explained then just give ½ mark for each.	
	Warehouse manager supervising the count	
	No division of responsibilities within each counting team	
	Internal audit teams should be checking controls and performing sample counts	
	No flagging of aisles once counting complete	
	Additional inventory listed on sheets which are not sequentially numbered	
	Inventory sheets not signed by counters	
	Damaged goods not moved to central location	
	Movements of inventory during the count	
	Warehouse manager not qualified to assess the level of work-in-progress	
	Warehouse manager not experienced enough to assess the quantities of raw materials	12
(b)	Up to 1 mark per well described procedure	
	Observe the counters to confirm if inventory count instructions are being followed	
	Perform test counts inventory to sheets and sheets to inventory	
	Confirm procedures for damaged goods are operating correct	
	Inspect damaged goods to confirm whether the level of damage is correctly noted	
	Observe procedures for movements of inventory during the count	
	Obtain a photocopy of the completed inventory sheets	
	Identify and make a note of the last goods received notes and goods despatched notes	
	Observe the procedures carried out by warehouse manager in assessing the level of work-in-progress	
	Discuss with the warehouse manager how he has estimated the raw materials quantities	
	Identify inventory held for third parties and ensure excluded from count	6

(c)   (i)   Up to 1 mark per well described procedure, max of 4 procedures
Calculate inventory days
Produce an aged inventory analysis to identify any slow moving goods
Cast the inventory listing
Select a sample of items for testing to confirm net realisable value (NRV)
   and/or cost
Recalculate cost and NRV for sample of inventory
Computer-assisted audit techniques (CAATs) can be used to confirm
   cut-off
CAATs can be used to confirm whether inventory adjustments noted
   during the count have been updated to inventory records.   4

(ii)   Up to 1 mark per well explained advantage
Test a large volume of inventory data accurately and quickly
Cost effective after setup
CAATs can test program controls as well as general IT controls
Test the actual inventory system and records rather than printouts from
   the system
CAATs reduce the level of human error in testing
CAATs results can be compared with traditional audit testing
Free up audit team members to focus on judgemental and high risk areas   4

(iii) Up to 1 mark per well explained disadvantage
Costs of using CAATs in this first year will be high
Team may require training on the specific CAATs to be utilised
Changes in the inventory system may require costly revisions to the
   CAATs
The inventory system may not be compatible with the audit firm's CAATs
If testing the live system, there is a risk the data could be corrupted or
   lost
If using copy files rather than live data, there is the risk that these files
   are not genuine copies
Adequate systems documentation must be available   4
                                                                                        ──
                                                                                        30

(a)

Deficiency (i)	Recommendation (ii)
The warehouse manager will supervise the inventory count and is not independent as he has overall responsibility for the inventory. He therefore has an incentive to conceal or fail to report any issues that could reflect badly upon him.	An independent supervisor should be assigned, such as a manager from the internal audit department.
Aisles or areas counted will not be flagged. This could result in items being double counted or not counted at all.	Once areas have been counted they should be flagged. At the end of the count the supervisor should check all areas have been flagged and therefore counted.
There is no-one independent reviewing controls over the count or test counting to assess the accuracy of the counts.	Instead of the internal auditors being involved in the count itself, they should perform secondary test counts and review controls over the count.

Deficiency (i)	Recommendation (ii)
Damaged goods are being left in their location rather than being stored separately. This makes it more difficult for finance to assess the level of damage to the goods and establish the level of write down needed. Also, if not moved, damaged goods could be sold by mistake.	Damaged goods should be clearly marked as such during the count and at the end of the count they should be moved to a central location. A manager from the finance team should then inspect these damaged goods to assess the level of allowance or write down needed.
Due to the continuous production process, there will be movement of goods in and out of the warehouse during the count, increasing the risk of double counting or failing to count inventory. This could mean inventory in the financial statements is under or overstated.	Although it is not practicable to disrupt the continuous production process, raw materials (RM) required for 31 December should be estimated and separated from the remainder of inventory. These materials should be included as part of work-in-progress (WIP). Goods manufactured on 31 December should be stored separately, and at the end of the count should be counted once and included as finished goods. Goods received from suppliers should also be stored separately, counted once at the end and included in RM. Goods despatched to customers should be kept to a minimum during the count.
The warehouse manager is going to estimate WIP levels. The warehouse manager is unlikely to have the necessary experience to estimate the WIP levels which is something the factory manager would be more familiar with. Alternatively a specialist may be needed to make the estimate. This could ultimately result in an inaccurate WIP balance in the financial statements.	A specialist should be used assess the work-in-progress.
The warehouse manager is going to approximate RM quantities. Although he is familiar with the RM, and on the basis that a specialist has been required in the past, the warehouse manager may not have the necessary skill and experience to carry out these measurements. This could result in an inaccurate RM balance in the financial statements.	As in previous years, a specialist should assess the quantities of raw materials, or at least check the warehouse manager's estimate to give comfort that the manager's estimates will be reasonable going forward.
There is no indication that inventory sheets are signed or initialled by the counting team, nor a record kept of which team counted which area. This means it will be difficult to follow up on any anomalies noted, as the identity of the counters may not be known.	Inventory sheets should be signed by both team members once an aisle is completed. The supervisor should check the sheets are signed when handed in.
Inventory not listed on the sheets is to be entered onto separate sheets. These sheets are not sequentially numbered and the supervisor will be unable to ensure the completeness of all inventory sheets.	Every team should be given a blank sheet on which they can enter any inventory counted which is not on their sheets. The blank sheets should be sequentially numbered with any unused sheets returned at the end of the count. The supervisor should then check the sequence of all sheets.

Deficiency (i)	Recommendation (ii)
The responsibilities of each of the two staff members within a counting team is unclear. It does not appear that one has been told to count and the other to check. Therefore errors in counting may not be picked up.	For each area one team member should be asked to count and the second member asked to check that the inventory has been counted correctly. The roles of each can then be reversed for the next area.

(**Note.** Only six deficiencies and six related recommendations were needed to gain 12 marks.)

(b)   **Procedures undertaken during the inventory count**

- For a sample of inventory items, carry out test counts from aisle to inventory sheet to test completeness and from inventory sheets to aisle to test existence.

- Obtain and record details of the last goods received notes (GRNs) and goods despatched notes (GDNs) for 31 December to form the basis for cut-off procedures at the audit.

- Observe whether teams carrying out the count are adequately following the inventory count instructions.

- For a sample of items marked as damaged on the inventory sheets, inspect the windows to verify that the level of damage has been correctly recorded.

- Observe the procedures for movements of inventory in and assess the risk that raw materials or finished goods have been missed or double counted.

- Photocopy the inventory sheets for follow up and use when performing procedures at the final audit.

- Ascertain how the warehouse manager is assessing the level of work-in-progress by observing the assessment and by reviewing his assumptions, and consider how consistent his estimate is with observed levels.

- Ask the warehouse manager how he has estimated the raw materials quantities and review his calculations and any assumptions for reasonableness. Re-perform a sample of the measurements of height and width forming the basis of any calculation to see if they are accurate.

- Confirm any third party inventory observed has been excluded from the count.

- Confirm that the procedures for identifying and separately storing damaged goods are operating effectively.

(**Note.** Only six procedures were needed to gain full marks).

(c)   **Computer assisted audit techniques**

(i)   **Audit procedures**

Software can be used to cast the inventory listing to confirm the total is complete and accurate.

Audit software could be used to extract a statistical sample of inventory items in order to verify their cost or net realisable value (NRV).

Calculations of inventory days or inventory turnover could be carried out by audit software, before being used to compare against the same ratios for the prior year or of competitors. This will help to assess the risk of inventory being overstated.

Audit software could be used to help extract an aged inventory analysis. This could in turn be used to identify any obsolete or slow moving items, which may require a write down or an allowance.

Audit software can be used to perform calculations during testing of inventory, such as recorded cost (eg weight or quantity multiplied by cost per kg or unit).

CAATs can be used to confirm whether inventory adjustments recorded during attendance at the count have been correctly recorded in the final inventory records forming the basis of inventory in the financial statements.

CAATs can be used to verify cut-off by testing whether the dates of the last GRNs and GDNs recorded relate to pre year end, and that any with a date after the year end have been excluded from the inventory records.

(**Note.** Only four procedures were required.)

(ii) **CAATs – Advantages**

- CAATs allow the audit team to test a large volume of inventory data more accurately and more quickly than if tested manually.

- CAATs decrease the scope for human error during testing and can provide evidence of a higher quality.

- By using CAATs, auditors can test actual inventory transactions within the system rather than working on printouts from spool or previewed files which are dependent on other software (and therefore could contain errors or could have been tampered with following export).

- Assuming the inventory system remains unchanged, CAATs used in the audit of Lily year on year should bring time (and therefore cost) savings in the long term, which should more than compensate for any set up costs.

- Auditors can utilise CAATs to test programme controls as well as general internal controls associated with computers.

- Results from CAATs can be compared with results from traditional testing. If the results correlate, overall confidence is increased.

- The use of CAATs allows audit team members more time to focus on risk areas and issues requiring judgement, rather than performing routine calculations that can be carried out by audit software.

(**Note.** Only four advantages were needed to gain full marks.)

(iii) **CAATs – Disadvantages**

- Setting up the software needed for CAATs in the first year is likely to be time consuming and expensive.

- Audit staff working on Lily's audit will need to be trained so they have a sufficient level of IT knowledge to apply CAATs when auditing the inventory system.

- If testing is performed on data in the live inventory system, there is a risk that live client data may be corrupted and lost.

- If the inventory system at Lily changed then it may be expensive and time consuming to re-design the CAATs.

- If the inventory system at Lily is not compatible with Daffodil & Co's CAATs then they will need to be tailored to Lily's system, which may be costly.

- If testing is performed on data from copies of the live files rather than the live data itself, there is the risk that these files have been affected by the copying process or have been tampered with.

- If there is not adequate systems documentation available, it will be difficult to design appropriate CAATs due to a lack of understanding of the inventory system at Lily.

(**Note.** Only four advantages were needed to gain full marks.)

149 Springfield Nurseries

> **Text reference.** Chapters 10, 12, 13 and 14.
>
> **Top tips.** You shouldn't find this 30 mark case-study question on the audit of revenue, non-current assets and inventory too tricky. Part (e) is probably the most difficult part. This question is typical of the sort of question you should expect on any of the main classes of assets or liabilities on your exam paper. You need to be able to explain issues and identify audit tests to gain sufficient evidence about them. You should also be ready to identify deficiencies in part of an accounting system and then suggest how these can be rectified. Remember to relate your answer to information provided in the scenario where possible.
>
> **Easy marks.** Parts (a) and (c) are the more straightforward parts of the question.
>
> For part (c) ensure that you deal with ownership and cost separately.

Marking scheme

		Marks
(a)	Tests of controls and substantive procedures Up to 1 mark per point to a maximum of	4
(b)	Assertions for non-current assets Up to 1 mark per point to a maximum of	5
(c)	Evidence available 0.5 marks per source of evidence to a maximum of	2
(d)	Audit procedures Up to 1 mark per point to a maximum of	5
(e)	Deficiencies and suggested solutions Up to 1 mark per explained deficiency and up to 1 point per suggested solution up to a maximum of	14
		30

(a) **Procedures**

    (i) *Tests of controls*

        Tests of controls are performed to obtain audit evidence about the operating effectiveness of controls preventing, or detecting and correcting, material misstatements at the assertion level. (ISA 330: para. 4(b))

        A test of control that may be carried out when auditing completeness of revenue is observing or verifying the process of matching of goods despatch notes (GDNs) to invoices. The auditor should also enquire how unmatched GDNs are investigated to ensure related sales are recorded where necessary.

    (ii) *Substantive procedures*

        Substantive procedures are audit procedures performed to detect material misstatements at the assertion level. They are generally of two types (ISA 330: para. 4(a)):

        • Substantive analytical procedures
        • Tests of detail of classes of transactions, account balances and disclosures

        An example of a substantive procedure is comparing monthly revenue with prior years, budgets and expectations (eg for expected seasonal peaks) and investigating any significant deviations.

(b) **Financial statement assertions for non-current assets**

Completeness

The amounts stated in the statement of financial position for non-current assets must represent all non-current assets used in the operations of the entity. Significant omissions could have a material effect on the financial statements. Where an entity has lots of small capital items, recording and tracking these can be an issue so good controls are important.

Existence

Recorded assets must represent productive assets that are in use at the reporting date. Where assets have been disposed, they must not be included in the statement of financial position. Items that are susceptible to misappropriation can also present issues.

Accuracy, valuation and allocation

Non-current assets must be stated at cost or valuation less accumulated depreciation. Whether an entity has a policy or not of revaluing certain categories of its non-current assets can have a material effect on its financial statements. The depreciation policy in place must be suitable as this can also have a significant bearing on asset values on buildings and larges items of plant and equipment.

Rights and obligations

This is a key assertion for non-current assets because the entity must own or have rights to all the recorded non-current assets at the reporting date. For example, where an asset is leased by the entity, it may not have substantially all the risks and rewards associated with ownership and therefore should not recognise the asset on its statement of financial position.

Classification

Tangible assets should be recorded in the correct accounts, and expenses which are not of a capital nature are taken to profit or loss.

Presentation

Non-current assets must be disclosed correctly in the financial statements.

(c) **Evidence available**

Asset	Ownership	Cost
Land and Buildings	Title deeds. These may be held at the bank or the client's solicitors.	The cost of the land and building can be traced to original invoices.
	It may be possible to obtain confirmation of ownership from the central land registry office.	The company may also have retained the original completion documents from the solicitor on the purchase of the land.
	The insurance policy should be reviewed to see whom the cover is in favour of.	

(d) **Procedures re depreciation**

The purpose of depreciation is to write off the cost of the asset over the period of its useful economic life.

(i) *Buildings*

To assess the appropriateness of the depreciation rate of 5%, the auditor should:

- Consider the physical condition of the building and whether the remaining useful life assumption is reasonable

- Review the minutes of board meetings to ensure there are no relocation plans

- Consider the budgets and ensure that they account for the appropriate amount of depreciation. If they do not, they may give an indication of management's future plans.

(ii)   *Computers and motor vehicles*

The reducing balance basis seems reasonable, given that computers and their software are updated frequently and therefore do wear faster early on in life, however the auditor should consider whether 20% is an appropriate rate given the speed at which technology develops.

The auditor should enquire and observe whether the assets are still in use.

The auditor should review the board minutes to ascertain whether there are any plans to upgrade the system.

The auditor should estimate the average age of the motor vehicles according to their registration plates and consider whether the life is reasonable in light of average age and recent purchases. Given that a number of vehicles are delivery vehicles and likely to heavily used, the auditor should look at recent profits and losses on disposals to see if large losses on disposal give an indication the 20% rate might be too low.

The auditor should ask management what the replacement policy of the assets is.

(iii)   *Equipment*

The equipment is depreciated at 15% per year, or over 6–7 years.

The auditor should consider whether this is reasonable for all the categories of equipment, or whether there are some assets for which the technology advances more quickly than others. Such assets may require a higher rate of depreciation.

(e)

Deficiency and explanation	Possible solution
There is a lack of segregation of duties. The site inventory controller is also the supervisor and count checker. The controller is therefore responsible for the physical assets as well as maintaining the book records. The site inventory controller is a position to cover up his or her own errors or theft of inventory.	An alternative senior member of staff should be made the inventory supervisor. Alternatively, inventory controllers could be rotated so they supervise the count of the garden centre they are not responsible for.
Transfer of inventory is permitted between centres, increasing the risk of double counting inventory. Also inventory may not be counted at it all if it is in transit during the count.	Movement of inventory between garden centres should not be permitted until all inventory has been counted.
Counters will be working on their own as there is only one allocated per area. This means the risk of error is increased compared to the normal situation where two counters are assigned.	Counts should be performed by pairs of counters, one counting and one checking.
Counters are provided with printed sheets with quantities already showing a quantity from the computer system and are only changed if found to be different from actual quantities. This may lead counters into the temptation of choosing to rely on the system and as a result failing to count all inventory lines.	Staff should be given sheets with items listed but no quantities. The staff should need to fill in the quantities as the count progresses.
Only one test count is carried out in each area by the inventory controller. This is unlikely to deter counters from being careless and the probability of errors being detected by the test count is low.	A larger sample should be test counted by the inventory controller. This could be determined statistically based on the estimated levels of inventory for each area per the system.

Deficiency and explanation	Possible solution
Damaged or old inventory quantities are crossed out and those items are given a nil quantity. This means all record of these items is lost and they may still have a value – they need to be assessed by more senior staff members.	Damaged or old inventory quantities should be maintained. They may be highlighted on the list. However, an appropriate independent senior staff member should carry out a separate review for damaged or old items and identify those which may need to included as part of an inventory provision.
Count sheets are to be discarded once the inventory system is updated. This means there will be no audit trail for inventory quantities and no way to verify how accurately the data has been entered.	Count sheets should be retained and, for a sample of inventory items, an independent person should verify that the quantities on the count sheets have been entered correctly.

150 Westra Co

Text references. Chapters 10, 11 and 16

Top tips. This 30 mark question is split into four parts so it is very important that you spend the appropriate amount of time on each part – do not get bogged down in one part and then find out that you do not have enough time to answer the other parts of the question.

In parts (a) and (b), you can score one mark for each audit procedure and one mark for explaining the purpose of that audit procedure, therefore half the marks available are for your explanations. Make sure that you do explain the reasons fully. An appropriate way of setting out your answer for those two parts would be in a table format. Such a format ensures that you link each audit procedure to an explanation.

In part (c), you are asked to 'describe' control procedures over the trade payables master file. This means that, again, you need to explain the control procedure fully – you will not score the full marks available if you do not do this.

In part (d), you are asked to discuss how CAATs can be used in the audit of payables at this client. Although you need to understand what CAATs are and how they can be used, it is very important that you apply your knowledge to this particular scenario. A general answer on CAATs will not score well unless it is relevant to the circumstances in this question.

Easy marks. This is a challenging question and there are no easy marks as such. However by using the information in the scenario, you should be able to score relatively well in parts (a) and (c), provided you explain your answers as required by the requirements.

Marks

(a) Audit procedures – purchases 12 marks. 1 for procedure and 1 for the reason. Limit to 5 marks in each category where stated briefly without full detail.

Audit procedure	Reason for procedure
Parts to GRN	Check completeness
Parts no GRN number	System error or cut-off error
GRN to computer	Parts received were ordered – occurrence
GRN agree to invoice	Completeness of recording
Review unmatched GRN file	Completeness of recording of liabilities
Paid invoice – GRN attached	Confirms invoice in PDB
Invoice details to payables ledger	Completeness and accuracy of recording
Review unmatched invoices file	Indicate understatement of liability (lack of completeness)

Payables ledger to purchase invoice	Liability belongs to Westra
Payables ledger to payments list	Liability properly discharged – payments complete
Payment list entries to invoice	Payment made for bona fide liability
Payments list to bank statement	Confirms payment to supplier
Bank statement entry to payments list	Confirms payment relates to Westra
GRN cut-off testing	Accuracy of cut-off
Maximum marks	**12**

(b) **Audit procedures – payables**, 8 marks. 1 for procedure and 1 for reason. Limit to ½ mark in each category where stated briefly without full detail.

Audit procedure	**Reason for procedure**
Obtain and cast list of payables	Ensure that the list is accurate
Total of payables to the general ledger and financial statements	Confirm that the total has been accurately recorded
Analytical procedures	Indicates problems with the accuracy and completeness of payables
Agree payables to supplier statements	Confirm balance due from Westra
Supplier statement reconciliation	Liabilities exist and belong to Westra
Reconcile invoices	Confirms completeness and cut-off assertions
Reconcile payments	Payment to correct supplier
Review ledger old unpaid invoices	Credits O/S or going concern indicator
After date credit notes	Payables not overstated
FS categorisation payables	Classification objective
Maximum marks	**8**

(c) **Controls over standing data**, 5 marks. 1 mark for explaining each control. ½ for poor/limited explanation.

Amendments authorised
How authorised (form or access control)
Reject deletion where outstanding balance
Keep record of amendments
Review list of suppliers – unauthorised amendments
Update supplier list on computer regularly
Review computer control log
Review list of suppliers – unauthorised additions
Other relevant points (each)
Maximum marks **5**

(d) **Use of CAATs**
Review computer control log
Identify old / obsolete – computer may already do this
Test data – online payments system
Use of CAATs – limited – lack of computer system integration
Need to assess computer controls prior to use of CAATs
Not cost effective – bespoke systems
Limited use of CAATs in suppliers ledger
Other relevant points (each)
Maximum marks **5**
30

(a)   **Substantive procedures**

Completeness

Audit procedure	Purpose
Perform analytical procedures on purchases, eg comparison to the prior year on a month-by-month basis, ratio of purchases to payables, gross profit % etc and investigate any significant fluctuations	To provide assurance on the completeness of amounts recorded in the accounts and to highlight any areas of concern for further investigation
For a sample of supplier invoices, trace amounts to the GRN, order and payables ledger	To confirm completeness of recording of purchases
Inspect the unmatched GRNs file and seek explanations for any old unmatched items and trace these to the year-end accruals listing	To provide assurance on completeness as these should be included in the year-end accrual
For a sample of amounts on the ledger, agree to the computerised payments list to verify the amount and supplier	To provide assurance that the payment list is complete and accurate

Occurrence

Audit procedure	Purpose
For a sample of amounts in the payables ledger, trace these to the invoice and other supporting documentation such as GRNs	To provide assurance on the occurrence assertion
For a sample of GRNs, agree back to the original order details	To provide assurance on occurrence
For a sample of payees on the computerised payments list, agree amounts back to the supporting documentation such as invoices and GRNs	To provide assurance that payment has been made for a *bona fide* liability of the company
For a sample of payments made after the year-end, trace back to the computerised payments list	To provide assurance that payment relates to the company
For a sample of payees on the computerised payments list, trace payment to post year-end bank statements	To confirm that payment was made to authorised suppliers of the company

Cut-off

Audit procedure	Purpose
For a sample of GRNs dated shortly before and after the year-end, agree that the amounts on invoices are posted to the correct financial year	To ensure that amounts are included in the correct financial period
Review the schedule of accruals and agree to GRNs, inspecting the date of receipt of goods to ensure that goods received after the year-end are not included	To ensure that amounts are included in the correct financial period
Inspect outstanding orders on the 'orders placed' file for any orders completed but not yet invoiced	To ensure that amounts are included in the correct financial period

(b) **Audit procedures on trade payables**

Audit procedure	Purpose
Cast the list of payables balances from the ledger at the year-end	To provide assurance that the list is complete and accurate
Reconcile the payables list from the payables ledger to the general ledger and accounts	To provide assurance that the figures are complete and accurate and correctly reflected in the financial statements
Perform analytical procedures on trade payables, comparing balance to prior year and investigating any significant fluctuations	To provide assurance on completeness and accuracy and to highlight areas of concern
For a sample of balances, trace amount to supporting supplier statements	To confirm the existence and accuracy of the amount outstanding at the year-end
Test cut-off by taking a sample of GRNs either side of the year-end and verifying that amounts are included on the payables ledger for goods received before the year-end	To ensure that amounts are included in the correct financial period
Review disclosure of payables in the draft financial statements	To ensure that payables have been disclosed appropriately in the statement of financial position and notes as either current or long-term liabilities

(c) **Control procedures over standing data on trade payables master file**

- Access to the trade payables master file is limited only to authorised staff

- Amendments to standing data can only be made by authorised staff and all amendments must be authorised prior to input

- Access to the file is controlled by logins and passwords and passwords must be prompted to be changed regularly (say, every 90 days)

- Computer log is reviewed regularly by IT department to detect any unauthorised access or attempts to access the trade payables master file

- The list of suppliers should be reviewed regularly by a senior manager and those no longer used should be removed from the system

(d) **Use of CAATs in audit of Westra**

CAATs could be used in the audit of purchases and payables at Westra in a number of ways.

For example, audit software could be used to generate a **sample of ledger balances** to be agreed to supplier statements. CAATs could also be used to **reperform** the cost of the total on the file to ensure the file is a complete record of transactions. CAATs can also be used to perform **ratio calculations** for analytical procedures on the purchases and payables data. **Test data** could be used to undertake some controls testing on the trade payables master file, such as on data access and payments to suppliers.

However, generally for this audit, the use of CAATs is somewhat **limited** as the company uses a mixture of manual and computerised systems, and where computerised systems are used, they are not fully integrated with each other.

151 Panda

Text reference. Chapter 1, Chapter 18 and Chapter 19.

Top tips. Part (a) is knowledge-based on the elements of assurance engagements and you should be able to score the full five marks here. In part (b), you first need to assess whether each of the issues is material or not so make sure you use the figures provided in the question for revenue and profit before taxation to make your assessment. Remember also to consider whether these are adjusting events or not. Each issue is worth six marks so assume there are three marks for explaining whether an amendment is required and three marks for the audit procedures. In part (c), you must fully explain how the non-disclosure/amendment relating to the explosion might affect the auditor's report – it is not enough to say that the opinion will be modified, for example; you must explain the basis of any modification and whether it is material or pervasive. Note that in this part you are only asked to discuss the explosion – you must not include a discussion of the defective chemicals as this has not been asked for.

Easy marks. Part (a) offers easy marks for explaining the elements of an assurance engagement.

Marking scheme

Marks

(a) Up to 1 mark per well explained element

- Intended user, responsible party, practitioner
- Subject matter
- Suitable criteria
- Appropriate evidence
- Assurance report

5

(b) Up to 1 mark per valid point, overall maximum of 6 marks per event

Event 1 – Defective chemicals
- Provides evidence of conditions at the year end
- Inventory to be adjusted to lower of cost and net realisable value
- Calculation of materiality
- Review board minutes/quality control reports
- Discuss with the directors, adequate inventory to continue to trade
- Obtain written representation re going concern
- Obtain schedule of defective inventory, agree to supporting documentation
- Discuss with directors basis of the scrap value

6

Event 2 – Explosion
- Provides evidence of conditions that arose subsequent to the year end
- Non-adjusting event, requires disclosure if material
- Calculation of materiality
- Obtain schedule of damaged property, plant and equipment and agree values to asset register
- Obtain latest inventory records to confirm damaged inventory levels
- Discuss with the directors if they will make disclosures
- Discuss with directors why no insurance claim will be made

6

(c)   Up to 1 mark per well explained valid point

- Disclosure required in 20X3 financial statements and adjustment to the assets in 20X4 financial statements
- Material but not pervasive misstatement, modified auditor's report, qualified opinion
- Basis for qualified opinion paragraph required
- Opinion paragraph – except for

3
___
20

(a)   **Elements of an assurance engagement**

There are five elements of an assurance engagement and these are explained below (IFAC, 2016).

A three party relationship

The three parties are the intended user, the responsible party and the practitioner. Intended users are the person, persons or class of persons for whom the practitioner prepares the assurance report. The responsible party is the person (or persons) responsible for the subject matter (in a direct engagement) or subject matter information of the assurance engagement.

The practitioner is the individual providing professional services that will review the subject matter and provide the assurance.

A subject matter

This is the data to be evaluated that has been prepared by the responsible party. It can take many forms including financial performance (eg historical financial information), non-financial performance (eg key performance indicators), processes (eg internal control) and behaviour (eg compliance with laws and regulations).

Suitable criteria

The subject matter is evaluated or measured against criteria in order to reach an opinion.

Evidence

Sufficient appropriate evidence needs to be gathered to support the required level of assurance.

Assurance report

A report containing the practitioner's opinion is issued to the intended user.

(b)   **Event 1: Defective chemicals**

A batch of chemicals produced before the year-end, costing £0.85m to produce, has been found to be defective after the year-end. Its scrap value is £0.1m. Inventory should be valued at the lower of cost and net realisable value in accordance with IAS 2 *Inventories* (IAS 2: para. 9). This is an adjusting event in accordance with IAS 10 *Events after the reporting period* (IAS 10: para. 3). As it stands, the inventory is overstated by £0.75m. This represents 13.4% of profit before tax and 1.4% of revenue and is therefore material to the financial statements.

Audit procedures to be performed

- Obtain a schedule to confirm the cost value of the defective batch of £0.85m and documentary proof of the scrap value of £0.1m.

- Discuss with management whether this is the only defective batch or whether there are likely to be other batches affected.

- Review quality control reports to assess the likelihood of other batches being affected and discuss results of testing with technical team members at Panda.

Event 2: Explosion

An explosion shortly after the year-end has resulted in damage to inventory and property, plant and equipment. The amount of inventory and property, plant and equipment damaged is estimated to be £0.9m. It has no scrap value. Inventory and property, plant and equipment are therefore overstated by £0.9m. This represents 16.1% of profit before tax and 1.6% of revenue, and is therefore material. The explosion represents a non-adjusting event in accordance with IAS 10 *Events after the reporting period*. It therefore does not require adjustment in the financial statements but should be disclosed as it is material (IAS 10: para. 10).

Audit procedures to be performed

- Obtain a schedule of the inventory and property, plant and equipment damaged in the explosion to verify the value of £0.9m.

- Visit the site where the explosion took place to assess damage.

- Discuss with directors the need to make disclosure in the financial statements and review any draft disclosure note drafted.

- Inspect insurance agreement to assess whether any claim can be made on the insurance.

(c) **Effect on auditor's report of the explosion**

The directors should make disclosures in the financial statements about the explosion and the effect on inventory and property, plant and equipment. This is because the amount involved is material and affects the value of opening inventory and property, plant and equipment in the following financial year.

If the directors refuse to make the disclosure, then the auditors would modify the opinion on the financial statements on the basis of a material misstatement. The opinion would be qualified 'except for' as the matter is material but unlikely to be pervasive. – spread everywhere

A 'Basis for qualified opinion' paragraph would be included in the auditor's report, describing the auditor's reason for modifying the opinion and the effect of the explosion on the opening balances in the financial statements for the following financial year (ISA 705: para. 20). The 'Basis for qualified opinion' would be placed immediately after the Opinion paragraph.

152 Rose

Marking scheme

Marks

(a) Up to 1 mark per well explained point, being ½ mark for the principle and ½ mark
for the explanation
Integrity
Objectivity
Professional competence and due care
Confidentiality
Professional behaviour   5

Marks

(b) Up to 1 mark per well described procedure
  (i) Trade payables and accruals
    Calculate trade payable days
    Compare total trade payables and list of accruals against prior year
    Discuss with management process to quantify understatement of payables
    Discuss with management whether any correcting journal adjustment
      posted
    Sample invoices received between 25 October and year end and follow
      to inclusion in year-end accruals or trade payables correcting journal
    Review after date payments
    Review supplier statements reconciliations
    Perform a trade payables' circularisation
    Cut-off testing pre and post year-end GRN   6

  (ii) Receivables
    For non-responses arrange to send a follow up circularisation
    With the client's permission, telephone the customer and ask for a
      response
    For remaining non-responses, undertake alternative procedures to
      confirm receivables
    For responses with differences, identify any disputed amounts, identify
      whether these relate to timing differences or whether there are
      possible errors in the records
    Cash in transit should be vouched to post year-end cash receipts in the
      cash book
    Review receivables ledger to identify any possible mispostings
    Disputed balances, discuss with management whether a write down is   5
      necessary

  (iii) Reorganisation
    Review the board minutes where decision taken
    Review the announcement to shareholders in late October
    Obtain a breakdown and confirm that only direct expenditure from
      restructuring is included
    Review expenditure to ensure retraining costs excluded
    Cast the breakdown of the reorganisation provision
    Agree costs included to supporting documentation
    Obtain a written representation
    Review the adequacy of the disclosures   4
                                                                       20

(a) **Fundamental principles** (ACCA Code of Ethics and Conduct: s. 100.5)

Principle	Explanation
Integrity	Members shall be straightforward and honest in all professional and business relationships.
Objectivity	Members shall not allow bias, conflicts of interest or undue influence of others to override professional or business judgements.
Professional competence and due care	Members have a continuing duty to maintain professional knowledge and skill at the level required to ensure that a client or employer receives competent professional services based on current developments in practice, legislation and techniques. Members shall act diligently and in accordance with applicable technical and professional standards.

Principle	Explanation
Confidentiality	Members shall respect the confidentiality of information acquired as a result of professional and business relationships and, therefore, not disclose any such information to third parties without proper and specific authority, or unless there is a legal or professional right or duty to disclose. Confidential information acquired as a result of professional and business relationships must not be used for the personal advantage of members or third parties.
Professional behaviour	Members shall comply with relevant laws and regulations and avoid any action that discredits the profession.

(b) **Substantive procedures**

(i) **Trade payables and accruals**

- Ask management about the action they have taken to establish the value of the misstatement of trade payables. If they have ascertained the value of the error assess the materiality of it and the impact of it remaining uncorrected.

- Enquire whether any correcting journal entry has been calculated and whether it has been processed in relation to the misstatement.

- For a sample of purchase invoices received between 25 October and the end of 31 October 20X2, verify that they are included within accruals or as part of trade payables via a journal adjustment.

- Reconcile supplier statements to purchase ledger balances, and investigate any reconciling items.

- Calculate and compare trade payables days to prior years. Significant differences should be investigated.

- Compare trade payables and accruals against the previous year and expectations. Investigate any significant differences and corroborate any explanations for differences to supporting evidence.

- Review the cash book payments and bank statements in the period immediately after the year end for evidence of payments relating to current year liabilities. Ensure any found are included in accruals, trade payables or the trade payables journal.

- For a sample of payable balances, perform a trade payables' circularisation. Any non-replies should be followed up and reconciling items between the balance confirmed and the trade payables' balance should be investigated.

- For a sample of goods received notes before the year end and after the year end, ensure the related invoices have been recorded in the period to which they relate.

(**Note.** Only six valid procedures were needed,)

(ii) **Receivables**

- For those receivables who don't respond, the team should arrange to send a follow up circularisation if agreed by the client.

- For non-responses to the follow up, and after obtaining client consent, the audit senior should telephone the customer and request the customer responds in writing to the circularisation request.

- Where all follow ups are unsuccessful, alternative procedures must be carried out to confirm receivables, such as reviewing after date cash receipts for year end receivables.

- Where responses highlight differences, these should be investigated to establish if any amounts are disputed or require adjustment.

- Where it is found that differences are in relation to disputed invoices, they should be discussed with management and the need for an allowance or write off assessed.

- For timing differences identified on responses or otherwise (eg cash in transit), these should be agreed to post year-end cash receipts in the cash book and bank statement.

- For those responses highlighting an unresolved difference, the receivables ledger should be reviewed for unusual entries that could suggest errors made when posting transactions.

(**Note.** Only five valid procedures were needed.)

(iii) **Reorganisation**

- Verify the announcement to shareholders was actually made in late October by inspecting documentary evidence of the announcement.

- Board minutes should also be reviewed to confirm the decision to reorganise the business was taken pre year end.

- Obtain an analysis of the reorganisation provision and confirm that only expenditure attributable to the restructuring is included.

- Cast the breakdown of the reorganisation provision to ensure it has been correctly calculated.

- Review the expenditure and confirm retraining costs are not included.

- Agree costs included within the provision to supporting documentation to confirm the appropriateness and accuracy of items included.

- Review the related disclosures in the financial statements to assess whether they comply with the requirements of IAS 37 *Provisions, contingent liabilities and contingent assets.*

- Obtain a written representation confirming management discussions in relation to the announcement of the reorganisation.

(**Note.** Only four valid procedures were needed.)

153 Donald

Text reference. Chapters 6, 8 and 16

Top tips. Part (a) was knowledge based and unrelated to a scenario. As long as you read the question correctly you should have scored well on this.

Part (b) is a common scenario related requirement where you needed to identify and describe **audit** risks and then explain the auditor's response to each risk. A tabular format would help ensure both mini requirements are addressed.

Note that we have emphasised that the risks are **audit** risks. For a risk to be an audit risk rather than just a general business risk it needs to have an impact on the financial statements being audited. Therefore you should include the assertion or area of the financial statements affected. If you do this it should become apparent if you have not come up with a audit risk as you will be unable to make the link. Make sure your responses to risks in a question like this are responses of the auditor, not of management.

Easy marks. The easy marks in this question were available in (a).

Examination Team's comments. In part (a) candidates performed satisfactorily. Where candidates did not score full marks this was because they failed to read the question properly. The scenario clearly excluded the procedure of external confirmation, however, a significant minority of candidates gave confirmations as a procedure.

In part (b) many candidates performed inadequately on this part of the question. As stated in previous examiner's reports, audit risk is a key element of the Audit & Assurance syllabus and candidates must understand audit risk.

A number of candidates wasted valuable time by describing the audit risk model along with definitions of audit risk, inherent risk, control and detection risk. This generated no marks as it was not part of the requirement.

The main area where candidates continue to lose marks is that they did not actually understand what audit risk relates to. Hence they provided answers which considered the risks the business would face or 'business risks,' which are outside the scope of the syllabus. Audit risks must be related to the risk arising in the audit of the financial statements and should include the financial statement assertion impacted.

The issue of the call centre closing and hence the workforce being made redundant was misunderstood by many. These candidates felt that this must mean that the company was having going concern issues, but there was no indication of this in the scenario. The risk related to the completeness of the redundancy provision.

Even if the audit risks were explained many candidates failed to provide a relevant response to the audit risk, most chose to give a response that management would adopt rather than the auditor.

Future candidates must take note audit risk is and will continue to be an important element of the syllabus and must be understood, and they would do well to practice audit risk questions.

Marking scheme

Marks

(a) Up to 1 mark per well explained procedure and up to 1 mark for a valid audit test, overall maximum of 2 marks per type of procedure and test.

Inspection
Observation
Analytical procedures
Inquiry
Recalculation
Performance

Maximum marks   **10**

(b) Up to 1 mark per well explained risk and up to 1 mark per response, overall maximum of 10.

Planes ordered may not exist at year end
Refurbishment of planes – capital or repairs
Loan of $25m not received yet
Recoverability of receivables
Completeness of income
Customer refunds
Redundancy provision

                                                                                                                     <u>10</u>
Maximum marks
                                                                                                                     <u>20</u>

(a) **Procedures to obtain audit evidence and examples relevant to auditing purchases and other expenses** (ISA 500: para. A14–A25)

Inspection

This is the examination of documents and records, both internal and external, in paper, electronic or other forms.

In the audit of purchases the auditor may inspect a sample of purchase invoices to ensure they agree to the amount posted to the general ledger.

Observation

This involves watching a procedure or process being performed.

An auditor may observe the checking of goods received against purchase orders in the goods received department.

Inquiry

This involves seeking financial or non-financial information from client staff or external sources.

An auditor may discuss with management whether there have been any changes in the key suppliers used and compare this to the purchase ledger to assess completeness and accuracy of purchases.

Recalculation

This consists of checking the mathematical accuracy of documents or records and can be performed through the use of IT.

The auditor may recalculate accruals and prepayments to gain evidence that other expenses are not over or understated.

Reperformance

This is the auditor's independent execution of procedures or controls that were originally performed as part of the entity's internal control.

The auditor may re-perform the payables ledger control account reconciliation to ensure it has been properly carried out.

Analytical procedures

This is evaluating and comparing financial and/or non-financial data for plausible relationships. Also include the investigation of identified fluctuations and relationships that are inconsistent with other relevant information or deviate significantly from predicted amounts.

The auditor could review expenses on a monthly basis to identify significant fluctuations and discuss them with management.

(**Note.** You may have come up with other valid examples relevant to purchases and expenses.)

(b) **Audit risks and responses**

Audit risk	Response to risk
Six planes have been ordered pre year end and it appears as though they may be delivered close to the year end. On average they are $3.33m each and there is a risk the assets and/or related liabilities are recorded in the wrong period, understating or overstating non-current assets.	Due to the monetary value of each aircraft all aircraft should be inspected and matched to those included in the Donald's accounting records. This will immediately highlight any planes recorded not received (ie those that don't exist at the year end date). It could also help to identify an asset received but not recorded.
The company has spent $15m on refurbishing aircraft. In order to classify this expenditure correctly (as either capital or revenue) accounting knowledge and judgement is required. Management at Donald may have classified the expenditure incorrectly either overstating or understating profit in the statement of profit or loss as a result.	An analysis of the refurbishment costs should be reviewed and traced to invoices. The invoice descriptions and supporting documents should be reviewed to assess the nature of the expenditure. Once established as either capital or revenue it should be traced to the general ledger and the financial statements to ensure it has been classified correctly as an asset or repairs.
Donald Co has capital commitments to fulfil having already ordered the planes, but has not yet secured funding because the bank loan of $25m has not been approved. This could cause going concern problems if the funding is refused.	Inquiries should be made as to the status of the loan application and progress in securing the funding should be monitored. A detailed going concern review is required.

Audit risk	Response to risk
Some of Donald's customers (the travel agents) are struggling to pay the amounts they owe to the company. This could result in irrecoverable debts not being written off and doubtful debts not being provided for. As a result the receivables balance and profit in the financial statements may be overstated	The detailed aged receivables analysis should be discussed with management and a value for a provision estimated for any potentially irrecoverable or doubtful debts. The review of amounts received by customers in respect of year end debts should be extended as far as possible.
Donald Co is making staff redundant as a result of the closure of their call centre which occurred pre-year end. There is a risk a redundancy provision has not been set up for staff not paid before the year end as required by IAS 37 *Provisions, contingent liabilities and contingent assets.* Profits may be overstated and provisions understated.	The auditor needs to establish the full redundancy cost through discussion with management and should corroborate to supporting evidence where necessary. The calculated redundancy cost should be compared to the actual provision included in the financial statements to ensure it is reasonable.

Top tips: Only five risks and five responses were needed to gain full marks, but other valid risks and responses are set out below.

Audit risk	Response to risk
Donald Co's website has consistently encountered difficulties with recording sales. This could result in sales of income recorded in the financial statements being incomplete.	Controls testing over the sales cycle should be increased to assess the extent of any potential understatement of revenue. Detailed testing should be performed over the completeness of income.
Tickets have been sold twice and some customers will require refunds. There is a risk that the tickets to be refunded have not been removed from sales.	The cut-off treatment of customer refunds should be reviewed around the year end to ensure that sales to be refunded are not included in the revenue figure in the financial statements.

154 Rocks Forever

Text reference. Chapters 12 and 13.

Top tips. In part (a) it is important to maintain a focus on the company in the scenario and not just write down general inventory risks. The high value of the inventory and the fact it is desirable gives rise to client specific risks.

Don't forget to explain the reason for using your procedures in part (b). Simply listing the procedures will not gain you the majority of the marks. We have included more points than necessary in our answer for your information, but you should stick to your time allocation on this part before moving on to the next.

Part (c) asks for factors to consider when placing reliance on the work of the expert. For five marks you need about five points so you will need to generate a few ideas. If you are not familiar with ISA 620 don't panic. You should be able to produce a reasonable answer with a bit of common sense. For part (d) the key is your accounting knowledge. Inventory should be valued at the lower of cost and net realisable value. Approach this part by thinking about the ways in which the cost of inventory can be confirmed. Then think about the way in which net realisable value can be established.

Easy marks. Overall this is a reasonably straightforward question looking at aspects of the audit with which you should be familiar. All the marks are reasonably achievable, which is good news although you do need to apply your knowledge to the scenario. Part (c) is probably the most straightforward as you can use your knowledge of ISA 620 *Using the work of an auditor's expert* to structure your answer.

		Marks
(a)	Risks associated with inventory in Rocks Forever Up to 1 mark per point to a maximum of:	3
(b)	1 mark for each procedure 1 for explaining the relevance of the procedure up to a maximum of:	8
(c)	Factors to consider when placing reliance on UJ Up to 1 mark per point to a maximum of:	5
(d)	Audit procedures to ensure jewellery is valued correctly Up to 1 mark per point to a maximum of:	4 20

(a) **Risks associated with inventory in Rocks Forever**

Rocks Forever is a company specialising in the sale of diamond jewellery. Inventory is therefore a material figure in the accounts of Rocks Forever.

Specific risks associated with inventory in Rocks Forever include existence – the nature of the inventory means that it is highly susceptible to theft and loss as it is a very attractive and valuable commodity.

Valuation is another key risk. The amount in the financial statements is material and the valuation of the jewellery is subjective as it is reliant on the judgement of expert valuers. The inventory should be valued at the lower of cost and net realisable value in accordance with accounting standards. However, given the nature of the inventory and the fact that sales are subject to changing trends and fashions, this is a key risk area.

(b) **Inventory count: procedures and reasons**

Audit procedures	Reason
Observe whether the client staff are following the inventory count instructions. This would include the following:	If proper procedures are not followed the auditor will not be able to rely on the count as relevant reliable audit evidence.
• Confirming that prenumbered count sheets are being used and that there are controls over the issue of count sheets.	Prenumbering of count sheets means that a completeness check can be performed and any missing sheets can be chased.
• Observing that counters are working in pairs of two.	This helps to prevent fraud and error.
• Confirming that inventory is marked once it has been counted.	Marking of inventory helps to prevent double counting of items.
• Confirming procedures to ensure that inventory is not moved during the count.	If inventory is moved eg sold during the count the counters may become confused as to which inventory has been counted and which has not. Movements of inventory would also make it more difficult to establish whether proper cut-off procedures have been followed.
• Confirming that inventory held for third parties is separately identified.	Customer jewellery held eg for repair should not be included in the inventory figure.
• Confirming that the counters are aware of the need to note down any items which they identify as damaged.	Damaged items may need to be written down to their recoverable amount. This will affect the overall value of inventory.

Audit procedures	Reason
Gain an overall impression of the levels and values of inventory held.	This will assist the auditor in the follow up procedures to judge whether the figure for inventory in the financial statements is reasonable.
Verify that all inventory sheets issued have been accounted for at the end of the count.	This provides evidence that a complete record of the results of the inventory count has been obtained. If missing count sheets were undetected inventory would be understated.
Take copies of the count sheets at the end of the inventory count and retain on file.	This prevents management from being able to adjust the figures subsequently. It also enables the auditor, in his follow up procedures to trace inventory counted to the final inventory calculation.
Obtain cut-off details ie record details of the last sales invoice issued before the count and the last goods in record before the count.	This information will allow the auditor to determine whether cut-off is correct. Items sold before the count should be included as sales and not recorded in inventory. Items received from suppliers before the count should be recorded as liabilities and in inventory. Sales and purchases after the inventory count should not be accounted for in this year's financial statements.
Discuss with the valuer the results of his findings (eg that the diamonds are genuine and any obsolete/damaged goods which have been identified).	This evidence will support the subsequent valuation of inventory.
Make an assessment as to whether the inventory count has been properly carried out.	This will help the auditor to determine whether the procedure is sufficiently reliable as a basis for determining the existence of inventory.

(c)   **Factors to consider**

- *The need for an auditor's expert*

  The auditor must consider the risk of material misstatement and whether there is the required expertise within the audit firm. In this case as inventory is material and this is the only client in the diamond industry which the firm has it would seem appropriate to use an expert. This need is increased by the specialised nature of the client's business.

- *The competence of the expert*

  The expert should be a member of a relevant professional body. The auditor should also consider the individual's experience and reputation in his field.

- *The objectivity of the expert*

  The opinion of UJ could be clouded if for example, if they were related in some manner to Rocks Forever. This could be a personal relationship or one of financial dependence.

- *The scope of the expert's work*

  If the auditor is to rely on this evidence it must be relevant to the audit of inventory. In this case UJ is considering issues which will impact on the valuation of inventory. This is of great importance to the auditor and is therefore relevant.

- *Evaluation of the work performed*

  The auditor will need to assess the quality of the work performed by the expert. The auditor will consider the following:

  - Source data used

  - Assumptions and methods used and their consistency with previous years

  - The consistency of the results of UJ's work with other audit evidence taking into account DeCe's overall knowledge of the business.

In spite of the fact that the auditor's expertise is limited in this field DeCe may test the data used by UJ. For example comparative price information may be available from other shops or industry sources.

(d)   **Inventory valuation: audit procedures**

The key principle is that inventory should be valued at the lower of cost and net realisable value.

Cost

For a sample of items agree the cost price to the original purchase invoice. Care should be taken to ensure that the invoice relates specifically to the item in question.

Net realisable value

Review the report produced by UJ for any indication that items are fake. (This is unlikely to be the case but should be confirmed.)

For a sample of items sold after the year end verify that the sales price exceeds cost. Where this is not the case the item should be written down to its net realisable value.

Confirm that items valued by the valuer have been included in the inventory total at this valuation. If there are discrepancies the inventory balance should be revised to include UJ's valuation.

Obtain a schedule of the ageing of inventory. For items identified as slow moving discuss with management the need to make an allowance.

155 Andromeda Industries Co

Text References. Chapters 8, 12, 13 and 19

Top tips. Note that in part (b) you are asked to consider the procedures you would carry out **before** and **during** the inventory count. One of the key procedures which the auditor must perform before the count is a review of the count instructions to determine whether the count is to be conducted in such a way that it will provide reliable evidence. Remember however it is not the auditor's responsibility to organise the count itself. That is the responsibility of management so make sure that you answer the question from the auditor's perspective. Other planning issues will be relevant, for example in this case there are a number of warehouses so the auditor will need to consider which counts to attend.

During the count, remember that the auditor carries out tests of controls and substantive procedures. The tests of controls provide evidence that the count is being conducted properly eg observing the count teams. Substantive procedures include the carrying out of test counts.

For the research and development expenditure, one approach would be to think about what the balance is made up of ie opening balance, plus additional expenses capitalised, less amortisation. Then think about how you would obtain evidence relating to each of these elements. For example the opening balances would be agreed to prior year financial statements and so on. You must also try to make your answer specific to the scenario. For example when you talk about the amortisation charge you should refer to the policy stated. This demonstrates that you are applying your knowledge and not just repeating a list of pre-learned procedures.

Part (c) asks you to consider the impact on the auditor's report. With this type of requirement, if you are given the information, calculate materiality and consider the implications of this in your response. If you decide that a modified opinion is required explain the grounds on which you think a modification is required (ie material misstatement or inability to obtain sufficient appropriate evidence) and the degree of seriousness (ie material or pervasive.

Easy marks. Part (a) should represent 4 easy marks. You should be comfortable explaining factors which influence the reliability of audit evidence.

Examination Team's comments. Candidates were firstly asked to explain four factors, which influence the reliability of audit evidence. One mark was available for each factor; candidates were required to either fully explain the factor or compare that factor to another source. This question was generally well answered. A minority of candidates did not fully describe each factor eg they noted written evidence was reliable but did not explain why it was reliable, or alternatively, did not make a comparison such as written evidence is stronger than oral evidence. It was pleasing that candidates planned their time carefully and generally only described the required number of factors.

Candidates were further provided with a short scenario based question and were required to describe audit procedures that would be performed before and during an inventory count (8 marks) and audit procedures in relation the research and development costs (4 marks). As in previous sittings and as noted in previous examiner's reports the provision of audit procedures relevant to particular circumstances was not well attempted by the majority of candidates.

Most candidates were able to identify that the count procedures should be obtained before the inventory count, however a significant number did not expand to explain the purpose of obtaining this information or the importance of the auditor reviewing the adequacy of these instructions. Candidates often then listed further details to be obtained eg location of count, assembling the audit team, whether to use an expert etc. A number of candidates referred to third party inventory however this was not mentioned in the scenario and therefore any related procedures were not valid. Only the better candidates suggested looking at prior year audit files or, considered the materiality of the sites and control issues.

Most candidates did note that during the count the auditor should observe the counters to ensure the instructions were being followed. However a significant number of candidates then proceeded to list the count procedures that the company's counting team should follow thereby straying into management responsibilities rather than the procedures relevant to the auditor. Some candidates correctly suggested undertaking test counts, while only a minority suggested obtaining copies of the completed count sheets. Overall it was disappointing that candidates did not seem familiar with the auditor's role at an inventory count.

In relation to research and development costs, some candidates correctly suggested that the auditor needed to ensure compliance with the capitalisation criteria in IAS 38 and also suggested recalculating the amortisation charge, but few candidates identified any other relevant procedures. Many candidates did not score any marks for this requirement. Although many candidates suggested a review of invoices, the procedure described was most often testing valuation or rights and obligations rather than to ensure correct classification.

Marking scheme

Marks

(a) Up to 1 mark per well explained point, maximum of 4 points.

- Reliability increased when it is obtained from independent sources

- Internally generated evidence more reliable when the controls are effective

- Evidence obtained directly by the auditor is more reliable than evidence obtained indirectly or by inference

- Evidence in documentary form is more reliable than evidence obtained orally

4

- Evidence provided by original documents is more reliable than evidence provided by copies

(b) (i) Up to 1 mark per well described procedure, overall maximum of 8 marks.

Before the count

- Review the prior year audit files to identify significant inventory issues from last year

- Discuss with management if any new warehouses or any sites have significant control issues

- Decide which of the 12 warehouses the audit team members will attend

- Review a copy of the proposed inventory count instructions

During the count

- Observe the counters to confirm if inventory count instructions are being followed
- Perform test counts inventory to sheets and sheets to inventory
- Confirm procedures for damaged goods are operating correctly
- Observe procedures for movements of inventory during the count
- Obtain a photocopy of the completed inventory sheets
- Identify and make a note of the last goods received notes and goods despatched notes
- Discuss with the internal audit supervisor how he has estimated the raw materials quantities

8

(ii)   Up to 1 mark per well described procedure, overall maximum of 4 marks.

- Cast the schedule of intangible assets
- Agree the opening balances to the prior year financial statements
- Agree the closing balances to the general ledger, trial balance and draft financial statements
- Recalculate amortisation charged in the year and confirm in line with the policy of straight line over five years
- For new projects, discuss with management the stage of development and if capitalised or expensed
- For those expensed as research, agree costs to invoices, supporting documentation and to inclusion in profit or loss
- For those capitalised as development, agree costs to invoice and confirm technically feasible by discussion with development managers or review of feasibility reports
- Review market research reports to confirm Andromeda has the ability to sell the product
- Review the disclosures in the financial statements in accordance with IAS 38 *Intangible assets*

4

(c)   Up to 1 mark per valid point, overall maximum of 4 marks.
- Discussion of issue
- Calculation of materiality
- Type of auditor's report modification required
- Impact on auditor's report

4
___
20

(a)   **Reliability of audit evidence**

The following factors or generalisations can be made when assessing the reliability of audit evidence:

- The reliability of audit evidence is increased when it is obtained from independent sources outside the entity.

- The reliability of audit evidence which is generated internally is increased when the related controls imposed by the entity, including those over its preparation and maintenance, are effective.

- Audit evidence obtained directly by the auditor is more reliable than audit evidence obtained indirectly or by inference.

- Audit evidence in documentary form, whether paper, electronic or other medium, is more reliable than evidence obtained orally.

- Audit evidence provided by original documents is more reliable than audit evidence provided by photocopies or facsimiles, the reliability of which may depend on the controls over their preparation and maintenance.

(b)   (i)   **Inventory count procedures**

Before the count

- Review the prior year audit files to identify whether there were any particular warehouses where significant inventory issues arose last year.

- Discuss with management whether any of the warehouses this year are new, or have experienced significant control issues.

- Decide which of the 12 warehouses the audit team members will attend, basing this on materiality and risk of each site.

- Obtain a copy of the proposed inventory count instructions, review them to identify any control deficiencies and if any are noted, discuss them with management prior to the counts.

During the count

- Observe the counting teams of Andromeda to confirm whether the inventory count instructions are being followed correctly. *completeness*

- Select a sample of inventory and perform test counts from inventory sheets to warehouse aisle and from warehouse aisle to inventory sheets. *existence*

- Confirm the procedures for identifying and segregating damaged goods are operating correctly, and assess inventory for evidence of any damaged or slow moving items.

- Observe the procedures for movements of inventory during the count, to confirm that all movements have ceased.

- Obtain a photocopy of the completed sequentially numbered inventory sheets for follow up testing on the final audit.

- Identify and make a note of the last goods received notes and goods despatched notes for 31 December in order to perform cut-off procedures.

- Discuss with the internal audit supervisor how any raw materials quantities have been estimated. Where possible, reperform the procedures adopted by the supervisor.

(ii)   **Research and development**

Obtain and cast a schedule of intangible assets, detailing opening balances, amount capitalised in the current year, amortisation and closing balances.

- Agree the opening balances to the prior year financial statements.

- Agree the closing balances to the general ledger, trial balance and draft financial statements.

- Recalculate the amortisation charge for a sample of intangible assets which have commenced production and confirm it is line with the amortisation policy of straight line over five years.

- For the five new projects, discuss with management the details of each project along with the stage of development and whether it has been capitalised or expensed.

- For those expensed as research, agree the costs incurred to invoices and supporting documentation and to inclusion in profit or loss.

- For those capitalised as development, agree costs incurred to invoices and confirm technically feasible by discussion with development managers or review of feasibility reports.

- Review market research reports to confirm Andromeda has the ability to sell the product once complete and probable future economic benefits will arise.

- Review the disclosures for intangible assets in the draft financial statements are in accordance with IAS 38 *Intangible assets*.

(c)   **Auditor's reports**

One of the projects Andromeda has developed in the year does not meet the recognition criteria under IAS 38 *Intangible assets* for capitalisation but has been included within intangible assets. This is contrary to IAS 38, as if the criteria are not met, then this project is research expenditure and should be expensed to profit or loss rather than capitalised.

The error is material as it represents 11.8% of profit before tax (0.98m/8.3m) and hence management should adjust the financial statements by removing this project from intangible assets and charging it to profit or loss instead. The finance director's argument that the balance is immaterial is not correct.

If management refuses to amend this error, then the auditor's report will need to be modified. As management has not complied with IAS 38 and the error is material but not pervasive, then a qualified opinion would be necessary.

A basis for qualified opinion paragraph would be needed and would explain the material misstatement in relation to the incorrect treatment of research and development and the effect on the financial statements. The opinion paragraph would be qualified 'except for'.

156 Squash Co

Study Text Reference: Chapters 12, 16

Top tips: Part (a) is an identify and explain requirement, so make sure you fulfil both parts of that requirement, do not simply list assertions. Try and use your learned knowledge to identify the key assertion, for example, issues 1 and 2 are **balances**, so the key issue is likely to be **existence**, **completeness**, **rights and obligations** or **accuracy, valuation and allocation** per the ISA. Issue three is a disclosure, and there is little issue with classification, so **accuracy, completeness and presentation** are the issues.

In part (b), think about what you want to gain evidence about before suggesting your procedures, and ensure that it is included in your procedure. A procedure should be an action and a reason, eg inspect the document to confirm the cost. It is fair to explain that a complete procedure such as this should gain a full mark, so you should be looking to produce as many explained procedures as there are marks available in each part. There will often be more potential procedures available than marks, as ACCA exams tend to allow a generous range of answers to their exam questions (as illustrated by the model answer).

Easy marks: Some of the more generic audit procedures relating to these three issues in part (b) represent the easy marks in this question – for instance, inspecting the purchase documents in respect of the customer list, verifying directors' salaries to payroll and bonus entitlements to their contracts.

Marks

(a) 1 mark per relevant identified assertion and 1 mark for valid explanation
(max of 3 for identifying assertions):

(i) Completeness (risk of understatement)
(ii) Valuation (risk of overstatement)
(iii) Presentation, completeness, accuracy (risk of incorrect
disclosure)

6

(b) 1 mark per appropriate audit procedure properly explained.

(i) Max of 4 marks
(ii) Max of 4 marks
(iii) Max of 5 marks

14

20

(a) **Assertions**

(i) **Payables: completeness**

Completeness is likely to be the riskiest assertion in relation to payables, as there is risk that Squash will want to understate liabilities to show a good position to the suppliers with whom it is in ongoing negotiations. In terms of detection risk, completeness may not be as easy to obtain evidence about this year due to the significant potential changes in the balance from previous years (as Squash will not have two credit balances at the year end that it customarily has had, but also because the company has stretched credit terms on its other suppliers). This may reduce the comparability between the two years and therefore also reduce the use of substantive analytical procedures.

(ii) **Intangible: Accuracy, valuation and allocation**

Valuation is the significant risk here. The directors want to carry the intangible at fair value, but this appears to be based on a management estimate which could be subject to bias, to improve the general impression of the financial statements for the benefit of shareholders or suppliers as discussed above. Estimates are inherently risky. Potentially Squash has no one qualified to estimate this value and they may not have similar assets on which to base the valuation, so detection risk is increased in relation to this assertion.

(iii) **Directors' emoluments: Presentation/completeness/accuracy**

This is a disclosure in the accounts, and the issue is that the disclosure will not be presented completely, accurately or understandably both generally, and specifically if the directors want to hide elements of their pay from interested parties (for example, the suppliers, who have had credit terms stretched if there is any question that these forms of 'finance' are simply lining the directors' pockets).

(b) **Substantive procedures**

(i) **Payables**

- Calculate prior year payables excluding the two affected suppliers and compare the trend with this years' payables (you would expect to see an increase in payables days to be consistent with the assertion that credit terms have been stretched for other suppliers)

- Read correspondence with the suppliers relating to the suspension of credit terms to confirm that these suppliers have ceased to offer the company credit and hence should not appear in the payables balance.

- Verify from any dates mentioned in that correspondence that credit balances should be missing at the year end.

- Review a sample of recent invoices from the suppliers and trace to payments on delivery dates to ensure that there should not be credit balances for these suppliers.

- Obtain supplier statement reconciliations and verify appropriateness.

- (Alternatively) obtain supplier statements for a sample of balances and reconcile these to purchase ledger accounts.

- Consider whether the results of supplier statement reconciliations suggest further work is required (for example, if invoices appear not to have been recorded by the company).

- Review goods received notes from immediately prior to the yearend and trace to invoice and purchase ledger to ensure that liabilities are accounted for in the correct period.

- Review bank reconciliation to ensure that purchase ledger payments for the end of the year were not recorded but delayed to improve the appearance of payables at the yearend (which would not affect the bank, as total liabilities would be the same, but might affect the ongoing negotiations with the suppliers if they consult audited financial statements when published).

(ii) **Intangible**

- Obtain purchase documents to verify the cost of the intangible asset (as this is the starting point for the fair value) and obtain any evidence about the validity of the useful life.

- Review the directors' estimate of fair value and consider the assumptions made for reasonableness.

- Consider whether the directors are qualified to estimate the value (for example, whether Squash owns any other comparable patents).

- Obtain third party evidence concerning valuation if possible (for example, refer to comparable industry data).

- Review sales information before and after the purchase and use of the patent to ensure it is adding value to the business and therefore should be capitalised not expensed.

- Consider whether the length of useful life is reasonable in relation to the legal terms of the patent.

- Recalculate amortisation.

- Obtain written representations from the directors confirming that they believe the assumptions made in estimating the fair value are reasonable.

(iii) **Directors' emoluments**

- Obtain the disclosure note concerning directors' emoluments and recalculate it to ensure it is accurate.

- Verify salary and bonus elements with the payroll to confirm they are accurate and complete.

- Review directors' contracts to ensure that salary and bonus payments are consistent with their agreements.

- Inquire what constitutes 'other payments'.

- Verify other payments to appropriate documentation, such as pension company statements.

- Review cash book for any transactions which appear to be payments to directors to ensure included in disclosure.

- Review board minutes for any references to payments to directors to ensure included in disclosure.

- Compare current year emoluments to prior year emoluments and assess whether differences are consistent with explanations received during the audit to ensure completeness.

- Ask each director to confirm whether they the disclosure is consistent with what they have received to give evidence of completeness.

157 Traffic Lights

Marking scheme

		Marks

(a)   1 mark per well-explained point:

- Expectation of comparability
- Controls
- Suitability of analytical procedures for particular assertions
- Nature of income and assets (donations, grants)
- Proof-in-total for depreciation   3

(b)   1 mark per well-explained procedure

(i)   Properties

- Review donated assets register for additions

- Compare value of properties with local valuation data, eg estate agents

- Consider time since previous revaluation of assets

- Calculate expectation of proof-in-total for depreciation on properties

- Compare calculation to trustee's calculation

- Enquire of trustees concerning any disposals

- Visit play premises/review any advertising to confirm   4
  disposals or not of premises

(ii) Play equipment

- Review purchased asset ledger for any donations in year

- Trace purchased assets to invoice/receipts (cost is likely to represent FV in this case)

- Review donated asset ledger for any donations/write offs in year

- Attend play sessions to assess whether any written off assets appear to be in use

- Compare fair value of donated assets to suitable evidence, eg:
    - Toy retailers' websites,
    - Ebay for quality used items
    - Local 'second-hand' shops

- Recalculate depreciation (as for properties)

- Review useful life

5

(c) (i) Legacies

- Review correspondence to assess existence of legacies in year

- Enquire of legal advisers about any legacies in year

- Review cash books for legacies (or any unspecified items), trace to bank statements

- Discuss whether any legacies have occurred with Trustees

2

(ii) Donations

- Observe cash counting

- Trace a sample of weekly bankings from cash books to bank statements

- Review cash books for unusual items, eg gaps

- Review correspondence to assess existence of donations from businesses/individuals

- Review cash books for donations, trace to bank statements

- Review local press for mention of donations to the charity, trace to bank statements

- Ask Trustees of any specific fundraising activity during the year relating to assets

- Cross check between new purchased assets and related donated funds

- Attend play sessions to gain an impression of any new equipment which might not be included in register

6

20

(a) **Use of substantive analytical procedures at TL**

When judging whether to use substantive analytical procedures, auditors must consider factors such as (ISA 520: para. 5):

- Internal controls in the related area
- The suitability of analytical procedures for particular assertions
- The auditor's expectation of comparability, given their understanding of the entity

Substantive procedures tend to be appropriate for large volumes of transactions which tend to be predictable over time.

In TL's case, given that income is donated and relatively low volume, there is likely to be a high degree of unpredictability. Donations related to play are voluntary and therefore are likely to be unpredictable, as are other income and legacies. In addition, asset donations are likely to be unpredictable.

It might be possible to establish a degree of correlations between particular appeals and subsequent donations, but given the assumption that controls are weak, it is unlikely that the auditor will judge that analytical procedures could give strong evidence over the completeness of income.

The local authority grants are applied for annually. This also implies a degree of unpredictability. However, actual practice over past years could be appraised, as it is possible that this is in fact predictable, if TL has been granted the same amount for a number of years and has a reasonable expectation of this continuing.

One area where Amber might be able to make use of analytical procedures is in relation to depreciation, where it will be possible to calculate an expectation of the depreciation charge for the year and compare it to TL's (a proof-in-total).

(b) **Procedures over valuation of assets**

(i) Donated property

The following procedures could be carried out in relation to the valuation of donated property:

- Review donated assets register to identify if there have been any additions in the year

- Compare the valuation of properties to third party evidence, for example, comparable properties in local estate agents, to assess reasonableness of valuation

- Consider length of time since previous revaluations and discuss with Trustees whether any class of asset requires revaluation to conform with accounting requirements

- Enquire of the Trustees of any disposals of properties

- Visit play premises to confirm they are still in use in the charity and hence fair value is reasonable (if properties are not in use their fair value may be affected)

- Review charity advertising to ensure all properties are in use (ie they have not been disposed of)

- Calculate an expectation of the depreciation charge on properties for the year and compare to the Trustees' calculation to assess whether the charge is reasonable

- Alternatively, recalculate depreciation

(ii) Play equipment

The following procedures could be carried out in relation to the valuation of play equipment:

- Review purchased asset register for any bought assets in the year

- Trace purchased assets to invoice as cost price should be a good indicator of fair value

- Consider assumptions relating to any difference in valuation between cost and fair value of purchased assets

- Review purchased asset register for any written off assets and attend play sessions to identify if written off assets are still in use in the centres.

- Review donated asset register for any additions/disposals in the year.

- Compare fair value of donated assets to suitable third party sources such as, toy retailers' websites, ebay for quality second hand toys, local second hand shops.

- As above, consider if revaluations have been considered on a timely basis (although second hand toys in frequent use are unlikely to increase in value, the trustees should be considering revaluations on a regular basis to comply with IAS 16)

- As above, perform a proof in total of depreciation and compare to Trustees'

- Alternatively, recalculate depreciation

- Review asset write offs to analyse whether a useful life of 10 years is appropriate (it seems potentially long for second-hand toys in frequent use)

- Consider whether the sub-category 'play equipment' is sufficient, or whether there are different classes of play equipment which may have different useful lives

(c) **Substantive procedures over income**

(i) Legacies

- Discuss whether any legacies have occurred with Trustees
- Review correspondence to assess occurrence of legacies in year
- Enquire of legal advisers about any legacies in year, to confirm occurrence and completeness
- Review cash books for legacies and trace to bank statements
- Review cash books and bank statements for unspecified items which might be legacies

(ii) Donations

Cash donations

- Observe a series of cash counts during the year under review and perform some cash counts to ensure accuracy

- Trace a number of entries in the branch cash book for donations to the bank statements

- Review the branch cash books for any weeks with lack of entries

- Discuss weeks with no entries with volunteers and assess reasonableness of answers (eg volunteer absence, centre closure)

- Corroborate answers where possible (for example, staff may have a rota which can be used to corroborate absence).

Tutor's note: It is important to remember here that you have been asked for substantive procedures – answers including tests of controls, for example, observing whether two staff carry out the cash count, will not receive credit.

Other donations

- Review correspondence to assess existence of donations from businesses/individuals

- Review cash books for donations, trace to bank statements

- Review bank statements for direct donations and trace to donation records

- Review local press for mention of donations to the charity, trace to bank statements

- Ask Trustees of any specific fundraising activity during the year relating to assets

- Cross check between new purchased assets and related donated funds having been recorded

- Attend play sessions to gain an impression of any new equipment which might not be included in register (as this could suggest that income re associated equipment has not been recorded)

158 Hawthorn Enterprises Co

Text references. Financial statement assertions are covered in Chapter 8. The audit of receivables, cash at bank and payables is covered in Chapters 14–16.

Top tips. The key issue for both part (a)(ii) and part (b) is the description of substantive procedures. There are two important points that you must bear in mind here. Firstly, make sure that you do not include any tests of controls. Confusing these two types of test is a common mistake identified by the examination team. A substantive procedure provides evidence regarding an assertion, whilst a test of control provides evidence regarding the effectiveness of controls operated by the entity. The second point is to note the use of the word 'describe'. Vague responses such as 'Check the year-end statements' will score no marks. You need to make it clear how you obtain the evidence and what the evidence actually is eg 'Select a representative sample of year-end supplier statements and agree the balance to the purchase ledger. If the balance agrees, then no further work is required'.

Easy marks. Part (a)(i) is straightforward but you must ensure that you explain the assertion as well as identifying it.

Marking scheme

		Marks

(a) Up to 1 mark per assertion, ½ mark for stating assertion and ½ mark for explanation, max of 4 marks; up to 1 mark per relevant revenue substantive procedure, max of 4 marks.
- Occurrence – explanation and relevant substantive procedure
- Completeness – explanation and relevant substantive procedure
- Accuracy – explanation and relevant substantive procedure
- Cut-off – explanation and relevant substantive procedure
- Classification – explanation and relevant substantive procedure

    8

(b) Up to 1 mark per well described procedure, overall maximum of 3 marks for supplier statement reconciliations, maximum of 4 marks for bank and maximum of 5 marks for receivables.

(i) Supplier statement reconciliation

- Select a sample of supplier statements and agree the balance to the purchase ledger

- Invoices in transit, confirm via GRN if receipt of goods was pre year end, if so confirm included in year-end accruals

- Cash in transit, confirm from cashbook and bank statements the cash was sent pre year end

- Discuss any further adjusting items with the purchase ledger supervisor to understand the nature of the reconciling item, and whether it has been correctly accounted for

    3

(ii) Bank reconciliation
- Check additions of bank reconciliation
- Bank balance to statement/bank confirmation
- Cash book balance to cash book
- Outstanding lodgements
- Unpresented cheques review
- Old cheques write back

    4

(iii) **Receivables**
- Aged receivables report to identify any slow moving balances
- Review the after date cash receipts
- Review customer correspondence to assess whether there are any invoices in dispute
- Review board minutes
- Calculate average receivable days
- Post year-end sales returns/credit notes
- Cut-off testing of GDN
- Agree to GDN and sales order to ensure existence

5

20

(a) **Assertions for classes of transactions and events** (ISA 315: para. 124)

Occurrence

Transactions and events that have been recorded or disclosed have occurred, and such transactions and events pertain to the entity.

Substantive procedures

Select a sample of sales transactions recorded in the sales day book; agree the details back to a goods despatched note (GDN) and customer order.

Review the monthly breakdown of sales per key product, compare to the prior year and budget and investigate any significant differences.

Completeness

All transactions and events that should have been recorded have been recorded, and all related disclosures that should have been included in the financial statements have been included.

Substantive procedures

Select a sample of GDNs raised during the year; agree to the sales invoice and that they are recorded in the sales day book.

Review the total amount of sales, compare to the prior year and budget and investigate any significant differences.

Accuracy

The amounts and other data relating to recorded transactions and events have been recorded appropriately, and related disclosures have been appropriately measured and described.

Substantive procedures

Select a sample of sales invoices and recalculate that the totals and calculation of sales tax are correct.

For a sample of sales invoices, confirm the sales price stated agrees to the authorised price list.

Cut-off

Transactions and events have been recorded in the correct accounting period.

Substantive procedures

Select a sample of pre and post year-end GDNs and agree that the sale is recorded in the correct period's sales day books.

Review the post year-end sales returns and agree if they relate to pre year-end sales that the revenue has been correctly removed from the sales day book.

Classification

Transactions and events have been recorded in the proper accounts.

Substantive procedures

Agree for a sample of sales invoices that they have been correctly recorded within revenue nominal account codes and included within revenue in the financial statements.

Presentation

Transactions and events are appropriately aggregated or disaggregated and clearly described, and related disclosures are relevant and understandable in the context of the requirements of the applicable financial reporting framework.

Substantive procedures

For an entity applying IFRS 15 *Revenue from contracts with customers*, obtaining a breakdown of trade receivables and for a sample of receivables, reviewing the related sales contract to ensure that the entity's right to consideration is not conditional. (Conditional consideration should be recorded as contract assets.)

(Tutorial note. Only four assertions and substantive procedures are required.)

(b) (i) **Substantive procedures for supplier statement reconciliations**

- Select a representative sample of year-end supplier statements and agree the balance to the purchase ledger of Hawthorn. If the balance agrees, then no further work is required.

- Where differences occur due to invoices in transit, confirm from goods received notes (GRN) whether the receipt of goods was pre year end, if so confirm that this receipt is included in year-end accruals.

- Where differences occur due to cash in transit from Hawthorn to the supplier, confirm from the cashbook and bank statements that the cash was sent pre year end.

- Discuss any further adjusting items with the purchase ledger supervisor to understand the nature of the reconciling item, and whether it has been correctly accounted for.

(ii) **Substantive procedures for bank reconciliation**

- Obtain Hawthorn's bank account reconciliation and cast to check the additions to ensure arithmetical accuracy.

- Agree the balance per the bank reconciliation to an original year-end bank statement and to the bank confirmation letter.

- Agree the reconciliation's balance per the cash book to the year-end cash book.

- Trace all the outstanding lodgements to the pre year-end cash book, post year-end bank statement and also to paying-in-book pre year end.

- Trace all unpresented cheques through to a pre year-end cash book and post year-end statement. For any unusual amounts or significant delays, obtain explanations from management.

- Examine any old unpresented cheques to assess if they need to be written back into the purchase ledger as they are no longer valid to be presented.

(iii) **Substantive procedures for receivables**

- Review the aged receivable ledger to identify any slow moving or old receivable balances, discuss the status of these balances with the credit controller to assess whether they are likely to pay.

- Select a significant sample of receivables and review whether there are any after date cash receipts, ensure that a sample of slow moving/old receivable balances is also selected.

- Review customer correspondence to identify any balances which are in dispute or unlikely to be paid.

- Review board minutes to identify whether there are any significant concerns in relation to payments by customers.

- Calculate average receivable days and compare this to prior year, investigate any significant differences.

- Inspect post year-end sales returns/credit notes and consider whether an additional allowance against receivables is required.

- Select a sample of goods despatched notes (GDN) before and just after the year end and follow through to the sales ledger to ensure they are recorded in the correct accounting period.

- Select a sample of year-end receivable balances and agree back to valid supporting documentation of GDN and sales order to ensure existence.

Chestnut

159   The correct answers are:

Review whether any payments have subsequently been made by this customer since the audit fieldwork was completed

Review the latest customer correspondence with regards to an assessment of the likelihood of the customer making payment

The audit concern here is that receivables are overstated as the balance from this customer does not appear to be recoverable. Audit procedures should therefore focus on the valuation of receivables. Vouching the balance owed by the customer at the year end to sales invoices will provide audit evidence in relation to the existence, rights and obligations of receivables, but not their valuation. Matching the total of the aged receivables' listing to the sales ledger control account will provide evidence of completeness.

160   The correct answer is:

Qualified 'except for'

The customer balance of $350,000 represents 1.2% (0.35/28.2m) of revenue, 6.3% (0.35/5.6m) of receivables and 7.3% (0.35/4.8m) of profit before tax, and as such is material but not pervasive.

If management refuses to provide against this receivable, the auditor's opinion will need to be modified. As the issue is restricted to receivables the error is material but not pervasive so a qualified 'except for' opinion would be necessary.

The opinion paragraph would state that the audit opinion is qualified 'except for'. A basis for qualified opinion paragraph would be needed and would include an explanation of the material misstatement in relation to the valuation of receivables, and of the effect on the financial statements.

161   The correct answer is:

Material	Financial statement impact
Yes	Gross profit may be overstated

Chestnut & Co was only appointed as auditors subsequent to Ash's year end and hence did not attend the year-end inventory count. Therefore, they have not been able to gather sufficient and appropriate audit evidence with regards to the completeness and existence of inventory. This may mean that closing inventory is over- or understated and this will have a resultant impact on gross profit and current assets.

Inventory is a material amount as it represents 21.3% (0.51/2.4m) of profit before tax and 5% (0.51/10.1m) of revenue.

162   The correct answers are:

Review the internal auditor's reports of the inventory count to identify the level of adjustments made to the records, in order to assess the reasonableness of relying on the inventory records for the purpose of the year end audit.

Perform test counts of inventory in the warehouse and compare these first to the inventory records, and then from inventory records to the warehouse, in order to assess the reasonableness of the inventory records maintained by Ash.

Audit procedures should focus on testing the accuracy of the work performed by the internal audit department at the year end in order to determine whether the year-end inventory quantity exists and is complete.

Testing the accuracy of the aged inventory report will provide evidence over the valuation of inventory.

Reviewing the sales order book for February, March and April 20X5 could provide audit evidence as to the quantity of inventory at the year-end but only if it is assessed to determine whether there would have been sufficient inventory at the year end to fulfil customer demand.

163   The correct answer is:

Audit opinion	Disclosure in the auditor's report
Qualified	Basis for qualified opinion

The auditor will need to express a modified opinion as they are unable to obtain sufficient appropriate evidence in relation to inventory. The effect of this is material but not pervasive. Therefore a qualified 'except for' opinion will be required.

The opinion paragraph will explain that the audit opinion is qualified 'except for'. A basis for qualified opinion paragraph will be required to explain the limitation in relation to the lack of evidence over inventory.

Humphries

164   D   All the procedures are valid in identifying subsequent events occurring up to the date of the auditor's report.

165   D   The flood damage does not provide evidence of conditions that existed at the year end, and therefore is not an adjusting event as defined by IAS 10 (IAS 10: para. 3). On this basis, the inventory should not be written down, but the nature and amount of expected uninsured losses may need to be disclosed. It is incorrect to recognise a contingent asset in the 20X1 financial statements: contingent assets should be disclosed, not recognised, and it should only be disclosed when an inflow of economic benefits is probable (IAS 37: paras. 31–35)).

166   A   Writing to the customer is likely to be unproductive. In addition, it would only provide persuasive evidence that the receivable existed at the year end, not that it was recoverable. Requesting a cash flow forecast is irrelevant, as it does not give evidence as to the recoverability of the receivable itself and there is no evidence that the going concern assumption needs to be revised.

167   C   The probable payment and anticipated adjustment needed is $0.6 million representing 8% of profit ($0.6m/$7.5m × 100%). This is material and if management refuse to adjust for the provision, the audit opinion will need to be modified on the basis management has not complied with IAS 37. The misstatement is material but not pervasive so a qualified opinion would be expressed. The opinion paragraph would state that 'except for' this issue the financial statements are presented fairly (or show a true and fair view). A basis for qualified opinion paragraph would explain the material misstatement in relation to the $0.6m not provided and will describe the effect on the financial statements.

168   D   Options A and B describe the auditor's responsibility with regards to subsequent events occurring before the date of the auditor's report. It is true that the auditor does not have any obligation to perform procedures or make enquiries, but should an adjusting event come to light, adjustments to the financial statements about to be issued must be considered and further audit procedures must be performed as necessary at the time, rather than deferring to next year, hence Option C is incorrect.

Minnie

169   The correct answers are:

As part of their completion procedures, auditors shall consider whether the aggregate of uncorrected misstatements in the financial statements is material

In deciding whether the uncorrected misstatements are material, the auditor shall consider the size and nature of the misstatements

The auditor must accumulate misstatements, even individually immaterial one, unless they are clearly trivial. Auditors are required to consider misstatements in relation to qualitative disclosures, as well as transactions and account balances.   .

170   The correct answer is:

Ask the directors to correct the specific misstatement, explaining that it is material to the financial statements.

The misstatement in relation to the property revaluation is 6% of profit before tax, and is therefore material. As a result, it is not enough to accumulate the misstatement along with other uncorrected misstatements – ISA 450 requires material misstatements to be identified individually and communicated to management (ISA 450: para. 12). We are at the finalisation stage of the audit, so the assessment of the management expert's (the valuer's) methodology should already have been done. It is inappropriate to modify the audit opinion before first asking management to correct the misstatement.

171   The correct answer is:

Material	Financial statement impact
Yes	Profit is understated

Land has been incorrectly depreciated – the depreciation of land is not permitted under IAS 16 (IAS 16: para. 58). The misstatement represents 7% of profit before tax ($0.7m/$10m) and is therefore a material misstatement. The effect of the incorrect depreciation understates profit and understates assets.

172   The correct answer is:

Audit opinion	Disclosure in the auditor's report
Unmodified	No related disclosure

Although legal action is being taken against the company for breach of copyright, the matter has been correctly disclosed as a contingent liability, in accordance with IAS 37. No modification of the audit opinion is required because the matter is appropriately disclosed. The uncertainty relating to the outcome of this litigation is not fundamental to users' understanding of the financial statements therefore no emphasis of matter paragraph is included in the auditor's report. Although the litigation might have implications for the company's ability to continue as a going concern, there is no indication that this would happen at this stage. Therefore, it is inappropriate to include a material uncertainty related to going concern paragraph.

173   The correct answer is:

5 March 20X8

The date of the letter must be as near as practicable to the date of the auditor's report but not after.

Greenfields

174   B   The audit team has already carried out some procedures in testing the calculations and assumptions relating to the warranty provision, and has found them to be in line with prior years (and presumably in accordance with expectations). All of the evidence to date is from internal sources, but there is unlikely to be readily available reliable external sources.

It will be difficult for anyone to predict how many warranty claims there will be in the future and the value of any future claims, and written representation on this matter will be one of the few sources of evidence available.

Management have offered a written representation over the recoverability of the receivables balance but have not allowed circularisation of the receivable. The written representation cannot be used as a substitute for evidence which should otherwise be available. The written representation proposed by management is focused on the recoverability and gives only weak evidence over the relevant assertions. Despite being in writing and more reliable than a verbal representation, the internally generated representation is not as good as evidence from an external source (such as any potential response from Yellowmix to the circularisation).

With the other evidence available being limited due to the lack of payment activity over the last six months, without further more compelling evidence, the representation alone would appear insufficient to conclude that receivables are free from material misstatement.

175   B   Reviewing correspondence with Yellowmix may provide details confirming the likelihood of the debt being repaid. If cash is received in after the period end from Yellowmix this provides evidence that the debt was recoverable at the period end.

Tracing a sample of goods despatched notes (option 2) provides evidence of completeness.

Tracing of entries in Yellowmix's account in the receivables ledger provides evidence of existence and accuracy.

176   A   Management has not provided a requested written representation, therefore ISA 580 *Written representations* requires the auditor to discuss the matter with management and ask why they will not provide the representation relating to the warranty provision.

ISA 580 also requires the auditor to re-evaluate the integrity of management and evaluate the effect this may have on the reliability of any other representations (such as on the Yellowmix balance) and audit evidence in general. (ISA 580: para. 19)

The auditor must then take appropriate actions, including determining the impact on the auditor's opinion in the auditor's report.

177   D   Given the limited evidence available other than the representation, the auditor will be unable to obtain sufficient appropriate evidence over the material warranty provision. Therefore a modification of the auditor's opinion is required. A qualified opinion will be issued because the misstatement, although material, will not be pervasive. A qualified or adverse opinion on the grounds of material misstatement would not be appropriate as the auditor has not been able to obtain sufficient evidence to determine whether a material misstatement has occurred or not.

178   C   The audit opinion would not be modified as the audit opinion relates to the financial statements and not the 'Other Information'. In accordance with ISA 700 *Forming an opinion and reporting on financial statements* (ISA 700: para. 32) and ISA 720 *The auditor's responsibilities relating to other information* (ISA 720: para. 21) the auditor's report would be required to include an Other Information section as other information is issued with the financial statements and is available to the auditors. As there is a material misstatement this would be disclosed in the Other Information section. An Other Matter paragraph is not used for these purposes.

Strawberry

179   D   The fall in inventory turnover days means that Strawberry is turning over its inventory more quickly, which if anything would improve its cash cycle and have a positive rather than negative impact on the ability of the company to continue. In this case the change is relatively small so is unlikely to be a significant factor either way.

180   B   In accordance with ISA 570 (ISA 570: para. 13) the assessment must cover a period of at least 12 months from the date of the financial statements. If the period covered is less than this the auditor must request that the assessment period is extended.

181   C   The receipt of the balance after the year end confirms that the debt is recoverable at the year end.

The written representation is written evidence but is internally generated.

The response to the circularisation provides evidence of existence but does not provide evidence of recoverability.

The correspondence between the lawyers is externally generated and from trusted parties but is less reliable than the receipt of the payment as it would still be possible for Grape Co to default.

182   D   As part of the going concern review the auditor must consider mitigating circumstances. In this case, the agreement with the alternative finance provider gives the most assurance as there is a greater degree of certainty that Strawberry will receive the cash. Options A, B and C may provide the cash required but this cannot be guaranteed. There is also a timing issue as the property may not sell for some time and costs savings will not have an immediate effect.

183   A   An adverse opinion would be issued as the matter is material and pervasive ie the auditors disagree with the whole basis on which the financial statements have been prepared. A description of the circumstances would be included in the Basis for Adverse Opinion paragraph in accordance with ISA 705 (ISA 705: para. 18).

A qualified opinion would apply if the issue were material, but not pervasive. Disclosure in the Material Uncertainty Related to Going Concern section is made when the auditor agrees with that the company is a going concern but believes that there is a material uncertainty which needs to be brought to the attention of the shareholders (ISA 570: para. 22). This does not apply in this case.

Clarinet

184   C   The uncorrected misstatement amounts to 15% of profit after tax and on this basis would be material (ie it is over 10% of PAT). It is an adjusting event as the discovery provides evidence as to the value of the inventory at the year end. The 20X4 financial statements should therefore be adjusted.

Adjustment in the 20X4 financial statements would not be required for non-adjusting events ie those which do not provide evidence of conditions which existed at the period end.

185   B   The entry of the competitor has resulted in a loss of market share and the loss of a major customer. There is a risk that this sizeable loss of market share will result in a significant loss of future revenues, as well as reducing future cash flows.

The overdraft has increased significantly and is due for renewal. This suggests liquidity problems. If the bank does not renew the overdraft, and the company fails to obtain alternative finance it may not be able to continue trading.

The failure of Clarinet's shareholders to invest indicate doubts in relation to the company's ability to generate healthy profits in future, or possible liquidity problems. It may also make it less likely for others to invest.

The existence of a bank loan in itself does not give rise to going concern issues. The bank loan is long term so there is no imminent requirement to repay the balance. To date all payments have been made therefore there is no breach of any loan terms which could trigger early repayment.

186   C   All of the procedures provide evidence regarding the assumption used in the cash flow forecast. However the review of post year-end sales and the order book is the most reliable as this shows sales which have actually taken place or sales to which the customer has shown a commitment. Procedures described in A, B and D are based on possible events.

187   A   The disclosures are set out in ISA 570 paragraph 25.

(4) is incorrect. The management assessment should be at least 12 months from the date of the financial statements. If not the auditors will ask that the assessment period is extended.

188   B   As the auditors agree with the basis of preparation of the financial statements and have concluded that the disclosures are adequate an unmodified opinion is issued. As a material uncertainty regarding going concern exists this must be highlighted for the benefit of the shareholders. In accordance with ISA 570 (ISA 570: para. 22) and ISA 701 (ISA 701: para. 15) this must be disclosed in a 'Material Uncertainty Related to Going Concern' section, and not as a Key Audit Matter.

Czech & Dawson

189   D   ISA 450 *Evaluation of misstatements identified during the audit* states that the auditor has a responsibility to accumulate misstatements identified during the audit, other than those that are clearly trivial (ISA 450: para. 5).

All the accumulated misstatements should be communicated to the appropriate level of management on a timely basis (ISA 450: para. 8). The auditor must request management to correct the misstatements.

If management refuses to correct some or all of the misstatements, the auditor must obtain an understanding of the reasons for not making the corrections, and take these into account when determining whether the financial statements are free from material misstatement (ISA 450: para. 9). This may affect the auditor's opinion if this results in the financial statements being materially misstated, but the refusal to correct the misstatements does not affect the opinion.

The auditor should determine whether uncorrected misstatements are material, both individually and in aggregate (ISA 450: para. 11).

190   A   Audit procedures should focus on determining the extent of research expenditure which has been incorrectly capitalised.

Whilst it is generally important to authorise expenditure the issue is not authorisation or occurrence but its classification.

191   C   Research expenditure of $2.1m has been capitalised within intangible assets. This accounting treatment is incorrect, as IAS 38 *Intangible assets* requires research expenditure to be expensed to profit or loss (IAS 38: para. 54).

The error is material as it represents 8% of profit before tax ($2.1m/$26.3m).

Management should adjust the financial statements by reversing it from the research expenditure from intangibles and debiting the amount to profit or loss.

If management refuse to make the adjustment, the auditor's opinion will need to be modified. As the error is material but not pervasive, a qualified opinion would seem appropriate.

The basis of opinion section would need to include a paragraph explaining the misstatement and its effect on the financial statements. The opinion paragraph would be qualified 'except for'.

192   C   Two months' worth of wages records have been lost and so audit evidence has not been gained in relation to this expense. Wages and salaries for the two month period represent 11% of profit before tax ($1.1m/$10m) and so wages and salaries may be materially misstated.

193   A   The auditors should seek alternative audit procedures to audit the wages and salaries account. If no alternative audit procedures are possible, the loss of data would constitute a lack of sufficient appropriate audit evidence.

The auditors will need to modify the auditor's opinion on the basis that they are unable to obtain sufficient appropriate evidence in relation to a material amount in the financial statements. As the two months' salary and wages are not pervasive, a qualified opinion would seem appropriate.

The basis of opinion section would require an explanation of the insufficient audit evidence in relation to wages and salaries. The opinion paragraph would be qualified on the grounds of an inability to obtain sufficient appropriate audit evidence.

Medimade

194   The correct answers are:

The going concern basis of accounting is used when the entity will be able to continue in business for the foreseeable future

The going concern basis of accounting assumes that the entity will be able to realise its assets and discharge its liabilities in the normal course of business

The term 'foreseeable future' is not defined within ISA 570, but IAS 1 deems the foreseeable future to be a period of 12 months from the end of the entity's reporting period (IAS 1: para. 25). When financial statements are prepared using the going concern basis of accounting, the assertion is that there is neither the intention nor the need to liquidate the company's operations.

195 The correct answers are:

Medimade now has to pay cash on delivery and this adds further cash flow strain imposed by the overdraft

Some suppliers may end their relationship with Medimade, preventing the company from producing its products, thus further reducing sales

Although all of the stated options are possible consequences, only these two options describe the most direct effect on going concern: cash flow difficulties and reducing sales. The main concern with bank covenants (which should already be in place) is that the bank can withdraw finance if and when the covenants are breached – bank covenants do not usually restrict the way in which a company conducts its business.

196 The correct answer is:

Review board minutes for meetings held after the year end for evidence which indicate further financial difficulties or evidence of alternative sources of finance

The bank letter will provide evidence of the current level of overdraft but not about the likelihood of the overdraft being renewed in future.

The scenario clearly states that the bank will not make a decision on the extension of the overdraft facility until after the auditor's report is signed, and banks will not agree to disclose such information to the auditor. While written representations are a valid form of audit evidence, they do not provide sufficient appropriate audit evidence on their own about any of the matters with which they deal.

197 The correct answer is:

Audit opinion	Disclosure in the auditor's report
Unmodified opinion	Describe the nature of the going concern uncertainty in the Material Uncertainty Related to Going Concern section

An unmodified opinion is issued as the auditor agrees with the used of the going concern basis of accounting and the level of disclosure provided. The existence of a material uncertainty in relation to going concern would be disclosed in the 'Material uncertainty related to going concern' section (ISA 570: para. 22). A qualified opinion would be issued if the going concern basis of accounting is appropriate, but a material uncertainty exists which is not adequately disclosed (ISA 570: para. 23). An adverse opinion would be issued where the going concern basis of accounting is inappropriate (ISA 570: para. 21). A disclaimer of opinion would be issued if the auditor is unable to form an opinion.

198 The correct answer is:

Discuss with management about their plans for the company and determine whether the 20X7 financial statements should now be prepared on a break-up basis. If yes, request management to adjust the financial statements, audit the adjustments and provide a new auditor's report

If Medimade is no longer able to continue its operations, this constitutes an adjusting event and the financial statements must be revised accordingly. IAS 10 states that an entity must not prepare its financial statements on a going concern basis if management determine after the year end that it has no other alternative but to liquidate the company (IAS 10: para. 14). Now that the bank has withdrawn its overdraft facility, closure has become a very real possibility. In this case, disclosure in the financial statements is no longer appropriate – the financial statements must be prepared on a break-up basis.

Before the financial statements are issued, the auditors have a passive duty to consider the impact of matters which, had they been known at the date of the auditor's report, would have caused the auditor to amend the auditor's report.

Mock exams

ACCA
Fundamentals Level
Paper F8
Audit and Assurance

Mock Examination 1

Specimen exam

Time allowed: 3 hours and 15 minutes

This question paper is divided into two sections:

Section A – ALL 15 questions are compulsory and MUST be attempted

Section B – ALL 3 questions are compulsory and MUST be attempted

Do NOT open this question paper until instructed by the supervisor.

Do NOT record any of your answers on the question paper.

This question paper must not be removed from the examination hall.

CANDIDATE ANSWER BOOKLET

SAMPLE PAGE ONLY

USE THIS PAGE TO RECORD ANSWERS TO MULTIPLE CHOICE QUESTIONS

- If your question paper has less than 60 questions, fill in the relevant answers only.

- Each multiple choice question has only one correct answer. Fill in one bubble only (A, B, C, or D) to indicate your choice of answer.

- The mark available for each question is indicated on your question paper. There is no penalty for incorrect answers or unanswered questions.

- No marks are awarded if you do not clearly indicate your final choice or if more than one bubble per question is filled in.

- To void a selected answer, place a cross (X) over the bubble.

HOW TO SHADE THE BUBBLES

EXAMPLE
Right mark   Wrong mark

To amend your selection place a cross over unwanted bubble

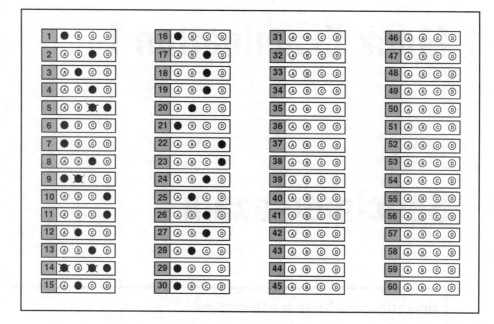

Section A – ALL FIFTEEN questions are compulsory and MUST be attempted

Each question is worth 2 marks.

The following scenario relates to questions 1–5.

You are an audit manager of Buffon & Co, and you have just been assigned the audit of Maldini Co (Maldini). The audit engagement partner who is responsible for the audit of Maldini, a listed company, has been in place for approximately eight years and her son has just been offered a role with Maldini as a sales manager. This role would entitle him to shares in Maldini as part of his remuneration package.

Maldini's board of directors is considering establishing an internal audit function, and the finance director has asked Buffon & Co about the differences in the role of internal audit and external audit. If the internal audit function is established, the directors have suggested that they may wish to outsource this to Buffon & Co. The finance director has suggested to the board that if Buffon & Co is appointed as internal as well as external auditors, then fees should be renegotiated with at least 20% of all internal and external audit fees being based on the profit after tax of the company as this will align the interests of Buffon & Co and Maldini.

1   From a review of the information above, your audit assistant has highlighted some of the potential risks to independence in respect of the audit of Maldini.

(1)   Audit partner has been in the position for eight years
(2)   Maldini has asked for advice regarding role of internal audit
(3)   Maldini has asked Buffon & Co to carry out internal audit work
(4)   Fees will be based on 20% of profit after tax

Which of the following options correctly identifies the valid threats to independence and allocates the threat to the appropriate category?

	Self-interest	Self-review	Familiarity
A	1 only	2 and 3	4 only
B	1 only	2 only	4 only
C	2 only	3 and 4	1 only
D	4 only	3 only	1 only

2   In relation to the audit engagement partner holding the role for eight years and her son's offer of employment with Maldini:

Which of the following safeguards should be implemented in order to comply with ACCA's Code of Ethics and Conduct?

A   The audit partner should be removed from the audit team
B   An independent review partner should be appointed
C   The audit partner should be removed if her son accepts the position
D   Buffon & Co should resign from the audit

3   **In line with ACCA's Code of Ethics and Conduct, which of the following factors must be considered before the internal audit engagement should be accepted?**

(1)   Whether the external audit team have the expertise to carry out the internal audit work
(2)   If the assignments will relate to the internal controls over financial reporting
(3)   If management will accept responsibility for implementing appropriate recommendations
(4)   The probable timescale for the outsourcing of the internal audit function

A   1, 2 and 3
B   2 and 3 only
C   1 and 4 only
D   1, 3 and 4

4 Following management's request for information regarding the different roles of internal and external audit, you have collated a list of key characteristics.

(1) Appointed by audit committee
(2) Reports are publicly available to shareholders
(3) Review efficiency and effectiveness of operations to improve operations
(4) Express an opinion on the truth and fairness of the financial statements

Which of the following options correctly allocates the above statements to the relevant auditor?

	External	Internal
A	2, 3 and 4	1 only
B	1 and 4	2 and 3
C	2 and 4	1 and 3
D	2 only	1, 3 and 4

5 If the internal and external audit assignments are accepted, what safeguards, if any, are needed in relation to the basis for the fee?

A As long as the total fee received from Maldini is less than 15% of the firm's total fee income, no safeguards are needed

B The client should be informed that only the internal audit fee can be based on profit after tax

C The fees should be based on Maldini's profit before tax

D No safeguards can be applied and this basis for fee determination should be rejected

The following scenario relates to questions 6–10.

Balotelli Beach Hotel Co (Balotelli) operates a number of hotels providing accommodation, leisure facilities and restaurants. You are an audit senior of Mario & Co and are currently conducting the audit of Balotelli for the year ended 31 December 20X4. During the course of the audit a number of events and issues have been brought to your attention:

Non-current assets and depreciation

Balotelli incurred significant capital expenditure during the year updating the leisure facilities at several of the company's hotels. Depreciation is charged monthly on all assets on a straight line basis (SL) and it is company policy to charge a full month's depreciation in the month of acquisition and none in the month of disposal.

6 During the audit of non-current assets, the audit team has obtained the following extract of the non-current assets register detailing some of the new leisure equipment acquired during the year.

EXTRACT FROM BALOTELLI'S NON-CURRENT ASSETS REGISTER

Date	Description	Original cost $	Depreciation policy	Accumulated depreciation $	Charge for the year $	Carrying value $
1 May 20X4	15 treadmills	18,000	36 months SL	0	4,000 ✓	14,000
15 May 20X4	20 exercise bikes	17,000	3 years SL	0	5,667	11,333
17 August 20X4	15 rowing machines	9,750	36 months SL	0	2,167	7,583
19 August 20X4	10 cross trainers	11,000	36 months SL	0	1,528	9,472
		55,750		0	13,362	42,388

In order to verify the depreciation expense for the year, you have been asked to perform a proof in total. This will involve developing an expectation of the depreciation expense for the year and comparing this to the actual expense to assess if the client has calculated the depreciation charge for the year correctly.

What is the expected depreciation expense for the above assets for the year ended 31 December 20X4 and the resultant impact on non-current assets?

A   Depreciation should be $10,660, assets are understated
B   Depreciation should be $18,583, assets are understated
C   Depreciation should be $9,111, assets are overstated
D   Depreciation should be $12,549, assets are overstated

---

7   The audit assistant who has been assigned to help you with the audit work on non-current assets has expressed some uncertainty over why certain audit procedures are carried out and specifically is unsure what procedures relate to the valuation and allocation assertion.

Which of the following audit procedures are appropriate to test the VALUATION assertion for non-current assets?

(1)   Ensure disposals are correctly accounted for and recalculate gain/loss on disposal

(2)   Recalculate the depreciation charge for a sample of assets ensuring that it is being applied consistently and in accordance with IAS 16 *Property, Plant and Equipment*

(3)   Review the repairs and maintenance expense accounts for evidence of items of a capital nature

(4)   Review board minutes for evidence of disposals during the year and verify that these are appropriately reflected in the non-current assets register

A   1 and 2
B   1, 3 and 4
C   2, 3 and 4
D   2 and 3 only

Food poisoning

Balotelli's directors received correspondence in November 20X4 from a group of customers who attended a wedding at one of the company's hotels. They have alleged that they suffered severe food poisoning from food eaten at the hotel and are claiming substantial damages. Management has stated that based on discussions with their lawyers, the claim is unlikely to be successful.

8   **In relation to the claim regarding the alleged food poisoning, which of the following audit procedures would provide the auditor with the MOST reliable audit evidence regarding the likely outcome of the litigation?**

A   Request a written representation from management supporting their assertion that the claim will not be successful

B   Send an enquiry letter to the lawyers of Balotelli to obtain their view as to the probability of the claim being successful

C   Review the correspondence from the customers claiming food poisoning to assess whether Balotelli has a present obligation as a result of a past event

D   Review board minutes to understand why the directors believe that the claim will not be successful

---

Trade receivables

Balotelli's trade receivables have historically been low as most customers are required to pay in advance or at the time of visiting the hotel. However, during the year a number of companies opened corporate accounts which are payable monthly in arrears. As such, the trade receivables balance has risen significantly and is now a material balance.

9 As trade receivables is a material balance, the audit partner has asked that the audit team carry out a trade receivables circularisation.

Which of the following are benefits of carrying out a trade receivables circularisation?

(1) It provides evidence from an independent external source
(2) It provides sufficient appropriate audit evidence over all relevant balance assertions
(3) It improves audit efficiency as all customers are required to respond
(4) It improves the reliability of audit evidence as the process is under the control of the auditor

A 1 and 2
B 1, 2 and 4
C 2 and 3
D 1 and 4 only

10 The results of the trade receivables circularisation carried out by the audit team on balances as at 31 December 20X4 are detailed below. You have been asked to consider the results and determine if additional audit procedures are required.

Customer	Balance per sales ledger $	Balance per customer confirmation $	Comment
Willow Co	42,500	42,500	
Cedar Co	35,000	25,000	Invoice raised 28 December
Maple Co	60,000	45,000	Payment made 30 December
Laurel Co	55,000	55,000	A balance of $20,000 is currently being disputed by Laurel Co
Oak Co	15,000		No reply

Which of the following statements in relation to the results of the trade receivables circularisation is TRUE?

A No further audit procedures need to be carried out in relation to the outstanding balances with Willow Co and Laurel Co

B The difference in relation to Cedar Co represents a timing difference and should be agreed to a pre year-end invoice

C The difference in relation to Maple Co represents a timing difference and should be agreed to pre year-end bank statements

D Due to the non-reply, the balance with Oak Co cannot be verified and a different customer balance should be selected and circularised

---

The following scenario relates to questions 11–15.

Cannavaro.com is a website design company whose year end was 31 December 20X4. The audit is almost complete and the financial statements are due to be signed shortly. Profit before tax for the year is $3.8 million and revenue is $11.2 million.

The company has only required an audit for the last two years and the board of directors has asked your firm to provide more detail in relation to the form and content of the auditor's report.

During the audit it has come to light that a key customer, Pirlo Co, with a receivables balance at the year end of $285,000, has just notified Cannavaro.com that they are experiencing cash flow difficulties and so are unable to make any payments for the foreseeable future. The finance director has notified the audit team that he will write this balance off as an irrecoverable debt in the 20X5 financial statements.

11 To explain to the board the content of the audit report, the audit partner has asked you to provide details as to why certain elements are included within an unmodified report.

Which of the following explains the purpose of the ADDRESSEE element of the unmodified audit report in line with ISA 700 *Forming an Opinion and Reporting on Financial Statements*?

A   It demonstrates the point at which sufficient appropriate evidence has been obtained
B   It clarifies who may rely on the opinion included within the report
C   It explains the role and remit of the audit
D   It sets out the location where the auditor practises

12 The audit assistant assigned to the audit of Cannavaro.com wants a better understanding of the effect subsequent events have on the audit and has made the following statements:

(1)   All material subsequent events require the numbers in the financial statements to be adjusted

(2)   A non-adjusting event is a subsequent event for which NO amendments to the current year financial statements are required

(3)   The auditor's responsibilities for subsequent events which occur prior to the audit report being signed are different from their responsibilities after the audit report has been issued

(4)   The auditor should request a written representation confirming that all relevant subsequent events have been disclosed

Which of the statements above in relation to subsequent events are TRUE?

A   1 and 3
B   2, 3 and 4
C   1, 2 and 4
D   3 and 4 only

13 The audit engagement partner has asked you to make an initial assessment of the materiality of the issue with the outstanding receivables balance with Pirlo Co and to consider the overall impact on the financial statements.

Which of the following correctly summarises the effect of the outstanding balance with Pirlo Co?

	Material	Financial statement impact
A	No	Revenue is overstated
B	No	Gross profit is understated
C	Yes	Profit is overstated
D	Yes	Use of going concern basis of accounting is in doubt

14 The audit engagement partner requires you to perform additional procedures in order to conclude on the level of any adjustment needed in relation to the outstanding balance with Pirlo Co.

Which TWO of the following audit procedures should be performed to form a conclusion as to whether the financial statements require amendment?

(1)   Discuss with management the reasons for not amending the financial statements
(2)   Review the cash book post year end for receipts from Pirlo Co
(3)   Send a request to Pirlo Co to confirm the outstanding balance
(4)   Agree the outstanding balance to invoices and sales orders

A   1 and 2
B   1 and 4
C   2 and 3
D   2 and 4

15 The finance director has asked you to outline the appropriate audit opinions which will be provided
    depending on whether the company decides to amend or not amend the 20X4 financial statements for the
    issue identified regarding the recoverability of the balance with Pirlo Co.

    **Which of the following options correctly summarises the audit opinions which will be issued depending
    on whether or not the 20X4 financial statements are amended?**

	Financial statements amended	Financial statements not amended
A	Unmodified	Unmodified with emphasis of matter
B	Unmodified with emphasis of matter	Qualified 'except for'
C	Unmodified	Adverse
D	Unmodified	Qualified 'except for'

    (Total = 30 marks)

Section B – ALL THREE questions are compulsory and MUST be attempted

Question 16

Milla Cola Co (Milla) manufactures fizzy drinks such as cola and lemonade as well as other soft drinks and its year end is 30 September 20X5. You are an audit manager of Totti & Co and are currently planning the audit of Milla. You attended the planning meeting with the audit engagement partner and finance director last week and the minutes from the meeting are shown below. You are reviewing these as part of the process of preparing the audit strategy document.

Minutes of planning meeting for Milla

Milla's trading results have been strong this year and the company is forecasting revenue of $85 million, which is an increase from the previous year. The company has invested significantly in the cola and fizzy drinks production process at the factory. This resulted in expenditure of $5 million on updating, repairing and replacing a significant amount of the machinery used in the production process.

As the level of production has increased, the company has expanded the number of warehouses it uses to store inventory. It now utilises 15 warehouses; some are owned by Milla and some are rented from third parties. There will be inventory counts taking place at all 15 of these sites at the year end.

A new accounting general ledger has been introduced at the beginning of the year, with the old and new systems being run in parallel for a period of two months. In addition, Milla has incurred expenditure of $4.5 million on developing a new brand of fizzy soft drinks. The company started this process in July 20X4 and is close to launching their new product into the market place.

As a result of the increase in revenue, Milla has recently recruited a new credit controller to chase outstanding receivables. The finance director thinks it is not necessary to continue to maintain an allowance for receivables and so has released the opening allowance of $1.5 million.

The finance director stated that there was a problem in April in the mixing of raw materials within the production process which resulted in a large batch of cola products tasting different. A number of these products were sold; however, due to complaints by customers about the flavour, no further sales of these goods have been made. No adjustment has been made to the valuation of the damaged inventory, which will still be held at cost of $1 million at the year end.

As in previous years, the management of Milla is due to be paid a significant annual bonus based on the value of year-end total assets.

Required

(a) Explain audit risk and the components of audit risk. **(5 marks)**

(b) Using the minutes provided, identify and describe **SEVEN** audit risks, and explain the auditor's response to each risk, in planning the audit of Milla Cola Co. **(14 marks)**

(c) Identify the main areas, other than audit risks, which should be included within the audit strategy document for Milla Cola Co; and for each area provide an example relevant to the audit. **(4 marks)**

The finance director has requested that the deadline for the 20X6 audit be shortened by a month and has asked the audit engagement partner to consider if this will be possible. The partner has suggested that in order to meet this new tighter deadline the firm may carry out both an interim and final audit for the audit of Milla to 30 September 20X6.

Required

(d) Explain the difference between an interim and a final audit. **(3 marks)**

(e) Explain the procedures which are likely to be performed during an interim audit of Milla and the impact which it would have on the final audit. **(4 marks)**

(Total = 30 marks)

Question 17

Baggio International Co (Baggio) is a manufacturer of electrical equipment. It has factories across the country and its customer base includes retailers as well as individuals, to whom direct sales are made through their website. The company's year end is 30 September 20X5. You are an audit supervisor of Suarez & Co and are currently reviewing documentation of Baggio's internal control in preparation for the interim audit.

Baggio's website allows individuals to order goods directly, and full payment is taken in advance. Currently the website is not integrated into the inventory system and inventory levels are not checked at the time when orders are placed.

Inventory is valued at the lower of cost and net realisable value.

Goods are despatched via local couriers; however, they do not always record customer signatures as proof that the customer has received the goods. Over the past 12 months there have been customer complaints about the delay between sales orders and receipt of goods. Baggio has investigated these and found that, in each case, the sales order had been entered into the sales system correctly but was not forwarded to the despatch department for fulfilling.

Baggio's retail customers undergo credit checks prior to being accepted and credit limits are set accordingly by sales ledger clerks. These customers place their orders through one of the sales team, who decides on sales discount levels.

Raw materials used in the manufacturing process are purchased from a wide range of suppliers. As a result of staff changes in the purchase ledger department, supplier statement reconciliations are no longer performed. Additionally, changes to supplier details in the purchase ledger master file can be undertaken by purchase ledger clerks as well as supervisors.

In the past six months, Baggio has changed part of its manufacturing process and as a result some new equipment has been purchased, however, there are considerable levels of plant and equipment which are now surplus to requirement. Purchase requisitions for all new equipment have been authorised by production supervisors and little has been done to reduce the surplus of old equipment.

Required

(a)   In respect of the internal control of Baggio International Co:

(i)   Identify and explain **SIX** deficiencies;

(ii)   Recommend a control to address each of these deficiencies; and

(iii) Describe a test of control Suarez & Co would perform to assess whether each of these controls, if implemented, is operating effectively.

Note. The total marks will be split equally between each part.   **(18 marks)**

(b)   Describe substantive procedures Suarez & Co should perform at the year end to confirm plant and equipment additions.

(2 marks)

(Total = 20 marks)

Question 18

Vieri Motor Cars Co (Vieri) manufactures a range of motor cars and its year end is 30 June 20X5. You are the audit supervisor of Rossi & Co and are currently preparing the audit programmes for the year-end audit of Vieri. You have had a meeting with your audit manager and he has notified you of the following issues identified during the audit risk assessment process:

Land and buildings

Vieri has a policy of revaluing land and buildings, this is undertaken on a rolling basis over a five-year period. During the year Vieri requested an external independent valuer to revalue a number of properties, including a warehouse purchased in January 20X5. Depreciation is charged on a pro rata basis.

Work in progress

Vieri undertakes continuous production of cars, 24 hours a day, seven days a week. An inventory count is to be undertaken at the year end and Rossi & Co will attend. You are responsible for the audit of work in progress (WIP) and will be part of the team attending the count as well as the final audit. WIP constitutes the partly assembled cars at the year end and this balance is likely to be material. Vieri values WIP according to percentage of completion, and standard costs are then applied to these percentages.

Required

(a)   Explain the factors Rossi & Co should consider when placing reliance on the work of the independent valuer.

(5 marks)

(b)   Describe the substantive procedures the auditor should perform to obtain sufficient and appropriate audit evidence in relation to:

(i)   The revaluation of land and buildings and the recently purchased warehouse; and   **(6 marks)**

(ii)   The valuation of work in progress.   **(4 marks)**

(c)   During the audit, the team has identified an error in the valuation of work in progress, as a number of the assumptions contain out of date information. The directors of Vieri have indicated that they do not wish to amend the financial statements.

Required

Explain the steps Rossi & Co should now take and the impact on the auditor's report in relation to the directors' refusal to amend the financial statements.   **(5 marks)**

(Total = 20 marks)

Answers

DO NOT TURN THIS PAGE UNTIL YOU HAVE
COMPLETED THE MOCK EXAM

Plan of attack

If this were the real Audit and Assurance exam and you had been told to turn over and begin, what would be going through your mind?

An important thing to say (while there is still time) is that it is vital to have a good breadth of knowledge of the syllabus because all the questions are compulsory. However, don't panic. Below we provide guidance on how to approach the exam.

Looking through the paper

Section A has three objective test cases, each with five questions. This is the section of the paper where the examination team can test knowledge across the breadth of the syllabus. Make sure you read these cases and questions carefully. The distractors are designed to present plausible, but incorrect, answers. Don't let them mislead you. If you really have no idea – guess. You may even be right.

Section B has three longer questions:

- **Question 16** is a 30-mark question focused on the planning stage, covering audit risk and the audit strategy document, with an unrelated coda on interim audits. Don't panic – take your time to read the scenario and what you are asked to do.

- **Question 17** is a 20-mark internal controls question. In part (a) it is crucial that you relate your answer to the scenario.

- **Question 18** is a 20-mark question dealing with a number of issues: an independent valuer, revaluations, work in progress, and auditor reporting.

Allocating your time

BPP's advice is to always allocate your time **according to the marks for the question**. However, **use common sense**. If you're doing a question but haven't a clue how to do part (b), you might be better off re-allocating your time and getting more marks on another question, where you can add something you didn't have time for earlier on. Make sure you leave time to recheck the OTQs and make sure you have answered them all.

Forget about it

And don't worry if you found the paper difficult. More than likely other candidates will too. If this were the real thing you would need to forget the exam the minute you left the exam hall and think about the next one. Or, if it is the last one, celebrate!

BPP
LEARNING MEDIA

Section A

1   D   Statement 1 – Partner has been in role for eight years, contravenes ACCA's Code of Ethics and Conduct and represents a familiarity threat (ACCA Code of Ethics and Conduct: para. 290.149).

Statement 3 – Providing internal audit services raises a self-review threat as it is likely that the audit team will be looking to place reliance on the internal control system reviewed by internal audit.

Statement 4 – This represents fees on a contingent basis and raises a self-interest threat as the audit firm's fee will rise if the company's profit after tax increases.

Statement 2 – Is not a threat to independence and therefore D is the correct answer.

2   A   If the engagement partner's son accepts the role and obtains shares in the company, it would constitute a self-interest threat but as the partner has already exceeded the seven-year relationship rule in line with ACCA's Code of Ethics and Conduct, the partner should be rotated off the audit irrespective of the decision made by her son. As Maldini is a listed company, an independent review partner should already be in place. It is unlikely that the firm needs to resign from the audit (due to stated circumstances) as the threats to objectivity can be mitigated.

Therefore option A is correct.

3   B   Statement 1 is inappropriate as the external and internal audit team should be separate and therefore consideration of the skills of the external audit team is not appropriate in the circumstances.

Statement 4 does not apply in that the timescale of the work is not relevant to consider the threats to objectivity.

Statement 2 and 3 are valid considerations – as per ACCA's Code of Ethics and Conduct providing internal audit services can result in the audit firm assuming a management role. To mitigate this, it is appropriate for the firm to assess whether management will take responsibility for implementing recommendations (ACCA Code of Ethics and Conduct: para. 290.161). Further, for a listed company the Code prohibits the provision of internal audit services which review a significant proportion of the internal controls over financial reporting as these may be relied upon by the external audit team and the self-review threat is too great (ACCA Code of Ethics and Conduct: para. 290.195).

Therefore option B is correct.

4   C   Internal audit are appointed by the audit committee (external audit usually by the shareholders) and it is the role of internal audit to review the effectiveness and efficiency of internal controls to improve operations. External audit looks at the operating effectiveness of internal controls on which they may rely for audit evidence and a by-product may be to comment on any deficiencies they have found but this is not a key function of the role.

Therefore statements 1 and 3 relate to internal audit.

The external auditor's report is publicly available to the shareholders of the company (internal audit reports are addressed to management/TCWG) and the external auditor provides an opinion on the truth and fairness of the financial statements.

Therefore statements 2 and 4 relate to external audit.

C is therefore the correct answer.

5   D   The proposal in relation to the fees is a contingent fee basis which is expressly prohibited by ACCA's Code of Ethics and Conduct and therefore the only viable option here is to reject the fee basis – D is therefore correct (ACCA Code of Ethics and Conduct: para. 290.220).

6   A   Depreciation should be calculated as:

Treadmills/exercise bikes = (18,000 + 17,000)/36 × 8 months =	7,778
Rowing machines/cross trainers = (9,750 + 11,000)/36 × 5 months =	2,882
Total	10,660

Therefore the correct answer is A and assets are currently understated as too much depreciation has currently been charged.

Option B is based on depreciation being applied for a full year instead of for the relevant months.

Option C is based on depreciation not being charged in the month of acquisition (ie seven and four months).

Option D is based on depreciation for the exercise bikes being divided by the three years instead of allocated on a monthly basis.

7	A	Test 4 is a test for existence and test 3 is for completeness. All other tests are relevant for valuation. Option A is correct.
8	B	While all procedures would be valid in the circumstances, only the written confirmation from the company's lawyers would allow the auditor to obtain an expert, third party confirmation on the likelihood of the case being successful. This would provide the auditor with the most reliable evidence in the circumstances. Therefore B is the correct answer.
9	D	As per ISA 505 *External confirmations*, the evidence obtained from the trade receivables circularisation should be reliable as it is from an external source and the risk of management bias and influence is restricted due to the process being under the control of the auditor (ISA 505: para. 2). Therefore 1 and 4 are benefits and option D is therefore correct.

Customers are not obliged to answer and often circularisations have a very low response rate. A circularisation will not provide evidence over the valuation assertion for receivables and therefore 2 and 3 are drawbacks of a circularisation.

10	B	A is incorrect as the balance with Laurel Co would need to be followed up due to the dispute.

C is incorrect as this represents a payment in transit and the payment would need to be agreed to post year-end bank statements – if the cash was received pre year end this would represent a cut-off issue as this should no longer be included in receivables.

D is incorrect as the sample chosen should be verified even if there is no response. As per ISA 505, the auditor should adopt alternative procedures (ISA 505: para.12).

Therefore B is the only statement which is true as this does represent a timing difference (invoice in transit) and should be agreed to a pre year-end invoice.

11	B	Addressee – sets out who the report is addressed to – usually the shareholders – and is there to clarify who can place reliance on the audit opinion. B is therefore the correct option.
12	D	Statement 1 is false as not all subsequent events will require an adjustment to the numbers within the financial statements. IAS 10 *Events after the reporting period* makes a distinction between an adjusting and non-adjusting event. Only material adjusting events would require an amendment to the figures within the financial statements (IAS 10: para. 8).

Statement 2 is false as while a non-adjusting event would not require a change to the numbers within the financial statements, IAS 10 may require a disclosure to be made. If the non-adjusting event is material, non-disclosure could still result in a modification to the audit report.

Statement 3 is true as the auditor is required to carry out procedures up to the date of the audit report to gain sufficient appropriate audit evidence that all relevant subsequent events have been identified and dealt with appropriately. After the audit report is issued, the auditor does not need to actively look for subsequent events but is only required to respond to subsequent events which they become aware of.

Statement 4 is true as ISA 560 *Subsequent events* requires the auditor to obtain written confirmation from management/those charged with governance that all subsequent events have been identified and dealt with in accordance with the appropriate reporting framework (ISA 560: para. 9).

D is therefore correct.

13	C	The outstanding balance with Pirlo Co is likely to be irrecoverable as the customer is experiencing financial difficulties.

The balance is material at 7.4% of profit before tax and 2.5% of revenue.

Currently profit and assets are overstated by $285,000. Therefore the correct option is C.

14   A   Writing to the customer/agreeing to invoices, while valid procedures during the audit to verify the existence of an outstanding balance, would not allow the auditor to assess the recoverability of the balance which is the key issue in determining whether an adjustment is required. Therefore options 3 and 4 are incorrect.

Post year-end cash testing is the best way for the auditor to assess if the balance is recoverable wholly or in part and therefore the cash book should be reviewed for any receipts which will change the assessment of the debt after the year end. The issue should also be discussed with management to understand their reasons for not wanting to amend the financial statements as this may be due to a change in circumstances.

15   D   The debt with Pirlo Co should be provided for and is material to the financial statements at 7.4% of profit before tax and 2.5% of revenue. This represents a material misstatement which is material but not pervasive. As such, if no adjustment is made the auditor will be required to provide a qualified 'except for' opinion. If the required change is made, then no material misstatement exists and therefore the auditor will be able to issue an unmodified opinion.

Section B

Question 16

		Marks
(a)	**Component of audit risk**	
	Explanation of audit risk	2
	Explanation of components of audit risk: Inherent, control and detection risk	3
		5
(b)	**Audit risks and responses** (only 7 risks required)	
	$5 million expenditure on production process	2
	Inventory counts at 15 warehouses at year end	2
	Treatment of owned v third party warehouses	2
	New general ledger system introduced at the beginning of the year	2
	Release of opening provision for allowance for receivables	2
	Research and development expenditure	2
	Damaged inventory	2
	Sales returns	2
	Management bonus based on asset values	2
	Max 7 issues, 2 marks each	14
(c)	**Audit strategy document**	
	Main characteristics of the audit	1
	Reporting objectives of the audit and nature of communications required	1
	Factors which are significant in directing the audit team's efforts	1
	Results of preliminary engagement activities and whether knowledge gained on other engagements is relevant	1
	Nature, timing and extent of resources necessary to perform the audit	1
	Restricted to	4
(d)	**Difference between interim and final audit**	
	Interim audit	2
	Final audit	2
	Restricted to	3
(e)	**Procedures/impact of interim audit on final audit**	
	Example procedures	3
	Impact on final audit	3
	Restricted to	4
Total marks		30

(a) **Audit risk and its components**

Audit risk is the risk that the auditor expresses an inappropriate audit opinion when the financial statements are materially misstated. Audit risk is a function of two main components being the risks of material misstatement and detection risk (ISA 200: para. 13(C)). Risk of material misstatement is made up of two components, inherent risk and control risk.

Inherent risk is the susceptibility of an assertion about a class of transaction, account balance or disclosure to a misstatement which could be material, either individually or when aggregated with other misstatements, before consideration of any related controls (ISA 200: para. 13(n)).

Control risk is the risk that a misstatement which could occur in an assertion about a class of transaction, account balance or disclosure and which could be material, either individually or when aggregated with other misstatements, will not be prevented, or detected and corrected, on a timely basis by the entity's internal control (ISA 200: para. 13(n)).

Detection risk is the risk that the procedures performed by the auditor to reduce audit risk to an acceptably low level will not detect a misstatement which exists and which could be material, either individually or when aggregated with other misstatements. Detection risk is affected by sampling and non-sampling risk (ISA 200: para. 13(e)).

(b) Audit risks and responses

Audit risk	Auditor response
Milla has incurred $5m on updating, repairing and replacing a significant amount of the production process machinery. If this expenditure is of a capital nature, it should be capitalised as part of property, plant and equipment (PPE) in line with IAS 16 *Property, Plant and Equipment*. However, if it relates more to repairs, then it should be expensed to the statement of profit or loss If the expenditure is not correctly classified, profit and PPE could be under or overstated.	The auditor should review a breakdown of these costs to ascertain the split of capital and revenue expenditure, and further testing should be undertaken to ensure that the classification in the financial statements is correct.
At the year end there will be inventory counts undertaken in all 15 warehouses. It is unlikely that the auditor will be able to attend all 15 inventory counts and therefore they need to ensure that they obtain sufficient appropriate audit evidence over the inventory counting controls, and completeness and existence of inventory for any warehouses not visited.	The auditor should assess which of the inventory sites they will attend the counts for. This will be any with material inventory or which have a history of significant errors. For those not visited, the auditor will need to review the level of exceptions noted during the count and discuss with management any issues which arose during the count.
Inventory is stored within 15 warehouses; some are owned by Milla and some rented from third parties. Only warehouses owned by Milla should be included within PPE. There is a risk of overstatement of PPE and understatement of rental expenses if Milla has capitalised all 15 warehouses.	The auditor should review supporting documentation for all warehouses included within PPE to confirm ownership by Milla and to ensure non-current assets are not overstated.
A new accounting general ledger system has been introduced at the beginning of the year and the old system was run in parallel for two months. There is a risk of opening balances being misstated and loss of data if they have not been transferred from the old system correctly. In addition, the new accounting general ledger system will require documenting and the controls over this will need to be tested.	The auditor should undertake detailed testing to confirm that all opening balances have been correctly recorded in the new accounting general ledger system. They should document and test the new system. They should review any management reports run comparing the old and new system during the parallel run to identify any issues with the processing of accounting information.
Milla has incurred expenditure of $4.5 million on developing a new brand of fizzy drink. This expenditure is research and development under IAS 38 *Intangible Assets*. The standard requires research costs to be expensed and development costs to be capitalised as an intangible asset (IAS 38: paras. 54 & 57).	Obtain a breakdown of the expenditure and undertake testing to determine whether the costs relate to the research or development stage. Discuss the accounting treatment with the finance director and ensure it is in accordance with IAS 38.

If Milla has incorrectly classified research costs as development expenditure, there is a risk the intangible asset could be overstated and expenses understated.	
The finance director of Milla has decided to release the opening balance of $1.5 million for allowance for receivables as he feels it is unnecessary. There is a risk that receivables will be overvalued, as despite having a credit controller, some balances will be irrecoverable and so will be overstated if not provided against. In addition, due to the damaged inventory there is an increased risk of customers refusing to make payments in full.	Extended post year-end cash receipts testing and a review of the aged receivables ledger to be performed to assess valuation and the need for an allowance for receivables. Discuss with the director the rationale for releasing the $1.5m opening allowance for receivables.
A large batch of cola products has been damaged in the production process and will be in inventory at the year end. No adjustment has been made by management. The valuation of inventory as per IAS 2 *Inventories* should be at the lower of cost and net realisable value (IAS 2: para 9). Hence it is likely that this inventory is overvalued.	Detailed cost and net realisable value testing to be performed to assess how much the inventory requires writing down by.
Due to the damaged cola products, a number of customers have complained. It is likely that for any of the damaged goods sold, Milla will need to refund these customers. Revenue is possibly overstated if the sales returns are not completely and accurately recorded.	Review the breakdown of sales of damaged goods, and ensure that they have been accurately removed from revenue.
The management of Milla receives a significant annual bonus based on the value of year-end total assets. There is a risk that management might feel under pressure to overstate the value of assets through the judgements taken or through the use of releasing provisions.	Throughout the audit, the team will need to be alert to this risk. They will need to maintain professional scepticism and carefully review judgemental decisions and compare treatment against prior years.

(c) **Audit strategy document**

The audit strategy sets out the scope, timing and direction of the audit and helps the development of the audit plan (ISA 300: para. 7). It should consider the following main areas:

It should identify the main characteristics of the engagement which define its scope. For Milla it should consider the following:

- Whether the financial information to be audited has been prepared in accordance with IFRS.
- To what extent audit evidence obtained in previous audits for Milla will be utilised.
- Whether computer-assisted audit techniques will be used and the effect of IT on audit procedures.
- The availability of key personnel at Milla.

It should ascertain the reporting objectives of the engagement to plan the timing of the audit and the nature of the communications required, such as (ISA 300: para. 8):

- The audit timetable for reporting and whether there will be an interim as well as final audit.
- Organisation of meetings with Milla's management to discuss any audit issues arising.
- Location of the 15 inventory counts.
- Any discussions with management regarding the reports to be issued.
- The timings of the audit team meetings and review of work performed.
- If there are any expected communications with third parties.

The strategy should consider the factors which, in the auditor's professional judgement, are significant in directing Milla's audit team's efforts, such as:

- The determination of materiality for the audit.

- The need to maintain a questioning mind and to exercise professional scepticism in gathering and evaluating audit evidence.

It should consider the results of preliminary audit planning activities and, where applicable, whether knowledge gained on other engagements for Milla is relevant, such as:

- Results of previous audits and the results of any tests over the effectiveness of internal controls.

- Evidence of management's commitment to the design, implementation and maintenance of sound internal control.

- Volume of transactions, which may determine whether it is more efficient for the audit team to rely on internal control.

- Significant business developments affecting Milla, such as the change in the accounting system and the significant expenditure on an overhaul of the factory.

The audit strategy should ascertain the nature, timing and extent of resources necessary to perform the audit, such as:

- The selection of the audit team with experience of this type of industry.
- Assignment of audit work to the team members.
- Setting the audit budget.

Tutorial note. The answer is longer than required for four marks but represents a teaching aid.

(d) **Differences between an interim and a final audit**

Interim audit

The interim audit is that part of the audit which takes place before the year end. The auditor uses the interim audit to carry out procedures which would be difficult to perform at the year end because of time pressure. There is no requirement to undertake an interim audit; factors to consider when deciding upon whether to have one include the size and complexity of the company along with the effectiveness of internal controls.

Final audit

The final audit will take place after the year end and concludes with the auditor forming and expressing an opinion on the financial statements for the whole year subject to audit. It is important to note that the final opinion takes account of conclusions formed at both the interim and final audit.

(e) Procedures which could be undertaken during the interim audit include:

- Review and updating of the documentation of accounting systems at Milla.

- Discussions with management on the recent growth and any other changes within the business which have occurred during the year to date at Milla to update the auditor's understanding of the company.

- Assessment of risks which will impact the final audit of Milla.

- Undertake tests of controls on Milla's key transaction cycles of sales, purchases and inventory, and credit control.

- Perform substantive procedures on profit and loss transactions for the year to date and any other completed material transactions.

Impact of interim audit on final

If an interim audit is undertaken at Milla, then it will have an impact on the final audit and the extent of work undertaken after the year end. First, as some testing has already been undertaken, there will be less work to be performed at the final audit, which may result in a shorter audit and audited financial statements possibly being available earlier. The outcome of the controls testing undertaken during the interim audit will impact the level of substantive testing to be undertaken. If the controls tested have proven to be operating effectively, then the auditor may be able to reduce the level of detailed substantive testing required as they will be able to place reliance on the controls. In addition, if substantive procedures were undertaken at the interim audit, then only the period from the interim audit to the year end will require to be tested.

Question 17

		Marks
(a)	**Control deficiencies, recommendations and tests of controls** (only 6 issues required)	
	Website not integrated into inventory system	3
	Customer signatures	3
	Unfulfilled sales orders	3
	Customer credit limits	3
	Sales discounts	3
	Supplier statement reconciliations	3
	Purchase ledger master file	3
	Surplus plant and equipment	3
	Authorisation of capital expenditure	3
	Max 6 issues, 3 marks each	18
(b)	**Substantive procedures for PPE**	
	Cast list of additions and agree to non-current asset register	1
	Vouch cost to recent supplier invoice	1
	Agree addition to a supplier invoice in the name of Baggio to confirm rights and obligations	1
	Review additions and confirm capital expenditure items rather than repairs and maintenance	1
	Review board minutes to ensure authorised by the board	1
	Physically verify them on the factory floor to confirm existence	1
	Other	—
	Restricted to	2
Total marks		20

(a) **Baggio International's (Baggio) internal control**

Deficiency	Control recommendations	Test of control
Currently the website is not integrated into the inventory system. This can result in Baggio accepting customer orders when they do not have the goods in inventory. This can cause them to lose sales and customer goodwill For goods despatched by local couriers, customer signatures are not always obtained. This can lead to customers falsely claiming that they have not received their	The website should be updated to include an interface into the inventory system; this should check inventory levels and only process orders if adequate inventory is held. If inventory is out of stock, this should appear on the website with an approximate waiting time. Baggio should remind all local couriers that customer signatures must be obtained as proof of delivery and payment will not be	Test data could be used to attempt to process orders via the website for items which are not currently held in inventory. The orders should be flagged as being out of stock and indicate an approximate waiting time. Select a sample of despatches by couriers and ask Baggio for proof of delivery by viewing customer signatures.

Deficiency	Control recommendations	Test of control
goods. Baggio would not be able to prove that they had in fact despatched the goods and may result in goods being despatched twice.	made for any despatches with missing signatures.	
There have been a number of situations where the sales orders have not been fulfilled in a timely manner. This can lead to a loss of customer goodwill and if it persists will damage the reputation of Baggio as a reliable supplier.	Once goods are despatched, they should be matched to sales orders and flagged as fulfilled. The system should automatically flag any outstanding sales orders past a predetermined period, such as five days. This report should be reviewed by a responsible official.	Review the report of outstanding sales orders. If significant, discuss with a responsible official to understand why there is still a significant time period between sales order and despatch date. Select a sample of sales orders and compare the date of order to the goods despatch date to ascertain whether this is within the acceptable predetermined period.
Customer credit limits are set by sales ledger clerks. Sales ledger clerks are not sufficiently senior and so may set limits too high, leading to irrecoverable debts, or too low, leading to a loss of revenue.	Credit limits should be set by a senior member of the sales ledger department and not by sales ledger clerks. These limits should be regularly reviewed by a responsible official.	For a sample of new customers accepted in the year, review the authorisation of the credit limit, and ensure that this was performed by a responsible official. Enquire of sales ledger clerks as to who can set credit limits.
Sales discounts are set by Baggio's sales team. In order to boost their sales, members of the sales team may set the discounts too high, leading to a loss of revenue.	All members of the sales team should be given authority to grant sales discounts up to a set limit. Any sales discounts above these limits should be authorised by sales area managers or the sales director. Regular review of sales discount levels should be undertaken by the sales director, and this review should be evidenced.	Discuss with members of the sales team the process for setting sales discounts. Review the sales discount report for evidence of review by the sales director.
Supplier statement reconciliations are no longer performed. This may result in errors in the recording of purchases and payables not being identified in a timely manner.	Supplier statement reconciliations should be performed on a monthly basis for all suppliers and these should be reviewed by a responsible official.	Review the file of reconciliations to ensure that they are being performed on a regular basis and that they have been reviewed by a responsible official.

Deficiency	Control recommendations	Test of control
Changes to supplier details in the purchase ledger master file can be undertaken by purchase ledger clerks. This could lead to key supplier data being accidently amended or fictitious suppliers being set up, which can increase the risk of fraud.	Only purchase ledger supervisors should have the authority to make changes to master file data. This should be controlled via passwords. Regular review of any changes to master file data by a responsible official and this review should be evidenced.	Request a purchase ledger clerk to attempt to access the master file and to make an amendment; the system should not allow this. Review a report of master data changes and review the authority of those making amendments.
Baggio has considerable levels of surplus plant and equipment. Surplus unused plant is at risk of theft. In addition, if the surplus plant is not disposed of, then the company could lose sundry income.	Regular review of the plant and equipment on the factory floor by senior factory personnel to identify any old or surplus equipment. As part of the capital expenditure process, there should be a requirement to confirm the treatment of the equipment being replaced.	Observe the review process by senior factory personnel, identifying the treatment of any old equipment. Review processed capital expenditure forms to ascertain if the treatment of replaced equipment is as stated.
Purchase requisitions are authorised by production supervisors. Production supervisors are not sufficiently independent or senior to authorise capital expenditure.	Capital expenditure authorisation levels to be established. Production supervisors should only be able to authorise low value items, any high value items should be authorised by the board.	Review a sample of authorised capital expenditure forms and identify if the correct signatory has authorised them.

(b) **Substantive procedures – additions**

- Obtain a breakdown of additions, cast the list and agree to the non-current asset register to confirm completeness of plant and equipment (P&E).

- Select a sample of additions and agree cost to supplier invoice to confirm valuation.

- Verify rights and obligations by agreeing the addition of plant and equipment to a supplier invoice in the name of Baggio.

- Review the list of additions and confirm that they relate to capital expenditure items rather than repairs and maintenance.

- Review board minutes to ensure that significant capital expenditure purchases have been authorised by the board.

- For a sample of additions recorded in P&E, physically verify them on the factory floor to confirm existence.

Question 18

Marks

(a) **Reliance on independent valuer**

ISA 500 requires consideration of competence and capabilities of expert   1

Consider if member of professional body or industry association   1

Assess independence   1

Assess whether relevant expertise of type of properties as Vieri Motor Cars   1

Evaluate assumptions   1

   5

(b) (i) **Substantive procedures for revaluation of land and buildings**

Cast schedule of land and buildings revalued this year   1

Agree the revalued amounts to the valuation statement provided by the valuer   1

Agree the revalued amounts included correctly in the non-current assets register   1

Recalculate the total revaluation adjustment and agree recorded in the revaluation surplus   1

Agree the initial cost for the warehouse to invoices to confirm cost   1

Confirm through title deeds that the warehouse is owned by Vieri   1

Recalculate the depreciation charge for the year   1

Review the financial statements disclosures for compliance with

IAS 16 *Property, plant and equipment*   1

Other

Restricted to   6

(ii) **Substantive procedures for work in progress (WIP)**

Discuss with management how the percentage completions are attributed to WIP   1

Observe the procedures carried out in the count in assessing the level of WIP; consider reasonableness of the assumptions used   1

During the count, agree a sample of percentage completions are in accordance with Vieri's policies   1

Discuss with management the basis of the standard costs   1

Review the level of variances between standard and actual costs   1

Obtain a breakdown of the standard costs and agree a sample of these costs to actual invoices   1

Cast the schedule of total WIP and agree to the trial balance and financial statements   1

Agree sample of WIP assessed during the count to the WIP schedule, agree percentage completion is correct and recalculate the inventory valuation   1

Other

Restricted to   4

(c) **Impact on audit report**

Discuss with management reasons for non-amendment   1

Assess materiality   1

Immaterial – schedule of uncorrected adjustments   1

Material not pervasive – qualified opinion   1

Basis for qualified opinion paragraph   1

Opinion paragraph – qualified 'except for'   1

Restricted to   5

Total marks   20

(a)   **Reliance on the work of an independent valuer**

ISA 500 *Audit evidence* requires auditors to evaluate the competence, capabilities including expertise and objectivity of a management expert. This would include consideration of the qualifications of the valuer and assessment of whether they were members of any professional body or industry association (ISA 500: para. 8).

The expert's independence should be ascertained, with potential threats such as undue reliance on Vieri Motor Cars Co (Vieri) or a self-interest threat such as share ownership considered.

In addition, Rossi & Co should meet with the expert and discuss with them their relevant expertise, in particular whether they have valued similar land and buildings to those of Vieri in the past. Rossi & Co should also consider whether the valuer understands the accounting requirements of IAS 16 *Property, plant and equipment* in relation to valuations.

The valuation should then be evaluated. The assumptions used should be carefully reviewed and compared to previous revaluations at Vieri. These assumptions should be discussed with both management and the valuer to understand the basis of any valuations.

(b)   (i)   **Substantive procedures for land and buildings**

- Obtain a schedule of land and buildings revalued this year and cast to confirm completeness and accuracy of the revaluation adjustment.

- On a sample basis, agree the revalued amounts to the valuation statement provided by the valuer.

- Agree the revalued amounts for these assets are included correctly in the non-current assets register.

- Recalculate the total revaluation adjustment and agree correctly recorded in the revaluation surplus.

- Agree the initial cost for the warehouse addition to supporting documentation such as invoices to confirm cost.

- Confirm through a review of the title deeds that the warehouse is owned by Vieri.

- Recalculate the depreciation charge for the year to ensure that for assets revalued during the year, the depreciation was based on the correct valuation and for the warehouse addition that the charge was for six months only.

- Review the financial statements disclosures of the revaluation to ensure they comply with IAS 16 *Property, plant and equipment*.

(ii)   **Substantive procedures for work in progress (WIP)**

- Prior to attending the inventory count, discuss with management how the percentage completions are attributed to the WIP, for example, is this based on motor cars passing certain points in the production process?

- During the count, observe the procedures carried out by Vieri staff in assessing the level of WIP and consider the reasonableness of the assumptions used.

- Agree for a sample that the percentage completions assessed during the count are in accordance with Vieri's policies communicated prior to the count.

- Discuss with management the basis of the standard costs applied to the percentage completion of WIP, and how often these are reviewed and updated.

- Review the level of variances between standard and actual costs and discuss with management how these are treated.

- Obtain a breakdown of the standard costs and agree a sample of these costs to actual invoices or payroll records to assess their reasonableness.

- Cast the schedule of total WIP and agree to the trial balance and financial statements.

- Agree sample of WIP assessed during the count to the WIP schedule, agree percentage completion is correct and recalculate the inventory valuation.

(c)   **Auditor's report**

Discuss with the management of Vieri why they are refusing to make the amendment to WIP.

Assess the materiality of the error; if immaterial, it should be added to the schedule of unadjusted differences. The auditor should then assess whether this error results in the total of unadjusted differences becoming material; if so, this should be discussed with management; if not, there would be no impact on the audit report.

If the error is material and management refuses to amend the financial statements, then the auditor's report will need to be modified. It is unlikely that any error would be pervasive as although WIP in total is material, it would not have a pervasive effect on the financial statements as a whole. As management has not complied with IAS 2 *Inventories* and if the error is material but not pervasive, then a qualified opinion would be necessary.

A basis for qualified opinion paragraph would need to be included after the opinion paragraph. This would explain the material misstatement in relation to the valuation of WIP and the effect on the financial statements. The opinion paragraph would be qualified 'except for'.

ACCA
Fundamentals Level
Paper F8
Audit and Assurance

Mock Examination 2

September 2016 CBE

Time allowed: 3 hours 15 minutes

This question paper is divided into two sections:

Section A – ALL 15 questions are compulsory and MUST be attempted

Section B – ALL 3 questions are compulsory and MUST be attempted

Do NOT open this question paper until instructed by the supervisor.

Do NOT record any of your answers on the question paper.

This question paper must not be removed from the examination hall.

ACCA

Fundamentals Level

Paper F8

Audit and Assurance

Mock Examination 2

September 2016 CBE

Time allowed 3 hours 15 minutes

This question paper is divided into two sections:

Section A – ALL 15 questions are compulsory and MUST be attempted

Section B – ALL 3 questions are compulsory and MUST be attempted

Do NOT open this question paper until instructed by the supervisor.

Do NOT record any of your answers on the examination paper.

This question paper must not be removed from the examination hall.

Section A – ALL 15 questions are compulsory and MUST be attempted

Each question is worth 2 marks.

The following scenario relates to questions 1–5.

You are an audit senior of Viola & Co and are currently conducting the audit of Poppy Co for the year ended 30 June 20X6.

Materiality has been set at $50,000, and you are carrying out the detailed substantive testing on the year-end payables balance. The audit manager has emphasised that understatement of the trade payables balance is a significant audit risk.

Below is an extract from the list of supplier statements as at 30 June 20X6 held by the company and corresponding payables ledger balances at the same date along with some commentary on the noted differences:

Supplier	Statement balance	Payables ledger balance
	$'000	$'000
Carnation Co	70	50
Lily Co	175	105

Carnation Co

The difference in the balance is due to an invoice which is under dispute due to faulty goods which were returned on 29 June 20X6.

Lily Co

The difference in the balance is due to the supplier statement showing an invoice dated 28 June 20X6 for $70,000 which was not recorded in the financial statements until after the year end. The payables clerk has advised the audit team that the invoice was not received until 2 July 20X6.

1   The audit manager has asked you to review the full list of trade payables and select balances on which supplier statement reconciliations will be performed.

Indicate on the table below if the following items should be included in, or excluded from, your sample.

Suppliers with material balances at the year end	INCLUDE	EXCLUDE
Suppliers which have a high volume of business with Poppy Co	INCLUDE	EXCLUDE
Major suppliers with nil balances at the year end	INCLUDE	EXCLUDE
Major suppliers where the statement agrees to the ledger	INCLUDE	EXCLUDE

2   **Which of the following audit procedures should be performed in relation to the balance with Lily Co to determine if the payables balance is understated?**

- ☐ Inspect the goods received note to determine when the goods were received
- ☐ Inspect the purchase order to confirm it is dated before the year end
- ☐ Review the post year-end cashbook for evidence of payment of the invoice
- ☐ Send a confirmation request to Lily Co to confirm the outstanding balance

3 **Which of the following audit procedures should be carried out to confirm the balance owing to Carnation Co?**

(1) Review post year-end credit notes for evidence of acceptance of return
(2) Inspect pre year-end goods returned note in respect of the items sent back to the supplier
(3) Inspect post year-end cash book for evidence that the amount has been settled

☐ 1, 2 and 3
☐ 1 and 3 only
☐ 1 and 2 only
☐ 2 and 3 only

---

4 The audit manager has asked you to review the results of some statistical sampling testing, which resulted in 20% of the payables balance being tested.

The testing results indicate that there is a $45,000 error in the sample: $20,000 which is due to invoices not being recorded in the correct period as a result of weak controls and additionally there is a one-off error of $25,000 which was made by a temporary clerk.

What would be an appropriate course of action on the basis of these results?

☐ The error is immaterial and therefore no further work is required
☐ The effect of the control error should be projected across the whole population
☐ Poppy Co should be asked to adjust the payables figure by $45,000
☐ A different sample should be selected as these results are not reflective of the population

---

5 To help improve audit efficiency, Viola & Co is considering introducing the use of computer assisted audit techniques (CAATs) for some audits. You have been asked to consider how CAATs could be used during the audit of Poppy Co.

Which of the following is an example of using test data for trade payables testing?

☐ Selecting a sample of supplier balances for testing using monetary unit sampling
☐ Recalculating the ageing of trade payables to identify balances which may be in dispute
☐ Calculation of trade payables days to use in analytical procedures
☐ Inputting dummy purchase invoices into the client system to see if processed correctly

---

The following scenario relates to questions 6–10.

You are an audit manager at Blenkin & Co and are approaching the end of the audit of Sampson Co, which is a large listed retailer. The draft financial statements currently show a profit before tax of $6.5m and revenue of $66m for the financial year ended 30 June 20X6. You have been informed that the finance director left Sampson Co on 31 May 20X6.

As part of the subsequent events audit procedures, you reviewed post year-end board meeting minutes and discovered that a legal case for unfair dismissal has been brought against Sampson Co by the finance director. During a discussion with the Human Resources (HR) director of Sampson Co, you established that the company received notice of the proposed legal claim on 10 July 20X6.

The HR director told you that Sampson Co's lawyers believe that the finance director's claim is likely to be successful, but estimate that $150,000 is the maximum amount of compensation which would be paid. However, management does not intend to make any adjustments or disclosures in the financial statements.

6   Blenkin & Co has a responsibility to perform procedures to obtain sufficient, appropriate evidence that subsequent events are appropriately reflected in the financial statements of Sampson Co.

Indicate on the timeline, up until which date the auditor should perform subsequent events procedures.

The date the subsequent events review is performed	The date of approval of the financial statement	The date of the auditor's report	The date the financial statements are issued
☐	☐	☐	☐

7   If, after the financial statements have been issued, Blenkin & Co becomes aware of a fact which may have caused its report to be amended, the firm should consider several possible actions.

Which TWO of the following are appropriate actions for Blenkin & Co to take?

☐ Discuss the matter with management and, where appropriate, those charged with governance

☐ Obtain a written representation from management

☐ Consider whether the firm should resign from the engagement

☐ Enquire how management intends to address the matter in the financial statements where appropriate

8   **Which of the following audit procedures should be performed to form a conclusion as to whether the financial statements require amendment in relation to the unfair dismissal claim?**

(1) Inspect relevant correspondence with Sampson Co's lawyers
(2) Write to the finance director to confirm the claim and level of damages
(3) Review the post year-end cash book for evidence of payments to the finance director
(4) Request that management confirm their views in a written representation

☐ 1, 2 and 3

☐ 1, 2 and 4

☐ 1, 3 and 4

☐ 2, 3 and 4

9   You are drafting the auditor's report for Sampson Co and the audit engagement partner has reminded you that the report will need to reflect the requirements of ISA 701 *Communicating Key Audit Matters in the Independent Auditor's Report.*

According to ISA 701, which of the following should be included in the 'Key Audit Matters' paragraph in the auditor's report?

☐ Matters which required significant auditor attention

☐ Matters which result in a modification to the audit opinion

☐ All matters which were communicated to those charged with governance

☐ All matters which are considered to be material to the financial statements

10   **Which of the following audit opinions will be issued if the unfair dismissal case is NOT adjusted for or disclosed within the financial statements?**

☐ A qualified audit opinion as the financial statements are materially misstated

☐ A qualified audit opinion as the auditor is unable to obtain sufficient appropriate evidence

☐ An unmodified opinion with an emphasis of matter paragraph

☐ An unmodified audit opinion

The following scenario relates to questions 11–15.

Sycamore & Co is the auditor of Fir Co, a listed computer software company. The audit team comprises an engagement partner, a recently appointed audit manager, an audit senior and a number of audit assistants. The audit engagement partner has only been appointed this year due to the rotation of the previous partner who had been involved in the audit for seven years. Only the audit senior has experience of auditing a company in this specialised industry. The previous audit manager, who is a close friend of the new audit manager, left the firm before the completion of the prior year audit and is now the finance director of Fir Co.

The board of Fir Co has asked if Sycamore & Co can take on some additional work and have asked if the following additional non-audit services can be provided:

(1)   Routine maintenance of payroll records
(2)   Assistance with the selection of a new financial controller including the checking of references
(3)   Tax services whereby Sycamore & Co would liaise with the tax authority on Fir Co's behalf

Sycamore & Co has identified that the current year fees to be received from Fir Co for audit and other services will represent 16% of the firm's total fee income and totalled 15.5% in the prior year. The audit engagement partner has asked you to consider what can be done in relation to this self-interest threat.

11   Complete the following sentences regarding the audit team by selecting from the options provided.

In relation to the composition of the current audit team, the fundamental principle of [   ] is at risk.

An appropriate safeguard to deal with this risk would be to [   ]

Fundamental principle	Safeguards
Confidentiality	reinstate the previous partner
Professional competence	appoint a completely new audit team
	resign from the engagement
	provide industry training for team members

12   **Which of the following identifies the threat which could arise as a result of the finance director's previous employment at Sycamore & Co and recommends an appropriate safeguard?**

☐   A self-review threat; review the work performed by the previous audit manager
☐   A familiarity threat; a different audit manager should be appointed
☐   A self-review threat; change the existing audit plan
☐   A familiarity threat; the firm should resign from the engagement

13   **Ignoring the potential effect on total fee levels, which of the following options correctly identifies the threats to independence from providing the above non-audit services?**

	Self-review	Self-interest	Advocacy
☐	2	1	3
☐	1	3	2
☐	1	2	3
☐	3	1	2

14   **Which of the following safeguards would NOT be relevant in mitigating the threat identified in relation to fees?**

☐   Disclosure to those charged with governance that fees from Fir Co represent more than 15% of Sycamore & Co's total fee income

☐   A pre-issuance review to be conducted by an external accountant

☐   The use of separate teams to provide the audit and non-audit services

☐   A post-issuance review to be conducted by an external accountant or regulatory body

15   During the course of the audit of Fir Co, a suspicious cash transfer has been identified. The audit team has reported this to the relevant firm representative as a potential money-laundering transaction.

Which of the following statements is true regarding the confidentiality of this information?

☐   Details of the transaction can only be disclosed with the permission of Fir Co

☐   If there is a legal requirement to report money-laundering, this overrides the principle of confidentiality

☐   Sycamore & Co is not permitted to disclose details of the suspicious transaction as the information has been obtained during the course of the audit

☐   In order to maintain confidentiality, Sycamore & Co should report their concerns anonymously

(Total = 30 marks)

Section B – ALL THREE questions are compulsory and MUST be attempted

Question 16

Heraklion Co is a manufacturer of footballs and is a new audit client for your firm. You are an audit supervisor of Spinalonga & Co and are currently preparing for the forthcoming interim and final audit for the year ending 31 October 20X6. You are required to document and assess the sales system, recommend control improvements to deal with a specific fraud issue as well as undertake substantive testing of revenue.

Sales ordering, goods despatched and invoicing

Heraklion Co sells footballs to a range of large and small sports equipment retailers in several countries. Sales are made through a network of sales staff employed by Heraklion Co, but new customer leads are generated through a third party company. Sales staff are responsible for assessing new customers' creditworthiness and proposing a credit limit which is then authorised by the sales director. The sales staff have monthly sales targets and are able to use their discretion in granting sales discounts up to a maximum of 10%. They then record any discount granted in the customer master data file.

The sales staff visit customer sites personally and orders are completed using a two-part pre-printed order form. One copy is left with the customer and the other copy is retained by the sales person. The sales order number is based on the sales person's own identification (ID) number.

The company markets itself on being able to despatch all orders within three working days. Once the order is taken, the sales person emails the finance department and warehouse despatch team with the customer ID and the sales order details and from this a pick list is generated. Sequentially numbered goods despatched notes are completed and filed in the warehouse.

Sequentially numbered invoices are generated using the pick lists for quantities and the customer master data file for prices. Standard credit terms for customers are 30 days and on a monthly basis sales invoices which are over 90 days outstanding are notified to the relevant sales person to chase payment directly with the customer.

Payroll fraud

The finance director, Montse Mirabelle, has informed you that a significant fraud took place during the year in the payroll department. A number of fictitious employees were set up on the payroll and wages were paid into one bank account. This bank account belonged to two supervisors, who were married, and were employed by Heraklion Co. One had sole responsibility for setting up new joiners in the payroll system and the other processed and authorized bank transfer requests for wages and supplier payments. These employees no longer work for the company and Montse has asked the audit firm for recommendations on how to improve controls in this area to prevent this type of fraud occurring again. Heraklion Co operates a Human Resources department.

Required

(a)   Describe **TWO** methods for documenting the sales system, and for each explain **ONE** advantage and **ONE** disadvantage of using this method.   **(6 marks)**

(b)   Identify and explain **SEVEN** deficiencies in the sales system of Heraklion Co and provide a recommendation to address each of these deficiencies.

      Note. Prepare your answer using two columns headed Control deficiency and Control recommendation respectively.   **(14 marks)**

(c)   In relation to the payroll fraud, identify and explain **THREE** controls Heraklion Co should implement to reduce the risk of this type of fraud occurring again and, for each control, describe how it would mitigate the risk.

                                                                                                                              (6 marks)

(d)   Describe substantive procedures the auditor should perform to obtain sufficient and appropriate audit evidence in relation to Heraklion Co's revenue.   **(4 marks)**

                                                                                                                        (Total = 30 marks)

Question 17

Elounda Co manufactures chemical compounds using a continuous production process. Its year end was 31 July 20X6 and the draft profit before tax is $13.6 million. You are the audit supervisor and the year-end audit is due to commence shortly. The following matters have been brought to your attention.

(i) **Revaluation of property, plant and equipment (PPE)**

At the beginning of the year, management undertook an extensive review of Elounda Co's non-current asset valuations and as a result decided to update the carrying value of all PPE. The finance director, Peter Dullman, contacted his brother, Martin, who is a valuer and requested that Martin's firm undertake the valuation, which took place in August 20X5. **(5 marks)**

(ii) **Inventory valuation**

Your firm attended the year-end inventory count for Elounda Co and ascertained that the process for recording work in progress (WIP) and finished goods was acceptable. Both WIP and finished goods are material to the financial statements and the quantity and stage of completion of all ongoing production was recorded accurately during the count.

During the inventory count, the count supervisor noted that a consignment of finished goods, compound E243, with a value of $720,000, was defective in that the chemical mix was incorrect. The finance director believes that compound E243 can still be sold at a discounted sum of $400,000. **(6 marks)**

(iii) **Bank loan**

Elounda Co secured a bank loan of $2.6 million on 1 October 20X4. Repayments of $200,000 are due quarterly, with a lump sum of $800,000 due for repayment in January 20X7. The company met all loan payments in 20X5 on time, but was late in paying the April and July 20X6 repayments. **(4 marks)**

Required

(a) Describe substantive procedures you should perform to obtain sufficient, appropriate audit evidence in relation to the above three matters.

Note. The mark allocation is shown against each of the three matters above.

(b) Describe the procedures which the auditor of Elounda Co should perform in assessing whether or not the company is a going concern. **(5 marks)**

(Total = 20 marks)

Question 18

You are an audit supervisor of Chania & Co and are planning the audit of your client, Sitia Sparkle Co which manufactures cleaning products. Its year end was 31 July 20X6 and the draft profit before tax is $33.6 million. You are supervising a large audit team for the first time and will have specific responsibility for supervising and reviewing the work of the audit assistants in your team.

Sitia Sparkle Co purchases most of its raw materials from suppliers in Africa and these goods are shipped directly to the company's warehouse and the goods are usually in transit for up to three weeks. The company has incurred $1.3 million of expenditure on developing a new range of cleaning products which are due to be launched into the market place in November 20X6. In September 20X5, Sitia Sparkle Co also invested $0.9 million in a complex piece of plant and machinery as part of the development process. The full amount has been capitalised and this cost includes the purchase price, installation costs and training costs.

This year, the bonus scheme for senior management and directors has been changed so that rather than focusing on profits, it is instead based on the value of year-end total assets. In previous years an allowance for receivables, made up of specific balances, which equalled almost 1% of trade receivables was maintained. However, the finance director feels that this is excessive and unnecessary and has therefore not included it for 20X6 and has credited the opening balance to the profit or loss account.

A new general ledger system was introduced in May 20X6; the finance director has stated that the data was transferred and the old and new systems were run in parallel until the end of August 20X6. As a result of the additional workload on the finance team, a number of control account reconciliations were not completed as at 31 July 20X6, including the bank reconciliation. The finance director is comfortable with this as these reconciliations were completed successfully for both June and August 20X6. In addition, the year-end close down of the purchase ledger was undertaken on 8 August 20X6.

Required

(a)   ISA 300 *Planning an Audit of Financial Statements* provides guidance to assist auditors in planning an audit.

     Required

     Explain the benefits of audit planning.   **(4 marks)**

(b)   Describe **SIX** audit risks, and explain the auditor's response to each risk, in planning the audit of Sitia Sparkle Co.

     Note. Prepare your answer using two columns headed Audit risk and Auditor's response respectively.
                                                                                      (12 marks)

(c)   In line with ISA 220 *Quality Control for an Audit of Financial Statements*, describe the audit supervisor's responsibilities in relation to supervising and reviewing the audit assistants' work during the audit of Sitia Sparkle Co.   **(4 marks)**

                                                                                      (Total = 20 marks)

Answers

DO NOT TURN THIS PAGE UNTIL YOU HAVE
COMPLETED THE MOCK EXAM

Answers

DO NOT TURN THIS PAGE UNTIL YOU HAVE
COMPLETED THE MOCK EXAM

Plan of attack

If this were the real Audit and Assurance exam and you had been told to turn over and begin, what would be going through your mind?

An important thing to say (while there is still time) is that it is vital to have a good breadth of knowledge of the syllabus because all the questions are compulsory. However, don't panic. Below we provide guidance on how to approach the exam.

Looking through the paper

Section A has three objective test cases, each with five questions. This is the section of the paper where the examination team can test knowledge across the breadth of the syllabus. Make sure you read these cases and questions carefully. The distractors are designed to present plausible, but incorrect, answers. Don't let them mislead you. If you really have no idea – guess. You may even be right.

Section B has three longer questions:

- **Question 16** is a 30-mark internal controls question mainly focused on control deficiencies and recommendations in a payroll system. You are also asked to consider controls that would help to prevent fraud. Don't panic – take your time to read the scenario and what you are asked to do. Try to relate your answers to the specific scenario as much as you can.

- **Question 17** is a 20-mark question on audit procedures relating to PPE, inventory, a bank loan and for assessing going concern. You have a number of individual areas to cover here so take care with timing.

- **Question 18** is a 20-mark planning and audit risk question. Make sure you have noticed that part (b) requires you to identify risks **AND** explain the auditor's response to these.

Allocating your time

BPP's advice is to always allocate your time **according to the marks for the question**. However, **use common sense**. If you're doing a question but haven't a clue how to do part (b), you might be better off re-allocating your time and getting more marks on another question, where you can add something you didn't have time for earlier on. Make sure you leave time to recheck the OTQs and make sure you have answered them all.

Forget about it!

And don't worry if you found the paper difficult. More than likely other candidates will too. If this were the real thing you would need to forget the exam the minute you left the exam hall and think about the next one. Or, if it is the last one, celebrate!

Section A

ALL 15 questions are compulsory and MUST be attempted

1

Suppliers with material balances at the year end	INCLUDE
Suppliers which have a high volume of business with Poppy Co	INCLUDE
Major suppliers with nil balances at the year end	INCLUDE
Major suppliers where the statement agrees to the ledger	EXCLUDE

Where completeness is the key assertion, the sample should be selected to verify where the balance may be understated and therefore should include suppliers with material balances, suppliers with a high volume of business with Poppy Co and major suppliers with no outstanding balance at the year end.

2   The correct answer is: Inspect the goods received note to determine when the goods were received.

In order to determine if the balance with Lily Co is understated, the auditor should determine if the goods should be included in payables at the year end by inspecting the goods received note.

3   The correct answer is 1 and 2 only

To confirm the balance with Carnation Co, the auditor must determine if the liability exists for the disputed items at the year end by reviewing pre year-end goods returned notes and post year-end credit notes to verify that the goods have been returned and the order cancelled by the supplier.

4   The correct answer is: The effect of the control error should be projected across the whole population.

Although the error is immaterial, the auditor must reach a conclusion on the sample selected and in order to do so the effect of the error must be considered in relation to the whole population.

5   The correct answer is: Inputting dummy purchase invoices into the client system to see if processed correctly

Test data involves inputting fake transactions into the client's system to test how the transactions are processed. The other options are examples of audit software.

6

The date the subsequent events review is performed	The date of approval of the financial statement	The date of the auditor's report	The date the financial statements are issued
☐	☐	✓	☐

As per ISA 560 Subsequent Events, the auditor has an active responsibility to carry out subsequent events procedures between the date of the financial statements and the date of the auditor's report.

7   The correct answers are:

Discuss the matter with management and, where appropriate, those charged with governance

Enquire how management intends to address the matter in the financial statements where appropriate

As per ISA 560 paragraph 15, in the circumstances described the auditor should initially discuss the matter with management and understand how management intends to address the matter in the financial statements.

8   The correct answer is 1, 3 and 4

The auditor is unlikely to ask the finance director, who is no longer an officer of the company and the party involved in the claim, to confirm the level of damages payable. All other procedures would be appropriate.

9   The correct answer is: Matters which required significant auditor attention

As per paragraph 9 of ISA 701 Communicating Key Audit Matters in the Independent Auditor's Report, in determining key audit matters, the auditor shall determine from the matters communicated to those charged with governance, those which required significant auditor attention.

10   The correct answer is: An unmodified audit opinion

The maximum damages of $150,000 is not material to the financial statements at 2.3% of profit before tax and 0.2% of revenue. Therefore no modification to the audit opinion is required.

11   In relation to the composition of the current audit team, the fundamental principle of **professional competence** is at risk.

An appropriate safeguard to deal with this risk would be to **provide industry training for team members**.

The fundamental principle at risk is professional competence as many of the audit team are new and do not have relevant experience in relation to the specialised industry in which Fir Co operates. It is not appropriate to reinstate the previous partner as in line with the ACCA Code of Ethics and Conduct, the previous partner has been rotated after seven years to prevent a familiarity threat. The audit firm should offer appropriate training for the audit team to ensure they have the necessary knowledge to carry out the work.

12   The correct answer is: A familiarity threat; a different audit manager should be appointed.

As the previous audit manager has taken up employment with the client as the finance director, there is a familiarity threat due to the ongoing relationship between the old and new audit manager. The familiarity threat is not so severe that the firm would need to resign but a new audit manager should be appointed.

13   The correct answer is

Self-review: 1
Self-interest: 2
Advocacy: 3

As per the ACCA Code of Ethics and Conduct, the following threats would be created from carrying out the non-audit services requested by Fir Co:

Payroll – Self-review as the auditor will also be involved in auditing the figures included in the financial statements in relation to wages and salaries.

Recruitment – Self-interest as the auditor would be involved in selecting an officer of the company who has significant influence over the financial statements.

Tax – Advocacy as the auditor may be perceived to be representing and promoting Fir Co's interest in liaising with the tax authority.

14   The correct answer is: The use of separate teams to provide the audit and non-audit services.

Using separate teams will not address the self-interest threat from the fee levels as separating the teams will not alleviate the firm's potential financial dependence on Fir Co and therefore the risk that work is not carried out independently for fear of the losing the client.

15   The correct answer is: If there is a legal requirement to report money-laundering, this overrides the principle of confidentiality.

As per ACCA Code of Ethics and Conduct (s140.7.b) – Confidential information may be disclosed when such disclosure is required by law.

Section B

Question 16

Marking scheme

		Marks	
(a)	**Methods for documenting the sales system**		
	• Narrative notes	3	
	• Questionnaires	3	
	• Flowcharts	3	
	Restricted to		**6**
(b)	**Control deficiencies and recommendations** (only 7 issues required)		
	• New customers' creditworthiness assessed by sales staff	2	
	• Sales staff have discretion to grant discounts up to 10%	2	
	• Access to master file data	2	
	• Inventory not checked by sales people prior to order being placed	2	
	• No copy of order with the sales ordering department, unable to identify unfulfilled orders	2	
	• Orders not sequentially numbered	2	
	• Warehouse despatch team do not receive a copy of the sales order	2	
	• Goods despatch notes filed by warehouse despatch team	2	
	• Salesperson responsible for chasing invoices over 90 days old	2	
	Max 7 issues, 2 marks each		**14**
(c)	**Controls to reduce risk of payroll fraud**		
	• Proof of identity checks undertaken for all new joiners	2	
	• Review of the number of employees per department to the payroll system	2	
	• Human resources department initiates request for new joiners	2	
	• Authorisation of all new joiners by payroll director	2	
	• Relatives not permitted to undertake interrelated processes	2	
	• Payroll system reviews same bank account name and number	2	
	• Bank transfer requests authorised by senior responsible official, independent	2	
	Restricted to		**6**

(d) **Substantive procedures for revenue**

	Marks
• Analytical review over revenue compared to budget and prior year	1
• Analytical review of main product categories of sales compared to prior year	1
• Gross margin review	1
• Agree sales prices for customers to price list or master file data	1
• Review credit notes	1
• Follow orders to goods despatched note to sales invoice to sales ledger	1
• Sales cut-off	1
Restricted to	4

Total marks 30

(a) **Documenting the sales system**

There are several methods which can be used to document the sales system.

Narrative notes

Narrative notes consist of a written description of the system; they would detail what occurs in the system at each stage and would include any controls which operate at each stage.

Advantages of this method include:

- They are simple to record; after discussion with staff members, these discussions are easily written up as notes.

- They can facilitate understanding by all members of the audit team, especially more junior members who might find alternative methods too complex.

Disadvantages of this method include:

- Narrative notes may prove to be too cumbersome, especially if the system is complex or heavily automated.

- This method can make it more difficult to identify missing internal controls as the notes record the detail but do not identify control exceptions clearly.

Questionnaires

Internal control questionnaires (ICQs) or internal control evaluation questionnaires (ICEQs) contain a list of questions; ICQs are used to assess whether controls exist whereas ICEQs assess the effectiveness of the controls in place.

Advantages of this method include:

- Questionnaires are quick to prepare, which means they are a timely method for recording the system.

- They ensure that all controls present within the system are considered and recorded; hence missing controls or deficiencies are clearly highlighted by the audit team.

  Disadvantages of this method include:

- It can be easy for the staff members to overstate the level of the controls present as they are asked a series of questions relating to potential controls.

- A standard list of questions may miss out unusual or more bespoke controls used by the company.

Flowcharts

Flowcharts are a graphic illustration of the internal control system for the sales system. Lines usually demonstrate the sequence of events and standard symbols are used to signify controls or documents.

Advantages of this method include:

- It is easy to view the system in its entirety as it is all presented together in one diagram.

- Due to the use of standard symbols for controls, it can be effective in identifying missing controls.

Disadvantages of this method include:

- They can sometimes be difficult to amend, as any amendments may require the whole flowchart to be redrawn.

- There is still the need for narrative notes to accompany the flowchart and hence it can be a time-consuming method.

Note. Full marks will be awarded for describing TWO methods for documenting the sales system and explaining ONE advantage and ONE disadvantage for each method.

(b)   **Deficiencies and controls over the sales system**

Control deficiency	Control recommendation
New customers' creditworthiness is assessed by a salesperson who sets the credit limit, which is authorised by the sales director. The sales staff have sales targets, and hence may suggest that new customers are creditworthy simply to meet their targets. This could result in sales being made to poor credit risks.	New customers should complete a credit application which should be checked through a credit agency with a credit limit set. Once authorised by the sales director, the limit should be entered into the system by a credit controller.
Sales staff have discretion to grant sales discounts to customers of up to 10%. This could result in a loss of revenue as they may award unrealistic discounts simply to meet sales targets. The discounts granted by sales staff are not being reviewed and could result in unauthorised discounts allowed.	All discounts to be granted to customers should be authorized in advance by a responsible official, such as the sales director. If not practical, then the supervisor of the sales staff should undertake this role.
Sales staff are able to make changes to the customer master data file, in order to record discounts allowed and these changes are not reviewed. There is a risk that these amendments could be made incorrectly resulting in a loss of sales revenue or overcharging of customers. In addition, the sales staff are not senior enough to be given access to changing master file data as this could increase the risk of fraud.	Sales staff should not be able to access the master data file to make amendments. Any such amendments to master file data should be restricted so that only supervisors and above can make changes. An exception report of changes made should be generated and reviewed by a responsible official.
Inventory availability does not appear to be checked by the sales person at the time the order is placed. In addition, Heraklion Co markets itself on being able to despatch all orders within three working days. There is a risk that where goods are not available, the customer would not be made aware of this prior to placing their order, leading to unfulfilled orders and customer dissatisfaction, which would impact the company's reputation.	Prior to the salesperson finalising the order, the inventory system should be checked in order for an accurate assessment of the availability of goods to be notified to customers.

Control deficiency	Control recommendation
Customer orders are recorded on a two-part pre-printed form, one copy is left with the customer and one with the sales person. The sales department of Heraklion Co does not hold these orders centrally and hence would not be able to monitor if orders are being fulfilled on a timely basis. This could result in a loss of revenue and customer goodwill.	The order form should be amended to be at least four-part. The third part of the order should be sent to the warehouse department and the fourth part sent to the finance department. The copy the sales person has should be stored centrally in the sales department. Upon despatch, the goods dispatch note should be matched to the order; a regular review of unmatched orders should be undertaken by the sales department to identify any unfulfilled orders.
Customer orders are given a number based on the sales person's own identification (ID) number. These numbers are not sequential. Without sequential numbers, it is difficult for Heraklion Co to identify missing orders and to monitor if all orders are being despatched in a timely manner, leading to a loss of customer goodwill.	Sales orders should be sequentially numbered. On a regular basis, a sequence check of orders should be undertaken to identify any missing orders.
The sales person emails the warehouse despatch team with the customer ID and the sales order details, rather than a copy of the sales order itself, and a pick list is generated from this. There is a risk that incorrect or insufficient details may be recorded by the sales person and this could result in incorrect orders being despatched, orders being despatched late or orders failing to be despatched at all, resulting in a loss of customer goodwill and revenue.	The third part of the sales order as mentioned previously should be forwarded directly to the warehouse department. The pick list should be generated from the original order form and the warehouse team should check correct quantities and product descriptions are being despatched, as well as checking the quality of goods being despatched to ensure they are not damaged.
Sequentially numbered goods despatched notes (GDNs) are completed and filed by the warehouse department. If the finance department does not receive a copy of these GDNs, they will not know when to raise the related sales invoices. This could result in goods being despatched but not being invoiced, leading to a loss of revenue.	Upon despatch of goods, a four-part GDN should be completed, with copies to the customer, warehouse department, sales department to confirm despatch of goods and a copy for the finance department. Upon receipt of the GDN, once matched to the fourth part of the sales order form, a clerk should raise the sales invoices in a timely manner, confirming all details to the GDN and order.
The sales person is given responsibility to chase customers directly for payment once an invoice is outstanding for 90 days. This is considerably in excess of the company's credit terms of 30 days which will lead to poor cash flow. Further, as the sales people have sales targets, they are more likely to focus on generating sales orders rather than chasing payments. This could result in an increase in bad debts and reduced profit and cash flows.	A credit controller should be appointed and it should be their role, rather than the salesperson, to chase any outstanding sales invoices which are more than 30 days old.

(c)   **Controls to reduce risk of payroll fraud**

Control	Mitigate risk
Proof of identity checks should be undertaken by the Human Resources (HR) department and recorded on individuals' personnel files for all new employees set up on the payroll system	This should reduce the risk of fictitious employees being set up, as in order to be set up on the system a fictitious set of identification would be required which would be an onerous process.
A count should be undertaken of the number of employees in each department of Heraklion Co; this should be reconciled to the number of employees on the payroll system.	This would identify if there are extra employees on the payroll system, which could then be investigated further.
The HR department should initiate the process for setting up new joiners by asking new employees to complete a joiner's form which will be approved by the relevant manager and HR. This request should then be forwarded to the payroll department, who should set up the employee.	This control introduces segregation of duties as in order to set up employees both the HR and payroll departments are involved. Without collusion with an HR employee, the payroll supervisor would be unable to set up fictitious employees.
All new joiners should be only be set up by payroll on receipt of a joiner's form and any additions to the system should be authorised by the payroll director. An edit report should be generated and reviewed by HR.	As all new joiners would be authorised by the payroll director, it is unlikely that payroll employees would risk establishing fictitious joiners. A further review by the HR department would also detect any employees without an authorized joiner form.
Where possible, employees who are related should not be allowed to undertake processes which are interrelated whereby they can breach segregation of duty controls for key transaction cycles. A regular review of job descriptions of related employees should be carried out by HR.	This should reduce the risk of related staff colluding and being able to commit a fraud.
The payroll system should be amended to run an exception report which identifies any employees with the same bank account name or number and this should be reviewed by HR.	Identifying the same bank account name or number will prevent multiple fraudulent payments being made to the same employees.
All bank transfer requests should be authorised by a senior responsible official, who is independent of the processing of payments; they should undertake spot checks of payments to supporting documentation, including employee identification cards/records.	This would introduce an additional layer of segregation of duties, which would reduce the risk of fraud occurring. In addition, the spot checks to employee identification cards/records would confirm the validity of payments.

(d)   **Revenue substantive procedures**

- Compare the overall level of revenue against prior years and budgets and investigate any significant fluctuations.

- Obtain a schedule of sales for the year broken down into the main product categories and compare this to the prior year breakdown and for any unusual movements discuss with management.

- Calculate the gross profit margin for Heraklion Co and compare this to the prior year and investigate any significant fluctuations.

- Select a sample of sales invoices for customers and agree the sales prices back to the price list or customer master data information to ensure the accuracy of invoices.

- Select a sample of credit notes raised, trace through to the original invoice and ensure the invoice has been correctly removed from sales.

- Select a sample of customer orders and agree these to the despatch notes and sales invoices through to inclusion in the sales ledger and revenue general ledger accounts to ensure completeness of revenue.

- Select a sample of despatch notes both pre and post year end and follow these through to sales invoices in the correct accounting period to ensure that cut-off has been correctly applied.

Question 17

Text references. Chapters 12, 13, 16 and 18

Top tips. This is a 20 mark audit evidence and going concern question. In part (a) the key is to note that you are being asked for substantive procedures relating to specific aspects eg **revaluation** of PPE, not all aspects of PPE. The examination team's report noted that in relation to inventory a significant proportion of candidates focused on inventory counts rather than **valuation** as required by the question. Make sure you read the information carefully noting important details like these.

You also need to ensure that you tailor your answer to the scenario rather than simply listing out standard audit procedures.

For part (b) make sure you understand the requirement. The question is asking for procedures, not going concern indicators.

Easy marks. Overall this is a demanding question due to the care required in reading the information and the need to tailor the answer specifically. However, you should have been able to pick up good marks for substantive procedures relating to the bank loan.

Marking scheme

			Marks
(a)	(i)	**Substantive procedures for revaluation of property, plant and equipment (PPE)**	
		• Cast schedule of PPE revalued this year and agree to TB/FS	1
		• Consider reasonableness of the valuer's qualifications, membership of professional body and experience	1
		• Discuss with management if the valuer has financial interests in the company which along with family relationship may impact his independence	1
		• Agree the revalued amounts to the valuation statement provided by the valuer	1
		• Consider if all items in the same class of assets have been revalued	1
		• Agree the revalued amounts included correctly in the non-current assets register	1
		• Recalculate the total revaluation adjustment and agree recorded in the revaluation surplus	1
		• Recalculate the depreciation charge for the year	1
		• Review the financial statements disclosures for compliance with IAS 16 *Property, Plant and Equipment*	1
		Restricted to	5
	(ii)	**Substantive procedures for inventory valuation**	
		• Cast a schedule of all raw materials, finished goods and work in progress (WIP) inventory and agree to TB/FS	1
		• Obtain breakdown and agree sample of WIP from the count to the WIP schedule, agree percentage completion	1

- For a sample, obtain relevant cost sheets and confirm raw material costs to recent purchase invoices, labour costs to time sheets or wage records and overheads allocated are of a production nature — 1
- For a sample of inventory items, review the calculation for equivalent units and associated equivalent unit cost and recalculate the inventory valuation — 1
- Select a sample of year-end finished goods and review post year-end sales Invoices to ascertain if net realisable value (NRV) is above cost or if an adjustment is required — 1
- Select a sample of items included in WIP at the year end and ascertain the final unit cost price, verifying to relevant supporting documentation, and compare to the unit sales price included in sales invoices post year end to assess NRV — 1
- Review aged inventory reports, identify slow moving goods, discuss with management — 1
- Compound E243, discuss with management plans for disposing of goods, why NRV is $400,000 — 1
- If any of defective goods have been sold post year end, agree to the sales invoice to assess NRV — 1
- Agree the cost of $720,000 for compound E243 to supporting documentation — 1
- Confirm the final adjustment for compound E243, discuss with management if adjustment made, if so, follow through the write down to confirm — 1
- Review the financial statements disclosures for compliance with IAS 2 *Inventories* — 1

Restricted to — 6

(iii) **Substantive procedures for bank loan**
- Agree the opening balance to the prior year audit file and FS — 1
- For loan payments made, agree to cash book and bank statements — 1
- Review the bank correspondence for late payment penalties, agree to statement of profit or loss — 1
- Obtain direct confirmation of year-end balance from bank, agree to the loan schedule — 1
- Review loan agreement for details of covenants and recalculate to identify any breaches — 1
- Agree closing balance to the trial balance and draft financial statements and review the disclosure of the current liability bank loan in the draft financial statements — 1

Restricted to — 4

(b) **Going concern procedures**
- Review cash flow forecasts — 1
- Review bank loan agreements, breach of key ratios or covenants — 1
- Review post year-end sales and order book — 1
- Review suppliers correspondence — 1
- Enquire of lawyers for any litigation — 1
- Subsequent events — 1
- Board minutes — 1
- Management accounts — 1
- Consider additional disclosures under IAS 1 Presentation of Financial Statements — 1
- Written representation — 1

Restricted to — 5

Total marks — 20

(a)   (i)   **Substantive procedures for revaluation of property, plant and equipment (PPE)**

- Obtain a schedule of all PPE revalued during the year and cast to confirm completeness and accuracy of the revaluation adjustment and agree to trial balance and financial statements.

- Consider the competence and capability of the valuer, Martin Dullman, by assessing through enquiry his qualification, membership of a professional body and experience in valuing these types of assets.

- Consider whether the valuation undertaken provides sufficiently objective audit evidence. Discuss with management whether Martin Dullman has any financial interest in Elounda Co which along with the family relationship could have had an impact on his independence.

- Agree the revalued amounts to the valuation statement provided by the valuer.

- Review the valuation report and consider if all assets in the same category have been revalued in line with IAS 16 *Property, Plant and Equipment*.

- Agree the revalued amounts for these assets are included correctly in the non-current assets register.

- Recalculate the total revaluation adjustment and agree correctly recorded in the revaluation surplus.

- Recalculate the depreciation charge for the year to ensure that for the assets revalued during the year, the depreciation was based on the correct valuation and was for 12 months.

- Review the financial statements disclosures relating to the revaluation to ensure they comply with IAS 16.

(ii)   **Substantive procedures for inventory valuation**

- Obtain a schedule of all raw materials, finished goods and work in progress (WIP) inventory and cast to confirm completeness and accuracy of the balance and agree to trial balance and financial statements.

- Obtain the breakdown of WIP and agree a sample of WIP assessed during the count to the WIP schedule, agreeing the percentage completion as recorded at the inventory count.

- For a sample of inventory items (finished goods and WIP), obtain the relevant cost sheets and confirm raw material costs to recent purchase invoices, labour costs to time sheets or wage records and overheads allocated are of a production nature.

- For a sample of inventory items, review the calculation for equivalent units and associated equivalent unit cost and recalculate the inventory valuation.

- Select a sample of year-end finished goods and review post year-end sales invoices to ascertain if net realizable value (NRV) is above cost or if an adjustment is required.

- Select a sample of items included in WIP at the year end and ascertain the final unit cost price, verifying to relevant supporting documentation, and compare to the unit sales price included in sales invoices post year end to assess NRV.

- Review aged inventory reports and identify any slow moving goods, discuss with management why these items have not been written down or if an allowance is required.

- For the defective chemical compound E243, discuss with management their plans for disposing of these goods, and why they believe these goods have a NRV of $400,000.

- If any E243 has been sold post year end, agree to the sales invoice to assess NRV.

- Agree the cost of $720,000 for compound E243 to supporting documentation to confirm the raw material cost, labour cost and any overheads attributed to the cost.

- Confirm if the final adjustment for compound E243 is $320,000 (720 – 400) and discuss with management if this adjustment has been made; if so follow through the write down to confirm.

- Review the financial statements disclosures relating to inventory and WIP to ensure they comply with IAS 2 *Inventories*.

(iii) **Substantive procedures for bank loan**

- Agree the opening balance of the bank loan to the prior year audit file and financial statements.

- For any loan payments made during the year, agree the cash outflow to the cash book and bank statements.

- Review bank correspondence to identify whether any late payment penalties have been levied and agree these have been charged to profit or loss account as a finance charge.

- Obtain direct confirmation at the year end from the loan provider of the outstanding balance and any security provided; agree confirmed amounts to the loan schedule and financial statements.

- Review the loan agreement for details of covenants and recalculate to identify any breaches in these.

- Agree closing balance of the loan to the trial balance and draft financial statements and that the disclosure is adequate, including any security provided, that the loan is disclosed as a current liability and disclosure is in accordance with accounting standards and local legislation.

(b) **Going concern procedures**

- Obtain Elounda's cash flow forecast and review the cash in and out flows. Assess the assumptions for reasonableness and discuss the findings with management to understand if the company will have sufficient cash flows to meet liabilities as they fall due.

- Discuss with management their ability to settle the next instalment due for repayment to the bank and the lump sum payment of $800k in January 20X7 and ensure these have been included in the cash flow forecast.

- Review current agreements with the bank to determine whether any key ratios or covenants have been breached with regards to the bank loan or any overdraft.

- Review the company's post year-end sales and order book to assess the levels of trade and if the revenue figures in the cash flow forecast are reasonable.

- Review post year-end correspondence with suppliers to identify whether any restrictions in credit have arisen, and if so, ensure that the cash flow forecast reflects the current credit terms or where necessary an immediate payment for trade payables.

- Enquire of the lawyers of Elounda Co as to the existence of litigation and claims; if any exist, then consider their materiality and impact on the going concern basis.

- Perform audit tests in relation to subsequent events to identify any items which might indicate or mitigate the risk of going concern not being appropriate.

- Review the post year-end board minutes to identify any other issues which might indicate financial difficulties for the company.

- Review post year-end management accounts to assess if in line with cash flow forecast and to identify any issues which may be relevant to the going concern assessment.

- Consider whether any additional disclosures as required by IAS 1 *Presentation of Financial Statements* in relation to material uncertainties over going concern should be made in the financial statements.

- Obtain a written representation confirming the directors' view that Elounda Co is a going concern.

Question 18

Marking scheme

		Marks
(a)	**Benefits of audit planning**	
	• Important areas of the audit	1
	• Potential problems	1
	• Effective and efficient audit	1
	• Selection of engagement team members and assignment of work	1
	• Direction, supervision and review	1
	• Coordination of work	1
	Restricted to	**4**
(b)	**Audit risks and responses** (only 6 risks required)	
	• Goods in transit from Africa	2
	• Research and development expenditure	2
	• Capitalisation of costs of plant and machinery	2
	• Senior management bonus scheme	2
	• Allowance for receivables	2
	• Introduction of new general ledger system	2
	• July 20X6 control account reconciliations not undertaken	2
	• Purchase ledger closed down on 8 August	2
	Max 6 issues, 2 marks each	**12**
(c)	**Supervising and reviewing audit assistants' work**	
	• Monitor the progress of the audit engagement to ensure the audit timetable was met	1
	• Consider the competence and capabilities of team members re sufficient available time, understanding of instructions and if work in accordance with planned approach	1
	• Address any significant matters arising, consider their significance and modifying the approach	1
	• Responsible for identifying matters for consultation/consideration by senior team members	1
	• Work performed in line with professional standards and other requirements	1
	• Work supports conclusions reached and properly documented	1
	• Significant matters raised for partner attention or further consideration	1
	• Appropriate consultations have taken place with conclusions documented	1
	Restricted to	**4**
	Total marks	**20**

(a) **Benefits of audit planning**

Audit planning is addressed by ISA 300 *Planning an Audit of Financial Statements*. It states that adequate planning benefits the audit of financial statements in several ways:

- Helping the auditor to devote appropriate attention to important areas of the audit.

- Helping the auditor to identify and resolve potential problems on a timely basis.

- Helping the auditor to properly organise and manage the audit engagement so that it is performed in an effective and efficient manner.

- Assisting in the selection of engagement team members with appropriate levels of capabilities and competence to respond to anticipated risks and the proper assignment of work to them.

- Facilitating the direction and supervision of engagement team members and the review of their work.

- Assisting, where applicable, in coordination of work done by experts.

(b) **Audit risk and auditors responses**

Audit risk	Mitigate risk
Sitia Sparkle Co purchases their goods from suppliers in Africa and the goods are in transit for up to three weeks. At the year end, there is a risk that the cut-off of inventory, purchases and payables may not be accurate and may be under/overstated.	The audit team should undertake detailed cut-off testing of purchases of goods at the year end and the sample of GRNs from before and after the year end relating to goods from suppliers in Africa should be increased to ensure that cut-off is complete and accurate.
Sitia Sparkle Co has incurred expenditure of $1.3 million in developing a new range of cleaning products. This expenditure is classed as research and development under IAS 38 *Intangible Assets*. The standard requires research costs to be expensed to profit or loss and development costs to be capitalised as an intangible asset. If the company has incorrectly classified research costs as development expenditure, there is a risk the intangible asset could be overstated and expenses understated. In addition, as the senior management bonus is based on year-end asset values, this increases this risk further as management may have a reason to overstate assets at the year end.	Obtain a breakdown of the expenditure and verify that it relates to the development of the new products. Undertake testing to determine whether the costs relate to the research or development stage. Discuss the accounting treatment with the finance director and ensure it is in accordance with IAS 38.
In September 20X5, the company invested $0.9 million in a complex piece of plant and machinery. The costs include purchase price, installation and training costs. As per IAS 16 *Property, Plant and Equipment*, the cost of an asset incudes its purchase price and directly attributable costs only. Training costs are not permitted under IAS 16 to be capitalised as part of the cost and therefore plant and machinery and profits are overstated.	Obtain a breakdown of the $0.9 million expenditure and undertake testing to confirm the level of training costs which have been included within non-current assets. Discuss the accounting treatment with the finance director and the level of any necessary adjustment to ensure treatment is in accordance with IAS 16.
The bonus scheme for senior management and directors of Sitia Sparkle Co has been changed; it is now based on the value of year-end total assets.	Throughout the audit, the team will need to be alert to this risk and maintain professional scepticism.

Audit risk	Mitigate risk
There is a risk that management might be motivated to overstate the value of assets through the judgements taken or through the use of releasing provisions or capitalization policy.	Detailed review and testing on judgemental decisions, including treatment of provisions, and compare treatment against prior years. Any manual journal adjustments affecting assets should be tested in detail. In addition, a written representation should be obtained from management confirming the basis of any significant judgements.
The finance director of Sitia Sparkle Co believes that an allowance for receivables is excessive and unnecessary and therefore has not provided for it at the year end and has credited the opening balance to profit or loss.	Review and test the controls surrounding how Sitia Sparkle Co identifies receivables balances which may require a provision to ensure that they are operating effectively in the current year.
There is a risk that receivables will be overvalued; some balances may be irrecoverable and so will be overstated if not provided for.	Discuss with the finance director the rationale for not maintaining an allowance for receivables and releasing the opening provision.
In addition, releasing the allowance for receivables will increase asset values and hence the senior management bonus which increases the risk further.	Extended post year-end cash receipts testing and a review of the aged receivables ledger to be performed to assess valuation and the need for an allowance for receivables.
A new general ledger system was introduced in May 20X6 and the old and new systems were run in parallel until August 20X6.	The auditor should undertake detailed testing to confirm that all of the balances at the transfer date have been correctly recorded in the new general ledger system.
There is a risk of the balances in May being misstated and loss of data if they have not been transferred from the old system completely and accurately. If this is not done, this could result in the auditor not identifying a significant control risk. In addition, the new general ledger system will require documenting and the controls over this will need to be tested.	The auditor should document and test the new system. They should review any management reports run comparing the old and new system during the parallel run to identify any issues with the processing of accounting information.
A number of reconciliations, including the bank reconciliation, were not performed at the year end, however, they were undertaken in June and August. Control account reconciliations provide comfort that accounting records are being maintained completely and accurately. At the year end, it is important to confirm that balances including bank balances are not under or overstated. This is an example of a control procedure being overridden by management and raises concerns over the overall emphasis placed on internal control.	Discuss this issue with the finance director and request that the July control account reconciliations are undertaken. All reconciling items should be tested in detail and agreed to supporting documentation.
The purchase ledger of Sitia Sparkle Co was closed down on 8 August, rather than at the year end 31 July. There is a risk that the cut-off may be incorrect with purchases and payables over or understated.	The audit team should undertake testing of transactions posted to the purchase ledger between 1 and 8 August to identify whether any transactions relating to the 20X7 year end have been included or any 20X6 balances removed.

(c)   **Supervision and reviewing of the assistants' work**

Supervision

During the audit of Sitia Sparkle Co, the supervisor should keep track of the progress of the audit engagement to ensure that the audit timetable is met and should ensure that the audit manager and partner are kept updated of progress.

The competence and capabilities of individual members of the engagement team should be considered, including whether they have sufficient time to carry out their work, whether they understand their instructions and whether the work is being carried out in accordance with the planned approach to the audit.

In addition, part of the supervision process should involve addressing any significant matters arising during the audit of Sitia Sparkle Co, considering their significance and modifying the planned approach appropriately.

The supervisor would also be responsible for identifying matters for consultation or consideration by the audit manager or engagement partner of Sitia Sparkle Co.

Review

The supervisor would be required to review the work completed by the assistants and consider whether this work has been performed in accordance with professional standards and other regulatory requirements and if the work performed supports the conclusions reached and has been properly documented.

The supervisor should also consider whether all significant matters have been raised for partner attention or for further consideration and where appropriate consultations have taken place, whether appropriate conclusions have been documented.

ACCA
Fundamentals Level
Paper F8
Audit and Assurance

Mock Examination 3

December 2016 exam

Time allowed: 3 hours 15 minutes

This question paper is divided into two section:

Section A – ALL 15 questions are compulsory and MUST be attempted

Section B – ALL 3 questions are compulsory and MUST be attempted

Do NOT open this question paper until instructed by the supervisor.

Do NOT record any of your answers on the question paper.

This question paper must not be removed from the examination hall.

Section A – ALL 15 questions are compulsory and MUST be attempted

Each question is worth 2 marks.

The following scenario relates to questions 1–5.

The board of directors of Sistar Co are concerned that they are not currently applying best practice in terms of corporate governance and are seeking to make improvements.

The company currently has three non-executive directors (NEDs) on the board, who are paid a fee which changes annually depending on company performance. The NEDs all sit on the audit, nomination and remuneration committees. There are currently no formal documents setting out the responsibilities of these committees.

At present, Sistar Co does not have an internal audit function but the directors are establishing a team which will be responsible for a range of internal audit assignments.

The following is the current proposed structure for the internal audit (IA) department.

The only role still to be filled is the Head of internal audit. There are two potential candidates: Paul Belling a consultant who helped design and implement the company's current control system, and Maria Marquez who is currently an audit manager at Rossi & Bell, an audit firm which has never been used by Sistar Co.

Out of the other three members of the proposed IA department, two of them have moved from other departments in Sistar Co and one of the audit assistants has audit experience.

1   Which of the following should be included in a formal document regarding the responsibilities of the audit committee?

 (1) To monitor and review the effectiveness of the newly established internal audit function
 (2) To evaluate the balance of skills, experience and independence of board members
 (3) To take responsibility for the appointment and removal of the external auditors
 (4) To monitor and review the effectiveness of internal financial controls established by the company

 A 1 and 2
 B 1 and 4
 C 2 and 3
 D 3 and 4

2 **Which of the following options correctly describes the deficiency relating to NEDs' remuneration and makes a valid recommendation for improvement?**

	Deficiency	Recommendation
A	Compromises NED independence	NEDs should be remunerated on the same basis as the executive team
B	Compromises the motivation of NEDs	NEDs' remuneration should be tied to profit targets
C	Compromises NED independence	NEDs' remuneration should be a set amount based on time committed
D	Compromises the motivation of NEDs	NEDs' remuneration should be linked to individual performance

3 The board is in the final stages of establishing the IA department.

Which of the following options provides appropriate recommendations which would improve the effectiveness and independence of the IA department?

	Reports to	Head of IA	Remaining staff members
A	Finance director	Maria Marquez	Appoint more senior staff with audit experience
B	Audit committee	Paul Belling	No changes needed
C	Chief executive	Paul Belling	All staff should be new to the company
D	Audit committee	Maria Marquez	Appoint more senior staff with audit experience

4 The board has started to compile a list of tasks for the IA department to carry out once it is up and running. It has been agreed that the first assignment to be completed will be for IA to review Sistar Co's processes over capital expenditure to verify if the right items are purchased at an appropriate time and competitive price.

What type of internal audit assignment does this represent?

A   A value for money audit
B   A management audit
C   A financial audit
D   An IT audit

5 **When deciding on the role of the IA department in undertaking operational audits, which of the following should the team NOT be involved in?**

A   Observing procedures carried out by Sistar Co's staff
B   Reperforming procedures documented in procedures manuals
C   Designing and implementing internal control procedures to address deficiencies
D   Reporting findings directly to the board of directors

The following scenario relates to questions 6–10.

You are an audit manager of Elm & Co and are finalising the audit of the financial statements of Oak Co for the year ended 31 May 20X6. You are reviewing the results of the final analytical procedures and other outstanding points on the audit file, prior to recommending the final audit opinion, which is due to be signed on 12 December 20X6.

The following ratio analysis has been completed as part of the final analytical procedures:

	20X6 Final	20X6 Planning	20X5 Final
Gross profit margin	9%	11%	12%
Quick ratio	0.2	0.6	0.8
Payables days	45	40	37
Inventory days	50	40	42

Discussions with the finance director have also revealed the following:

(1)   Oak Co lost a major customer, Beech Co, in May 20X6, but new business has been won post year end which has mitigated the impact of the loss of Beech Co.

(2)   Oak Co is due to repay a substantial loan on 31 January 20X7. Oak Co is currently negotiating revised terms with the bank but it is unlikely that negotiations will be concluded before the auditor's report is signed. This will be disclosed in the financial statements.

The financial statements for the year ended 31 May 20X6 have been prepared on a going concern basis.

6   As part of the going concern assessment, the following additional issues have been noted on the audit file:

(1)   A number of personnel in the purchasing department left during the year and have not been replaced

(2)   A major supplier to Oak Co has just gone out of business with a number of unfulfilled orders

(3)   A new product which was due to account for 30% of revenue has proved to be unsuccessful

(4)   A litigation claim has been raised against Oak Co after the year end with potential damages totalling 3% of this year's profit

Which of the issues identified could individually cast doubt over the use of the going concern basis of accounting for Oak Co?

A   1 and 3
B   2, 3 and 4
C   2 and 3 only
D   1, 2 and 4

7   As part of your review of the final analytical procedures, you compare the results to the following comments on the audit file:

(1)   The company has increased the sales prices charged to customers while maintaining costs at a level comparable to 20X5

(2)   The company has become more reliant on its overdraft facility during the year

(3)   Due to cash restrictions, the company has encountered delays in paying suppliers

(4)   At the year-end inventory count, a lower level of slow moving inventory was noted compared to prior year

Which of the above comments are INCONSISTENT with the results of the final analytical procedures?

A   1 and 2
B   1 and 4
C   2 and 3
D   3 and 4

8   **Which of the following procedures would provide the MOST reliable evidence in relation to the new business won post year end?**

A   Review of post year-end sales orders from the new customer
B   Inspect email correspondence between the sales director of Oak Co and the new customer
C   Obtain a written representation confirming the level of business agreed with the new customer
D   Review of board minutes discussing the contract with the new customer

9   The initial going concern assessment conducted by the management of Oak Co covers the period to
     30 November 20X6.

     Which of the following is an appropriate course of action in the circumstances described above?

     A   Request management extend the assessment to the date of the auditor's report

     B   Design and carry out procedures to only assess going concern in the period from 31 May 20X6 to the
          date of the auditor's report

     C   Request management extend the assessment to cover at least until 31 May 20X7

     D   Accept the timeframe used by management as the going concern review is their responsibility

10   The audit engagement partner has concluded that the disclosure included in the financial statements in
     relation to the loan negotiations is adequate. Additionally, the audit partner has commented that this
     disclosure is fundamental to the users' understanding of the financial statements.

     What form of auditor's report should be issued?

     A   Modified opinion with a material uncertainty related to going concern paragraph
     B   Unmodified opinion with a material uncertainty related to going concern paragraph
     C   Modified opinion with an other matter paragraph
     D   Unmodified opinion with an other matter paragraph

The following scenario relates to questions 11–15.

You are an audit senior at Jones & Co and are currently performing the final audit of Walker Co for the year ended
31 October 20X6. The company is a manufacturer and retailer of shoes and boots. The current audit senior is ill and
you have been asked to complete the audit of payroll in their absence.

On arrival at the head office of Walker Co, you determine the following data from a review of the current year and
prior year audit files:

(1)   As at 31 October 20X5, Walker Co had 500 employees

(2)   On 1 November 20X5, 10% of staff were made redundant, effective immediately, due to discontinuation of a
      product line

(3)   On 1 January 20X6, all remaining staff received a 6% pay rise

(4)   Over the course of the year, sales levels met performance targets which resulted in a fixed bonus of $1,500
      being paid to each employee on 31 October 20X6

11   **Which of the following statements explains the CUT-OFF assertion for wages and salaries?**

     A   Wages and salaries have been fairly allocated within the statement of profit or loss

     B   Wages and salaries have been appropriately calculated taking into account all relevant taxation costs
          and adjustments

     C   Wages and salaries which have been incurred during the period have been accounted for in respect
          of all personnel employed by Walker Co

     D   Wages and salaries accounted for relate to the current year ended 31 October 20X6

12   The following audit evidence has been gathered relating to the accuracy of wages and salaries for Walker Co:

     (1)   Proof in total calculation performed by an audit team member

     (2)   Written representation from the directors of Walker Co confirming the accuracy of wages and salaries

     (3)   Verbal confirmation from the finance director of Walker Co confirming the accuracy of wages and
           salaries

     (4)   Recalculation of the gross and net pay for a sample of employees by an internal audit team member
           of Walker Co

What is the order of reliability of the audit evidence starting with the MOST RELIABLE first?

- A   1, 2, 3, 4
- B   1, 4, 2, 3
- C   4, 1, 2, 3
- D   4, 1, 3, 2

13   The prior year financial statements for Walker Co included $17m for wages and salaries in the statement of profit or loss.

What would be the estimated current year wages and salaries expense, ignoring redundancy costs, based upon the data gathered from the review of the audit files?

- A $16,740,000
- B $16,893,000
- C $16,815,000
- D $18,600,000

14   **Which of the following are substantive ANALYTICAL PROCEDURES for wages and salaries?**

(1)   Trace and agree the total wages and salaries expense per the payroll system to the draft financial statements

(2)   Recalculate the gross and net pay for a sample of employees, agree to payroll records and investigate discrepancies

(3)   Compare the current year total payroll expense to the prior year and investigate any significant differences

(4)   Perform a proof in total calculation and compare expected expense to actual expense within the draft financial statements

- A   1 and 2
- B   1 and 3
- C   2 and 4
- D   3 and 4

15   You have been given a list of procedures to carry out on revenue and you have decided to prioritise those which deal with the key assertion of occurrence.

Which of the following substantive procedures provide evidence over the OCCURRENCE assertion for revenue?

(1)   Compare the reported revenue figure to the budget and to the previous year, investigating any significant differences

(2)   Select a sample of goods despatched notes (GDNs) and agree to invoices in the sales day book

(3)   Select a sample of invoices from the sales day book and agree to GDNs

(4)   Select a sample of invoices and recalculate the invoiced amount agreeing to price list

- A   1 and 2
- B   1 and 3
- C   2 and 4
- D   3 and 4

(Total = 30 marks)

Section B – ALL THREE questions are compulsory and MUST be attempted

Question 16

You are an audit supervisor of Ant & Co and are planning the final audit of Centipede Co, which is a listed company, for the year ended 31 December 20X6. The company purchases consumer packaged goods and sells these through its website and to wholesalers. This is a new client for your firm and your audit manager has already had a planning meeting with the finance director and has provided you with the following notes along with financial statement extracts.

Client background and notes from planning meeting

Rather than undertaking a full year-end inventory count, the company undertakes monthly perpetual inventory counts, covering one-twelfth of all lines monthly. As part of the interim audit which was completed earlier in the year, an audit assistant attended a perpetual inventory count in September and noted that there were a large number of exceptions where the inventory records were consistently higher than the physical inventory in the warehouse. When discussing these exceptions with the finance director, the assistant was informed that this had been a recurring issue all year. In addition, the audit assistant noted that there were some lines of inventory which, according to the records, were at least 90 days old.

Centipede Co has a head office where the audit team will be based to conduct the final audit fieldwork. However, there are four additional sites where some accounting records are maintained and these sites were not visited during the interim audit. The records for these sites are incorporated monthly through an interface to the general ledger. A fifth site was closed down in 20X5, however, the building was only sold in 20X6 at a loss of $825,000.

One of Centipede Co's wholesale customers is alleging that the company has consistently failed to deliver goods in a saleable condition and on time, hence it has commenced legal action against Centipede Co for a loss of profits claim.

The directors have disclosed their remuneration details in the financial statements in line with International Financial Reporting Standards, which does not require a separate list of directors' names and payments. However, in the country in which Centipede Co is based, local legislation requires disclosure of the names of the directors and the amount of remuneration payable to each director.

FINANCIAL STATEMENT EXTRACTS FOR THE YEAR ENDED 31 DECEMBER

	Draft 20X6 $'000	Final 20X5 $'000
Revenue	25,230	21,180
Cost of sales	(15,840)	(14,015)
Gross profit	9,390	7,165
Operating expenses	(4,903)	(3,245)
	4,487	3,920
Inventory	2,360	1,800
Trade receivables	1,590	1,250
Cash	–	480
Trade payables	3,500	2,800
Overdraft	580	–

Required

(a) Describe the matters which Ant & Co should have considered prior to accepting the audit of Centipede Co.

(5 marks)

(b) Calculate **SIX** ratios, for **BOTH** years, which would assist you in planning the audit of Centipede Co.

(6 marks)

(c)   From a review of the above information and the ratios calculated, describe **SEVEN** audit risks and explain the auditor's response to each risk in planning the audit of Centipede Co.

   Note. Prepare your answer using two columns headed Audit risk and Auditor's response respectively.

(14 marks)

The finance director of Centipede Co informed Ant & Co that one of the reasons they were appointed as auditors was because of their knowledge of the industry. Ant & Co audits a number of other consumer packaged goods companies, including Centipede Co's main rival. The finance director has enquired how Ant & Co will keep information obtained during the audit confidential.

Required

(d)   Explain the safeguards which Ant & Co should implement to ensure that this conflict of interest is properly managed. **(5 marks)**

(Total = 30 marks)

Question 17

Caterpillar Co is a clothing retailer which operates 45 stores throughout the country. The company's year end is 31 March 20X7. Caterpillar Co has an internal audit department which has undertaken a number of internal control reviews specifically focusing on cash controls at stores during the year. The reviews have taken place in the largest 20 stores as this is where most issues arise. You are an audit supervisor of Woodlouse & Co and are reviewing the internal controls documentation in relation to the cash receipts system in preparation for the interim audit which will involve visiting a number of stores and the head office.

Each of Caterpillar Co's stores has on average three or four cash tills to take customer payments. All employees based at the store are able to use each till and individuals do not have their own log on codes, although employees tend to use the same till each day. Customers can pay using either cash or a credit card and for any transaction either the credit card payment slips or cash are placed in the till by the cashier. Where employees' friends or family members purchase clothes in store, the employee is able to serve them at the till point.

At the end of each day, the tills are closed down with daily readings of sales taken from each till; these are reconciled to the total of the cash in the tills and the credit card payment slips and any discrepancies are noted. To save time, this reconciliation is done by the store's assistant manager in aggregate for all of the store tills together. Once this reconciliation has taken place, the cash is stored in the shop's small safe overnight and in the morning it is transferred to the bank via collection by a security company. If the store is low on change for cash payments, a junior sales clerk is sent by a till operator to the bank with money from the till and asked to change it into smaller denominations.

The daily sales readings from the tills along with the cash data and credit card payment data are transferred daily to head office through an interface with the sales and cash receipts records. A clerk oversees that this transfer has occurred for all stores. On a daily basis, he also agrees the cash transferred by the security company has been banked in full by agreeing the cash deposit slips to the bank statements, and that the credit card receipts have been received from the credit card company. On a monthly basis, the same clerk reconciles the bank statements to the cash book. The reconciliations are reviewed by the financial controller if there are any unreconciled amounts.

Required

(a)   State **TWO** control objectives of Caterpillar Co's cash receipts system.   **(2 marks)**

(b)   Identify and explain **THREE CONTROL STRENGTHS** in Caterpillar Co's cash receipts system and describe a **TEST OF CONTROL** the auditor should perform to assess if each of these controls is operating effectively.

   Note. Prepare your answer using two columns headed Control strength and Test of control respectively.

(6 marks)

(c)   Identify and explain **SIX DEFICIENCIES** in Caterpillar Co's cash receipts system and provide a recommendation to address each of these deficiencies.

   Note. Prepare your answer using two columns headed Control deficiency and Control recommendation respectively.

(12 marks)

(Total = 20 marks)

Question 18

You are an audit manager of Snail & Co and you are in charge of two audits which are due to commence shortly. Insects4U Co is a registered charity which promotes insect conservation and has been an audit client for several years. Spider Spirals Co, also an existing audit client, manufactures stationery products and its draft total liabilities are $8.1 million. Both clients' financial year ended on 31 October 20X6. The following matters have been brought to your attention for each company.

Insects4U Co

(i) **Completeness of income**

Insects4U Co is a not-for-profit organisation which generates income in a number of ways. It receives monthly donations from its many subscribers and these are paid by bank transfer to the charity. In addition, a large number of donations are sent through the post to the charity. Insects4U Co also sells tickets for their three charity events held annually. During the audit planning, completeness of income was flagged as a key risk.

Note. Assume that the charity adopts International Financial Reporting Standards. **(4 marks)**

Spider Spirals Co

(ii) **Trade payables**

The finance director of Spider Spirals Co has informed you that at the year end the purchase ledger was kept open for one week longer than normal as a large bank transfer and cheque payment run was made on 3 November 20X6. Some purchase invoices were received in this week and were recorded in the 20X6 purchase ledger as well as the payment run made on 3 November. **(6 marks)**

(iii) **Trade receivables**

Spider Spirals Co has a large number of small customers; the normal credit terms offered to them is 30 days. However, the finance director has informed you that the average trade receivables days have increased quite significantly this year from 34 days to 55 days. This is partly due to difficult trading conditions and also because for six months of the year the role of credit controller was vacant. The company has historically maintained on average an allowance for trade receivables of 1.5% of gross trade receivables. **(5 marks)**

Required

(a) Describe substantive procedures the auditor should perform to obtain sufficient, and appropriate audit evidence in relation to the above three matters.

Note. The mark allocation is shown against each of the three matters above.

(b) The finance director of Spider Spirals Co has informed you that he is not proposing to make an adjustment for the trade payables payment run made on 3 November, as the total payment of $490,000 would only require a change to trade payables and the bank overdraft, both of which are current liabilities.

Required

Discuss the issue and describe the impact on the auditor's report, if any, should this issue remain unresolved. **(5 marks)**

(Total = 20 marks)

Answers

DO NOT TURN THIS PAGE UNTIL YOU HAVE
COMPLETED THE MOCK EXAM

Plan of attack

If this were the real Audit and Assurance exam and you had been told to turn over and begin, what would be going through your mind?

An important thing to say (while there is still time) is that it is vital to have a good breadth of knowledge of the syllabus because all the questions are compulsory. However, don't panic. Below we provide guidance on how to approach the exam.

Looking through the paper

Section A has three objective test cases, each with five questions. This is the section of the paper where the examination team can test knowledge across the breadth of the syllabus. Make sure you read these cases and questions carefully. The distractors are designed to present plausible, but incorrect, answers. Don't let them mislead you. If you really have no idea – guess. You may even be right.

Section B has three longer questions:

- **Question 16** is a 30-mark question focused on the planning stage, covering analytical procedures, audit risk, acceptance procedures and ethics. Read the requirements carefully, taking note in particular of the number of ratios that you have been asked to calculate and that they must be calculated for both years.

- **Question 17** is a 20-mark internal controls question. Here you need to consider strengths in the system as well as identifying weaknesses.

- **Question 18** is a 20-mark question dealing with substantive procedures relating to income, trade payables and trade receivables. You are also asked to consider the impact on the auditor's report of any unresolved issues.

Allocating your time

BPP's advice is to always allocate your time **according to the marks for the question**. However, **use common sense**. If you're doing a question but haven't a clue how to do part (b), you might be better off re-allocating your time and getting more marks on another question, where you can add something you didn't have time for earlier on. Make sure you leave time to recheck the OTQs and make sure you have answered them all.

Forget about it

And don't worry if you found the paper difficult. More than likely other candidates will too. If this were the real thing you would need to forget the exam the minute you left the exam hall and think about the next one. Or, if it is the last one, celebrate!

Section A

1   B   In accordance with best practice these are responsibilities of the audit committee.

2   C   If NED pay is dependent on profits decisions may be influenced by personal gain rather than the best interests of the company.

3   D   The audit committee is not involved in the day-to-day running of the business. Maria Marquez would be new to the company. Only a junior team member currently has audit experience.

4   A   Value for money audits examine economy, efficiency and effectiveness of activities.

5   C   If IA designs and implements systems they will no longer be able to monitor effectiveness impartially.

6   C   1 and 4 are not significant individually.

7   B   (1) is inconsistent with the fall in the gross profit margin.
(4) is inconsistent with an increase in inventory days.

8   A   Sales actually taking place confirms that the new business has been won.

9   C   This is 12 months from the date of the financial statements.

10   B   As the disclosure is adequate an unmodified opinion can be issued. The material uncertainty paragraph is required as the issue is fundamental to the understanding of the financial statements.

11   D   Cut-off relates to the recognition of transactions in the correct accounting period.

12   B   Auditor generated evidence is more reliable than internally generated evidence. Written evidence is more reliable than oral evidence.

13   A $17{,}000{,}000 \times 90\% \times 2/12 = 2{,}550{,}000$

                $(17{,}000{,}000 \times 106\%) \times 90\% \times 10/12 = 13{,}515{,}000$

                $450 \times 1{,}500 = 675{,}000$

                $2{,}550{,}000 + 13{,}515{,}000 + 675{,}000 = 16{,}740{,}000$

14   D   Comparisons with prior years and proof in total calculations are examples of substantive analytical procedures.

15   B   (2) provides evidence that goods despatched have been invoiced
(4) provides evidence of accuracy

Section B

Question 16

Marking scheme

			Marks
(a)	**Matters to be considered prior to accepting the audit of Centipede Co**		
	• Compliance with ACCA's *Code of Ethics and Conduct*	1	
	• Competent	1	
	• Reputation and integrity of directors	1	
	• Level of risk of Centipede Co audit	1	
	• Fee adequate to compensate for risk	1	
	• Write to outgoing auditor after obtaining permission to contact	1	
	• Previous auditor permission to respond	1	
	• Review response for any issues	1	
	Restricted to		5
(b)	**Ratio calculations** (½ mark for each year)		
	• Gross margin	1	
	• Operating margin	1	
	• Inventory days/Inventory turnover	1	
	• Receivable days	1	
	• Payable days	1	
	• Current ratio	1	
	• Quick ratio	1	
	Restricted to		6
(c)	**Audit risks and responses** (only 7 risks required)		
	• New client, increased detection risk	2	
	• Perpetual inventory count adjustments	2	
	• Valuation of inventory	2	
	• Branch records	2	
	• Disposal of building	2	
	• Legal case	2	
	• Directors remuneration disclosure	2	
	• Revenue growth	2	
	• Misclassification of costs between cost of sales and operating	2	
	• Going concern	2	
	Max 7 issues, 2 marks each		14

			Marks
(d)	**Safeguards to deal with conflict of interest**		
	•	Notify Centipede Co and its competitor	1
	•	Advise seek independent advice	1
	•	Separate engagement teams	1
	•	Procedures prevent access to information	1
	•	Clear guidelines on security and confidentiality	1
	•	Confidentiality agreements	1
	•	Monitoring of safeguards	1
	Restricted to		**5**
Total marks			**30**

(a) **Matters to be considered prior to accepting the audit of Centipede Co**

ISA 220 *Quality Control for an Audit of Financial Statements* provides guidance to Ant & Co on the steps they should have taken in accepting the new audit client, Centipede Co. It sets out a number of processes which the auditor should perform prior to accepting a new engagement.

Ant & Co should have considered any issues which might arise which could threaten compliance with ACCA's Code of Ethics and Conduct or any local legislation, such as the level of fees from Centipede Co, to ensure they are not unduly reliant on these fees, as well as considering whether any conflicts of interest arise with existing clients. If issues arise, then their significance must be considered.

In addition, they should have considered whether they were competent to perform the work and whether they would have appropriate resources available, as well as any specialist skills or knowledge required for the audit of Centipede Co.

Ant & Co should have considered what they already know about the directors of Centipede Co; they needed to consider the reputation and integrity of the directors. If necessary, the firm may have wanted to obtain references if they do not formally know the directors.

Additionally, Ant & Co should have considered the level of risk attached to the audit of Centipede Co and whether this was acceptable to the firm. As part of this, they should have considered whether the expected audit fee was adequate in relation to the risk of auditing Centipede Co.

Ant & Co should have communicated with the outgoing auditor of Centipede Co to assess if there were any ethical or professional reasons why they should not have accepted appointment. They should have obtained permission from Centipede

Co's management to contact the previous auditor; if this was not given, then the engagement should have been refused. Once received, the response from the previous auditor should have been carefully reviewed for any issues which could affect acceptance.

(b) **Ratios**

Ratios to assist the audit supervisor in planning the audit:

	20X6	*20X5*
Gross margin	9,390/25,230 = 37.2%	7,165/21,180 = 33.8%
Operating margin	4,487/25,230 = 17.8%	3,920/21,180 = 18.5%
Inventory days or	2,360/15,840 × 365 = 54 days	1,800/14,015 × 365 = 47 days
Inventory turnover	15,840/2,360 = 6.7	14,015/1,800 = 7.8
Receivables days	1,590/25,230 × 365 = 23 days	1,250/21,180 × 365 = 22 days
Payables days	3,500/15,840 × 365 = 81 days	2,800/14,015 × 365 = 73 days
Current ratio	3,950/4,080 = 0.97	3,530/2,800 = 1.26
Quick ratio	(3,950 – 2,360)/4,080 = 0.39	(3,530 – 1,800)/2,800 = 0.62

(c) **Audit risks and auditor's responses**

Audit risk	Auditor's response
Centipede Co is a new client for Ant & Co and is a listed company. As the team is not familiar with the accounting policies, transactions and balances of the company, there will be an increased detection risk on the audit.	Ant & Co should ensure they have a suitably experienced team. Also, adequate time should be allocated for team members to obtain an understanding of the company and the risks of material misstatement, including attendance at an audit team briefing.
The company utilises a perpetual inventory system at its warehouse rather than a full year-end count. Under such a system, all inventory must be counted at least once a year with adjustments made to the inventory records on a timely basis. Inventory could be under or overstated if the perpetual inventory counts are not complete. During the interim audit, it was noted that there were significant exceptions with the inventory records being higher than the inventory in the warehouse. As the year-end quantities will be based on the records, this is likely to result in overstated inventory.	The completeness of the perpetual inventory counts should be reviewed and the controls over the counts and adjustments to records should be tested. In addition, the level of adjustments made to inventory should be considered to assess their significance. This should be discussed with management as soon as possible as it may not be possible to place reliance on the inventory records at the year end, which could result in the requirement for a full year-end inventory count.
During the interim audit, it was noted that there were some lines of inventory which according to the records were at least 90 days old. In addition, inventory days have increased from 47 to 54 days. It would appear that there may be an increase in slow moving inventory. The valuation of inventory as per IAS 2 *Inventories* should be at the lower of cost and net realisable value. Hence there is a risk that obsolete inventory has not been appropriately written down and inventory is overvalued.	The aged inventory report should be reviewed and discussed with management to assess if certain lines of products are slow moving. Detailed cost and net realisable value testing to be performed to assess whether an allowance or write down of inventory is required.
Centipede Co maintains accounting records at four additional sites which were not visited during the interim audit, and the records from these sites are incorporated monthly into the general ledger.	Discuss with management the significance and materiality of the records maintained at the four sites. The team may then need to visit some of these sites during the final audit to undertake testing of the records held there.
Ant & Co need to ensure that they have obtained sufficient appropriate audit evidence over all the accounting records of the company, not just for those at head office. There is a detection risk if the team does not visit or undertake testing of the records at these sites. Further, if the interface does not occur appropriately, there is a risk that accounting records are incomplete.	In addition, computer-assisted audit techniques could be utilised by the team to sample test the monthly interface of data from each site to head office to identify any errors.

Audit risk	Auditor's response
During 20X6 a building was disposed of with a loss on disposal of $825,000. There is a risk that the disposal has not been removed appropriately from the accounting records or that the loss on disposal calculation is incorrect. In addition, significant profits or losses on disposal are an indication that the depreciation policy for land and buildings may not be appropriate. Therefore depreciation may be understated and consequently assets overstated.	Agree that the asset has been removed from the non-current assets register, recalculate the loss on disposal calculation and agree all items to supporting documentation. Discuss the depreciation policy for land and buildings with the finance director to assess its reasonableness. Review the level of losses on disposal generated from other asset sales to ascertain if this is a more widespread issue.
A customer of Centipede Co has commenced legal action against Centipede Co for a loss of profits claim. If it is probable that the company will make payment to the customer, a legal provision is required. If the payment is possible rather than probable, a contingent liability disclosure would be necessary. If Centipede Co has not done this, there is a risk over the completeness of any provisions and the necessary disclosure of contingent liabilities.	Ant & Co should write to the company's lawyers to enquire of the existence and likelihood of success of any claim from the wholesale customer. The results of this should be used to assess the level of provision or disclosure included in the financial statements.
The directors have not disclosed the individual names and payments for each of the directors' remuneration. This is in line with IFRS but disclosure of this is required by local legislation. In cases where the local legislation is more comprehensive than IFRS, it is likely the company must comply with the local legislation. The directors' remuneration disclosure will not be complete and accurate if the names and individual payments are not disclosed in accordance with the relevant local legislation and hence the financial statements will be misstated as a result of the non-compliance.	Discuss this matter with management and review the requirements of the local legislation to determine if the disclosure in the financial statements is appropriate.
Revenue has grown by 19% in the year; however, cost of sales has only increased by 13%. This is a significant increase in revenue and along with the increase in gross margin may be due to an overstatement of revenue.	During the audit a detailed breakdown of sales will be obtained, discussed with management and tested in order to understand the sales increase. Also increased cut off testing should be undertaken to verify that revenue is recorded in the right period and is not overstated.
Gross margin has increased from 33.8% to 37.2%. Operating margin has decreased from 18.5% to 17.8%. This movement in gross margin is significant and there is a risk that costs may have been omitted or included in operating expenses rather than cost of sales.	The classification of costs between cost of sales and operating expenses will be compared with the prior year to ensure consistency. Also increased cut-off testing should be performed at the year end to ensure that costs are complete.

Audit risk	Auditor's response
The overall liquidity of the company is in decline with the current and quick ratios decreasing from 1.26 to 0.97 and 0.62 to 0.39 respectively. In addition, the cash balances have decreased significantly over the year, and the company now has an overdraft of $580,000 at the end of the year. Further, the trade payable days have increased from 73 to 81 days, implying the company is struggling to meet their liabilities as they fall due. All of these changes in key ratios could signal going concern difficulties.	Detailed going concern testing to be performed during the audit as there may be a doubt over going concern and the basis of accounting should be discussed with management to ensure that the going concern basis is reasonable.

(d) **Safeguards to deal with conflict of interest**

- Both Centipede Co and its rival competitor should be notified that Ant & Co would be acting as auditors for each company and, if necessary, consent obtained.

- Advising one or both clients to seek additional independent advice.

- The use of separate engagement teams, with different engagement partners and team members; once an employee has worked on one audit, such as Centipede Co, then they should be prevented from being on the audit of the competitor for a period of time.

- Procedures to prevent access to information, for example, strict physical separation of both teams, confidential and secure data filing.

- Clear guidelines for members of each engagement team on issues of security and confidentiality. These guidelines could be included within the audit engagement letters.

- Potentially the use of confidentiality agreements signed by employees and partners of the firm.

- Regular monitoring of the application of the above safeguards by a senior individual in Ant & Co not involved in either audit.

Question 17

Text reference. Chapters 9 and 10

Top tips. This is a 20 mark question on controls and tests of controls in the cash system. Part (b) of the question asks you to identify strengths in the system and tests of controls. Make sure you can distinguish between tests of controls and substantive procedures. Tests of controls aim to provide evidence that controls are operating effectively.

Part (c) should be a familiar requirement asking for the identification of weaknesses and recommendations to address each weakness. This type of requirement is typically well answered but take care when making your recommendations. Examination team comments have often referred to the fact that recommendations are often phrased in vague terms. Make sure you explain clearly the procedure which needs to be performed, and if possible who should perform it.

Easy marks. These are available in part (a).

Marks

(a) **Control objectives – cash receipts system**
- To ensure that all valid cash receipts are received and deposited promptly in the bank 1
- To ensure all cash receipts are recorded in the cash book 1
- To ensure that all receipts are recorded at the correct amounts in the cash books 1
- To ensure that cash receipts are correctly posted to the general ledger 1
- To ensure that cash receipts are recorded in the correct accounting period 1
- To ensure that cash is safeguarded to prevent theft 1
- To ensure that management has accurate and timely information regarding the cash position 1

  Restricted to 2

(b) **Control strengths and tests of control** (3 strengths required)
- Internal audit department which undertakes cash control reviews at stores 2
- Daily sales readings taken from tills and reconciled to cash and credit card payment slips, exceptions noted 2
- Cash collected daily and taken to the bank by security company 2
- Daily interface to head office for sales, cash and credit card data into sales and cash receipts books 2
- Daily agreement of cash banked by security company and cash received from credit card company into bank statements 2
- Monthly bank reconciliations undertaken 2

  Max 3 issues, 2 marks each 6

(c) **Control deficiencies and recommendations** (only 6 issues required)
- Internal audit only visits 20 largest stores rather than all 45 2
- All employees able to use tills and no individual log on codes 2
- Employees can serve friends and family members at the till points 2
- Daily till reading reconciliations performed in aggregate for all tills in store rather than individually 2
- Cashing up of tills undertaken by just one individual 2
- Cash stored on site overnight 2
- Junior sales clerks given cash and sent to the bank to change notes into smaller denominations 2
- Lack of segregation of duties in head office for recording and reconciling of cash 2
- Bank reconciliations not always reviewed by the financial controller 2

  Max 6 issues, 2 marks each 12

Total marks 20

(a) **Control objectives – cash receipts system**

- To ensure that all valid cash receipts are received and deposited promptly in the bank.
- To ensure all cash receipts are recorded in the cash book.
- To ensure that all receipts are recorded at the correct amounts in the cash book.
- To ensure that cash receipts are correctly posted to the general ledger.
- To ensure that cash receipts are recorded in the correct accounting period.
- To ensure that cash is safeguarded to prevent theft.
- To ensure that management has accurate and timely information regarding the cash position.

(b)   **Caterpillar Co's cash cycle strengths and tests of control**

Control strength	Test of control
Caterpillar Co has an internal audit (IA) department which has undertaken a number of internal control reviews, which specifically focused on cash controls at stores during the year. This is a strong monitoring control as stores will aim to ensure that company procedures are maintained as they would not wish IA to report any exceptions at their store.	Discuss with IA the programme of their visits to stores and the areas addressed on these visits. This will assess the strength of this monitoring control. In particular, enquire of IA whether over a rolling period all stores will be visited. Review the IA department files for the results of the store visits, to confirm that the 20 stores programmed to be visited did all actually take place and for exceptions noted and actions taken.
At the end of each day, the tills are closed down with daily readings of sales taken; these are reconciled to the total of the cash in the tills and the credit card payment slips and any discrepancies are noted. Daily cashing up procedures should ensure that the cash is controlled and reduces the risk of fraud as employees are aware that the assistant manager will be looking for cash discrepancies.	For a sample of stores visited, the auditor should review the file of daily reconciliations to ascertain if end of day till reconciliations have taken place on a daily basis. For reconciliations with discrepancies, discuss with the store manager what actions were taken and how these differences were resolved.
Cash received from customers is taken to the bank daily via collection by a security company. This ensures that cash is safeguarded and that the risk of theft when transferring to the bank is minimised.	During the store visits, enquire of staff how the cash is transferred to the bank. A sample of invoices from the collection company should be reviewed and confirmed that they are charging Centipede Co on a daily basis. In addition, during these visits observe the cash collection process carried out by the security company.
The daily sales readings from the tills along with the cash and credit card data are transferred to head office through a daily interface into the sales and cash receipts records. This should ensure that sales and cash records are updated on a prompt basis and are complete and accurate.	During the interim audit at head office, compare the daily sales readings from individual stores, including some visited by the audit team, to the sales and cash receipt records within the general ledger. Review the date on which the sales and cash receipt records were updated to ensure this occurred promptly. Any discrepancies should be discussed with the clerk responsible for overseeing this process.
On a daily basis the clerk agrees that the cash banked and the credit card receipts from the credit card company have been credited to the bank statements in full. This should ensure the completeness of cash receipts, as they are transferred in from two sources, being the security company and the credit card operator.	Discuss with the clerk responsible for reconciling the cash and credit card receipts, the process he undertakes. Review the daily reconciliations he has completed to confirm the process has been undertaken as described.
Bank reconciliations are undertaken on a monthly basis. This should ensure that any discrepancies between the cash book and the bank statements are identified promptly.	Review the file of bank reconciliations to ascertain if there is one for each month and that they are either fully reconciled, or the financial controller has evidenced their review of any unreconciled amounts.

(c)   **Caterpillar Co's cash system deficiencies and controls**

Control deficiency	Control recommendation
The IA department only undertake cash control visits to the 20 largest stores as they feel this is where most issues arise. However, Caterpillar Co has 45 stores in total which means over half of the stores are not being checked. This increases the likelihood of control errors, as these stores may not comply with company procedures and with it being a cash business heightens the chance of frauds occurring.	Caterpillar Co's IA department should have a rolling programme of visits to all 45 stores. This programme can have a bias to large and high risk stores, but it should ensure that all stores are visited on a cyclical basis.
All store employees are able to use each till and none have an individual log on code when using the tills. Allowing all employees access to the till points increases the risk of fraud and error arising. Also in the event of cash discrepancies arising in the tills, it would be difficult to ascertain which employees may be responsible as there is no way of tracking who used which till.	Only employees for whom criminal record/credit checks have been undertaken should be able to use the tills to take customer payments. Each employee should have a designated till and a log on code, which is required for each payment transaction.
Where employees' friends or family members purchase clothes in store, the employee is able to serve them at the till point. There is a significant fraud risk as employees could fail to put the goods through the till, but retain the cash paid by the friend/family members. Additionally, they could give the goods away for free or undercharge for goods sold, thereby granting unauthorised discounts.	Caterpillar Co should instigate a policy whereby employees are unable to serve friends or family members at the till points. They should be required to request that a manager or supervisor put these goods through the till. In addition, CCTV cameras could be placed in the shops, near to the till points to record the daily till transactions. This would act as a deterrent to employees as well as provide evidence in the case of fraudulent transactions occurring. Also Caterpillar Co should carry out regular inventory counts to identify if goods in the stores are below the levels in the inventory records, as this could identify goods being given away for free.
The daily reading of sales and reconciliations to the tills is performed in aggregate rather than for each till. This means if exceptions arise, it will be difficult to identify which till caused the difference and therefore which employees may require further till training or have undertaken fraudulent transactions.	The reconciliations should be undertaken on an individual till by till basis rather than in aggregate.
The cashing up of tills along with the recording of any cash discrepancies is undertaken by just one individual, the assistant store manager. There is a fraud risk as the store manager could remove some of the cash and then simply record that there was an exception on this till.	The cashing up process should be undertaken by two individuals together, ideally the assistant and the store manager. One should count the cash and the other record it. Any exceptions to the till reading should be double checked to confirm that they are not simply addition errors.

Control deficiency	Control recommendation
The cash is kept at the store overnight in a small safe. Although in a safe, this is not secure as it is likely that the cash sales for one day would be a significant sum. This cash is at risk of being stolen overnight.	The cash should continue to be collected daily by the security company, but rather than in the morning it should be collected as the store closes in the evening so that cash does not have to be stored overnight.
If a store needs change, a junior sales clerk is sent to the bank by a till operator to change it into smaller denominations. There is a risk of the cash being misplaced or stolen on the way to the bank or collusion between the junior clerk and till operator as no record appears to be kept of the money removed from the till in these instances and no confirmation of how much cash is returned is carried out.	Caterpillar Co's head office should stipulate a float amount per till and how the note denominations should be comprised. When assigning the cash float in the morning, the store manager should ensure that this policy is adhered to. If during the day, further smaller denomination notes are required, the store manager should authorise a member of staff to obtain cash from the bank and should fully record movements in and out of the till.
One clerk is responsible for several elements of the cash receipts system. He oversees the daily interface from stores, agrees that cash has cleared into the bank statements and undertakes the bank reconciliations. There is a lack of segregation of duties and errors will not be identified on a timely basis as well as increasing the risk of fraud.	These key roles should be split between a few individuals, with ideally the bank reconciliations being undertaken by another member of the finance team.
The bank reconciliations are only reviewed by the financial controller if there are any unreconciled amounts. The bank reconciliation could reconcile but still contain significant errors as there could be compensating errors which cancel each other out. In addition, for a cash based business, the bank reconciliation is a key control which reduces the risk of fraud. If it is not reviewed, then this reduces its effectiveness.	The bank reconciliations should be reviewed by the financial controller on a monthly basis, even if there are no exceptions, and he should evidence his review by way of signature on the bank reconciliation.

Question 18

Text references. Chapters 14, 16 and 19.

Top tips. This is a 20 mark question which tests substantive procedures relating to income, trade payables and trade receivables, together with auditors' reports. In part (a) you must read the scenario carefully and tailor your substantive procedures. In the past the examination team has commented that candidates often provide lists of standard audit work without consideration of the facts in the question. Also note that in relation to income the question considers the assertion of completeness specifically. Again you must ensure you address this in your answer.

In part (b) the key is to note that you need to discuss the issues as well as commenting on the impact on the auditor's report. Your discussion should support the conclusion you have come to.

Easy marks. No specific part of this question is straightforward but there are some easier marks available in part (b).

Marks

(a) (i) **Substantive procedures for completeness of Insects4U Co income**
- Cast schedule of all of the company's income ... 1
- Compare individual categories of income to prior year ... 1
- Trace monthly donations from bank statements to cash book ... 1
- New subscribers agree subscription forms to donations received account, cash book and bank statements ... 1
- For donations, review correspondence from donors, agree to donations account, cash book and bank statements ... 1
- Perform proof in total of tickets sold multiplied by ticket price, compare to actual and investigate significant difference ... 1

Restricted to ... 4

(ii) **Substantive procedures for Spider Spirals Co trade payables**
- Calculate trade payable days ... 1
- Compare total trade payables and list of accruals against prior year ... 1
- Discuss with management process to quantify misstatement of payables ... 1
- Sample invoices received between 1 to 7 November, if post year end, then agree excluded from ledger ... 1
- Review after date payments ... 1
- Review supplier statements reconciliations ... 1
- Perform a trade payables' circularisation ... 1
- Cut-off testing pre and post year-end GRN ... 1

Restricted to ... 6

(iii) **Substantive procedures for Spider Spirals Co trade receivables**
- Aged receivables report to identify any slow moving balances ... 1
- Review customer correspondence to assess whether there are any invoices in dispute ... 1
- Review the after date cash receipts ... 1
- Review board minutes ... 1
- Calculate level of irrecoverable receivables, assess if material and discuss with management ... 1
- Recalculate allowance for receivables ... 1
- Post year-end sales returns/credit notes ... 1

Restricted to ... 5

(b) **Effect of uncorrected misstatement and impact on auditor's report**
- Discussion of issue ... 1
- Calculation of materiality ... 1
- Type of auditor's report modification required ... 2
- Impact on auditor's report ... 1

Restricted to ... 5

Total marks ... 20

(a) (i) **Substantive procedures for Insects4U Co income**

- Obtain a schedule of all Insects4U Co's income and cast to confirm completeness and accuracy of the balance.

- Compare the individual categories of income against prior year and investigate any significant differences.

- For monthly donations, trace a sample of donations received in the bank statements to the cash book to ensure that they are recorded completely and accurately.

- For a sample of new subscribers in the year, agree from their completed subscription form the monthly sum and start date, trace to the monthly donations received account and agree to the cash book and bank statements.

- For donations received in the post, review correspondence from donors, agree to the donations account and trace sums received to the cash book and bank statements to ensure all completely recorded.

- For the charity events, undertake a proof in total calculation of the number of tickets sold multiplied by the ticket price, compare this to the income recorded and discuss any significant differences with management.

(ii) **Substantive procedures for Spider Spirals Co trade payables**

- Calculate the trade payables days for Spider Spirals Co and compare to prior years and investigate any significant difference, in particular any decrease for this year due to the payment run on 3 November.

- Compare the total trade payables and list of accruals against prior year and investigate any significant differences.

- Discuss with management the process they have undertaken to quantify the misstatement of trade payables due to the late payment run and cut-off error of purchase invoices and consider the materiality of the error in isolation as well as with other misstatements found.

- Select a sample of purchase invoices received between the period of 1 and 7 November, ascertain through reviewing goods received notes (GRNs) if the goods were received pre or post year end, if post year end, then confirm that they have been excluded from the ledger or follow through to the correcting journal entry.

- Review after date payments; if they relate to the current year, then follow through to the purchase ledger or accrual listing to ensure they are recorded in the correct period.

- Obtain supplier statements and reconcile these to the purchase ledger balances, and investigate any reconciling items.

- Select a sample of payables balances and perform a trade payables' circularisation, follow up any non-replies and any reconciling items between the balance confirmed and the trade payables' balance.

- Select a sample of GRNs before the year end and after the year end and follow through to inclusion in the correct period's payables balance, to ensure correct cut-off.

(iii) **Substantive procedures for Spider Spirals Co trade receivables**

- Review the aged receivables listing to identify any slow moving or old receivables balances, discuss the status of these balances with the finance director to assess whether they are likely to pay.

- Review customer correspondence to identify any balances which are in dispute or unlikely to be paid.

- Review whether there are any after date cash receipts for slow moving/old receivables balances.

- Review board minutes to identify whether there are any significant concerns in relation to payments by customers.

- Calculate the potential level of receivables which are not recoverable and assess whether this is material or not and discuss with management.

- Recalculate the allowance for receivables and compare to the potentially irrecoverable balances to assess if the allowance is adequate.

- Inspect post year-end sales returns/credit notes and consider whether an additional allowance against receivables is required.

(b) **Impact on auditor's report**

The company made a payment run of $490,000 for payables on 3 November, which is post year end. The trade payables which were outstanding at the year end have been understated as they have been recorded as being paid. In addition, the bank overdraft is overstated as the payments are recorded as coming out of the year-end bank balance. This is evidence of window dressing, as the company has attempted to record a lower level of payable obligations at the year end. The finance director's argument that no adjustment is necessary because the balances affected are both current liabilities is irrelevant, as although both balances are liabilities, they should each still be materially correct.

The amount of the payment run is $490,000 which represents 6.0% of total liabilities (490/8,100) and hence is a material matter.

If management refuses to adjust for the post year-end payment run, the auditor's report will need to be modified. As trade payables are understated and the bank overdraft is overstated and there is a material misstatement which is not pervasive, a qualified opinion would be necessary. A basis for qualified opinion paragraph would need to be included subsequent to the opinion paragraph. This would explain the material misstatement in relation to the treatment of the trade payables and bank overdraft and the effect on the financial statements. The opinion paragraph would be qualified 'except for'.

BPP
LEARNING MEDIA

Review Form – Paper F8 Audit and Assurance (02/17)

Name: _____ **Address:** _____
_____
_____

How have you used this Kit?
(Tick one box only)

☐ On its own (book only)
☐ On a BPP in-centre course _____
☐ On a BPP online course
☐ On a course with another college
☐ Other _____

Why did you decide to purchase this Kit?
(Tick one box only)

☐ Have used the complimentary Study Text
☐ Have used other BPP products in the past
☐ Recommendation by friend/colleague
☐ Recommendation by a lecturer at college
☐ Saw advertising
☐ Other _____

During the past six months do you recall seeing/receiving any of the following?
(Tick as many boxes as are relevant)

☐ Our advertisement in *Student Accountant*
☐ Our advertisement in *Pass*
☐ Our advertisement in *PQ*
☐ Our brochure with a letter through the post
☐ Our website www.bpp.com

Which (if any) aspects of our advertising do you find useful?
(Tick as many boxes as are relevant)

☐ Prices and publication dates of new editions
☐ Information on product content
☐ Facility to order books
☐ None of the above

Which BPP products have you used?

Study Text	☐	*Passcards*	☐	*Other*	☐
Practice & Revision Kit	☑	*i-Pass*	☐		

Your ratings, comments and suggestions would be appreciated on the following areas.

	Very useful	Useful	Not useful
Passing F8			
Questions			
Top Tips etc in answers			
Content and structure of answers			
Mock exam answers			

Overall opinion of this Practice & Revision Kit	*Excellent* ☐	*Good* ☐	*Adequate* ☐	*Poor* ☐

Do you intend to continue using BPP products?   *Yes* ☐   *No* ☐

The BPP author of this edition can be emailed at: accaqueries@bpp.com

Please return this form to: Head of ACCA & FIA Programmes, BPP Learning Media Ltd, FREEPOST, London, W12 8AA

Review Form (continued)

TELL US WHAT YOU THINK

Please note any further comments and suggestions/errors below.